The Changing Mood in America

The Changing Mood in America

Eroding Commitment?

Faustine Childress Jones, Senior Fellow
Institute for the Study of Educational Policy
Howard University
WITH THE ASSISTANCE OF
Cynthia Smith, ISEP
John McClendon, ISEP
Reginald Hildebrand, ISEP

HOWARD UNIVERSITY PRESS, Washington, D.C., 1977

Library of Congress Cataloging in Publication Data
Jones, Faustine Childress, 1927- The changing mood in America.

  Bibliography: p.
  Includes index.
  1. Afro-Americans--Social conditions--1964–1975.   2. United States--Race question.   I. Title.
E185.86.J65   301.45'19'6073   76–52380
ISBN 0–88258–073–6

Acknowledgments are gratefully extended to the following:

   Thomas Y. Crowell Company, Inc., for permission to reprint an excerpt from *Rich Man, Poor Man* by Herman P. Miller, copyright © 1964 by Thomas Y. Crowell Co., Inc., with permission of the publisher.

   Irving Kristol for permission to reprint an excerpt from "Welfare: The Best of Intentions, the Worst of Results," copyright © 1971 by Irving Kristol. Reprinted with permission.

   Newsweek, Inc., for permission to reprint excerpts from the July 29, 1963, October 25, 1965, and June 30, 1969 issues; copyright © 1963, 1965, 1969, respectively, by Newsweek, Inc.

   The University of Michigan's Institute for Social Research for permission to reprint excerpts from *Black Racial Attitudes: Trends and Complexities* by Howard Schuman and Shirley Hatchett, copyright © 1974 by the University of Michigan; and for excerpts from *White Attitudes Toward Black People* by Angus Campbell, copyright © 1971 by The Institute for Social Research, the University of Michigan.

   This report was made possible by a grant from the Ford Foundation.

ACKNOWLEDGMENTS

This book was made possible by the support of the Institute for the Study of Educational Policy at Howard University. Appreciation is expressed to the Director, Kenneth S. Tollett, for his constant assistance and encouragement. A debt of gratitude is happily acknowledged to the Senior Fellows of the Institute, Elizabeth Abramowitz, John Fleming, and Samuel Wong, for their helpful suggestions, positive critical comments, and continued reinforcement as the "changing mood" affected my mood.

Dr. Cynthia Smith, Visiting Fellow, ISEP and John McClendon of the Institute are the co-authors of the subsection on the changing tone that is evident in three black periodicals. Appreciation is expressed to them for accepting and executing the responsibility for this portion of the book.

Absolutely essential to its preparation was the research assistance of Reginald Hildebrand and Michal F. Settles. Their willing efforts and thorough attention to the details of the topic provided invaluable material for the paper. Also most helpful with specific subtopics were Herschelle Reed, Gary Ayers, and Susan Johnson. The work of Yvonne Dianne Jones provided necessary information on impoundment. The thoughtful insights of John McClendon, Julius Hobson, Jr., and other Institute staff members permitted no easy answers to the hard questions posed by the topic.

Jane Midgley provided valuable editorial assistance. Betty Fortune, Margaret Sullivan, and Teresa Bragg deserve tremendous credit for typing the several drafts through which this book has gone. At early stages, Geneva Sanders and Virginia Finch gave necessary assistance in typing and research, respectively. Dr. Marilyn Keilson's willingness to comment on an early draft is appreciated. The constructive criticisms of Dr.

Edmonia W. Davidson, Dr. Peter Sola, and Dr. Barbara D. Lyles were extremely helpful.

It should be clear that this book is a team effort, and I thank the team members for jobs well done. What errors and omissions may occur are my own responsibility.

FOREWORD

The Institute for the Study of Educational Policy (ISEP) developed out of the need for both a national clearinghouse and a research center on the issues affecting equal educational opportunities in higher education. As a national clearinghouse, ISEP aims to serve policy makers and interested researchers by keeping abreast of developments in higher education, within the public and private sectors. In addition, ISEP assumes responsibility for reporting such information to its constituents.

As a research and policy center, ISEP has three program objectives:

To prepare a periodic critical assessment of the dynamic status and needs of blacks in higher education

To assess the impact of law and social science research on the status of blacks in higher education

To use old models creatively and to develop new models and theories of higher education with implications for elementary and secondary education.

Through its annual reports and monographs, through its seminars and conferences, as well as through its announcements and public testimony, the Institute for the Study of Educational Policy attempts to fill a vacuum in the organized body of knowledge about higher educational opportunities of blacks and other minorities. In doing so, ISEP attempts to make a significant contribution to the formulation and evaluation of contemporary educational policy.

In conjunction with our second program objective, Institute staff members monitor and evaluate the purposes, operation, and effect of social science research upon the status, needs, aspirations, and participation of blacks in higher education. This is necessary because the product of social science research may be the genesis, validator, or rationalizer of public policy which will affect blacks positively or negatively, depending upon the character of the research and its findings and recommendations. Such monitoring and evaluating behavior is reactive, but necessary, in light of the American social structure. In a positive vein, the Institute encourages position papers and original research on social science questions and public policy.

All programs of the Institute must take into account a change of mood in the country. The mood is shifting from helping the underprivileged and racial minorities to a great social concern for the middle-income and affluent classes. This change has been camouflaged with euphemistic language, thus making the state of regression less descernible. It is the responsibility of the Institute to monitor, research, and expose the inequitable social consequences which will flow from this changing mood.

This book is an evaluation of this changing mood and, therefore, is a position paper which combines reactive and affirmative elements. It is not an Institute document, but represents the viewpoint of an Institute staff member, and was written under the Institute's second program objective.

Kenneth S. Tollett, Director ISEP
and Chairman ISEP National Advisory Board

PREFACE

This book examines the current social climate in the United States in order to determine whether there is an eroding societal commitment to equal opportunity for blacks and other minorities and the poor. Gunnar Myrdal's classic work, *An American Dilemma,* forms the conceptual framework for this discussion of a changing mood in the dominant society. In addition, the book looks at the black population, America's largest minority group, to see whether a changing mood exists in this segment of the citizenry. The book documents the conclusion that there is a changing mood in the dominant society, in the black population, and in all three branches of the federal government, and shows how the changes have occurred. It also discusses the effect of the changing mood on educational policy and how the mood might be altered to a positive concern for American society and its underprivileged groups.

Specific emphasis is placed on social changes at the national level, including the magnitude of the changes, the span of the changes, and the effect of the changes on subgroups in the society. Of particular concern is how these changes affect and reflect the mood of the country, and how that mood affects policy in higher education, particularly the higher education of blacks. The basic assumption is that change both reflects and affects mood, and mood affects public policy in general and educational policy in particular.

This presentation focuses on publications of groups and institutions as units of analysis. Data for this book are drawn from previously published documents and obtained through library research that reviews the literature and makes a survey of writings related to the topic.

Five key terms will be used repeatedly in this presentation:

1. *Mood*—predominant emotion, prevailing attitude, temporary state of mind with regard to passion, feeling, or disposition, as

"The crowd was in an angry mood because the scheduled singer had not appeared, and it was an hour past the posted opening time."

2. *Changing*—transforming, making visibly different.

3. *Social change*—the *process* of shifting the sentiments and commitments of society from one direction to another in terms of such group relationships as majority/minority, white/black interactions, and the *result* of that process, the attainment of the end.

4. *Conservatism*—the attitude and practice of stressing established institutions and social practices and preferring gradual development to swift and/or pervasive change; a nostalgia for the past *(status quo ante)*, which is perceived to be superior to the present in terms of prevailing conditions contributing to social order.

5. *Dominant group*—the white majority in America, whose behavior and appearance are considered to be the norm, for example, the authoritative standard that guides, controls, or regulates proper and acceptable behavior. The dominant group creates and enforces the social norms, which it in turn rewards. It is also able to control economic and political power so as to keep minorities in subordinate positions against their will. Subordination is a result of the exercise of power, in the sense that the dominant group can exercise its will despite the wishes of minorities. The dominant group is not monolithic, however. Subgroupings of importance within the dominant group, which receive attention in this book, are the white working class, influential intellectual leaders, and affluent youth.

The following areas of study and analysis will be covered in the presentation, chapter by chapter: (1) *An American Dilemma* as the conceptual framework for examining the changing mood, (2) the changing mood in the dominant society since 1969, (3) the changing mood in the black population since 1969, (4) the changing tone of the federal government since 1969, (5) the changing mood and education, and (6) the changing mood and the future.

I have not attempted a systematic refutation of negative views toward blacks and other minorities and the poor. Such a refutation would have resulted in another work the size of *An American Dilemma*. Therefore the reader must look primarily for documentation of a changing mood, with minimal evaluative comment about the neoconservative views that cause and reflect it.

Nevertheless, I have a distinct point of view, and this book is not "value neutral." I am a staunch advocate of equality and justice in this lifetime. Having borne all the responsibilities of citizenship, I believe in procuring all its rights and privileges. To the extent that the changing mood interferes with this process, the mood is perceived as injurious.

Being essentially optimistic in outlook, I believe that the changing mood can be shifted toward a positive concern for those Americans who have yet to attain all the benefits of the American dream and promise.

Faustine Childress Jones

CONTENTS

The Changing Mood in America

INTRODUCTION

Following the *Brown* v. *Board of Education of Topeka* decision in 1954 and continuing through the mid-1960s, a growing feeling of optimism pervaded America. The feeling was that ideals of equality and justice could be realized for black Americans, that segment of the populace so long denied equity. The mood of Americans generally was positive and supportive of the quest for equality and justice; the mood of black Americans was jubilant.

This jubilance began with the *Brown* decision and increased as that decision was buttressed by federal action. Presidents John F. Kennedy and Lyndon B. Johnson enforced the legal interpretation of equal rights. Kennedy, for example, sent federal troops to the University of Mississippi to ensure that James Meredith, a black citizen, would receive an education in his home state. In addition, the *Brown* decision was reinforced by Congress through the passage of the Civil Rights Act of 1964 and the Voting Rights Act of 1965.

Public sensibilities were stirred as the country watched televised newscasts, heard radio reports, or read vivid accounts of intimidation and brutality suffered by blacks as they sought to exercise their rights of citizenship. The populace was indignant about the violence and chicanery perpetrated against black citizens and their white supporters by white extremists who sought to restore the *status quo ante*. The educational shambles at Central High School in Little Rock, Arkansas, the assassination of Medgar Evers, the bombing of a Birmingham, Alabama, church in which four black children were killed, the brutality of Theophilus Eugene "Bull" Connor, the severe treatment of white and black freedom riders and voter registration workers, Governor George Wallace's stand in the University of Alabama's door, and other such events showed the American public, in explicit terms, that black Americans were in fact denied their rights of citizenship. The American public reacted against the blatant violence of white extremists, supporting the idea that democratic tenets should be realistically attainable for black citizens.

These legal, political, social, and educational events occurred in a period of economic growth and increasing affluence. The expanding economy could absorb more blacks and other minorities, as well as women of all groups, in newly created and growing industries and in different ways than had been the case historically. This absorption could occur with minimal threat to the previously employed, predominantly white, male group since it also was prospering in the expanding economy.

However, the relative condition of some whites was not improving. In fact, some whites were only superficially better off than the black minority. This segment of the white populace perceived black gains as "too much, too fast," and felt the upward mobility of blacks as a group (or class) to be a threat to them as a group (or class). They began to express negative feelings toward structural changes that benefited blacks collectively in a form that was labeled "backlash" by the society. Their disenchantment with the political process was aimed at the Democratic party, with which most of them had been affiliated since the era of Franklin D. Roosevelt. The size of this group of whites, as well as their political strength, increased with the rate of unemployment and inflation. By 1967 their economic position had deteriorated enough to make them believe that a change in national leadership from Democratic to Republican (in the 1968 national election) was necessary for survival.

At the same time that nondiscrimination was being emphasized at the federal level, several states passed discriminatory laws in reaction to the *Brown* decision. Louisiana, Florida, Virginia, Alabama, Georgia, Mississippi, South Carolina, and California passed laws between 1956 and 1964 which were discriminatory against blacks on such points as blood banks, beaches, eating and sanitary facilities, entertainment, sports and games, public facilities, business clientele, and housing.[1] Also, there was state legislation to thwart school desegregation in Alabama, South Carolina, Virginia, Arkansas, North Carolina, Louisiana, Georgia, and Florida.[2] These laws reinforced the status quo, but were counter to the federal emphasis on nondiscrimination.

Opposition to liberal Supreme Court decisions was expressed openly by some groups. A particularly graphic expression of this opposition appeared in the form of billboard advertisements across the nation urging the people to "impeach Earl Warren," who, as chief justice, was helmsman of the court.

From 1964 to 1969 these positive and negative cross-currents were visible throughout American society. By 1969 the optimistic mood of the late fifties and early sixties had changed; a new mood had clearly begun to shift in the opposite direction. The inauguration of Richard M. Nixon as president of the United States in January 1969 is one benchmark of the shift in national focus from the plight of black Americans toward other domestic concerns. "Law and order," for example, replaced "justice in our time" as a national priority.*

From 1969 to the present, this trend has continued. It is the belief of most black Americans in 1976 that there is clearly a changing mood in the nation, compared to that of the 1950s and early 1960s—one that indicates an unwillingness on the government's part to intervene on behalf of black progress. At best, the current mood can be described as one of "benign neglect" toward blacks.

This shift of attitude has been a cyclical recurrence in American history. In the twentieth century this recurrence or shift has been from (1) Woodrow Wilson's progressive legislative policies to the Republicanism of the 1920s, (2) the liberalism of Franklin D. Roosevelt to the more reserved policies of Dwight D. Eisenhower, and (3) the progressive social programs of John F. Kennedy and Lyndon B. Johnson to the retrogressive social programs of Richard M. Nixon and Gerald R. Ford.

---

*The 1974 revelation of White House complicity in the high-level conspiracy against law and order, which resulted in the Watergate break-in, is a painful reminder of the danger of political expediency, of which the changing mood is a by-product.

I

AN AMERICAN DILEMMA: CONCEPTUAL FRAMEWORK FOR EXAMINING THE CHANGING MOOD

The most comprehensive study of the black–white problem and modern American democracy is *An American Dilemma* by Gunnar Myrdal.* This classic work describes and analyzes the conflict between American values and ideals on the one hand, and the actual social status accorded the Negro† in American life on the other. Myrdal viewed the "Negro problem" as primarily a moral issue in the minds of white Americans and postulated that the solution to the American dilemma lay in changing the attitudes of white Americans.

While visible progress has occurred in that direction in the thirty-odd years since *An American Dilemma* first appeared, continuing controversy surrounding black people in the United States indicates that white attitudes continue to be obstacles to the full inclusion of Negroes in the American social, political, and economic system. The moral problem, the central theme of Myrdal's classic work, still persists in the United States in the 1970s.

Despite Myrdal's claim that the "American Creed" represents our common core of values, that it is the "higher" set of valuations and the unifying force in American life, the social reality of 1976 demonstrates the depth of continued dominant-group subscription to secondary valuations, or "low order" valuations. A review of Mydral's theory of social

---

*Work has begun on *An American Dilemma Revisited: The Racial Crisis in the United States in Perspective,* with Gunnar Myrdal as principal author, assisted by Kenneth Clark and others. It is expected that the publication of this book is at least two years away. Whereas the first study was a field study, the second will focus on analyzing data gathered since 1944.

†"Negro" was the acceptable term for Americans with African heritage when *An American Dilemma* was published in 1944. Since that time, the term "black" has become increasingly acceptable in the minority community to describe itself. The terms, "Negro" and "black" will be used interchangeably in this book.

change is appropriate in explaining how his theory might account for the changing mood.

MYRDAL'S THEORY

Gunnar Myrdal's theory of social change can be described as an "engineering" theory, as well as a multifactor theory, which is based on a dynamic conception of the social system in which all social forces interact. Man's intelligence is assigned a causative role in the creation and maintenance of constructive social change, founded on moral and ethical premises. Thus Myrdal perceived man to be a purposive, self-determining being whose potentialities can be actualized by virtue of his basic human need for consistency and for rational and logical action.

In *An American Dilemma,* Myrdal emphasized the great gap between the nation's ideals (the American Creed) and its day-to-day practices. Myrdal's view is that Americans have two sets of ideas about what is valuable, a higher set and a lower set. The higher set he calls the "American Creed"; it is made up of those ideas which apply without qualification to all mankind, mainly ideas of liberty, equality, and justice. It is the unifying force in American life, and the test of our system is the degree to which the society realizes the creed. Another way of referring to the American Creed is to call it "primary valuations" or "high-order valuations." These primary valuations, which refer to mankind as a whole, are *morally* higher in America. They also are given the sanction of religion and legal processes; they are principles which should rule American society.*

The lower set of ideas regarding what is valuable may be called "secondary valuations" or "low-order valuations." This lower set applies to some individuals but not to others; it emphasizes personal and local interests and includes such ideas as economic benefit, social relationships, and status and prestige allocations. The secondary valuations are often referred to as "irrational" or "prejudiced" and are defended by

---

*According to Myrdal *(An American Dilemma,* 1:8), essential components of the American Creed, briefly stated, are (1) belief in the essential dignity of man, (2) belief in the perfectibility of man, (3) the feeling that the gains of government are mass gains, designed for the many and not the few, (4) confidence in the value of the consent of the governed, and (5) confidence in the value of decisions arrived at by common counsel rather than by violence and brutality. These postulates are grounded in (1) reason in regarding the essential nature of the political man, (2) observation, experience, and inference, and (3) the belief that fulfillment of the democratic ideals is strengthened by faith in the final triumph of ideals of human behavior in general and political behavior in particular.

their holders as useful, traditional, or expedient. They may be identified in such American day-to-day practices as exclusionary housing sales and rentals or school busing controversies.

Because these two sets of valuations are incompatible, they give rise to conflicts within society, between groups, and within the conscience of the individual. Thus the root of social problems in America, for Myrdal, is the moral dilemma between valuations on different levels of consciousness and generality. In fact, the title of his book, *An American Dilemma,* represents the constant conflict between the high-order valuations exhibited on the general level, or the American Creed, where Americans talk, think, and behave under the influence of lofty national and religious precepts, and, on the other hand, the low-order valuations exhibited in day-to-day living, where personal and group prejudice against particular individuals or groups of people is shown, and where miscellaneous wants, impulses, and habits dominate the lives of people.

The problem is complicated by the fact that the moral conflict between valuations is exhibited not only between groups and persons, but that conflicting valuations are held by the same person. For survival purposes, individuals, groups, and the society have tended to rationalize the discrepancy and to compartmentalize various departures from the general valuations, so that a discrepancy in one realm appears not to be related to discrepancies in other realms of life. Out of this process Americans have developed a facility for believing that things, although disjointed, will somehow work out all right. Myrdal calls this a "bright fatalism," which is unmatched in the Western world and which has become a part of the national ethos.

American behavior thus has become a moral compromise. There are no longer homogeneous attitudes underlying human behavior but, instead, "a mesh of struggling inclinations, interests, ideals, some held conscious and some suppressed for long intervals but all active in bending behavior in their direction."[1] Thus American behavior often is not logical. For example, in an attempt to conceal the conflict between the two planes of valuations, Americans keep some valuations from awareness by focusing attention on others. In fact, Myrdal found that Americans "twist and mutilate their beliefs of how social reality actually is" in their attempt to conceal the contradictions in their valuations. He found a great many firmly entrenched popular beliefs in America concerning the Negro and his relations to the larger society which were blatantly false and which could be understood only as one remembered the purpose they served—consistency, or what Leon Festinger, renowned American social psychologist, terms "reduction of cognitive dissonance."

The two major social "statics" in Myrdal's system are valuations and beliefs. Valuations are ideas about how reality ought to be (or ought to have been); they are norms, or "oughts," that is, value judgments. These value judgments, of "rightness," "fairness," and "desirability" cannot be judged by the scientific method. Valuations are centered in the belief in equality and in the rights to liberty. Beliefs are descriptive accounts of how social reality actually is or was; beliefs are knowledge, and may be true or false. Beliefs and valuations may vary in generality. Myrdal is most interested in beliefs having to do with social reality rather than those pertaining to the inanimate environment. He stresses the fact that beliefs differ in their degree of rationality; they can be more or less accurate and more or less complete. Their degree of accuracy or rationality can be determined by the scientific method.

Beliefs and valuations converge in daily living patterns. Myrdal found that when Americans express motives for specific actions or inactions, their underlying beliefs and valuations are chosen in relation to the expediencies of the situation, or opportunistically. People give "good" reasons rather than "true" reasons; that is, they rationalize their behavior. However, when people or groups criticize each other on moral grounds, they usually appeal to the higher valuations that are held in common. Also, the leeway for false beliefs, which makes rationalizations of valuations more suited for their purpose, has been much reduced in this age of developed science and extensive education. The result, Myrdal feels, is that, despite the great American dilemma, Americans have cultural unity because they hold most valuations in common. This cultural unity is the basis for discussion between persons and groups, and it is the foundation upon which the democratic process rests.

Additionally, Myrdal found that Americans want to be rational. In a complex, literate society such as the United States, scientific truth seeking and education are slowly rectifying beliefs and thereby influencing valuations. Myrdal discovered that in a rational, civilized society, the valuations not only shape the beliefs, but also depend on the beliefs. As a result, there is a striving for consistency between the two which would not be present in a primitive or a nonliterate society. This desire for consistency also has direction: a desire to make the low-order valuations compatible with the high-order valuations. The principle of consistency is one of the dynamics of Myrdal's theory.

Another dynamic principle in Myrdal's theory is the principle of cumulation, which holds that a whole cluster of variables, such as laws, economic conditions, education, beliefs, valuations, housing, nutrition, clothing, health, stability in family relations, manners, cleanliness, orderliness, trustworthiness, law observance, loyalty to society at large, criminality, etc., cause the social phenomenon of the inferior status of the Negro. Not only do these variables cause the phenomenon, they are interrelated, so that a change in one brings about some change in all the others. Therefore, because of the interrelations and the fact that the variables cumulate, an improvement in one variable will effect an improvement in all the other variables. Specifically, improvement in the employment situation of the Negro will tend to increase earnings, raise standards of living, improve health, education, manners, law observance, and so on, through the whole system of variables.

Myrdal has called this a "circular cumulative accelerating process," because the effects of the process accumulate and the social changes are accelerated. This spiraling effect brings improvement much more rapidly than would be the case if the process were not circular. Furthermore, as the plane of living or life condition of the Negro improves, white prejudice against the Negro decreases. Therefore, the better the life condition of the Negro, the less prejudice against him from the dominant group. However, deterioration in any of the factors begins a downward spiral which continues until it is counteracted by some outside force—a process Myrdal called the "vicious circle." [2] Deterioration in any factor is detrimental for the Negro.

This principle of cumulation, or reciprocal reinforcement, makes Myrdal's theory desirable from the standpoint of social engineering, for it emphasizes that changes for the better may be produced out of proportion to the apparent value of the initial variable. However, because the process works in both directions, it is also important to prevent, or to ward off, undesirable changes in the variables because a change in an unfavorable direction may start the spiral effect downward in a vicious circle.

Myrdal has an interesting conception of equilibrium in the American social system. He rejects the theories of static or stable equilibrium which hold that social equilibrium is adjustment between society and a particular set of conditions, disruption, and "restoration" of a new equilibrium. Myrdal believes society is never in a state of static equilibrium but is always in the process of cumulative change in one direction or another. He presents "processes of systems actually rolling in one direction or the other, systems which are constantly subjected to all sorts of pushes from outside through all the variables, and which are moving because of the cumulative effect of all these pushes and the interaction between the variables." [3]

Thus it appears, from Myrdal's statement, that the major statics of his theory—beliefs and valuations—are as much in movement as the minor statics and the dynamic processes. One way this movement shows itself is in the changing relationship between the secondary valuations and the primary valuations, and in the fact that the secondary valuations are modified upward; they are slowly becoming more consistent with the primary valuations.

Another important idea in Myrdal's theory is the "opinion explosion," which may occur within a person, a group, or the total society. It takes place when it is no longer possible to hold to the low-order valuations, when rationalization and compartmentalization fail, when the strain toward consistency is too great to permit holding to both the low- and the high-order valuations. An opinion explosion is actually a social crisis, which results in either a rapid social change or a revolution-seeking change. Fundamental to this analysis is Myrdal's contention that neither beliefs nor valuations are fixed and static; they are always in movement. As long as a state of cynicism does not spread, American society strives toward greater consistency in valuations and moves in the direction of the more general (high order) valuations. It is clear that an opinion explosion brings about visible change.

As social stress develops within the society as a result of change, groups that have advantages resist what they perceive to be a reduction of those advantages. They move to protect themselves and in order not to have to change their deeply held beliefs. Myrdal holds that if issues are continuously brought before the public through discussion and if inconsistencies are pointed out and documented to the extent that there is no further hiding place in false logic—if false beliefs are repeatedly confronted by facts and evidence—ultimately man will go one way or the other. Myrdal felt that the direction would be upward toward the high-order valuations, the American Creed.

ANALYSIS AND CRITIQUE OF MYRDAL'S THEORY

Any sociological study of the magnitude and scope of *An American Dilemma* would be expected to draw considerable critical analysis, and Myrdal's work has drawn such analysis. Moreover, the rest of time can be applied to the study to determine if its basic tenets were valid and, thirty-two years after their first publication, are still valid.

Ralph Ellison, a leading black American writer, critiqued Mydral's work in *"An American Dilemma:* A Review," in *Shadow and Act.*[4] Ellison held that Myrdal's survey was at bottom a theatrical gesture sponsored by a capitalist institution, the Carnegie Corporation, which sought to discover the techniques "for a more effective exploitation of the South's natural, industrial, and human resources." Ellison felt that Myrdal experienced his own personal dilemma in conducting the study:

> In interpreting the results of this five-year study, Myrdal found it confirming many of the social and economic assumptions of the Left, and throughout the book he has felt it necessary to carry on a running battle with Marxism. Especially irritating to him has been the concept of class struggle and economic motivation of anti-Negro prejudice which to an increasing number of Negro intellectuals correctly analyzes their situation.[5]

Ellison reacted vigorously to Myrdal's idea of the "rank order of discrimination" held by blacks and whites. Myrdal asserted that "the Negro's own rank order is just about parallel, but inverse, to that of the white man." In practical terms, this means that whites are most concerned about preventing intermarriage and legal sexual intercourse among the races; the breakdown of etiquette; the increase of intimate relationships between races; the desegregation of public facilities, schools, and churches; political disfranchisement; discrimination in the courts; and discrimination in securing jobs, credit, land, and welfare. If these priorities, which are presented in descending order, are reversed, they are applicable to black concerns. Ellison felt that Myrdal's analysis was shortsighted and that, since Myrdal felt the Negro's life and opinions are to be considered mainly as secondary reactions to more primary pressures from the dominant white majority, his analysis was inadequate. Ellison asked:

> But can a people (its faith in an idealized American Creed notwithstanding) live and develop for over three hundred years simply by *reacting?* Are American Negroes simply the creation of white men, or have they at least helped to create themselves out of what they found around them? Men have made a way of life upon the horns of the white man's dilemma.[6]

An informed intellectual critique of Myrdal's basic theory, fundamental assumptions, and underlying sociological imagination has been delivered by Stanford M. Lyman in *The Black American in Sociological Thought: A Failure of Perspective.*[7] Lyman, in his 1972 analysis, questions the extent of the humanistic and dynamic theory of *An Ameri-*

can Dilemma. He asserts that Myrdal has not moved very far from his conservative sociological forebears—Sumner, Ward, Park, Ogburn—although Myrdal was critical of them in his book. Reduced to its most basic elements, Myrdal's theory is gradualist and cautionary, according to Lyman, and Myrdal does not provide "a new sociology rooted in free will or in man's inherent capacity to remake the world." [8]

Lyman questions the entire body of Myrdal's argument in four ways: (1) it is possible, in theory and reasonably based on evidence, to postulate that racism is not a lower and local set of values but a complex value premise, equal in every respect to that of the American Creed; (2) even if it is accepted that racism is a morally inferior value to most Americans, it is quite possible for an individual to maintain contradictory beliefs without suffering excruciating pangs of conscience or seeking to bring his beliefs into line with logical consistency; (3) Myrdal's theory of value consistency in complex societies stands in sharp contradiction to an alternative theory of social complexity and normative pluralism; and (4) Myrdal's proposals for amelioration of the race problem, when analyzed, turn out to be a commitment to a unified value system and a mechanical equilibrium model which generates cautious, slow, and gradualist policies—a program which is modest in scope. Lyman supports Ellison's point that Myrdal failed to recognize the existence of a black subculture, which had developed (to some degree) in the racial isolation of America. As a result of this failure, Myrdal ascribed to the Negro the role of reacting to the negative features of society, and this role is quite inadequate.

Lyman's succinct conclusion is worth noting in full:

> Gunnar Myrdal's theory of an American dilemma is, despite his disclaimers, another study in the tradition of classical American sociology. Devoted to depicting black life in America, Myrdal imprisons it within a single value culture to which it can respond only by ultimate assimilation. Convinced that both individuals and institutions are subject to strain caused by the disparity between prejudicial actions and the public promise of equality, Myrdal couches his optimism about the eventual solution to the black problem in terms of his belief that such contradictions cannot for long be countenanced. Thus he exchanges the teleology of the traditional mores of the past for the teleology of a value-consistent psyche of the future. His practical solutions are on the same order as those of his conservative predecessors: slow, gradual steps consistent with age-old beliefs, guided by intelligent benevolence, and eschewing social tumult.

Myrdal sees the black as existing in the shadow of American
culture, dependent on its slow but inexorable changes subject to its
cultural, social, and idiosyncratic whims, to be liberated by eventual
absorption into the American system which will then have
triumphed in the final solution to the black problem.[9]

Accepting Ellison's and Lyman's critical analyses of Myrdal's
theory as valid, one still wants to add his own specific criticisms. It
seems indisputable that education and public discussion exert powerful
influences on man's growth in matters relating to his intellectual and social development, as Myrdal claims. What he proposes, then, is not
beyond the realm of possibility; man's intelligence and his conscious,
purposeful attack on the great American problem *can* affect the future
of the nation in a positive manner. But whether man *will* do so is another
matter. It seems true that the American Creed is slowly and gradually
realizing itself, in the sense that America has been moving steadily, although slowly, toward a greater understanding of democratic principles.
The creed is now asserting its ideals in the political and economic
spheres and in international organizations. For example, the American
Creed is changing to include a decent standard of living and economic
security among the liberties and rights which are given its highest moral
sanction. Also, overt resistance to black equality has been greatly
reduced in the South, where such resistance was an integral aspect of the
mores of white Southerners for an extended period of time.

It has been true, as Myrdal claims, that as the level of Negro living
has increased, white prejudice has decreased, and there have been cumulative and spiral effects from particular improvements in the conditions
of life. Further, many Americans are troubled about the inconsistency
between ideals and practice and would like them to be consistent. Myrdal did not err when he said the race problem is one of the critical
problems that America faces today. But it seems that while Myrdal is
correct to a large extent, his theory is not sufficient to solve the American dilemma; if it were sufficient, many more far-reaching changes
should have already taken place in America. Let us examine some of the
problems with Myrdal's theory.

Myrdal has claimed that his is a multifactor theory of social change
which is applicable to all advanced societies. However, he seems to have
elevated a single factor, the American Creed, to a primary position,
which means that he negated his own multifactor claim. Because of this
elevation of the American Creed, it would seem that his theory no longer
applies to all advanced societies but only to advanced democratic socie-

ties, or, more specifically, only to American society. Even though we may grant that the American Creed is a very powerful weapon in America, there are difficulties with its use in attacking the black–white racial dilemma in the United States.

First, there is a wealth of evidence to show that even if all Americans believe in the fundamental tenets of the creed—freedom, equality, and justice for all mankind—its tenets do not have the same meaning to all individuals or to all groups. There are divergent and conflicting interpretations of these high principles, which would indicate that the democratic tradition itself needs to be clarified before it can be used as a means of integrating American society. Because these varying interpretations exist, the creed could very well divide, rather than unite, the American people. These conflicts must be resolved before the American Creed could be the unifying force that Gunnar Myrdal suggests.

Second, Myrdal does not admit that racism has existed alongside the American Creed ever since the assumption of power by the dominant group in this country, and that the weight of racism has been equal to that of the creed in societal practices. The genocide of the native Indians, the enslavement of Africans on American shores, the Chinese Exclusion Act, and the incarceration of Americans of Japanese descent in concentration camps show that the lofty ideals of the American Creed have been, and can be, compromised by the society when the human rights of people of differential visibility appear to conflict with the needs and interests of the people in power.

Myrdal seems to underestimate the power of regional norms which are very strong and very old, just as the American Creed is very strong and very old. These regional norms, coupled with subcultures of strong ethnicity, are powerful forces that counteract the American Creed and thereby make its unifying job far more difficult than Myrdal points out.

Myrdal also seems to underestimate psychological forces which are powerful and widespread; for example, the "in group" perceives itself as superior to the "out group." It has been established that many lower-class whites have a psychological need to enhance their egos by looking down on some other group which is perceived to be inferior to them. This need has been met by looking down on the Negro, and when efforts are made to raise the social position of the Negro, this class of Caucasians offers strenuous objections. Furthermore, does even a rational middle-class or upper-class person, confronted with contradictions, change for the better? As often as some people change, others defend their egos, self-interests, and positions when they are "threatened."

How can Myrdal's principle of cumulation be reconciled with the fact that white prejudice, especially in times of economic crisis, often increases, rather than decreases as the Negro becomes a more effective competitor? In fact, white interest groups seek to put an end to such programs as affirmative action, which aim to redress historic inequities. Additionally, social systems are not closed systems; so spiraling cannot go on forever. When a system is not closed, the elements within it are connected with elements outside the system. Therefore, such interconnections with outside elements may slow the spiraling process. For example, wages earned by the Negro are related to the wage level of all workers and to the availability of jobs in the economic system; so when there are insufficient jobs, as is presently the case, the Negro's job and wage potentials are limited and the spiraling process is hampered.

Despite the respect Americans express in theory for high ideals and for the legal system, most have relatively little respect for law and order in day-to-day living practices. This is true particularly when it concerns their personal behavior and when it seems to be a threat to their freedom. Hence, there is a defeatist attitude toward the possibility of generating social change by means of legislation, and most appeals to the collective interest have not been successfully sustained. This has come about because of negative experiences with clever lawyers, unsavory politics, bureaucracy, and the like, and has led to a kind of political fatalism, which has resulted in lack of respect for the law.

Myrdal recognizes this state of affairs but believes it is reversible. His argument is that social change can be generated by legislation because similar changes are effected by such means in other parts of the world. Better-prepared, better-administered laws, Myrdal argues, are means to the end. The problem in America has been that we have conflicting laws in the same state, among the several states, and between state and federal laws. Even when humane laws have been passed, they have not been enforced consistently over time; they have, therefore, been ineffective. The question then arises, How does one get consistency in law enforcement in America? The Nixon and Ford administrations, for example, did not enforce civil rights laws in the seventies to the degree that the Johnson and Kennedy administrations did in the sixties.

Despite these problems with Myrdal's theory, one may admit that he is a rational theorist who has offered something constructive to Americans. He has made Americans more conscious that our social problems, if left alone, will not just fade away; they will become American dilemmas. He has shown us that to solve this very serious race problem, we must work on it, consciously and consistently and, on as many fronts as possible, using all the resources we possess to cause opinion to explode in the direction of greater consistency with high national ideals.

MYRDAL'S THEORY AND THE CHANGING MOOD

The nature of the social change which has occurred in America since 1969 was predictable from Myrdal's theory; the specific forms the change has taken depended on time, circumstances, and societal conditions. By combining Myrdal's notion of social equilibrium and his theory of cumulation (reciprocal reinforcement), one would know that if a dynamic equilibrium is operating, there are forces that want to retain the status quo, which dominants call "stability," just as there are forces operating for modification and change. Therefore, as blacks moved increasingly for social change in the early and mid-1960s and accumulated more forces for changing their status in America in the direction of more equality, there were forces acting and reacting to keep blacks "in their place." Hence, when the forces are strengthened or weakened in either direction, the forces in one direction will always bring resistance from the other, until a crisis is reached. Figure 1-1 illustrates the process, as set out by Myrdal.

The crisis stage, when reached, does not mean that all hope is lost for the Negro to improve his status in America. What emerges from the crisis depends on the strength of one set of forces and the erosion of strength in the other. If the forces to improve Negro status are removed, Negro status reverts to its former plane. For example, an economic crisis means that blacks are laid off work; this results in unemployment, which in turn results in inability to pay bills, which results in foreclosure of mortgages, poor diets, family disharmony, inability to send offspring to college—all of which, collectively, means that black status goes down. Another example would be nonenforcement of the civil and voting rights laws passed in 1964 and 1965. This nonenforcement results in the inability of blacks to exercise the right which exists in theory (e.g., voting in Mississippi) and to elect officials sympathetic to blacks. Thus there are fewer laws and appointed officials to maintain earlier gains, resulting in a collective decline in black political and economic status. Thus the weakening of a strong force or forces, designed to improve the status of blacks, ultimately reduces the aggregate black status; and weakened forces produce a vicious circle for the Negro. The weakening of key forces since 1969 seriously upsets the black population today.

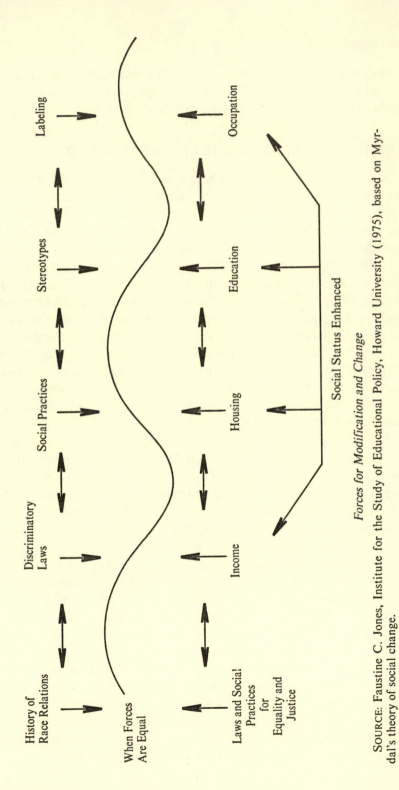

Forces to Retain Status Quo of Negroes

History of Race Relations · Discriminatory Laws · Social Practices · Stereotypes · Labeling

When Forces Are Equal

Laws and Social Practices for Equality and Justice · Income · Housing · Education · Occupation

Social Status Enhanced

Forces for Modification and Change

SOURCE: Faustine C. Jones, Institute for the Study of Educational Policy, Howard University (1975), based on Myrdal's theory of social change.

FIGURE 1–1. CUMULATION, DYNAMIC EQUILIBRIUM, AND SOCIAL CHANGE

Therefore, given the civil rights thrusts of black Americans in the late 1950s and early 1960s, it was predictable, from Myrdal's theory, that a white "backlash" would occur. It was also predictable that divisions would appear in the ranks of black people, based on differing perceptions of how to reach the ultimate goals of equality and justice and resulting in the effectuation of differing strategies designed to reach the same end. Thus the social stress between the races, which has been visible in the last twenty years, was predictable by using Myrdal's social theory about the United States.

Also, the societal stress that is evident between social classes was predictable from Myrdal's work. Classes that have advantages (the upper-middle and upper classes) resist what they perceive to be a reduction of those advantages. Given these societal stresses, it was predictable that advantaged groups and classes would exert political and economic pressure on all change agents, such as the media and the federal government, to stop those agents from assisting disadvantaged minorities in their attempt to make further advances. The advantaged perceived these advances as a threat to their economic, social, political, and/or educational well-being.

What was not directly predictable from Myrdal's theory was the current economic crisis, simultaneously characterized by depression and inflation. This crisis impinges on the lives of all salaried and working-class Americans, regardless of color, class, race, sex, or religion, and affects their attitudes, based on their perceived self-interest and personal/family security.

Nor, prior to the current economic crisis, was the effect of the wars in Southeast Asia on the American economy and on the minds of the American people predictable from Myrdal's theory. To state the obvious, his ideas were first published in 1944 and the research for them was completed in the late 1930s; so it was not possible to predict specific wars from his publication. Nevertheless, it is necessary to cite the effect of these wars on the American economy and the American people: the Vietnam War helped to remove the primary concern from domestic problems, including the problem of race relations. It also helped to remove federal monies from domestic assistance programs, under the rubric that it was possible for the country to have guns and butter at the same time, but the butter would have to be spread less liberally than originally hoped.* Thus the Vietnam War reduced the role of the federal

---

*Lyndon B. Johnson, "The Budget of the United States Government for the Fiscal Year

government as a change agent, working to enhance the status of blacks, the poor, women, and other disadvantaged groups in society. Since the federal government had been the primary source on which disadvantaged groups could rely for assistance, the reduced role of the executive, judicial, and legislative branches has negatively affected the upward movement of these groups.

It is important to state that, prior to the heightened United States involvement in Vietnam and the current economic crisis, the deepest and most pervasive feelings within the changing mood were directly traceable to changes in black–white relations and to perceived black gains within the American social system. In the lay culture, black–white relationships are perceived as a zero-sum game in which what blacks win, whites must lose (and vice versa) in a declining economy. So long as this social and psychological orientation obtains, the goals of democracy—equality, justice, liberty—will not be realized. Until American society is willing to work out ways so that life is not in fact a zero-sum game, the American dilemma will obtain in this society. The class divisiveness and racial hostilities will endure. Added to those problems is increasing sexual divisiveness, which again is based on the reality of daily living in America under the zero-sum concept. What women gain, men must lose; the battle of the sexes is now added to the battles of the races and the classes.

It is clear that the economic growth of the country, or lack of such growth, is a key factor in class, race, and sex relations. All such relations can be enhanced in times of economic affluence and growth, so it appears that the American Creed is being realized; but these same relations suffer and decline in a no-growth period, contributing to a new vicious circle for Negroes and other disadvantaged people and moving them away from actualization of the promises of the American Creed. Yet the high level of expectation continues for all groups, since all Americans want to live comfortably, equitably, and justly. All individuals and groups must meet the economic costs of such necessities as food, housing, clothing, transportation, and insurance. If disparate groups

---

Ending June 30, 1967" (excerpts), *U.S. Department of State Bulletin 54* (Feb. 14, 1966), p. 247. In his budget message for 1966 (transmitted Jan. 24, 1966), President Johnson noted that his administration was "determined to press confidently toward the Great Society." Yet he acknowledged that this would have to be done "at a pace which reflects the claims of our commitments in Southeast Asia upon the Nation's resources."

could really learn to look beyond such superficialities of differential visibility as race, sex, and class, they would see that vast numbers of them have the same, identical problems in living in the American system. Therefore they would do better to cooperate in seeking realizable solutions, rather than continue to fight with each other, competing for scarce jobs, housing, and the like. The cooperative vision and understanding, however, are too long coming, and so the relation of black–white racial competition to democratic norms is still the primary unsolved problem of American society—and the American dilemma continues.

SUMMARY AND CONCLUSIONS

The modern classic, *An American Dilemma,* has profound and continuing significance for intergroup relations in the United States. The book examines the fundamental value system into which all Americans are socialized, as well as the contradictions within that value system which occur in the course of daily human associations. These contradictions, coupled with the inconsistent behavior which results from and/or is permitted by them, result in confusion in people as well as in institutional policies and practices.

The book's author, Gunnar Myrdal, examined the relationship between life conditions and prejudice, with primary emphasis on the low status of Negroes in the United States, the world's leading democracy. He found that relationship to be mutual and cumulative. When the life condition of the Negro improves, prejudice against the group diminishes; when the life condition of the Negro declines, prejudice increases. Basic changes in the relationship of blacks and whites in America could occur, Myrdal held, and in fact were occurring (in 1944 and 1962) in an upward direction, consistent with America's highest values.

Bearing out Myrdal's views, the nation witnessed, during the decade of the fifties, a continuation of the positive changes of the forties, followed by negative counterthrusts, such as the public school confrontation in Little Rock, Arkansas. These negative acts were not to prevail, however, and the decade of the sixties brought social change favorable to the Negro of a magnitude never before witnessed in the United States. In fact, some social theorists feel that the rapidity of change in the twenty-year period, 1948–1968, was the greatest in the history of human relations; and this change was for the most part highly favorable to the Negro. There has been some retrogression in the seventies, and much still needs to be done to solve America's most crucial problem, black–white relations. Nevertheless, Myrdal felt that the American

Creed would prevail over time, and a major factor in that triumph would be education—equal and universal public education.

The values of the American Creed prevail in times of great crisis and also in a growing economy. Those same values often are compromised in a no-growth economic period and when social equilibrium is relatively stable. The promises and hopes of the American Creed can be realized as societal contradictions are worked out, deliberately and systematically, by knowledgeable, sensitive leaders who have the will to achieve social progress.

II

THE CHANGING MOOD IN THE DOMINANT SOCIETY SINCE 1969

As stated in the introduction, most black Americans believe there is a changing mood in this nation, compared to the late fifties and early sixties, and that the mood has shifted from institutional intervention on behalf of black progress. Black Americans feel that a significant proportion of the white population has shifted priorities, from eliminating the vestiges of racial discrimination as the major goal in this society to reviving a feeling that blacks have had as much help as they need and deserve; therefore, social policy should shift in the seventies toward other primary concerns, such as ecology, women, and the needs and interests of white ethnics.

To what extent are the beliefs and feelings of blacks verifiable by evidence? Is there, in fact, a changing mood in the dominant society?

SURVEYS OF WHITE ATTITUDES

The Survey Research Center at the University of Michigan studied white racial attitudes in fifteen cities in early 1968, using a cross-section of the white population. The center also studied cross-sectional samples of the national white population in the fall of 1964, 1968, and 1970. Angus Campbell, director of the University of Michigan's Institute for Social Research, has published the results of these studies in a monograph, *White Attitudes toward Black People*, issued in August 1971 by that institute. From the fifteen-city study of 1968, Campbell reported the following findings.

The Nature of White Attitudes

The white population varied greatly in its feelings about race and no typical person could be identified as representative of the total. White Americans in the cities were not predominantly located at either extreme of the scale of racial attitudes; one-fifth to one-third were generally positive in racial outlook in the sense that they tended to accept interracial contact, were sensitive to racial discrimination, and were sympathetic to various forms of black protest. By the same criteria, an equal proportion of the responses ranged from negative to very hostile. The remaining perceptions and attitudes were ambiguous and conflicting. [1] The three attitude scales that were used to measure white opinions toward race focused on

1. Segregation and white acceptance of more equalitarian interracial relationships
2. Degree of racial discrimination witnessed by respondents in their immediate environments
3. Sympathy with the black protest

Attitudes toward Social Action

In response to a series of proposals for social action submitted by the Survey Research Center to samples of the white population of fifteen Northern cities, the collective responses were as follows: (1) laws should be instituted to prevent discrimination in hiring and promotion, (2) majorities should have substantial representation in federal programs that give aid to cities, (3) a long-term solution to the disorder problem requires more than simply building up the police force, and (4) almost unanimous opposition to whites' taking the law into their own hands in case of a racial disturbance. White respondents equivocated only on the question of open housing ordinances. On this matter whites were more evenly divided than on questions of employment, federal programs of aid to cities, use of police, or taking the law into their own hands.[2]

Campbell concluded that the prevailing white attitude in these cities was far from the monolithic opposition to change that it is sometimes represented to be. However, Campbell found a strong inclination of white people in these cities to believe that the main responsibility for action to improve the lot of black people should belong to blacks themselves. He discovered that most of the white population had given up the belief that blacks are inherently incapable of competing equally with whites, but had not accepted the alternative argument that black deficiencies are due to environmental barriers. These same people believed that the poor education, low employment status, and substandard housing of urban blacks were due primarily to their failure to better themselves; they believed that blacks lack the will to succeed as other minorities have done in preceding generations.[3] Thus there was the clear tendency in this white majority to place the burden of blacks on blacks themselves and thereby to deny the reality of society's imposed problems on this group.

The Social Location of White Attitudes

Campbell acknowledged that the white family is the primary instrument of acculturation and socialization for its young, instilling positive and negative attitudes about race early in the lives of their children. Obviously, this socialization pattern is later influenced by the larger community, as the young move into other dimensions of the world than the family. Given that base of understanding, Campbell found that it is accurate only in a limited sense to speak of American white society as having a common orientation toward race.[4] He discovered that the differences in whites in some respects corresponded to common expectations—that people of Southern origin are conservative in their racial views, that Jews are liberal.

What was striking was how little difference Campbell found in racial attitudes associated with precollege school experience or Protestant or Catholic churches. The contribution of public elementary and secondary schools and churches as major forces of acculturation with respect to racial patterns has been to preserve the status quo. But college attendance made a difference. Campbell discovered that racial attitudes were changing most dramatically among young people who have been educated in the nation's colleges since 1948. The post–World War II generation of white college students has had a different campus experience with respect to race from that of their parents. Racial justice has become an article of faith for a large proportion of the college educated.[5]

Racial Differences in the Quality of Urban Life

In the fifteen cities, the objective circumstances of life of urban blacks were, on average, more modest than those of their white neighbors; actually, blacks in these cities fell far short of the standard of living which whites had attained. Also, the experience of life was less satisfying to blacks than to whites. Campbell raised the question whether the major source of discontent and protest among urban blacks was their below-average income, occupational status, and housing or, instead, the pattern of exclusion, subordination, and denigration which white society has traditionally assigned them. It seems impossible, however, to separate the two categories because the pattern of exclusion, subordination, and denigration is inextricably related to below-average income, occupation, and housing—continuing problems that are faced by the majority of black people.

Moreover, even blacks with middle-income levels and higher educational status are not characterized by higher satisfaction levels with respect to the quality of urban life, even when they express satisfaction with respect to income level. It appears that their racial status, which continues to include aspects of exclusion, subordination, and denigration, is the major factor in dissatisfaction of middle-income blacks.

Relation of White Attitudes to Dissatisfaction and Powerlessness

Although Campbell acknowledged the limitations of information in this respect, as well as the need for further longitudinal research, he concluded that white people who are dissatisfied with their city government and local community services are much more likely to exhibit hostility toward blacks than whites who describe themselves as satisfied. This hostile reaction seemed to be greater than immediate dissatisfactions and frustrations, though related to them. Hostility seemed to be part of a general racial orientation which had built up over the individual's lifetime.

White Attitudes in the Suburbs

The attitudes and perceptions of whites in the cities and in the suburbs did not show any important differences. Campbell found that suburban residents were more likely than city residents to live in all-white neighborhoods and were more sensitive to the idea of blacks moving into their neighborhoods. Aside from this specific difference, Campbell concluded that whites in the cities and suburbs could be described as sharing a common attitude toward race.[6]

Stability and Change in Racial Attitudes, 1964–70

The survey data from which Campbell drew his conclusions about stability and change in racial attitudes were drawn from representative samples of the national population, taken by the University of Michigan's Survey Research Center in the fall of 1964, 1968, and 1970. In this six-year period, public incidents showed a strong polarity in the racial attitudes of individual white and black Americans, such as George Wallace's rhetoric and the antiwhite rhetoric of some black militant leaders. Also visible was white resistance to change in the desegregation of schools and neighborhoods.

Campbell's primary focus, though, was on the collective attitudes of whites and blacks. His question emerged as "Did the collective attitudes of whites and blacks become more polarized over the six years; was the nation moving toward two separate societies as the Kerner Commission reported?" Campbell's evidence made him conclude that the report of the Kerner Commission was not true, although he admitted his inquiry was limited and that more penetrating questions might have been asked. Nevertheless, Campbell did not find a deterioration or widening of relationships between the races between 1964 and 1970. On the contrary, he found that on many questions of principle and policy white and black attitudes moved closer together.

What Campbell failed to make clear is that it is with the *implementation* of principle and policy that black–white relationships begin to break down. That is, when people seek to put principle and policy into practice through *programs,* divisiveness occurs, as with the use of busing as a tool to implement the principle and policy of desegregation. Another example is the attack on affirmative action programs, which are designed to implement the principle and policy of equality of opportunity.

Campbell noted increasing impatience within the black population in 1970 with the pace and accomplishments of the movement for racial equality. He felt that if this frustration became more intense, it would have major implications for black–white relationships in the future.

The Present and the Future

Campbell concluded that the racial situation in the United States defies understanding; the complexity and range of relationships between blacks and whites is so great that both groups tend to rely on simplistic generalities which serve to reduce the problem to manageable terms. At worst, this process degenerates into a crude form of racism, with blanket stereotyping of each race and naive beliefs about racial superiority. At the least, it creates a tendency to forget that intraracial diversity is as great as interracial diversity and that no characteristic is held universally within either race.[7]

Given this broad understanding, Campbell proceeded to specifics, as follows, on the quality of white attitudes:

a. The white population in the cities is not universally racist nor can it be divided into contrasting categories called racist and nonracist. White Americans are racist in varying degrees.

b. Resistance to change is the traditional pattern of race relations, and while not universal among whites, it is very widespread and is shown in one form or another by the white population. Forms of change such as increasing racial integration in the work situation seem to be accepted relatively easily by whites, but integration in the more private areas of life disturb many whites.

c. The central theme of conventional racist doctrine, innate racial superiority, was largely missing from white attitudes from 1964 to 1970. Acknowledging that in this period it was unfashionable to be openly racist, Campbell nevertheless felt that the interview techniques made respondents free to express themselves openly and anonymously about their attitudes; so they could have expressed racist attitudes if they had felt them. More important, Campbell concluded that over the past twenty-five years the explanation whites give for blacks' conditions has moved from the genetic to the motivational. He felt this shift implies far-reaching consequences for social policies that are seen as appropriate for meeting social problems.

d. The clear consequences of socialization patterns and an individual's lifetime experiences are visible in racial attitudes of white groups, for example, in Southern conservative socialization patterns and the more liberal Jewish experiences, which are different in character from those of the general white population. But most social characteristics which are not associated with regional or ethnic divisions, such as age, sex, income, occupation, or suburban living, show relatively little relationship to racial attitudes.

e. In the white population, the general characteristic which is dramatically related to racial orientation is college education. High school education or less has little effect on white attitudes about race, nor did college education prior to the end of World War II. However, white men and women who have attended college since World War II are more positive in their racial views than white people of the same generation who did not attend college or people of the prewar generation who did. It appears that this positive change in white racial attitudes can be attributed to a significant change in the intellectual climate on the nation's campuses concerning questions of race. Thus college experience since World War II has contributed significantly to a positive change in traditional white attitudes toward race in this country.

f. White attitudes can be classified into two groups: the first group expresses a preference for racial separation, a denial of discriminatory practices, and a resistance to change in racial patterns; the second group expresses a more hostile attitude through willingness to condone violence directed toward blacks. This second group, a small minority of the white population, is characterized by a low educational level, lack of association with a church, and dissatisfaction with the community in which it lives. They criticize black people and show little or no sympathy for their problems. They believe the civil rights movement is pushing too fast. Because they are disaffected, this group of whites exhibits a readiness for violent answers to racial questions. Their grievances against their communities are displaced by hostility directed toward black people. Thus these whites, already frustrated, who may be first and most directly affected by changes in political and economic conditions, can be expected to show an increasing hostility toward blacks.[8] (This process is called scapegoating, projection, displacement, and works as a defense mechanism for this second group of whites with respect to their attitudes about blacks. Nevertheless, the consequences of these attitudes are felt to be very real by blacks. This writer believes that politicians play to these feelings, as well as to the resistance to change in racial patterns displayed in attitudes of the first group of whites.)

The Future of White Attitudes

Campbell spoke with assurance on a massive shift in the racial attitudes of white Americans since World War II. This shift has been demonstrated by opinion polls taken since World War II and by the passage of local, state, and federal legislation designed to protect the civil rights of blacks. This does not mean that whites are fully committed to racial equality and justice, but there has been movement away from the traditional belief in white superiority and its concomitant patterns of segregation and discrimination toward a more equalitarian view of the races and race-associated relationships, such as those in work situations. The shift has been uneven, and many whites have not moved with it, but the direction of collective change is clear. However, Campbell was not sure that this positive shift in white attitudes would continue. He felt that persistence forecasting would say the trend toward racial equality would be maintained, but there are significant cross-currents which create great uncertainty for the future. Such cross-currents are the white ethnic backlash, the white attitudinal set of noncompliance with busing policies of school systems, and encouragement of such attitudinal sets by Presidents Nixon and Ford in their public statements about "forced busing." Despite these cross-currents, however, there are positive patterns:

1. Interracial contact is increasing in the work force, in the schools, and in public places. Contact as peers provides increasing opportunities for interaction and could produce more favorable attitudes between the races. (Myrdal's thesis is supported.)

2. A significant upgrading of educational achievement is taking place in the younger black population. There has also been a growing number of blacks moving into white-collar jobs. The gap in educational and occupational levels between the races is still substantial, but the continuing upward mobility of black people should reduce the sense of class difference felt by whites and weaken the basis of prejudice. (Myrdal's thesis is supported.)

3. The increasing numbers of white youth attending college and the fact that colleges are producing successive classes of young people whose racial attitudes are in the main more positive toward blacks than those of previous generations are desirable factors in race relations. If these positive attitudes do not regress as college-educated youth move into the adult world and positions of influence and prestige, they should increase the pressure for change away from traditional patterns of racial inequality. (Myrdal's thesis is supported.)

4. The future of white attitudes cannot be considered apart from the future of black attitudes, since they influence each other. If black people determine to separate themselves from the mainstream of American life, the positive trends discernible in white attitudes and behavior would not continue. Apartheid, with all its ramifications, is a logical prediction for American society if blacks demand separation. If, however, separation is only a stage in the process of eventual acculturation and assimilation, it is possible that the black minority will move beyond its present rhetoric and behavior and achieve a secure sense of American identity. However, it is clear that even if blacks choose the acculturation/assimilation goal once again, reaching it will not be easy and will not be achieved in the decade of the 1970s. (Conclusions are in harmony with Myrdal's thesis.)

Campbell concluded in this way:

> We are at present [1971] at a point of uneasy confrontation. The black demands for change are insistent and sometimes abusive [sic]. Most white people agree that change should occur but they want to move gradually and they are repelled by the violent aspects of black rhetoric and action. Change is taking place but black ex-

pectations rise as achievements rise. American society is developing a new pattern of relationships between white and black and the period of change is a time of tension for both races.[9]

Campbell's study has been summarized in some length because it was based on two sets of survey research conducted throughout the years of change, 1964–1970, with explanations extending into 1971. The writer agrees with Campbell's general conclusions. But the findings and conclusions of the Survey Research Center differ from those of the better-known, more widely publicized, but soon-buried Kerner Commission Report, which was issued in March 1968. This latter report pictured America as a divided nation, moving toward two societies—separate and unequal.

THE KERNER REPORT ON WHITE ATTITUDES

The eleven-member Kerner Commission was appointed by President Lyndon Johnson on July 27, 1967, and was composed of persons noted for their moderate political positions. Known radicals or militants, white or black, were excluded from the commission. Two of its members were black and one was female; thus the membership was overwhelmingly white male, moderate, respectable, responsible, and middle class, though not monolithic in viewpoint on the racial question.

Charged with examining the causes of civil disorders and recommending solutions, the commission found that their root causes go beyond civil rights and unemployment, quality education and poverty. The fundamental cause of civil disorders was found to be white racism, that is, white refusal to accept blacks as human beings—as social and economic equals. The belief that blacks were inferior permitted white individuals and institutions to treat blacks in ways which could be characterized as "subhuman" at worst (the perpetuation of slum ghettos, with their totality of human miseries) to "different" at best (the college-educated black, who was permitted to buy a home in suburbia and have a secure job, offering upward mobility). But regardless of the differential circumstances, blacks as a group were always unequal to whites.

In its search for solutions to racial conflict, the commission rejected plans that were characterized as "white moderation," such as continuing the failing efforts toward an integrated society, including the current (1968) proportions of national monetary resources devoted to domestic social and economic programs. It also rejected plans characterized as "black separatism," which essentially meant abandonment of integration as a goal, of commitment of increased resources to make ghetto life better, and provision of a separate territory within the nation which would be assigned to the black population for occupancy. The commission recommended "a policy which combines ghetto enrichment with programs designed to encourage integration of substantial numbers of Negroes into a society outside the ghetto." The overall strategy was "affirmation of common possibilities, for all, within a single society." [10] In the commission's words, "only a commitment to national action on an unprecedented scale can shape a future compatible with the historic ideals of American society. . . .The major need is to generate new will— the will to tax ourselves to the extent necessary to meet the vital needs of the nation."[11] That major need still exists in 1976.

The commission's identification of white racism as the root cause of civil disorders was received by the American power structure and the dominant group with various reactions: denials from some sectors and alienated resignation from others. Probably no other report in the last twenty years has received so much publicity as the Kerner Commission Report, or been filed and forgotten so rapidly.

In retrospect, the commission's language sounds temperate. To say that the nation was divided was an accurate perception. To say that it was moving *toward* two societies, separate and unequal, was an understatement; America has always been two societies—separate and unequal, black and white. Perhaps the hopefulness between the late 1950s and the mid-1960s should be characterized by this paper as "the changing mood," rather than the shift from hopefulness to "benign neglect" in 1969 and thereafter. Viewed in historical perspective, the temper of the 1970s is more like regression, or reversion to type, than a changing mood —except in the precise sense that there is an altered social climate in the limited time perspective of the late 1950s and mid-1960s to 1969–76.

FLETCHER KNEBEL ON WHITE ATTITUDES

In 1969 Fletcher Knebel, former syndicated columnist and reporter, made a mood assessment of the country from Boston to San Diego. The results of this survey were published in the November 18, 1969, issue of *Look* magazine. His broad findings, itemized below, indicated that the prevailing mood in America encompassed many more facets than those directly traceable to race relations. Knebel found that—

1. People were disturbed, anxious, apprehensive. They were sick of

the Vietnam War, baffled by the young, nervous about change —but somehow optimistic.

2. The "kids" had become the symbol of almost everything that alarmed or irritated their elders.
3. The boy-girl sexual revolution was deep and wide, and Puritan America was gone forever.
4. The gleaming new superhighways, with their concrete stanchions, cloverleaf approaches, and spiraling ramps, were our architectural splendors, our pyramids.
5. To older Americans, the kids robbed, rioted, dropped out, seized, mocked, goofed off, wore long hair, and scorned the noble work on which their parents had built their lives.
6. One sensed, along with the tensions, a turbulence of ideas, a growing determination of thinking Americans to "do something" about national domestic problems.[12]

With respect to race relations, Knebel reported finding a great amount of fear in whites arising from the black revolution. He also found that some blacks experienced many of the same fears. Knebel stated that many whites viewed the black uprising with hostility, resentment, and anger, and were arming to protect whatever they had gained. At the same time, he sensed a feeling or a hope that the peak of racial confrontation had passed and that perhaps things would get better between the races. His feeling was based on the fact that finally white Americans were beginning to meet thousands of black Americans in positions of economic parity, and that racial contact had increased tremendously due to the increased visibility of blacks in jobs that were visible to the public. These blacks tried harder and were warmer, more helpful, and more cheerful than their white counterparts, Knebel reported. Further, Knebel found that, outside the dead-end ghettos, blacks were more zestful and optimistic than whites; he felt that the injection of black blood on all-WASP boards of directors would lend an exuberance that was lacking in such places.

Knebel concluded that his pessimism about America's future was deeper than that expressed by most people with whom he talked. However, despite his pessimism, he still had faith in this country to work out the obvious problems. Knebel also saw a spurt of individual effort by such people as Ralph Nader and Pete Seeger to contribute positively to America's future.

It is evident that neither Knebel (using observation and survey methods) nor Campbell (using survey data from two distinct efforts) perceived race relations to be as bleak as painted by the Kerner Commission Report. At the same time, they found no grounds for boundless optimism. Campbell explained that

> despite the changes we have noted and the trends we foresee, the white population of this country is far from a general acceptance of the principle and practice of racial equality. There is little doubt that while there is collective movement of a positive character there are many white individuals whose attitudes have hardened in response to the persistent black pressure for change. These people are being confronted by demands to open their neighborhoods, integrate their labor unions, desegregate their schools, increase the black proportion of their police force, and otherwise accept changes which they consider intolerable. As we have seen, these people are found at all levels of the population and it is not likely that they will soon disappear.[13]

ETHNIC BACKLASH IN THE 1970s

Campbell's survey revealed latent hostility in white people against blacks. These whites were generally frustrated, dissatisfied, and felt themselves to be powerless in their communities and in the American system. This latent hostility appeared to be independent of immediate dissatisfaction and frustrations, but reflected aspects of a general racial orientation built up over the individual's lifetime.* Coupled with fear and/or misunderstanding, this hostility has emerged in the seventies as a threat to the progress of blacks in the quest for equality and justice in our time. These white people view black progress as a threat to their own strivings and achievements. The phenomenon can be explained partially by the aforementioned psychological factors and partially by the fact that this group knows the practical meaning of the zero-sum concept as it operates in America—what blacks win, whites must lose, and vice versa. If, for example, there are not enough jobs so that all qualified persons may be employed in an appropriate slot, who is to be left out? White ethnics do not want to be the persons left out and neither do blacks. Since these groups are in competition for the same employment opportunities and housing options, as well as slots in professional schools, group animosities emerge and often become violent confronta-

---

*See also Gordon Allport, *The Nature of Prejudice* (Cambridge, Mass.: Addison-Wesley, 1954), and Gertrude J. Selznick and Stephen Steinburg, *The Tenacity of Prejudice: Anti-Semitism in Contemporary America* (New York: Harper & Row, 1969).

tions, as with the recent opposition to school busing in Boston, Massachusetts. When family socialization patterns are reinforced by peer associations with other whites whose attitudes have hardened as a result of black pressure for change, the collective response is backlash. This phenomenon comes largely from working-class whites who subscribe to ethnic group identifications.

A body of literature has emerged in the seventies which examines the attitudes and feelings of working-class whites. Representative of the type are *Why Can't They Be like Us?* (Greeley, 1969), *White–Town, U.S.A.* (Binzen, 1970), the second edition of *Beyond the Melting Pot* (Glazer and Moynihan, 1970), *The Middle Americans* (Coles, 1971), *The World of the Urban Working Class* (Fried, 1973), *Unmeltable Ethnics* (Novak, 1973), and *Divided Society* (Greer, 1974). While these works are by no means identical, there is a commonality in their attention to the resurgence of ethnicity in the seventies and in their denial that this resurgence is simply the resurgence of racism.

What characteristics of the ethnics, or the white working class, emerge from these books?† The following generalities can be found.

Labels:	Silent majority, forgotten American, little man, troubled American, the man in the middle.
Stereotype:	Nativism of the hard-hat, blue-collar variety.
Educational attainment:	High school or less.
Occupation:	Truck driver, policeman, turret-lathe operator, white-collar office worker.
Income:	$5,000–$10,000 a year in 1970.
Housing status:	Homeowner of modest but respectable dwelling.
Ethos:	Strong believer in Puritan/Protestant ethic; strongly family oriented, including extended family; steady worker; exhibits old-fashioned patriotism; religious (often Roman Catholic or fundamentalist conservative Protestant); nonpermissive parent–child relationship, tending toward

---

†See Binzen (1970), chaps. 1 and 8 for details of these summarized characteristics. See also Andrew M. Greeley, "Ethnics Know Who's on Their Side—and Who Isn't," *Washington Star*, June 8, 1975, pp. B-1 and B-4.

authoritarianism, especially with females; values his neighborhood as an extension of himself and his home and family.

Watchword: Law and order.

Political affiliation: Democratic party, but many voted for George Wallace in 1968 and Richard Nixon in 1972.

Verbal habits: Outspoken; exhibits distrust for most politicians and contempt for the white rich and the black poor; expresses support for the neighborhood school concept.

Gripes: Their low status—a kind of inferiority, even though white; past humiliations of their group in America, e.g., "No Irish need apply."

Problems: Basically economic—income just above family subsistence level; poor neighborhood services from the city; tarnished national image; working-class and some occupational identities have lost status and respect in America.

Opposed to: Open housing, school busing, hippies, Yippies, draft dodgers and the like, admitting Negroes into unions, China in the United Nations; even against his church when it gets embroiled in civil rights causes.

Generalized concerns: Crime in the streets; his community may be ruined and property values drop; unfair and burdensome taxes; inadequate transportation; high credit rates; better housing; high medical costs; high cost of entertainment; financial burden of parochial education; poor mental health facilities; high cost or lack of opportunity for higher education.

Visceral reactions to: Black power, black militancy, the upward thrust of blacks in politics, jobs, housing, education; blacks on welfare (AFDC).

Personal contact with blacks:	Limited in nature and scope.
Self-description:	"We are honest, hard-working people with children we love dearly."
Other-description:	"The working American—the average white ethnic male . . . the ordinary employee in factory and office, blue collar and white, who lives in the 'gray area' fringe of central cities and constitutes the majority of the nation's work force."[14]

These general characteristics of ethnics have been epitomized in the television program *All in the Family.* The fictional character, Archie Bunker, and his loyal, usually subservient wife Edith, represent the attitudes and feelings of the white working class.

Preceding this popular television program was a movie, *Joe,* which appeared in 1970. Some think that the reception this movie received gave Norman Lear the idea for the Archie Bunker character. Woven into the film were all the elements of the white ethnic's hostility, fear, and distrust toward upper-middle-class whites, distaste for the youth rebellion, and dislike of blacks and their quest for equality.

A sense of alienation and powerlessness because of fear, misunderstanding, the rapid social change in the last twenty years, and the black push for equality (seen as a threat, real or imagined) can merge to form a lethal combination on a local, state, or national level when they are focused on any single issue. And school busing is an example of such an issue. Busing is one method, currently in use, to implement the desegregation of public elementary and secondary schools.

As a method of getting children to their schools, busing has been long accepted in this country. Buses are still used to transport children to consolidated schools in rural areas, often covering long distances in the process. They have also been used to transport white children to all-white schools, past a black school, and black children to all-black schools, past a white school. Buses also convey children to parochial schools, past all the public schools that are closer to their homes, and transport children to specialized schools that provide maximum development for their talents (art, music, science) or that compensate for handicaps (schools for the deaf, mute, blind, physically or mentally handicapped).

Despite this long-accepted tradition of busing, the white working class's reaction to busing as a device for school desegregation has been violent. Buses have been overturned and burned, and children spat upon by working-class whites as the youngsters tried to enter or leave these vehicles. Working-class whites say they fear a drop in quality education, as well as social relationships that might develop into intermarriage, when schools have a substantial black enrollment. They also feel that blacks are being forced on them, and not upon upper-middle-class or upper-class whites.

Further, the neighborhood concept is a valued idea to working-class whites, and this includes the neighborhood school. Busing is viewed as a threat to homogeneity as well as to schooling. Greeley examines the feelings of whites when faced with the fact that "their" neighborhoods are no longer inviolable:

> Invasion by a "foreign" ethnic group is a profound threat; not only does it imply a decline in sales value of one's own house; it is also a challenge to friendship patterns, churches, familiar landscape and shopping areas, and all those things a man has come to value in that particular area he thinks of as his own.[15]

Lack of understanding can be seen, for example, in white perceptions of the role of the black male. Many white working-class people believe that most black men desert their families and are apathetic or lazy. As a result, they believe, black families are poor, but "the fact is, of course, that there are many, many working-class and middle-class Negro and Puerto Rican men, working hard and supporting families—indeed, far more than those who are not—but they are rarely considered."[16]

Working-class whites express hostile feelings against affluent whites, liberals, agitators of all sorts (colored and white), their overeager sympathizers among the well-to-do and "respectable," Catholic priests who marched and worked in the civil rights movement, and the federal government. Essentially this hostility is based on a perception that all these individuals and groups are working for blacks at the expense of the ethnics, and as a result the ethnics are all alone.[17]

There is some pity for the plight of blacks in this country, but working-class whites do not feel that the total burden for solving the problem in terms of daily behavior should be placed on them. Novak has "not found one who does not agree that Blacks get the worst deal in American life, and that the number one injustice in America is the treatment of Blacks. But their persistent question is why the gains of Blacks should be solely at their expense." [18]

It is increasingly clear in 1976 that, as the economy stands still, the lower classes will be increasingly confronted with this mode of thinking. It should eventually become clear to both whites and blacks that many problems are class problems masquerading as race problems.

Coles, like Novak, was told by a white working-class woman: "I am against a lot of them [blacks] because I think they don't do enough for themselves, but I think they have a worse time than the rest of us, and no matter what they do and no matter how good they'd be, there are a lot of people who wouldn't have them living nearby. . . . I feel sorry for them; I really do."[19]

These statements give little comfort to black Americans, who are acutely conscious that the black experience has been one of slavery and second-class citizenship for the 357 years that blacks have been in America. Even the brief periods from 1865 to 1877 and from 1961 to 1968 were not characterized by total effort at positive social change, although blacks received some relief from oppression in the forms of federal assistance and societal support. Blacks at the bottom of the economic and social scale were affected little in either period. Given the state of national affluence and enlightenment in the 1960s, the failure to mount and sustain an all-encompassing societal effort is intolerable.

No other group (except the American Indian) has had such a long history of deprivation and repression, or such totality of exclusion from the possibility of equality, as the black American. There have been no prolonged, sustained, all-encompassing societal efforts to assist the black masses to overcome the effects of slavery, the neoslavery which followed it, and modern incarceration in urban ghettos. It is true that individual blacks and families have "made it" in spite of the system, but the collective black poor cannot do so without a new national will to commit sufficient resources over an extended period of time to alleviate their plight.

Must this commitment occur at the expense of working-class whites? The answer is "yes"—as the American economic system now operates in domestic matters; this is the effect of the zero-sum concept. Thus the practical reality is that such a commitment to raise the lot of the black poor will not be forthcoming on a continuous, sustained basis in terms of policies and programs, because its political effect would be alienation of large numbers of white ethnics. The real societal question, however, is why working-class people of all races and ethnic groups, along with the more seriously disadvantaged of all groups, seem not to learn that such a commitment is not made for the disadvantaged of *any* group. If they could learn this very basic fact, they might see beyond such superficialities as skin color and begin to work together for the implementation and maintenance of policies and programs which would help them all in improving the quality of their lives.

Do the authors we have surveyed recommend solutions to this aspect of the American dilemma and the changing mood? Novak argues for a coalition of the black and white lower classes. Irving Levine (cited by Binzen) argues for specific solutions to specific problems, such as organizing security agents (e.g., block wardens) to be responsible for safety on their blocks and to combat crime in the streets. These authors represent conventional thought and offer piecemeal, "safe" solutions— even if they could be actualized.

What will it take for working people—regardless of economic status, color, sex, or religion—to realize that the domestic social problems of the 1970s are larger than any class, race, sex, or religion? High salaries are eroded by inflation and by unfair, burdensome taxes. Dehumanization is real, with evidence that the CIA and FBI have maintained secret folders on citizens. Personal mail has been opened illegally by government officials and phones have been tapped. Assassination of national leaders and alleged assassination plots against foreign leaders demonstrate that human life is not sacred, and that to take a leadership role with a commitment to solving human problems may mean signing one's own death certificate.

Further, the specter of unemployment hangs over all in America. The unemployed Ph.D. or the displaced engineer is no better off than the unemployed construction worker or the displaced automobile factory worker. The credit system, in which so many Americans are deeply immersed, provides for foreclosure on homes and repossession of cars and furniture, regardless of education or previous payment patterns, when payments are two months overdue. This knowledge is readily available to the ordinary person who consults his daily newspaper with regularity.

Unless all working, salaried Americans can find a way to overcome provincial differences and work collectively to solve the massive domestic social problems of the 1970s, there is little real hope for meaningful social change for any dispossessed group. Only superficial changes will occur in response to pressures from particular groups, and these superficial changes will be at the expense of another group. To pay more Social Security benefits to the elderly, for example, requires that all workers, including the young, be more highly taxed, up to $16,500 in annual income. It is a vicious circle from which we will never emerge, so long as group animosities and rivalries allow the divide-and-conquer strategy to prevail as a given in American life.

Despite the continuing American dilemma, made worse by the general economic condition, the total picture is by no means completely negative for blacks in 1977 with respect to white attitudes. For example, the *New York Times* of August 18, 1975, carried a front-page article by Paul Delaney which reported the findings of the Institute for Social Research at the University of Michigan from a series of surveys it conducted between 1964 and 1974 on white attitudes toward blacks. The broad findings were (1) whites reported their contacts with blacks had increased slowly but steadily between 1964 and 1974; (2) the increased contacts had brought a change in attitude of whites toward blacks from negative to positive; and (3) there appeared to be a growing acceptance of blacks by whites. The surveys were taken in 1964, 1968, 1970, 1972, and 1974, and approximately 10,000 persons were interviewed (10 percent were black).[20]

Dr. Angus Campbell, director of the institute, was quoted as saying that the survey data reveal "pretty clearly that white people have a strong sense of feeling of more change taking place now in their contact with blacks in all phases of life than in the past."[21] Also, the survey data showed that (1) whites' contact with blacks is clearly associated with education: college graduates had most contact and whites with little schooling had least contact with blacks; young whites and those with more education became more favorable toward blacks between 1964 and 1974; (2) the proportion of whites who believed in strict segregation (under the *Plessy* decision) declined from one-fourth to one-tenth; (3) the percentage of whites who believed the federal government should protect the rights of blacks to equal accommodation rose from 56 to 75 percent; (4) the percentage of whites who felt that blacks should have the right to move into any neighborhood they could afford rose from 65 to 87 percent; and (5) regional differences were smaller at the end of the ten-year period than at the beginning. All of these findings are positive for blacks.

Two areas in which negative attitudes prevailed were desegregation of jobs and schools and the federal role in desegregation efforts. In 1964, less than half of the whites contacted said the federal government should see that blacks get fair treatment in jobs. The proportion of whites with this belief was about the same a decade later.[22] In 1966, less than half the whites who were interviewed felt that the federal government should see that white and black children attend the same schools. By 1970 the percentage had climbed a bit, to a small majority. However, since 1970 white support has dropped sharply, to just over one-third. This is the lowest point in the ten-year period.[23]

Dr. Campbell and his research assistant, Shirley Hatchett, also noted the importance of the breaking down of negative racial attitudes about blacks on the part of whites. However, they agreed that there was little correlation between expressed attitudes and action. Dr. Campbell thought the data showed that whites felt satisfied with racial progress and had become less enthusiastic about civil rights. Along with perceived racial progress over this decade, whites saw black faces on television and blacks move into high-level federal positions. This gave whites the feeling that racial injustice no longer existed in America.

This latter expression, the satisfaction of whites with racial progress and increased visibility of blacks in public places, is another example of Ralph Barton Perry's "egocentric predicament." Each group, white and black, views the extent of racial progress (or lack of it) from its own perspective and its particular position in the social structure of the country. Therefore, whites are satisfied with the rate and amount of racial progress in the last decade, but blacks are not.

Viewed from the black perspective, the areas where negative white attitudes prevail are critical because they are antecedent to the possibility of progress in areas where white attitudes are positive. For example, it takes equality of employment opportunities for blacks to be able to buy a house of their choice and move into any neighborhood. If one cannot make the money, housing alternatives are necessarily limited. In like manner, it has taken the federal government's intervention to safeguard the rights of blacks, since neither state and local governments nor private enterprise would do so. Without the compulsions of national laws and court orders, the gains that blacks have procured in the last decade, including increased contacts with whites, could not have been achieved. Therefore blacks are skeptical about the possibility of a reduced federal role in desegregation efforts, especially with respect to jobs and education generally.

Although blacks view the advancement of other blacks to high-level federal positions as a positive gain, they also believe this is tokenism, in the sense that these persons are few in number and rarely in key or crucial decision-making roles. The increased visibility of blacks in the media (especially television) and sports is also regarded as progress by the minority population. However, this advancement does not reach the core of black problems or the large numbers of under- or unemployed blacks. Progress for this large group of people has been almost nonexistent over the last decade.

This leads to the obvious question, Has progress occurred for the black minority in the last decade, and if so, how much progress and in what areas of American life? This question will be answered in chapter 3.

CHANGING ATTITUDES OF SELECTED WHITE INTELLECTUALS AND AFFLUENT WHITES

Who, by definition, are white intellectual leaders and affluent whites? White intellectual leaders are engaged in activity that requires the creative use of intelligence, who are expected to be guided chiefly by the intellect rather than by emotion or experience. Affluent whites are those who possess a generous or sufficient and typically increasing supply of material possessions and creature comforts in American society. Individuals may fit into one or both of these categories. Most of the intellectuals discussed in this section are former liberals who received new recognition and appreciation during the 1960s, as John F. Kennedy and Lyndon B. Johnson turned to the "brains" of the country for solutions to social problems. A kind of euphoria resulted for intellectuals, who had generally been ignored as "ivory tower" types during the Truman and Eisenhower years.

By the late 1960s, having lost John and Robert Kennedy to assassinations and having witnessed the complexity and difficulty of resolving long-standing domestic social problems, as well as encountering the rigidities of entrenched bureaucracies most interested in retaining their self-interests, these former liberals lost the nerve, interest, and willingness to continue their efforts to effect social, political, and economic change. Also, these liberals had come under attack by George Wallace in his 1968 presidential campaign; he characterized them as "pointy headed," a term of derision designed to elicit popular support for his cause. Later, in 1969 and 1970, intellectuals were to be subjected to further verbal abuse from Spiro Agnew, then vice president, who labeled them "effete intellectual snobs."

Under attack, and finding no easy answers to complex social and racial problems, these white intellectuals retreated. Now they speak and write in a neoconservative vein, compared with the former liberal style. They have retreated into secure positions and are now concerned with the maintenance and stability of an order which has rewarded them.

It must nevertheless be emphasized that not every white intellectual or liberal-affluent white person has changed to the neoconservative position. There are individuals of note who define themselves as left of center—intellectuals who have not changed their liberal stance, which was evident in the 1960s and earlier. They continue to exhibit knowledge of, and interest in, the continuing domestic social problems, writing and speaking in the interests of the common man. In this sense they represent a countertrend to the divide-and-conquer theory and a continuation of the thought and commitment of the early 1960s, which sought to effect meaningful social change for the dispossessed. Unfortunately, these intellectuals do not receive the same publicity as intellectuals who have become neoconservative. Their writings do not trickle from the scholarly and professional journals to the popular magazines in the same degree as those of the neoconservatives, nor does one hear of them as referents on televised newscasts and issue-oriented programs to the same extent as the neoconservatives. Therefore, even though these intellectuals retain their liberal stance, their effect is muted in comparison with the effect of the neoconservatives on American social policy. A few intellectuals who are of this continuing liberal persuasion are Eugene Genovese, Lewis Coser, Irving Howe, and Herbert Aptheker.

There are other intellectuals who are not left of center, whose views have not changed in the 1970s. Thomas Pettigrew and John Rawls of Harvard University, as well as Robert O'Neil of Indiana University at Bloomington and Clarence J. Karier of the University of Illinois at Urbana, are such persons. They represent some of the few who today are speaking out for equality, justice, and continued effort toward societal integration.

How can the changing white intellectuals be characterized? According to Joseph Epstein, author and editor, the new intellectual conservatives are "reputable . . . mostly men of solid achievement in the social sciences or intellectual journalism, many of them having themselves once been figures of impeccable liberal and radical standing."[24] In addition to their solid achievement, the new intellectual conservatives are highly educated people, often faculty members at prestigious colleges or universities—people who received their postsecondary education in the 1940s or early 1950s (prior to 1954). They have ample resources of time, funds, and research assistance to study social problems and to comment on them verbally and in writing. They are (or have been) heard by presidents and congressmen as advisors or have held important appointive posts. Intellectuals who are associated with this rightward conservative movement are Norman Podhoretz, Irving Kristol, Nathan Glazer, Edward Banfield, and Daniel P. Moynihan, among others.

The discourse indicating retrenchment in social commitment on the part of these influential white intellectuals and others of their bent can be classified into several streams: (1) the reopening of genetic inferiority theories, (2) the contention that the poor are largely responsible for their condition, (3) the idea that governmental and institutional intervention in individual affairs makes no substantial difference, and (4) the pseudo-meritocracy.*

In 1969 Arthur R. Jensen, an educational psychologist at the University of California at Berkeley, rekindled the nature–nurture controversy which had raged in American intellectual circles at the turn of the century and through the 1920s, but which had been muted since 1954. Writing in the winter 1969 issue of the *Harvard Educational Review,* Jensen argued that the intellectual potential of the poor generally, and blacks particularly, was restricted by inherent genetic limitations.[†] Thus, because of genetic deficits, there was no need for massive social and/or educational programs designed to improve the lot of blacks or the poor. The causes of low incomes and inferior social status were not environmental (nurture) but were genetically determined (nature); therefore, little could be done to remedy the inequalities. Jensen's viewpoint concurred with that of Richard Herrnstein, H. J. Eysenck, and William Shockley, a Nobel Prize–winning physicist at Stanford University. Wide publicity has been given to these men and/or their ideas in *U.S. News and World Report, Saturday Review, Newsweek, Education Digest, School and Society,* the *New York Times Magazine, Life,* and other periodicals.[††] Thus the ideas flowed from scholarly journals to the more popular press, where a large audience was reached. Large audi-

---

*For detailed analyses see Bernard C. Watson, *Stupidity, Sloth and Public Policy: Social Darwinism Rides Again,* a 1973 publication of the National Urban Coalition; also see *Social Policy* (May/June 1972) editorial comment (pp. 2–4), as well as S. M. Miller and Ronnie Steinberg Ratner, "The American Resignation: The New Assault on Equality," in the same issue (pp. 5–15).

†Genetic explanations had been supplanted by environmental explanations in the 1930s. Jensen's article was also intended to be a means of explaining why federal domestic programs of the Great Society failed.

††See, for example, *U.S. News and World Report* 66:48–51 (10 March 1969); *Saturday Review,* pp., 52–68 (17 May 1969) and 244:9 (Summer 1972); *Newsweek* 72:84 (31 March 1969); *Education Digest* 35:1–4 (October 1969); *School and Society* 96: 127–28 (2 March 1968); *New York Times Magazine,* pp. 10–11 (31 August 1969); and *Life* 68:58b–58d (12 June 1970).

ences also are reached via television, where genetic inferiority ideas have had exposure.

Other scholars reacted to Jensen's article in the spring 1969 issue of *Harvard Educational Review,* pointing out contradictory evidence and questioning Jensen's methodology and conclusions. However, the contradictory evidence has not had the same publicity. Also, various Americans seem to have forgotten their own group experiences when they were similarly labeled as genetically inferior. For example, the charge was made in 1921 that Italians, Poles, and Jews were feebleminded; so to continue to permit large numbers of them to immigrate to the United States would dilute the mental abilities of the populace. This argument was used to encourage Congress to pass a restrictive immigration law in 1921, which was supplanted by the Immigration Act of 1924. The latter discriminated strongly against people from southern and eastern Europe and favored people from northern and western Europe. In 1977, some of the people most discriminated against in 1921 and 1924 (or their descendants) seem to want to believe that blacks are in fact genetically inferior, and therefore beyond the help of social and educational policies designed to more nearly equalize the human condition. Thus this debate, reopened by Jensen in 1969, continues unabated into 1976.

The second stream of neoconservatism in intellectual discourse, which states that the poor are largely responsible for their condition, can be linked with the third stream, the idea that governmental and institutional intervention in individual affairs makes no substantial difference. To illustrate the connection of these two themes, it is necessary to recall that in the years of Kennedy's New Frontier the goals included a struggle, and that in the years of Johnson's Great Society an "unconditional war on poverty" was declared, again using federal funds as ammunition. Before this "war on poverty" could be won, priorities were altered because of the war in Vietnam. Both wars could not be won simultaneously; the nation could not in fact have guns and butter in equal amounts at the same time. Guns were the priority, and domestic programs were reduced in scope and received less funding and governmental attention. As a result, the domestic programs failed to achieve the lofty goals that had been set for them originally, and the people at whom the programs were aimed remained poor for the most part. Instead of intellectuals recognizing the situation as it was, many of them became disillusioned with what was called the failure of the war on poverty and placed the blame on poor people—the victims—instead of placing it on a society which allocated too little resources and effort over too short a period of time to make a significant difference. Also, these intellectuals have played down the hostility of local power groups which the federal government had to circumvent in its antipoverty programs.

Thus the common intellectual argument becomes: Governmental intervention occurred to help the poor, but it did not remove them from poverty. Therefore governmental intervention makes no substantial difference and is an unnecessary expense. The poor remain poor because they are lazy, unmotivated, apathetic, or live in "a tangle of pathology."

Daniel P. Moynihan became known for the preceding phrase with respect to the Negro family, about which he wrote in 1965. While stressing that this "pathological" state was the result of three centuries of mistreatment, Moynihan concluded that the "tangle" cannot be unraveled by the amelioration of social conditions. According to Moynihan, it becomes the fault of the Negro family that it is in a generally depressed state when compared with the white family in the United States. By 1969 Moynihan's writings indicated that he felt the poverty programs failed because they had encouraged the poor to hope for more than they could get.[25] Given the fact that Moynihan has been chosen by four presidents for appointive and/or advisory posts and roles, his influence on those presidents and in the society has been far from negligible.

In *The Unheavenly City,* which appeared in 1968, Edward C. Banfield asserted that most of the people caught up in the culture of poverty were unable to sacrifice immediate gratifications in favor of future ones, or to accept the disciplines that are required in order to get and to spend. Extreme "present orientedness," then, is the principal cause of poverty, not lack of income. Improvements in external circumstances can affect poverty only superficially; one dilemma of a multiproblem family is no sooner solved than another arises. According to Banfield, raising such a family's income would not necessarily improve its way of life, and could conceivably make things worse.

Regarding institutional intervention in relation to education, the most recent widely publicized attack was made by Christopher Jencks. His book, *Inequality: A Reassessment of the Effect of Family and Schooling in America,* appeared in 1972. The book's jacket says:

> Christopher Jencks' *Inequality* is a landmark in social and educational thought in America—for it presents the evidence to overturn the most cherished assumptions of liberal reform in our society. Jencks and his associates challenge much of contemporary social policy with these startling conclusions:

educational reform cannot bring about
economic or social quality;

genes and IQ scores have relatively
little effect on economic success.[26]

This book was soon used by opponents of school busing, legislators who opposed increasing expenditures for schools, and other school critics. Jencks declared that it was not his intent that his book be used to justify limiting educational expenditures or abandoning efforts at desegregation. Nevertheless, whatever his intent, his book has provided additional ammunition for the troops who war against liberal reforms as appropriate social and educational policy.

The fourth stream of neoconservatism is the pseudomeritocracy, which says that adult success comes solely, or primarily, from merit. Supposedly, when people work hard enough (Puritan/Protestant ethic), develop their natural talents, and demonstrate their capability, as well as possess appropriate credentials, they will be rewarded because they merit jobs, salaries appropriate to the jobs, and accompanying status. Therefore, what blacks and other underprivileged persons need to do is apply themselves, work hard, and prove that they are capable, and the rewards will follow. However, the reality in America is that although some people who have followed this course have been rewarded, many have not (e.g., many Asian Americans). The job selection process, especially at high levels, is more often based on personal contacts, skin color, sex, cultural background, or favoritism than on ability, presumed or demonstrated.

The revelations in 1975 in daily papers (such as the *Washington Post*) about abuses in the Civil Service system in grades GS 13–15 illustrate the faults in the selection process. What we read is that, more often than not, jobs at these levels are filled, or the persons have actually been selected, prior to advertising the vacancies. The process of advertising is merely perfunctory, because it is required by law, and means little or nothing to job applicants. Further, jobs at these levels most often are filled by persons already within the system, which means that equally qualified persons outside the system do not have an equal chance to get the jobs, no matter how meritorious they may be. Even within the system, white males are overwhelmingly chosen for these upper-level jobs—more often than blacks, Chicanos, Puerto Ricans, Asians, and women. Therefore white males are considered, *ipso facto,* more meritorious than any other group. Yet the social policy of affirmative action is under attack by white males, who cry "reverse discrimination" when people other than themselves are selected in larger than token numbers for jobs from which they had been excluded in the past. People who have power never relinquish it willingly; so to the extent that white males have power to get and hold the best jobs, they fight efforts to share that power.

But what of affluent whites who may not properly be classified as intellectuals? What has been their position with respect to the changing mood? Upper-middle-class white youth (who will be used as an example of affluent whites) in the middle sixties participated in freedom rides and in voter registration drives throughout the South. (At least two of them, Schwerner and Goodman, lost their lives in Mississippi.) These youths also exhibited great concern for public-interest law, so that law school curricula expanded to emphasize problems of tenants, disadvantaged groups, debtors, and civil rights. Young white lawyers worked in OEO-funded Neighborhood Legal Services programs around the country and fought for the best human interests of migrants, senior citizens, the poor, prisoners, American Indians, and other powerless people. They also accepted positions in public-interest organizations, either sponsored by foundations or funded by the government. These organizations worked for equal employment opportunities, consumers' rights, and preservation of the environment. The young white lawyers were so energetic that leading politicians, such as Ronald Reagan and Spiro Agnew, found it necessary to speak out against these young "troublemakers" who, they said, were creating problems in a society which would otherwise be orderly.

Many of these energetic young whites became alienated from the civil rights movement as it became increasingly black in tone, based on the "black power" utterances of militant leaders such as Stokely Carmichael. Others became alienated from the society, because of the war in Vietnam and apparent hypocrisies. They turned their energies to protesting the war and/or to such hedonistic indulgences as marijuana, LSD, communal living, and "free" sex. Still others turned to such good and just causes as the American Indian movement, the women's movement, and ecology programs. However, they ignored the continuing good and just causes of blacks and the poor. These shifts in the interests, efforts, influence, and funds of affluent young whites from one deserving cause to another, before any problem was solved, have contributed to the changing mood since 1969. Their efforts helped end the war in Vietnam, but all the domestic problems remain unsolved.

Public-interest law is also on the decline among these young people. Hostile to OEO, the Nixon administration undercut it. Inflation and recession have reduced foundations' funds to public-interest law groups, and the Internal Revenue Service is reexamining the tax-exempt status of public-interest law groups. Lawyers, like all other Americans, must earn a living, no matter what their personal interests may be. Eliminating the funding for public-interest law groups has meant that many of the ambitious, energetic young people have been forced to take their legal expertise somewhere else, and the underprivileged are left once again powerless, at the mercy of society. Therefore, by personal choice or by economic necessity, the young affluent whites who were so active in the 1960s are not active in the 1970s. This contributes to the changing mood of the 1970s.

Where does it all end? How do we regroup? *Can* we regroup? Where do we go from here? Miller and Ratner suggested in *Social Policy* that

> what is needed is a politics of equality that will join many groups in America together behind a positive program of change. This is a gloomy moment to think about such a politics of change. But if Nixon can go to China, cannot those liberals dismayed by the retreat from liberalism, those radicals drawn to large-scale change, those victims of the economic and social structures of the nation begin to struggle together for the kinds of changes that would produce a more egalitarian society—with less spent on the military and more on social amenities, with equal distribution of economic goods and with economic controls to promote equality rather than perpetuate unfairness, with greater liberty rather than repression, with less elitism. In short, cannot we work together to create the kind of society that does not manipulate or coerce commitments but rather attracts them?[27]

Their suggestion, made in 1972, is even more valid in 1976.

CHANGING TONE OF THREE WHITE-ORIENTED PERIODICALS

As in the altered attitudes in the writings of some key intellectuals since 1969, there is a changing tone in many intellectually oriented periodicals since that time. Examples of the changing tone of such journals can be found by surveying *Commentary, Public Interest,* and *Atlantic Monthly* over the past ten or twelve years, and by reviewing articles pertaining to vital domestic issues of the time with respect to blacks and the poor.*

The changing tone of *Commentary* has been noted by Bernard Rosenberg and Irving Howe in *The New Conservatives: A Critique from the Left.* In their article "Are American Jews Turning toward the Right?" these men note what seems to be a rightward turn among Jewish intellectuals, which can be seen in one instance in the

> recent evolution of *Commentary,* which under the editorship of Norman Podhoretz, and with the help of Milton Himmelfarb, has been conducting a fierce campaign not only against the New Left (or its shattered remnants) but also against some of the ideas traditionally associated with socialism, social democracy, and even liberalism. Irritable and overreaching as this campaign has been its thrust has thus far seemed not so much toward a conservative ideology as against recent versions of what Podhoretz takes to be vulgarizations of liberalism. . . . To what extent *Commentary* reflects growing sentiments within the Jewish community, or to what extent it runs counter to the dominant sentiments of that community, no one really seems to know.[28]

Following the same line of thought on the attack on liberalism and social democracy, Miller and Ratner noted that a liberal retreat was verifiable in 1972. They explained four main themes in what they called "the new assault on equality": (1) there is nothing wrong with America that lowering our aspirations won't solve, (2) things are much better than people seem to think, (3) blaming the victim, and (4) things will get worse if you try to make them better.[29] The editor of *Social Policy,* Frank Reissman, summed up the negative arguments of the seventies by saying that former liberals, now turned conservative, hold that the effort at social change failed in the sixties and it is now necessary to return to old ways, such as "benign neglect," acceptance of the basic inferiority of the poor, and the stability provided by traditional values, meaningless hard work, and pseudo meritocracy.[30]

Between 1960 and 1967, *Commentary* consistently published articles depicting the need for a common democratic commitment, across racial, ethnic, religious, and class lines, to solve race and social problems which were evident in the United States. While specific strategies for actualizing the commitment differed from one author to another, the commitment was visible in this journal. However, beginning in January 1969

---

*The review of these journals ended with the December 1974 issue in each case.

and continuing through 1974, *Commentary* consistently published articles that backed away from that common democratic commitment, including affirmative action, busing, the IQ controversy, and open admissions.

The intellectual attack on liberation in the pages of *Commentary* has been led by Harvard (or former Harvard) University professors of national prominence, such as Nathan Glazer, Daniel P. Moynihan, Edward Banfield, and Richard Herrnstein. They have been joined by Irving Kristol and Sidney Hook of New York University, Robert A. Nisbet of Columbia University, Paul Seabury of the University of California at Berkeley, and, more recently, Hadley Arkes of Amherst. The stature of these authors and the prestige of their institutions give credibility and great weight to their analyses and conclusions. Only rarely, in the seventies, are authors published in *Commentary* who vigorously defend the quest for equal rights. And only occasionally, in the seventies, does *Commentary* publish the views of black authors (most notably, Bayard Rustin is given the opportunity to be heard).

Below is a sampling of *Commentary* articles during the periods of democratic commitment (1963–67), change (January to April 1969), and conservatism (1970–74). In February 1963 Norman Podhoretz, editor of *Commentary,* wrote the journal's lead article, "My Negro Problem—and Ours," in which he acknowledged his personal feelings of fear, envy, and hatred of Negroes, which had been learned through years of association (mostly negative) in Brooklyn. Podhoretz also expressed the feeling that most white Americans are twisted and sick in their feelings about Negroes, and despair of the push toward integration. He stressed, however, that his "own twisted feelings about Negroes" conflicted with his moral convictions and that he was acknowledging the feelings so they could be controlled (a kind of catharsis) and ultimately disregarded in favor of the moral convictions. The article was published with a disclaimer from the magazine and the sponsoring organization, stating that Podhoretz's views were not representative of their views. This article, identified by *Commentary* as a landmark, set the tone for subsequent articles addressed to race problems in the United States. A selection of these articles has been reissued as *Commentary Reports* and assembled in a body for retrospective reading. The selection is reviewed below.

February, 1964   In "The Meaning of Negro Strategy," David Danzig was supportive of the concept of collective struggle over individual achievement as the road to Negro freedom. He was supportive also of Negro tactics in Birmingham.

September 1964   Midge Decter was very supportive of the Negro quest for better schooling in New York and of the idea that all children are of value.

February 1965   Bayard Rustin, a black, identified by *Commentary* as a leading tactician of the civil rights movement, wrote the lead article, which supported the black movement, from civil rights activities to a total social movement. Rustin expressed his belief that the Democratic party could be shaped into a consensus party which could be the vehicle for social reconstruction. He requested federal government action to help achieve the goal of integration of blacks into the mainstream of America.

March 1966   Rustin was critical of the McCone Report on Watts and repeated his proposal for a massive public works program to create new jobs. He felt the nation should begin to develop the $100 billion "freedom budget" advocated by A. Philip Randolph to solve the problems of blacks.

April 1966   In an article both explanatory and conciliatory, John Slawson wrote "Mutual Aid and the Negro," in which he said Negroes in 1966 were basically opposed to the idea of self-help or mutual aid as the primary vehicle for changing the overall condition of blacks because the idea of self-help or mutual aid had become a covert way of implying that the Negro is responsible for his condition.

September 1966   In "Black Power: Two Views," David Danzig wrote "In Defense of 'Black Power' " and Bayard Rustin wrote "Black Power and Coalition Politics." Danzig defended the idea of black power, saying the Negro lacked a network of unifying social traditions and must therefore depend on political action through color consciousness as his main instrument of solidarity. He stressed, however, that black efforts would fail if based exclusively on self-interest. Rus-

tin was against the popularized conception of black
power; he advocated actualization of Randolph's
$100 billion freedom budget through coalitions and
aiming for integration.

Though Danzig's and Rustin's views were somewhat opposed to
each other, both were in the vein of a common democratic commitment
to solve race and social problems within the established framework of
American society. Both points of view appeared to be in line with the
stated aims of *Commentary:* fighting bigotry and protecting human
rights, as well as being hospitable to diverse viewpoints and beliefs.

The year 1966 seems to have been one in which *Commentary* articles bore the liberal banner, espousing the common democratic commitment. In addition to the articles reviewed above, "An Agenda for
American Liberals" appeared in June 1966. In this article John Kenneth
Galbraith expressed the thought that the age of liberals had arrived and
he set forth a general agenda from which American liberals should
work.

Commentary continued to feature the ideas of Bayard Rustin in
1967. They were consistent with his previous thoughts, in line with the
democratic commitment. For example:

April 1967   In "The Lessons of the Long Hot Summer" Rustin
                    itemized the lessons learned, set forth social goals,
                    and urged that the basic injustices and contradic-
                    tions woven into the political and economic fabric be
                    corrected in keeping with the ideals of American
                    society. He continued to advocate integration and
                    use of coalitions.

A change in tone can be seen in *Commentary* articles in 1968, as in
Daniel P. Moynihan's August presentation, "The Professors and the
Poor." Moynihan stressed that the war on poverty, like the war in Vietnam, was preeminently the work of liberal intellectuals who came to
power in the early 1960s under the presidency of John F. Kennedy. A
key element in the war on poverty was the idea of community action,
and a key exclusion from it was an adult employment program, especially one for the employment of adult males. Moynihan held that both
this inclusion and this exclusion were errors in judgment by white intellectuals who knew very little about urban Negro poverty but were key

policy makers. In fact, "no Negro was involved in any significant way at any significant stage in planning the Economic Opportunity Act of 1964."[31]

Moynihan then argued that a Negro intellectual/academic tradition, which was in full force a generation ago, had somehow faltered in 1968; most of the burgeoning literature on poverty was being written from the research of whites. He claimed that Negro social scientists were few and far between, and those who were held in greatest respect were so overextended and in such demand that they produced less than would otherwise be the case. The literature of poverty "involves the dissection of unusually unsuccessful groups by representatives of unusually successful ones."[32]

Moynihan felt that social science greatly needed a considerable widening of its ethnic, social, regional, and religious base so that social scientists, observing a given milieu, could compare their judgments with the judgments of other social scientists. The society could then be more confident of the results. Moynihan also believed that American social science should be characterized by rigorous inquiry, and in this case it should be inquiry into what social process keeps people in poverty or leads them out of it. Moynihan concluded by saying, in the liberal vein, that "there are promises to keep. In the dark hours of 1964 a bright and shining commitment was made. That commitment stands, and intellectuals, having played a major role in its establishment, now have a special responsibility both for keeping it alive and for keeping it on the proper track."[33]

By January 1969 the positive tone toward social and racial issues, so evident in Moynihan's preceding note, had begun to change in the pages of *Commentary,* and Earl Raab's "The Black Revolution and Jewish Question" clearly signals the change. Raab reviewed the nature of "the Jewish question" in America, where Jewish people had moved from a stage of nonacceptance in 1920 to a stage of near acceptance in the post–World War II era. When their almost complete acceptance was evident, the defensive energies and apparatus of the Jewish community moved from the Jewish question to the Negro question, based on the fellow-Americans concept and on the Jewish impulse to help other people who experience less than first-class citizenship. Raab then noted that the black revolution had progressed through the stages of equal opportunity, antipoverty, and black positiveness to a stage of black expressivism which was anti-Semitic in tone. The black revolution was stirring the Jewish community and America in general into a renewed understanding of pluralistic politics, and was alienating many Jewish people. Raab emphasized that the alienation is not a Jewish backlash but a regrouping, and that the key question for Jewish people would have to become "Is it good for the Jews?"

This question was to set the tone for the articles and editorial comments which have appeared in *Commentary* in the 1970s. The general theme became that Jewish people are not "horned and leprous bigots" but people who have troubles of their own, a dignity of their own, and a growing sense that they are being left out. What this meant to Raab was that there would have to be a new agenda for the United States, with less attention to blacks and more attention to the lower class. He concluded with the observation that the Jewish question is alive again because the American political structure and its traditional coalitions are in naked transition.

Milton Himmelfarb, continuing the discussion started by Raab, analyzed what he saw as the Jewish situation in America in the March 1969 issue of *Commentary* under the title "Is American Jewry in Crisis?" He concluded that it was, because of the resurgence of anti-Semitism on the part of black militants, teachers, professors, other intellectuals, and community leaders, which was expressed in print, on the radio, on television, and at hearings of the New York City Board of Education. He also believed a crisis existed because of the reintroduction of the idea of a quota system. Himmelfarb maintained that the Jewish situation was serious and warranted a more concerned response from the Jewish community than uneasy apprehension.

The third article in this series came the next month, April 1969, and was written by Nathan Glazer. Glazer pointed out that Raab and Himmelfarb had raised the issue of blacks' anti-Semitism, its extent, its sources, and its dangers. Glazer's article addressed three key questions: (1) are Jews actually threatened by black anti-Semitism? (2) is an alliance, or potential alliance, developing between black militants and the WASP establishment? and (3) if there is a threat to Jews, how can it best be countered?

In the issues of *Commentary* from 1970 through 1974 the more conservative trend, evident in Raab's, Himmelfarb's and Glazer's 1969 articles, had become a dominant theme. That conclusion is reached by analyzing the key articles, by counting the articles whose tone is negative or questionable on the actualization of concepts such as equality and justice in America, and by noting which authors' ideas have been published. A spirit of "benign neglect" seems to have taken hold of *Com-*

mentary from 1970 through 1974, with 1972 being the "banner year"— the apex of a hands-off policy in terms of actualization of equality and justice for blacks in America.

A sampling of articles from 1970 through 1974 will demonstrate the general tone of neoconservatism which has prevailed in *Commentary* in the early and mid-seventies. That general tone is occasionally broken by a liberal article, but an overall neoconservatism comes through a thinly veiled cloak of classical-liberal rhetoric which imparts enough ambivalence to key articles that the reader must proceed carefully, lest he be lost in specious reasoning. Dissenters from *Commentary's* main thrust of the seventies can still be heard in the section "Letters from Readers," but that is about the only forum in the magazine still open to liberal opinion on such issues as equality, racial and ethnic relations, affirmative action programs, open admissions, and the division of wealth and power.

Nathan Glazer's "The Limits of Social Policy," which appeared in *Commentary* in September 1971, gives the tone of many *Commentary* articles. Glazer's point of view is that

1. Social policy is an effort to deal with the breakdown of traditional ways of handling distress. These traditional mechanisms are located primarily in the family, but also in the ethnic group, the neighborhood, and in such organizations as the church and the *landsmanschaft.*
2. In its effort to deal with the breakdown of these traditional structures, however, social policy tends to encourage their further weakening. There is, then, no sea of misery against which we are making steady headway. Our efforts to deal with distress themselves increase distress.

   I do not mean to suggest any automatic law. I do suggest processes.[34]

Glazer's view means that, as a process, federal intervention into human affairs is a mistake since federal intervention is accomplished through the efforts of public authorities, thereby weakening or undermining traditional structures such as the family, neighborhood, ethnic associations, and the church. He overlooks the fact that these traditional structures had already been seriously undermined by industrialization, automation, and geographical mobility and that they had declined in vigor and effectiveness in the turbulence of urbanization and upward mobility since World War II.

Glazer defined the limits of social policy as (1) limitation of resources, (2) inevitable professionalization of services, and (3) lack of knowledge.

> But aside from these problems of cost, of professionalization, and of knowledge, there is the simple reality that every piece of social policy substitutes for some traditional arrangement in which public authorities take over, at least in part, the role of the family, of the ethnic and neighborhood group, or of the voluntary association. In doing so, social policy weakens the position of these traditional agents, and further encourages needy people to depend on the government, rather than on the traditional structures, for help. Perhaps this is the basic force behind the ever growing demand for social policy, and its frequent failure to satisfy the demand.[35]

Thus the conclusion is that public authorities should do as little as possible, or nothing, to help people in terms of social policy. Who, then, is to help people, given the decline of traditional institutions under social forces that are not of their making and are not within their control? Glazer does not say; he simply says who is *not* to help them.

Nineteen seventy-two marked the turning point in *Commentary's* pages for the publication of neoconservative articles and opinions which had distinctly negative overtones with respect to the struggle for equality and justice for blacks, the poor, women, and other minorities in America. A listing and summary of 1972's articles and opinions will verify this point.

January 1972   "Quotas by Any Other Name" by Earl Raab. Raab's article, an attack on affirmative action in San Francisco, occupied a second lead position on the magazine's cover.

February 1972   "How Washington Enforces New Forms of Discrimination in the Name of Equal Opportunity" by Paul Seabury. This article is an attack on affirmative action as conceived by HEW in relation to universities. This was the issue's lead cover article, titled "HEW and the Universities," on p. 38.

"Community Control Revisited" by Diane Ravitch. She concluded that no one gained educationally from the Ocean Hill–Brownsville experiment in community control.

Editorial by Norman Podhoretz: "Is It Good for the Jews?" His opinion was that analyses of social issues must ask this as the key question for Jewish people.

March 1972   "Is Busing Necessary?" by Nathan Glazer. He concluded that busing was not necessary at that time. His article occupied the second lead cover position.

Editorial by Norman Podhoretz: "School Integration and Liberal Opinion." Podhoretz found Glazer's arguments entirely convincing.

April 1972   "Does IQ Matter?" by David K. Cohen. Cohen's article departs from the neoconservative tone; it is a balanced presentation of 1972's IQ controversy. *Commentary* gave it second lead position on the cover.

May, 1972   "The Pottinger Papers," an exchange on affirmative action, consisted of letters from readers, pro and con, reacting to Seabury's article in the February issue and Seabury's response to those letters.

"Sword of the Law," by Milton Himmelfarb, points out the failure of civil libertarians who did not denounce Georgia legislator Julian Bond, who was quoted in the *New York Post* of February 5, 1972, as saying blacks should take the law into their own hands to eliminate dope pushers in their neighborhoods. However, Himmelfarb says their silence is not the important point; what is important is that Bond's remarks tell the society that some old questions are still alive when the society wanted to think them dead. When evildoers are not punished by the sword of the law, for whatever reason, tolerable life in society becomes impossible. If the law allows its sword to be blunted, people will look elsewhere for a sharp one to protect them.

June 1972   "Liberalism versus Liberal Education," by James Q. Wilson, argued that in the modern period liberal education has become the adversary of liberalism by challenging the values of prevailing society and setting students apart from it, as well as by eroding the bases of authority and legitimacy of those institutions that define and defend civil liberties.

July 1972

"An Exchange on Busing." Letters from readers, pro and con, reacting to Glazer's article in the March issue, and Glazer's response to those letters.

"Banfield's Heresy," by T. R. Marmor, is about controversial reception of Edward Banfield's *The Unheavenly City*. Overall analysis is balanced; however, he concludes that the Banfield case and others serve as examples of "the intemperate and intimidating atmosphere in which the discussion of social policy has come to be conducted in America."

Editorial by Norman Podhoretz: "A Call to Dubious Battle." He assails the "assault on equality" camp as illustrated by Professor William Ryan and *Social Policy* magazine.

August 1972

"Dr. Coles among the Poor," by Joseph Epstein, is critical of Coles' *Children of Crisis,* based on the difficulty of classifying it, Coles' excessive detail without analysis, and the two-sidedness of every subject Coles touches upon, resulting in ambivalence. He also criticizes Coles as the prototypical liberal who, by virtue of understanding everything, finally disqualifies himself from taking a position on anything.

September 1972

"Serrano vs. the People," by Chester E. Finn Jr. and Leslie Lenkowsky, attacks the *Serrano* decision as a simple financial solution to a nonfinancial problem; questions whether legal decisions are appropriate to resolve economic, social, and educational questions of uncommon complexity.

October 1972

"The Quota Commission," by Elliot Abrams, attacks the Equal Employment Opportunity Commission (EEOC) for its efforts to enforce affirmative action.

November 1972   "About Equality" by Irving Kristol, a lead article, expressed the idea that equality had become, in the past two decades, a major political and ideological issue. It had become an idea that represented the self-interested ideology of "a mass of several millions of 'intellectuals' who are looking at their society in a highly critical way" because they "are engaged in a class struggle with the business community for status and power";[36] intellectuals want to run the society.

December 1972   "The Idea of Merit" by Paul Seabury, a lead article, gives historical case for a meritocracy; argues against the idea of preferential treatment for blacks, women, ethnics, or age groups.

The prevailing mood of these 1972 articles is disillusionment with the liberal ideas of the 1960s. The overriding suggestion is that minorities and women are asking too much (in the form of affirmative action, quotas, and busing) and trying to proceed too fast in social matters with the aid of the federal government. These articles stress the belief that declining expectations should prevail in the United States, and that the society should maintain the social order as it was at that time. Social change would come about through the operation of "natural forces" and traditional institutions.

The following year, 1973, saw fewer articles of this type published in *Commentary,* but the flow did not stop. For example:

February 1973   "Higher Education for All? The Case of Open Admissions" by Martin Mayer, a lead article, questioned the results of the policy of open admissions at City University of New York.

"An Exchange on Equality." Letters from readers, pro and con, reacting to Irving Kristol's article in November 1972 issue, and Kristol's reply to those writers.

March 1973   "Prison, Politics and the Attica Report" by Roger Staff, a lead article, found the McKay Report's account of the Attica riot was similar to other official reports of civil disturbances (e.g., the McCone, Kerner, and Scranton commissions). "It is hard to see how the tenor of the McKay Commission's Report will do other than make more plausible the rationalizations that impede rehabilitation; more difficult the administration of criminal justice; more resistant to prison reform the great majority of Americans who are fearful of jeopardizing their own safety for the uncertain benefit of inmates; and more shaky the plight of the victims in the cities of the nation."[37]

"The Intellectuals and the People," by James Hitchcock, said that in the decade of the sixties intellectuals had been dupes of fads and absurdities. In recent years the general populace had preserved its sanity in the face of the peculiar hysteria of the highly educated—the reverse of the historical situation where intellectuals usually remain cool in the face of popular hysteria. "Anything like a healthy progressivism in American politics will depend in the future on maintaining the delicate balance between the bias toward change inherent in the upper middle-class, and the often sullen skepticism and love of stability inherent in the mass of the white population."[38]

April 1973

"Black Progress and Liberal Rhetoric" by Ben J. Wattenberg and Richard M. Scammon, a lead article, said more than half of black Americans had reached "middle class" status. This remarkable development could be attributed to breaking the "logjam" in the 1960s so that blacks could move up in America. A blanket of silence seemed to envelope the liberal community on this point. Why had the data of black advancement been kept secret by those who presumably had no interest in making them known? The public policy of liberals and civil rights workers had been to downplay any acknowledgment or celebration of black accomplishments in order to maintain the moral and political pressure of the administration on public opinion. This strategy was mistaken and counterproductive.

"On Challenging an Orthodoxy" was R. J. Herrnstein's defense of his article on IQ which appeared in the *Atlantic Monthly* in September 1971. He described the antagonism this article engendered against him on college campuses throughout the country, repeated his ideas that genetic factors are paramount with respect to IQ and social class, and explained that the egalitarian-environmental outlook encourages a false belief in the equality of human endowment, which leads to inflexible expectations, often doomed to frustration, and then to anger.

Editorial by Norman Podhoretz, "The New Inquisitors," sympathized with Herrnstein and decried the fact that "colleges and universities continue their degenerative mutation from sanctuaries for free discussion into inquisitorial agents of a dogmatic secular faith."

May 1973

"Nixon, the Great Society and the Future of Social Policy," a lead article, was a symposium that featured the ideas of Edward C. Banfield, Nathan Glazer, Michael Harrington, Tom Kahn, Christopher Lasch, Robert Leckachman, Bayard Rustin, Gus Tyler, and George F. Will in a three-way breakdown of opinion, as follows:

Neoconservative Position	*Moderate Position*
Edward C. Banfield	Robert Lekachman
Nathan Glazer	Bayard Rustin
George F. Will	Gus Tyler

Liberal Position
Michael Harrington
Tom Kahn
Christopher Lasch

"An Exchange on Open Admissions." Letters from readers, pro and con, reacting to Martin Mayer's article in the February issue.

July 1973   "An Exchange on IQ: R. J. Herrnstein & Critics."
                       Letters from readers, pro and con, reacting to
                       Herrnstein's article in the April issue.

September 1973   "The New Egalitarianism and the Old," by Charles
                       Frankel, defined "the new egalitarianism" as
                       redemptive egalitarianism which transfers what he
                       called supernaturalistic perspectives to secular poli-
                       tical problems, and contrasted the new egalitarian-
                       ism with the old, which he called corrective egalitar-
                       ianism; disapproved of John Rawls' *A Theory of
                       Justice.*

October 1973   "Gentlemen and Scholars," by Milton Himmelfarb,
                       invoked Jewish tradition and theory in support of his
                       argument against admitting students to college and
                       professional schools by lottery in the name of equali-
                       ty.

This resurgence of conservatism continued into 1974's issues of
Commentary. In the September 1974 issue Nathan Glazer, in "Ethnicity and the Schools," examined the wave of ethnic feeling pervading
America, especially with relation to its place in the schools as reflected
by demands for ethnic-group studies in the curriculum and by the funding by foundations of a number of projects in ethnicity. Some of these
projects were research oriented, some oriented toward community action, and some oriented toward "directing pre-existing bodies of ethnic
sentiment into a liberal political direction."[39]

Glazer asked two sets of questions about the rise of ethnicity: (1) Is
the rise authentic? and (2) What does the new ethnicity mean for relations among the different groups in America and for the future of the
country? He concluded with the observation that the United States is
one nation, created of many stocks, and that this complex reality should
not be suppressed. But neither should the nation be "presented with a
false and distorted picture in which every group is the equivalent of
every other and in which our common heritage as a nation is either de-
famed or made to disappear."[40]

The October 1974 issue of *Commentary* continued the discussion
by featuring as the lead article "Why Ethnicity?" by Nathan Glazer
and Daniel P. Moynihan. The authors felt that the rise of ethnicity was
new in the sense that its emphasis was on the economic and social inter-

ests of the members of the group. The strategies of the group became (1) making claims against the government for resources and (2) pressuring for group equality. As an example of the first strategy the authors cited the Civil Rights Act of 1964, by which blacks, in essence, made a claim against the government and the government employed "ethnic categories as a basis for distributing its rewards."[41] What they were really saying, or certainly implying, was that the withdrawal to "ethnicity" had been caused by the fact that some social groups could not "make it" under the established norms and therefore had fallen back on "ethnicity" to excuse their lower group-success rates and to seek different social solutions to group problems.

The November 1974 issue of *Commentary* carried an article that was different in kind, in the sense that it was an attack on an individual rather than an attack on issues. Titled "The Problem of Kenneth Clark" and written by Hadley Arkes of Amherst, the article focused on Clark as a social scientist and as a public man. Clark was taken to task on the quality of his scholarship as a social scientist, which is the basis for his claims to leadership as a public man. Arkes found Clark's scholarship lacking in—

1. Presenting evidence to the U.S. Supreme Court that racial segregation caused psychological damage to Negro children (Arkes said that in no case did Clark pick out a study that tested the effects of segregation on the educational performance or disabilities of black children)

2. The doll studies he did with his wife between 1939 and 1950* (Arkes found them modest affairs)

---

*The doll studies, performed by psychologist Kenneth Clark and his wife, Mamie, also a psychologist, are well known through published psychological literature. As early as 1939 these researchers began to publish their findings on the effects of race on the self–identity of black children. In the 1940s the Clarks used black dolls and white dolls with black children to assess whether these three-to-seven-year olds could correctly identify dolls by race, whether there was an expressed preference for dolls by racial classification, and, if so, what that preference was. Three-fourths of the children could correctly identify the dolls by race, and there was an "unmistakable preference for the white doll and a rejection of the brown doll," even among the three-year-old black children. The doll studies were carried on for several years in such diverse locations as Arkansas, Pennsylvania, and Massachusetts.

The Clarks felt that racism and forced segregation caused psychological damage to black children, as indicated by these test results, and by other research studies they conducted. Forced segregation was experienced by black children in many ways, but long exposure to separate, unequal public schools had a particularly telling negative effect, the Clarks felt. As a result, Kenneth Clark prepared testimony to this effect; that testimony was presented to the Supreme Court as part of the evidence of the NAACP in asking that the *Plessy* decision be overturned.

3. The ways he interpreted the meaning and intent of the *Brown* decision

4. How he had dealt with evidence

5. Addressing himself, in a patient and demanding way, to the grounds or principles for his teachings. Arkes also found Clark lacking in his role as a public figure, stating that "Clark seems to be animated in his public moves by the simple recoil of his disappointments over one scheme or another, and by a notable want, on his own side, of political insight or prudence."[42]

No attempt has been made here to refute the very questionable ideas and presentations in these *Commentary* articles through the end of 1974—although there are many articulate refutations of all their controversial arguments about IQ, affirmative action, busing, quotas, meritocracy, ethnicity, and open admissions. The purpose of this review has been to show the changing tone of *Commentary* between the sixties and the seventies as representative of the changing tone of many intellectual journals in the seventies. Through this changing tone, *Commentary* seeks to influence public opinion and public policy.

It can be determined from the synopses of the preceding articles that between 1964–67 and 1969–74 *Commentary* made a complete shift in tone, from a democratic commitment across racial, ethnic, religious, and class lines to solving race and special problems in the United States, to disillusionment with such issues, and then to a neoconservatism which suggested that declining expectations must prevail. Some of the factors which explain this change are (1) negative feelings engendered by years of association with blacks, (2) perceptions of anti-Semitism among blacks, (3) pro-Arab support from various sectors in the United States, (4) the Ocean Hill–Brownsville controversy in the New York school system, (5) a perceived threat to the Jewish position from affirmative action programs, with accompanying goals and timetables, and from open admissions programs, and (6) the economic dimension, as reflected in (a) threats perceived by intellectuals-turned-neoconservatives who fear affirmative action because of the possibility of their students' being displaced by women and/or minorities in a tighter academic job market or (b) middle-class whites who resent financial subsidies for the poor and for blacks "at their expense," through the tax system, particularly since the middle class is experiencing the inflationary/recession squeeze.

Inspection of *The Public Interest* reveals that many of the same authors' beliefs are published in its pages, as well as in *Commentary*. For that reason, a detailed survey of *The Public Interest* will not be necessary. The views of Irving Kristol, Daniel P. Moynihan, Nathan Glazer, Christopher Jencks, James Q. Wilson, and others are essentially the same in both *The Public Interest* and *Commentary*. They express increasing disillusionment with social intervention programs and increasing despair that the lot of the constituencies at whom the programs are aimed (the poor and the black, particularly) can be improved by federal spending and planning.

The Public Interest's first issue was published in the fall of 1965, nineteen years after the first publication of *Commentary*. Because the former periodical began with a neoconservative tone, which recurs with regularity, a "changing tone" is not a completely accurate description of its content. The articles, which are written by "elite intellectuals"* who find attentive ears among the powerful, are distressing to those who read them from a black or disadvantaged perspective. However, *The Public Interest* prints a number of articles which are positive with respect to the continuing quest for equality and justice in America on the part of groups seeking full inclusion in the society. Such articles seek to be objective, displaying scholarly detachment while analyzing public policy.

The appearance of neoconservative articles as well as other articles which are more positive and objective toward the realization of expressed ideals of the American Creed, reflects the viewpoint of the editors of *The Public Interest*. In the first editorial, Daniel Bell and Irving Kristol pointed out that there is no such thing as the public interest: "There are only private interests—of individuals, groups, classes—which maneuver to obtain the greatest amount of public influence and public power, and each of which discerns 'the public interest' in its own image."[43] This suggests that the leaders or spokesmen of powerful private interests are vying to be heard and jockeying for position and influence in this era of rapid social change.

A few outstanding persons are heard over and over, and their opinions are expressed in leading journals; these people are not just individuals, they are leaders and spokesmen for powerful interests which seek to shape public opinion and public policy in a given direction. Sometimes these individuals are compelled to relate their particular interest to the general welfare because of the need to procure the coopera-

---

*For an analysis of this group, see "Who Are the Elite Intellectuals?" by Charles Kadushin in *The Public Interest,* 29 (Fall 1972): 109–25.

tion of other groups or because of the practical necessities of a given situation. But they are really fighting for particular interests, and each
group has a program designed to serve that interest. This point is clearly
stated in William O. Stanley's *Education and Social Integration*.[44]
Some examples of "conservative chic" articles in *The Public Interest,*
which blacks and other underprivileged persons find potentially negative
in terms of public policy, follow.

In the first issue of *The Public Interest,* Daniel P. Moynihan and
Nathan Glazer (in separate articles) criticized the legislative programs
of the Great Society, especially those related to the war on poverty. The
futility or counterproductivity of governmental intervention in such domestic problems is the neoconservative thread that runs through these
two articles. Also, both authors were critical of Michael Harrington's
book *The Other America,* which is an analysis of poverty in America.
The kind of writing exemplified here by Moynihan and Glazer is often
referred to as "the new conservative-chic literature," which has a dual
influence in public policy formulation: (1) it molds thought in the conservative direction and serves as an initiator of conservative social and
economic policies, and (2) it records, reflects, rationalizes, and legiti-
mates a conservatism which periodically lies dormant and at other times
flares up, asserting itself forcibly.

Christopher Jencks, writing in the winter 1966 issue, posed the
critical question, "Is the Public School Obsolete?" He followed with the
equally provocative and suggestive question of whether the public school
should survive if it cannot compete with the private school in open competition. Such an article has potentially dire consequences for shaping
public policy in education.

Less strident were James S. Coleman's articles, "Equal Schools or
Equal Students" (summer 1966) and "Toward Open Schools" (fall
1967). He said that "the task of increasing the achievement of lower-
class children cannot be fully implemented by school integration, even if
integration were wholly achieved—and the magnitude of racial and
class concentrations in large cities indicates that it is not likely to be
achieved soon."[45]

In the winter 1968 issue, Daniel Patrick Moynihan negatively discussed the plight of the poor in an article titled "The Crisis in Welfare."
As Moynihan criticized the status of welfare in America, he advocated
abolition of programs which failed to solve the problems of blacks and
the poor. He did not say what should be implemented in lieu of those
programs to help these groups. Moynihan also cautioned the nation

about the lack of academic planning and dearth of research in welfare reform.

John H. Kain and Joseph J. Persky, in the winter 1969 issue, were highly critical of the majority of blacks who inhabit the ghettos and of their lifestyle. To put it mildly, they suggested that the poor are poor because they want to be poor. Both writers were against a redistribution of wealth and power in this country, not necessarily because it would take from those who have but because it would be futile to give to the "have nots." Finally, Kain and Persky were scornful of the domestic legislation passed during the Johnson administration because it merely increased the economic dependence of an already dependent group. Although these writers remained positive on the issue of equality on an abstract level, this view was inconsistent with the overall tone of the article.

Discussion of the welfare crisis continued in the summer 1969 issue with Edward C. Banfield's "Welfare: A Crisis without Solutions." Concerned with the social costs of welfare, Banfield argued that the "government should use its power to take from some and give to others, not for the sake of the others, but only for that of the whole society."[46] Since this does not appear to be the case, Banfield asserted that the welfare system caused the breakup of many families:

> The Moynihan Report of a few years ago theorized that male Negro unemployment caused the breakup of the Negro family and that this in turn caused dependency rates to soar. I suggest that this theory would work better in reverse: it is high AFDC rates that are causing the breakup of the poor—and hence the Negro—family. The fact is that the AFDC program offers low-income parents strong financial incentives to separate.[47]

He maintained that the welfare system enabled a great many people to escape work who should work. Banfield believed that the welfare system deterred people from moving to places where their opportunities could be better and where the costs of supporting a family could be less. He also believed the system offered an incentive to wholesale lying and cheating.

Banfield concluded that "there would be no 'welfare crisis' if welfare were practiced the way originally conceived—that is, for helping those poor people who, because of unemployment or other causes beyond their control, are temporarily in need."[48] To think in terms of welfare reform as an instrument for a redistribution of income is erroneous. "The experience of recent years demonstrates welfare cannot in and of itself constitute a satisfactory answer to the problem of income redistribution."[49]

In the fall 1969 issue, Moynihan stated in "Toward a National Urban Policy":

> The Civil Rights Act of 1964 was the culmination of the political energies generated by the earlier period. The provisions which forbade employers, universities, government, or whatever to have any knowledge of the race, religion, or national origin of individuals with which they dealt marked in some ways the high-water mark of Social Darwinism in America, its assumption that "equality" meant only equal opportunity did not long stand opposed. Indeed, by 1965 the federal government had already, as best one can tell, begun to require ethnic and social census of its own employees, and also of federal contractors and research grant recipients. To do so violated the spirit of the Civil Rights Act, with its implicit model of the lone individual locked in equal—and remorseless—competition in the market place, but very much in harmony with the emergency sense of the 1960's that groups have identities and entitlements as well as do individuals. This view is diffusing rapidly.[50]

Moynihan indicated that two tendencies appeared to dominate the period: (1) the sense of general community was eroding, and with it the authority of existing relationships, and (2) at the same time, a powerful quest for a specific community was emerging in the form of an even more intense assertion of racial and ethnic identification. This is simply to say that the emerging doctrine of black nationalism was coming into direct conflict with the ethos of the white working class. More succinctly, this same white working class, that favored the civil rights movement in the early 1960s, had begun to challenge the concept that any school which had 50 percent or more black students was racially unbalanced.

The same issue carried an article by Edward Harwood, "Youth Unemployment—A Tale of Two Ghettoes," in which Harwood wrote that since the early 1960s the nation's unemployment rate had dropped precipitously in most cities, yet unemployment among youths, especially Negro teenagers, remained high. Instead of attributing this condition to inadequate education or to the difficulty of attracting business that had begun to flourish in the suburbs back to the cities, Harwood stated that many underprivileged blacks and whites were unemployed or underemployed because they could afford to be or they preferred to be: "So long as lower class youth find 'action,' of one form or another, on the streets, they may continue to opt for leisure despite government efforts to move them into jobs."[51]

Harwood made the following conclusions about joblessness:

(1) Boys are under-employed or sub-employed because they value leisure as much as money.

(2) Because many youths support only themselves, their preference for underemployment may be based on a reasoned calculation of self-interest. Why should we expect ghetto youths to settle down at age 17 or 18 to the discipline of a year-round–full-time job that, in effect, denies them the leisure for 'identity-building' we extend to college youths?

(3) Education is not the barrier, but rather child labor laws and insurance regulations, rather than the inferiority often referred to in the ghetto school system.[52]

Moving into the decade of the seventies, in "Policy vs. Program in the 70's" (summer 1970) Daniel P. Moynihan discussed the anomalies of the 1960s. He felt that this had been a period in which an extraordinary effort was made to institute a viable and lasting social policy. He also felt that the vast majority of Americans shared his sentiments, and that this was most evident in the maelstrom of social dissatisfaction. Apparently, the Great Society had too much defined policy in the form of program. Moynihan concluded that we must have a government by policy, not one by program.

Two years later, in spring 1972, Moynihan strongly contended that poverty was inextricably associated with family structure in "The Schism in Black America." He would have us believe that this schism was between the able and the less able, between the well prepared and those who were ill prepared. He agreed with, and quoted, Andrew Brimmer, who said in a 1970 speech at Tuskegee Institute that

> this deepening schism can be traced in a number of ways, including the substantial use in the proportion of Negroes employed in professional and technical jobs while the proportion in low-skilled occupation also edges upward; in the sizable decline in unemployment—while the share of Negroes among the long-term unemployed rises, in the persistence of inequality in income distribution within the black community—while a trend toward greater equality is evident among white families, above all in the dramatic deterioration in the position of Negro families headed by females.[53]

The summer 1972 issue of *The Public Interest* carried a controver-

sial research report, "The Evidence on Busing" by David J. Armor, that
reported that social science research findings had been inextricably in-
terwoven with policy decisions on school desegregation at every step,
from the 1954 *Brown* decision to the federal busing orders of 1970.
Armor also reported his detailed findings from the Boston METCO
study, as well as findings from other comparable studies on busing. With
respect to policy, Armor concluded that—

> (1) massive mandatory busing for purposes of improving student
> achievement and interracial harmony is not effective and should not
> be adopted at this time, and

> (2) voluntary integration programs such as METCO, ABC, or Proj-
> ect Concern should be continued and positively encouraged by sub-
> stantial federal and state grants.[54]

The fall 1972 issue carried (in lead position) a three-part section,
"On Equality," with selections by Daniel Bell, Daniel P. Moynihan, and
Seymour Martin Lipset. Bell's article, "Meritocracy and Equality,"
analyzed the growing societal tension between meritocracy and equality
as the appropriate philosophical basis for policy making, emphasizing
the stresses between populism and meritocratic elitism. Bell focused on a
central social and ethical current issue. A diffuseness of argument is apparent in the article, which conformed to the "chicness" of the day.

Moynihan's article, "Equalizing Education: in Whose Benefit?"
began with a complaint against legal service lawyers' fighting for plain-
tiffs who were bringing legal action against federal, state, and local governments. It continued with an attack on court decisions, such as the
Serrano decision, as being well meaning but not for the good of the
people. The article also presented the argument that increased expenditures would have the major effect of increasing the pay of teachers (salaries being the largest component of school expenditures), thus providing
the middle class with a greater income and in the short run increasing
income inequality. He then presented a case for judicial restraint in the
policy question of equalizing educational expenditures so that the nation
could "avoid another miserable encounter between the courts and the
political system of democracy."[55]

Lipset's article was the only one in this three-part section which
spoke to the continuing needs of black Americans in light of their unequal status in 1972. In "Social Mobility and Equal Opportunity" he
provided evidence that equality of opportunity had not declined in
America and that social mobility was more easily possible in some re-

spects in American society in 1972 than in former years. However, mobility patterns have differed for minority groups over time, including whites from southern and eastern Europe who came to the United States around the turn of the century. But in 1972 it was the black population which remained most handicapped in terms of being able to move upward in the occupational class system.

Quoting Blau and Duncan, Lipset said that—

1. Negroes are handicapped at every step in their attempts to achieve economic success, and these cumulative disadvantages are what produces the great inequalities of opportunities under which the Negro American suffers.

2. The multiple handicaps associated with being an American Negro are cumulative in their deleterious consequences for a man's career.

3. Education, which we have seen opens all sorts of doors for whites, even many of quite low social origin, did not work in the same way for blacks.[56]

He followed this with a statement of the significant social and economic progress made by black Americans during the last decade, but noted that, despite this

considerable progress of certain segments of the black community, whites are still enormously advantaged by the presence of a racial minority which (together with other minority groups) handles a heavily disproportionate share of the less rewarded jobs and status positions.[57]

Thus 1972 was the year in which questions of equality and inequality, with particular reference to education and economic benefit, were repeatedly discussed in *Commentary, Public Interest,* and the society. The publication of Jencks' *Inequality: A Reassessment of the Effect of Family and Schooling in America* and Mosteller and Moynihan's *On Equality of Educational Opportunity* are also examples of 1972 publications that discussed these issues. A review essay of Jencks' book by Nathan Keyfitz, appeared in the spring 1973 issue of *Public Interest.* Titled "Can Inequality Be Cured?" it concluded that Americans did not want inequality "cured" at that time, and predicted "a combination of the process by which visible social inequality will increase effort and hence production and hence income, and the income will be used to purchase the symbols of social inequality."[58]

Although the majority of *The Public Interest's* articles are neocon-servative, there were a few published between 1967 and 1973 which would be considered positive from a minority perspective. The following are several examples.

Otis Dudley Duncan, "After the Riots" (fall 1967)

Aaron Wildavsky, "The Empty-Head Blues: Black Rebellion and White Reaction" (spring 1968)

Howard Hubbard, "Five Long Hot Summers and How They Grew" (summer 1968)

Andrew Effrat, Roy E. Feldman, and Harvey M. Sarpolsky, "Inducing Poor Children to Learn" (spring 1969)

Norton E. Long, "The City as a Reservation" (fall 1971)

Thomas F. Pettigrew, Marshall Smith, Elizabeth L. Useem, and Clarence Normand, "Busing: A Review of 'the Evidence'" (winter 1973)

The authors of the preceding articles supported their beliefs with evidence and the articles are persuasive, well written, and lucid. These authors vigorously supported the quest for equality and justice in this time as realizable societal goals. However, their names do not recur repeatedly, as do those of the neoconservative intellectuals.

Representative of objectivity in reporting and presenting a societal question, and of policy related to that question, is the special (volume 34) issue of *The Public Interest, The Great Society: Lessons for the Future* (winter 1974). Diverse viewpoints are aired on the "politics of social intervention of the 1960's" in comprehensive fashion. Objectivity in reporting and presentation is as clear in the introduction as in the concluding essay, both of which were written by Eli Ginzberg and Robert M. Solow, who also had editorial responsibility for this special, enlarged issue. These scholars met their own criteria of combining "scholarly detachment with a lively interest in public policy."[59]

Some black intellectuals have had their beliefs printed in the pages of *Public Interest,* such as Orlando Patterson on "The Moral Crisis of the Black American" (summer 1973) and Andrew F. Brimmer and Charles V. Hamilton in an examination of the Great Society (winter 1974). Brimmer's analysis was "Economic Developments in the Black Community" and Hamilton's was "Blacks and the Crisis of Political Participation." Thomas Sowell described a successful public school in "Black Excellence: The Case of Dunbar High School" in the spring

1974 issue of *Public Interest*. Black authors have not been totally excluded from this forum of public expression, although they appear infrequently. Additionally, these authors are not generally regarded as militants in either black or white circles.

The third journal we have surveyed is *Atlantic Monthly*. Oldest of the three, it was founded in 1857 and is in its second century of continuous publication. The magazine relies upon competent authors, giving them freedom to express conflicting and even controversial opinions in the belief that the free expression of ideas has made the United States what it is. The magazine is also pledged to be politically nonpartisan.

Atlantic Monthly is part of what Charles Kadushin called a "literary circle." Using a new computer technique developed by Richard Alba, Kadushin identified six rather distinctive clique structures in contemporary intellectual circles, the fifth of which is this "literary circle." The journals in the circle were identified as *Atlantic, Harper's, The New Yorker,* and *New York Review of Books*—to name a few.

Three of Kadushin's six cliques were arranged in interconnected circles:

> Clique 4. The largest of these structures, with about one third of the intellectual elite as members, consisted of both social scientists and literary men. The majority of this circle, especially its social scientists, do not live in New York, and it has a strong Cambridge-Boston representation. The members of what we might call the Social Science–Literary Circle characteristically write for *The Public Interest* and *Commentary,* and to a lesser extent, for *Partisan Review* and *Dissent*.

> Clique 5. Then there was a Literary Circle, almost three quarters of whom live in New York. They tend to write for journals such as *New Yorker, Harper's, Atlantic, New York Review of Books,* and others, but hardly ever for *Commentary* or *The Public Interest.*

> Clique 6. The last and perhaps the most interesting circle may best be called the Center Circle, for its members overlap with both the Literary and the Social Science–Literary Circles. This Center Circle resides almost wholly in New York. Generally somewhat older and more prestigious than members of other circles, the intellectuals in this set also tend to write for a variety of the very top journals.[60]

Kadushin also named the seventy most prestigious contemporary

American intellectuals as of 1970, but he did not place them within one of the three overlapping circles. However, if one accepts his listing and uses it to determine which of the seventy intellectual elitists who currently espouse neoconservative views have written for *Atlantic* (as well as for *Commentary* and *Public Interest)* since 1969, several names correspond. Most notable are Sidney Hook and his "The War against the Democratic Process" *(Atlantic,* February 1969), Irving Kristol and his "Welfare: The Best of Intentions, The Worst of Results" (August 1971), and James Q. Wilson and his "The Sick Sixties" (October 1973). Wilson also appeared in the March issue of *Atlantic,* where he commented on "law and order," a theme that was popularized by the incoming Nixon administration.

Probably the most controversy-producing article from the perspective of the black minority in the pages of *Atlantic* since 1969 was Richard Herrnstein's "I.Q." (September 1971). Herrnstein's article was introduced by an editorial comment, which concluded on this note: "The subject of intelligence is such an issue—important because social legislation must come to terms with actual human potentialities, painful because the actualities are sometimes not what we vainly hope."[61] This comment seems to give tacit support to Jensen's thesis that blacks and whites differ in inherited intelligence, since it followed a summary statement of Jensen's article in the *Harvard Educational Review* and the reactions to that article.

Herrnstein addressed the history of the measurement of intelligence (IQ testing) and the implications of IQ. He related Jensen's findings in some detail, which could be interpreted as evidencing a degree of agreement with them. However, Herrnstein skirted the question of race and intelligence:

> Using the procedures of quantitative genetics, most experts estimate that I.Q. has a heritability between .80 and .85, but this is based almost entirely on data from whites. We may, therefore, say that 80 to 85 percent of the variation among whites is due to the genes. Notwithstanding some preliminary reports of slightly lower heritabilities for blacks, we still cannot make a comparable statement for them. But let us simply assume, for the sake of discussion, that .8 is the heritability for whites and blacks taken together. What could we say about the racial differences in I.Q. then? The answer is that we could still say nothing positive about it. . . .
>
> Although there are scraps of evidence for a genetic component in the black-white difference, the overwhelming case is for believing

that American blacks have been at an environmental disadvantage. To the extent that variations in the American social environment can promote or retard I.Q., blacks have probably been held back. But a neutral commentator (a rarity these days) would have to say that the case is simply not settled, given our present stage of knowledge. To advance this knowledge would not be easy, but it could certainly be done with sufficient ingenuity and hard work.[62]

This cautious skirting of the critical question of race and intelligence is belied by blurbs in bold type atop the pages where the question is discussed and where Jensen is cited in detail. The top of one page reads "How much can we boost I.Q. and scholastic achievement? Not very much." And on the following page it is reported, in heavy type, "Jensen concluded (as have most of the other experts in the field) that the genetic factor is worth about 80 percent and that only 20 percent is left to everything else." This suggests very strongly that the author and/or the editors selected these ideas for emphasis, as characterizing features of the main ideas in the body of the article.

Herrnstein's article drew both supportive and antagonistic comments from the intellectual community. Most of these comments centered on race and intelligence, but the overlapping areas of class, race, and intelligence must not be overlooked in Herrnstein's article.

Making the cautious conclusion that the upper class scores about 30 IQ points above the lower class, and noting that IQ is tied to occupation and that occupation affects social standing, Herrnstein said it follows logically that IQ affects social standing. He predicted, somewhat sadly, that the fiction of Michael Young's meritocracy may become reality in America through "the growth of a virtually hereditary meritocracy arising out of the successful realization of contemporary political and social goals."[63]

Does this sound benign? Not when you link the notion of the "inevitability" of the growing meritocracy with the continued use of IQ testing. When one does that, he gets a *wedding* of the two, which is not innocent from the viewpoint of the lower class and minorities. Herrnstein concluded his article with the following:

> The measurement of intelligence is one of the yardsticks by which we may assess the growing meritocracy, but other tests of human potential and performance should supplement the I.Q. in describing a person's talents, interests, skills, and shortcomings. The biological stratification of society looms whether we have tests to gauge it or not, *but with them a more humane and tolerant grasp of*

human differences is possible. And at the moment, that seems our best hope. [author's italics][64]

Commentary allowed Herrnstein space in its April 1973 issue to defend his article which had appeared in *Atlantic.* In this defense he stated his belief that genetic factors dominate with respect to IQ, as well as social class, and explained that the environmental viewpoint provides a false belief in the equality of human endowment which leads to unrealistic expectations, is doomed to frustration, and results in hostility. In this same issue, Podhoretz, *Commentary's* editor, sympathized with Herrnstein.

Thus we see that neoconservative intellectuals reinforce each other and provide access to leading intellectual journals for one another. Access and frequency of publication become key critical matters as the societal debate goes on and as diverse segments of the public seek to realize their part of the "public interest" by influencing policy makers.

From the viewpoint of the black minority, this "conservative chic" classical liberal rhetoric, emanating from elite white intellectuals and the journals they control, represents a cyclical occurrence in United States history. It was pointed out in 1973 by this writer that

> there is a cyclical aspect, a *deja vu* quality, to the current combined writing of Moynihan, Glaser, Herrnstein, Armor, Banfield, Jensen, et al. It appears that when the black race as a race (an identifiable entity) seeks, and begins to accomplish verifiable social, economic, and political gains toward the end (goal) of equality as human beings in America, prominent social scientists of the period emerge with sociological, psychological, and/or evolutionary "evidence" for retrenchment in social policies and political action. This "evidence" is designed to provide proof that the black race is inferior and therefore undeserving of social, economic, political and educational equality, or of social programs designed to contribute to the pursuit of such equality; further, they deny that such social programs can make a difference en masse.
>
> The social, political, and educational reforms attempted in the 1960s in the U.S. have been compared with the far-reaching reforms attempted in the Reconstruction period following the Civil War. The retrenchments in, and withdrawal of, moral and financial support for continuation of those reforms in the 1970s have been deemed analogous to the "undoing" of similar political, social and educational reconstruction in the 1890s and early 1900s. Retrenchment in, and abandonment of, social reforms suggest that deliberate efforts at social change almost invariably fail.[65]

In this vein, the black minority has seen leading magazines and newspapers present hostile articles about the group at an earlier time in this century, 1901–18. Today's articles are not precisely the same in tone—the social and cultural climate of 1976 is distinctly improved over that of the earlier period—but there is a parallel. Rayford W. Logan, historian, presented a survey of representative Northern magazines and newspapers which mirrored "preponderantly hostile attitudes to the Negro" in *The Betrayal of the Negro. (Atlantic Monthly* was one of the magazines surveyed by Dr. Logan.)

Logan made two sets of concluding comments in this discussion, one following his analysis of magazines and the other following his analysis of newspapers. In the case of the former, he said:

> One must conclude that the principal literary magazines in the United States had made slim contribution to a clear understanding of a problem that after the war became even more complicated and pressing—an increased determination to deny, and an increased insistence to gain, equal rights for Negroes.[66]

Logan remarked about newspapers:

> On balance, the newspapers surveyed did not give strong support to Negroes in their struggle for equal rights. One can only conjecture as to the influence on the American mind of this continuing, though lessening, evidence of the violations of the basic principals of American democracy.[67]

The state of affairs is not so bleak today, but if one paraphrases Logan's two comments and combines them, a fairly accurate picture is procured for this era. We could use his words to say that

> one must conclude that three leading intellectual journals in the United States are making slim contributions to a clear understanding of the continuing race and class problems which have become ever more complicated and pressing. Neither the poor nor minorities of color are receiving strong support in their struggle for equal rights. One can only conjecture as to the influence on the American mind, and on the minds of policy makers, of this continuing flow of neoconservative chic literature.[68]

SUMMARY AND CONCLUSIONS

There is a changing mood in the dominant society. This changing mood is more negative than positive with respect to the aspirations of blacks, other minorities, and the poor, but it is by no means completely negative. The mood shifts have been documented by surveys conducted by the Survey Research Center at the University of Michigan, by research conducted by the National Advisory Commission on Civil Disorders (Kerner Commission), and by the personal observations of Fletcher Knebel. The changing mood is experienced by American people as they go about daily living in this society, and this may be termed participant-observer verification. The latter is by no means scientific, nor would verifications from individuals necessarily be identical; the change is nevertheless real.

Three examples from the dominant society illustrate the changing mood and show how the shifts occurred from the mid-'60s to the mid-'70s. The first example is the white working class and its ethnic backlash, the second is key intellectual leaders, and the third is the changing tone of three influential and intellectually oriented periodicals.

The ethnic backlash was shown to have emerged out of the fears of working-class whites and out of the perceived threat to them from blacks' advances, particularly in employment, housing, and school desegregation. Yet even in the midst of hostility against blacks, white working-class people admit that blacks have had a worse time than other Americans.

This group of whites also expresses distrust for most politicians and contempt for the affluent class of whites. Public schools have become battle grounds between white ethnic groups and blacks, especially in the North. Boston is the clearest example of the struggle, where the interrelated complexities of inequality, racism, class differences, and politics can be seen most clearly. Yet in the midst of the conflict and confusion, Judge Arthur Garrity took a responsible leadership role to try to solve the problems, and most of Boston's schools were reasonably quiet—with the exception of South Boston High. Moreover, the teachers' union has supported desegregation. The Boston school situation is illustrative of the cross-currents in the changing mood as it applies to white ethnics and blacks.

The changing stance of key white intellectual leaders was the second example used to illustrate the changing mood. The primary point was that certain intellectuals have influence on public policy, including educational policy. In an era when knowledge is a primary resource, these leaders command respect, based on their personal achievements and because they are often employed in top positions in elite universities and colleges. They influence policy, directly and indirectly. Direct influence comes from social scientists who accept roles in government, where they have access to policy makers. Indirect influence, less tangible but nevertheless real, comes from their research and publications which define and explain social problems and communicate those ideas to the public through scholarly journals, lay magazines, newspapers, and televised programs. To the extent that these key intellectuals were liberal in the '60s, they assisted the aspirations of blacks and the poor. The extent to which they have become neoconservative in the '70s is harmful and injurious to the desires of blacks and the poor.

This changing stance of white liberals was predictable, according to Clarence J. Karier. In *Roots of Crisis: American Education in the Twentieth Century* he said:

> Weaknesses in the liberal ideology are exposed during times of crisis . . . liberals in crisis directly or indirectly have usually supported the existing power structure. They were, in fact, *Servants of Power*. If, indeed, the unfortunate time shall come when the left meets the right in open battle, little doubt should remain where many liberals will stand.[69]

Karier maintains that they will stand on the right of the political spectrum.[70]

The third example that was used to illustrate the changing mood was the changing tone of three influential and intellectually oriented periodicals. These journals publish the writings of elite intellectuals and express a viewpoint through editorial statements. They seem to be taking a rightward turn in what is printed in both their editorial statements and the articles they select to be printed.

Neither the poor nor minorities are receiving strong support in their struggle for equality and justice in the seventies from these three periodicals. Since these journals have some influence on policy makers and on the American mind, their rightward turn is interpreted as harmful to the progress of blacks and the poor. The precise degree of such influence is indeterminate at this time.

From the perspective of blacks and the poor, the changing mood in the dominant society must be reversed, for the negative effects could become a self-fulfilling prophecy. When blacks and the poor are labeled as inferior, this confirms a "natural rightness" for assigning them an inferior status in society, with all the resulting effects of that status. Myrdal's "vicious circle" is the outcome.

Merton addressed this problem of the self-fulfilling prophecy in *So-*

cial Theory and Social Structure in 1949. Beginning with the theorem of W. I. Thomas, "if men define situations as real, they are real in their consequences," Merton explained that "public definitions of a situation (prophecies or predictions) become an integral part of the situation and thus affect subsequent developments."[71] He stated that in the beginning the self-fulfilling prophecy is a *false* definition of the situation, which evokes a new behavior, which makes the false conception come *true* (italics his). Thus "the specious validity of the self-fulfilling prophecy perpetuates a reign of error," and "it is the self-fulfilling prophecy which goes far toward explaining the dynamics of ethnic and racial conflict in the America of today."[72]

Merton stated that application of the Thomas theorem also suggests how the vicious circle of self-fulfilling prophecies in ethnic and racial conflict can be broken:

> The initial definition of the situation which has set the circle in motion must be abandoned. Only when the original assumption is questioned and a new definition of the situation introduced, does the consequent flow of events give the lie to the assumption. Only then does the belief no longer father the reality.[73]

The vicious circle and the self-fulfilling prophecy can be broken by enacted, deliberate, appropriate institutional change. Deliberate institutional controls with appropriate administrative conditions, do not occur automatically. Prejudices die by eliminating the sustenance provided them by certain societal institutions. Planning human relations is possible, according to Merton, and must be done to eliminate the conditions that nourish the self-fulfilling prophecy with respect to race and ethnic relations.

III

THE CHANGING MOOD
IN THE BLACK POPULATION SINCE 1969

The changing mood in American society has not been restricted to the white population; blacks in this country also have shown shifting attitudes. Whether the changing mood in the black population is a response to the negative features of American society —such as the economic, social, political, or educational circumstances—or to the positive assertion of blacks' will to experience equality and justice at this time, the changes are visible and verifiable.

In the 1950s blacks appeared to be striving for conventional middle-class assimilation by such traditional means as educational attainment and political representation. The decade of the 1960s witnessed many great shifts in the black mood, which never was monolithic: nonviolent civil rights activities, urban upheavals, a desire for self-determination, increased identification with the motherland, Africa, and "black power." Activity in the 1970s is more subtle and less dramatic because discrimination is less overt and more subtle. In this decade, blacks are exerting continued efforts to demolish educational barriers, making use of the increased political representation at all levels, and supporting affirmative action forces in an attempt to gain equal employment opportunity and equal promotion opportunity, once employed. The songs and slogans of the sixties are part of history; charismatic leaders such as Martin Luther King and Malcolm X are dead—assassinated; and organizations such as SNCC and CORE have little practical or functional meaning or funding.

The past twenty-five years have indeed witnessed a changing mood in the black population. It has gone from hopeful traditional assimilation to activism to alienation to relative passivity, punctuated now and again by sporadic efforts to effectuate black progress within the system. How did it happen? Where are blacks today? Where do blacks go from here? To understand the changing mood of the black population (which again, is not monolithic) it is necessary to review the conditions and circumstances of blacks in America.

Black people constitute the largest racial-ethnic minority in the United States, roughly 11 percent of the population, or 24 million people in March 1975.* Blacks are also the "oldest" minority group, dating from 1619 when the first blacks were brought to the English colonies for settlement.† General sociological literature maintains that this minority group holds the lowest status or rank of the racial and ethnic groups in the United States. The term *caste* or the phrase *caste-like status* is often used to describe the position of blacks in the social stratification scheme or social continuum of America.

This social position is directly traceable to historic circumstances in the United States. Historically, most blacks were brought forcibly to these shores to be slaves in the plantation sector of the American economic and social system. Built into the maintenance of the slave system was the idea that slaves were inferior as human beings. It is necessary only to recall, for example, the *Dred Scott* decision of 1857, which stated that blacks had no rights which whites were bound to respect. In effect, then, blacks were property—not people—in the eyes of the dominant group. Once the idea of inferiority took hold, it perpetuated itself through a kind of self-fulfilling prophecy. Blacks were bought and sold at the whim of the master, often beaten, and sometimes slain. They were always treated as less than human and often denied adequate food, shelter, and clothing. They were not allowed to marry and keep their children; they were bred against their will. Education was forbidden to them, and there was no chance of obtaining freedom for most blacks. The portion of the population that was free was forced into social isolation.

Given this set of totally inhuman circumstances, which prevailed from 1619 to 1865, most blacks could not develop personally, economically, socially, politically, or educationally. It is, in fact, a miracle that so many survived the trying experience.

From 1865 to 1877 blacks experienced a brief period when the federal government took a leadership role in making conditions more

---

*This is the official count of the Census Bureau; however, blacks are undercounted traditionally, for reasons which are well known.

†Indians did not officially become a minority group until 1871; prior to that time the official relationship between Indians and whites was that of one sovereign nation to another.

palatable for them. During this period the Thirteenth, Fourteenth, and Fifteenth Amendments were added to the United States Constitution. The Freedmen's Bureau was established and made meaningful differences in the lives of blacks and poor whites, especially in providing some educational opportunity. Blacks temporarily enjoyed civil rights, including the right to vote and some access to elected public offices. Federal effort to help blacks reached a zenith in passage of the Civil Rights bill of 1875.

In 1883 the Supreme Court declared this bill unconstitutional. The court's decision let the Southern states (where most blacks lived) know that the federal government would no longer insist upon equal rights for the black population. The *Plessy* v. *Ferguson* decision in 1896 institutionalized the separate and unequal conditions which were to be foisted upon blacks until 1954, when the *Plessy* decision was overturned by *Brown.* "Jim Crow" laws were passed by Southern states to enforce a pattern of discrimination and segregation on black people. As a result, blacks were prevented from voting, holding office, and securing most remunerative work outside the black community. Equal educational opportunity was systematically denied blacks. The effect of these laws was to keep blacks as a group in a servile state, in societally imposed inferiority. But discrimination was not restricted to the Southern states. Customs and practices in all areas of the country restricted blacks to designated neighborhoods, particular kinds of jobs, and specified schools. Sectional differences were differences in degree, not in kind.

But some positive aspects of public policy were being formulated at the federal level. In the 1930s, for example, equal pay clauses were included in Tennessee Valley Authority (TVA) legislation. In fact, in all the agencies developed by Franklin D. Roosevelt (such as the Works Progress Administration) the concept of equal pay for equal work prevailed for blacks and whites. Roosevelt deserves accolades for his beliefs in this respect, for this was the first time in the South that blacks received equal pay for equal work. Roosevelt did not challenge the laws of segregation in the South, but he challenged the economics of the Southern situation.

Further, the Fair Employment Practices Commission (FEPC) was established in 1941 as a result of Executive Order 8802, actually written by Fiorello LaGuardia and presented by Walter White. To get the FEPC legislation passed, much organized effort was required. In most of the major cities, local FEPC organizations, composed of blacks and whites, acted as pressure groups to push for enactment. This means there were organized and sustained interracial group efforts at the local as well as the national level to effect legislation which would make for social change in employment practices.††

Another positive aspect of public policy that was formulated at the federal level was President Truman's executive order desegregating the armed forces. This order was issued in the late 1940s. Also at this time the NAACP was winning its cases before the Supreme Court with respect to the illegal inequality of higher education provided for blacks by the states.

By 1954 black Americans had begun to feel that their life and conditions in this country could be made equal. In that year the Supreme Court's *Brown* decision overturned the *Plessy* decision, stating that

---

††Using standard interview techniques, this writer talked with several black women and men over 65 years of age about strategies and methods used by blacks in the 1930s and 1940s to bring about social change directed toward the attainment of equality. These older persons stressed the use and effectiveness of interracial group efforts, as well as organized black endeavors headed by tireless, dedicated leaders. They attribute some of the current slowdown in momentum on the part of blacks to attain equality to a lack of leadership, but they emphasize that a larger problem of blacks is that we are prone to criticize society and to stop with that criticism. Instead, we should be reshaping our organizations and participating in them, as well as in other organizations dedicated to black interests. It is coordinated, sustained group effort under effective leadership that results in positive social change, according to these respondents. They say, for example, that there are many criticisms of the NAACP from blacks, but that blacks are failing to work through that organization and others, as they did in the 1930s and 1940s, to effect social change. Further, the young adult black population (under age 30) seems not to know the contributions of the NAACP and other organizations of its type to black progress. Nor does this group know that even into the 1950s membership in the NAACP and other such groups was a personal and economic threat to blacks, but many joined and worked despite the possible consequences. For example, older black adults say that they worked through the National Negro Congress, which was organized in the mid-1930s. More leftist in orientation than the NAACP, the National Negro Congress was dissolved in the 1950s under the investigations of McCarthy, who succeeded in labeling it pro-Communist. In fact, McCarthy succeeded in labeling many of the interracial, international organizations pro-Communist, which dismantled them in terms of practical value. These organizations have not been replaced by equally efficient organizations in the 1970s.

Another dimension stressed by older blacks with respect to changes in public policy in the 1930s and 1940s was the role of black women in challenging the status quo. They describe black women of that time as "free spirits" in the sense that they were free to take on the tasks of attaining freedom and equality without the fear of economic reprisals faced by black men. These black women worked through groups and organizations to make their voices heard on social issues. Some of the organizations were the National Council of Negro Women, the National Association of Colored Women's Clubs, and church-based organizations through which black and white women worked collectively toward attaining social justice for black people.

"separate but equal" could not be equal. Blacks were pleased at the change of concept, even though they knew there had never been any systematic attempt to make education "separate but equal." Further, blacks knew the long, arduous, and costly legal fight which had been led and waged by the NAACP through a series of cases to get to the stage of *Brown*. Therefore the group was hopeful about the possibilities expressed by the *Brown* decision but also was very reality oriented, based on a long history of negative experiences, realizing that *Brown* did not signal the end of the struggle for equality, justice, and liberty for blacks in America. Blacks were right—as the remaining years of the 1950s would demonstrate, with the 1955–56 Montgomery bus boycott (following Rosa Parks' refusal to give her seat to a white man), the Central High School confrontation in Little Rock (1957), and other schoolhouse battles at every level of education.

These facts of life were demoralizing, but the hope engendered by *Brown* was not to be extinguished by the fact that evasive tactics were used by Southerners to keep from obeying the decision of the Supreme Court. In addition to evasive tactics by white Southerners, the economic condition of America took a downturn, and the black population always suffers first and longest under adverse economic conditions. But even economic conditions would not deter black efforts to gain equality and justice.

In Greensboro, North Carolina, young black college students in 1960 started a sit-in movement to gain access to public eating facilities. They were "sitting in" to stand up for their rights. The sit-ins led to the freedom rides—and the black struggle gained momentum in the early 1960s.

New organizations arose to help in the struggle as the nation heard of the Student Nonviolent Coordinating Committee (SNCC), the Congress of Racial Equality (CORE), and the Southern Christian Leadership Conference (SCLC). The fight for equality and justice moved from the courts to restaurants to the streets, and even to jail. One success led to another effort.

In the White House, John F. Kennedy was much more voluntarily supportive of black efforts than his predecessor, Dwight D. Eisenhower. Kennedy's strength lay in enforcement of the law. Lyndon B. Johnson, who ascended to the presidency after Kennedy's assassination, continued the Kennedy practice of law enforcement. Johnson's strengths were his personal charisma and his ability to use relationships which had been painstakingly built through years of associations as a congressman.

Black legal and political progress was substantial throughout the Johnson administration.

In 1963 and 1964, black efforts to attain social justice leaped "from crisis to crisis, escalating the racial problems to new frontiers of strife and controversy."[1] In 1963 there were more than 2,000 demonstrations across the nation, and more than 10,000 demonstrators, black and white, were arrested.[2] Was this a nonviolent revolution, brought on by the exertion of Negro power? Lerone Bennett, author and editor, concluded that the "1960–64 convulsion . . . met some of the basic tests of a classic upheaval: the direct intervention of the masses . . . and the reliance on direct action."[3] Bennett said in 1964:

> Semantics apart, the cataclysm in the streets is real enough, and it proceeds from revolutionary premises. The fundamental premise is that old forms and old ways are no longer adequate and that the social system, as organized, is incapable of solving, through normal channels, the urgent problem presented to it by history. The second major premise is allied to the first: that the social system, as organized, is part of the problem and cannot be appealed to or relied upon as an independent arbiter in power conflicts of which it is a part. The third major premise is that white Americans, generally speaking, lack the will, the courage, and the intelligence to voluntarily grant Negroes their civil rights and that they must be forced to do it by pressure.[4]

Bennett explained the 1960–64 period by saying that at the base of the upheaval was a cataclysmic shift in the mood of Negroes, a shift that was seen in changing patterns of protest and social contention. The causes of the shift were traceable to the long preparatory work. The seeds of the black protest and efforts to attain equality "were sown in the last decade of the nineteenth century by Negro intellectuals who refused to accept the place prepared for them. In the dawn years of the twentieth century, Negro intellectuals and reform-minded whites formed an uneasy alliance. Out of this alliance came the NAACP and the National Urban League."[5]

His analysis said the actual rebellion of the '60s was the result of a "parallelogram" of four contextual forces which had developed between 1930 and 1945 but which required a spark to ignite them to social action:

1. The development of a new self-conception in the Negro psyche and the growth of a revolutionary will to dignity

2. The development of a new principle of leadership which abandoned the elite concept of selected agents acting for the masses in various theaters of power
3. The development of a social myth which provided a new script of roles and models for Negro youth
4. The existence of a competing ideology in a world power struggle which made wholesale repression embarrassing, if not distasteful.[6]

The protests and demonstrations which came after the spark of the *Brown* decision were a direct cause of Congress's passage of the Civil Rights Act of 1964. This act provides for (1) recognition of a sixth-grade education as a presumption of literacy for voting purposes, (2) outlawing segregation and discrimination in places of public accommodation, (3) desegregation of public facilities (parks, playgrounds, libraries), (4) filing of school desegregation suits by the attorney general, (5) outlawing discrimination in all federally assisted activities, (6) outlawing discrimination by employers or unions with one hundred or more employees or members, and (7) authorizing the attorney general to intervene in private suits in which persons allege denial of equal protection of the laws under the Fourteenth Amendment.

It is important to remember, however, that the 1964 Civil Rights Act was not effective in school desegregation until Section VII was enforced. The denial of money changed the behavior of school officials with respect to school desegregation in the South. Federal funds had to be withheld from discriminating districts before those districts would obey the law; following some withholding, the threat of denial of funds became sufficient to cause compliance. Enforcement of the law was thus the central ingredient in black progress with respect to school desegregation in the South. However, the same enforcement had not yet been tried in the North. In Chicago, for example, when federal funds were withheld from the schools by HEW in the mid-sixties, it was alleged that a telephone call from Mayor Daley to President Johnson resulted in a restoration of monies to Chicago. A common political argument is that economic sanctions were intended to remedy *de jure* segregation in the South, not *de facto* Northern desegregation.

Under the 1964 Civil Rights Act, blacks were ensured the right to vote in all elections, but when they attempted to register in the South they were met with threats and intimidation by the entrenched white power structures. Three male volunteers, working to get Mississippi's large black population registered to vote, were murdered: Chaney who was black, and Goodman and Schwerner, both white. Efforts by organizations to get blacks registered focused on Alabama, where voter registration attempts had failed. A march was planned from Selma to Montgomery to dramatize the problem (televised coverage of the events made a major difference). This march met with violence, exercised by white police; two whites and one black were killed and many were wounded. This march stimulated passage of the Voting Rights Act of 1965, which made it possible for blacks in the South to actually register and vote—ninety-five years after passage of the Fifteenth Amendment (1870), which constitutionally provided blacks the right to vote.

The Selma to Montgomery march was the last mass demonstration of the civil rights movement. A march was attempted in June 1966 in Mississippi, where James Meredith was shot, and the march was aborted.

In 1965 a major uprising occurred in Watts, the black ghetto of Los Angeles. Another civil disturbance took place in Cleveland, Ohio, in 1966 and was followed in 1967 by similar major uprisings in Newark and Detroit. Alphonso Pinkney, educator and author, reported that in 1967 these uprisings took place in "56 cities, in 31 states and resulted in at least 84 deaths, 3,828 injuries, 9,550 arrests, and hundreds of millions of dollars in property damage."[7] Pinkney defined the Watts uprising as signaling the end of the monopoly previously held by the advocates of nonviolence as a method of protest among blacks.

The Northern revolts may have occurred because the problems of Northern blacks were not being addressed in the civil rights movement. Such uprisings are triggered by incidents which seem minor in nature, but their underlying causes are the festering resentment and hostility of blacks who are forced to live in urban slums under conditions of poverty and deprivation. Pinkney's analysis is that "they [blacks] utilize the uprisings as a means of bringing their economic plight (unemployment and low earnings) maintained by white racism to the attention of public officials who have generally been insensitive to their status."[8]

In June 1966, shortly after James Meredith had been shot, civil rights leaders tried to effect a second stage of the Meredith Mississippi Freedom March. When the marchers reached Greenwood, Mississippi, a mass meeting was held. Stokely Carmichael spoke to the gathering and used a new and controversial slogan for the first time: "black power."[9] Martin Luther King, Jr., who was at the meeting, expressed reservations about the use of this slogan in the civil rights movement, and his associates from the Southern Christian Leadership Conference agreed with him. The leaders of SNCC and CORE approved use of the black-power slogan as appropriate, however, and it became part of the nomenclature of the civil rights movement.

Some literature indicates that the uprisings or riots in the cities and the voices proclaiming black power collectively *caused* a "white backlash," because the majority group became infuriated and empathy for blacks disappeared. Martin Luther King, Jr., did not agree with this easy explanation for the backlash. He held that the change in mood among the dominant group preceded Watts and the black-power slogan; he also believed the white backlash had always lain below the surface and sometimes on the surface of American life.[10] However, King, Pinckney, and Bennett were in agreement that the initial phase of the civil rights movement came to an end with Selma and the Voting Rights Act in 1965.[11]

Southern blacks, particularly, benefited from the passage and initial enforcement of the Civil Rights Act of 1964 and the Voting Rights Act of 1965. They could, in the late sixties, actually vote for public officials. They could also, without intimidation, use public facilities for the first time. The libraries, parks, and swimming pools for which their taxes had partially paid—but which they could not use—were now open to blacks, although some communities closed public swimming pools rather than let blacks and whites use the facilities together. Restaurants and hotels, if they were open to the public, were forced to admit the black portion of the American public for the first time. Southern blacks in the late 1960s began to experience the token equality which blacks outside the South had already achieved.[12] This represented significant progress in overcoming overt discrimination and segregation against blacks, especially in the South.

Businessmen, not wanting legal action taken against them or continued public displays in their businesses, became courteous to black customers. Hotels accepted black conventions. Politicians, seeking office, moderated the demagogic appeals in their campaign speeches. Interpersonal contacts between races increased in number and frequency and were no longer relationships of superordinate–subordinate, white-over-black quality.

What the two congressional acts did *not* represent was realization of full equality and justice for blacks throughout the country. Legislation and court decrees are (and have been) necessary to the realization of those goals, but are not sufficient. Fundamental, long-standing problems remain. Poverty, unemployment, job discrimination, inadequate housing, and educational barriers still exist throughout America as grave problems for the black minority. There is no doubt that the civil rights movement of the 1960s resulted in progress for blacks, but if we assess those gains in retrospect and in light of the problems which remain in 1977 it has to be said quite candidly that this progress was modest. The status of black Americans has not been altered significantly, although many individual black persons and their families have benefited. The changes in the 1960s represented more progress for blacks than in the hundred years since Reconstruction, but in the 1970s blacks are still the lowest group of minority citizens, proportionally.

Blacks still are represented in the lower class in disproportionate numbers because the great efforts of the sixties were directed at symptoms, not fundamental causes, of the black predicament. The system of segregation imposed by the *Plessy* decision was a symptom of something more basic—the belief that blacks were inferior to whites and as a result could and should be separated. The fact of separation plus the "mandate" which accompanied it belied the platitudes of justice and equality so often heard in patriotic speeches. When the *Brown* decision overturned *Plessy* it overruled the symptom but not the cause. However, since *Plessy* was in effect so long, it had become the reason or cause for societal practices. One can see the circularity and progression of symptom–cause–symptom from *Plessy* to *Brown*. Segregation was not the real issue; forced segregation could end without ending black oppression or correcting blacks' economic plight. The real issues are the deeply ingrained beliefs that blacks are inferior and therefore can be oppressed, and thus deserve their economic plight. The real issues are the most difficult to solve, which is why we are where we are today as a society.

Today, and since about 1967, some black leaders and intellectuals have tried to internationalize the struggle of various peoples throughout the world, especially in Asia, Africa, and Latin America, to attain equality and justice.* The international effort is called a Third World

---

*Some contemporary black authors describe this movement as if it were a new phenomenon. It is not. The reader may recall that W. E. B. DuBois held a pan-African philosophy as early as 1917 and worked to internationalize the struggle of people of color. In the 1940s Paul Robeson was chairman of the Board of the Council on Africa, an organization with similar goals. Horace Mann Bond organized the American Committee on Africa. George Haynes worked toward these ends through the Federal Council of Churches. Blacks lent support to the East-West Association, organized by Pearl Buck, and to groups lobbying for the independence of India. These efforts were made in the 1940s, for the most part. The efforts of the late 1960s and beyond represent a revival of earlier concern. One difference is that in the contemporary period black militant expressions of revolution have been added.

quest for the elimination of poverty, discrimination, racism, and war. Other black leaders and intellectuals in the mid-1970s have turned to ideas of socialism and Marxism in their efforts to find solutions to the continuing American dilemma.

There is, moreover, little collective effort between blacks and whites or minority groups to effect meaningful social change in realizing the goals of the American Creed. The nation stands at the crossroads—will it go forward, toward actualizing its expressed democratic ideals, or will it regress toward the *status quo ante?* White Americans believe that establishing the principle of legal equality as public policy is sufficient to the realization of actual equality. Also, white Americans generally are satisfied with the idea that a very gradual pace is acceptable with respect to the actualization of equal rights for blacks and other minorities. Blacks, on the other hand, know from their group experience over time that principles often are one thing and real-life practices another. They also know that the group is a long way from one-on-one equality in the professions, the trades, and the decision-making processes. The pace of progress is equally disturbing to blacks who must meet the responsibilities and obligations of citizenship and daily living but are asked to wait for their rights.

Resistance to change, or slowing the pace of change, results primarily from the unwillingness of white Americans to give up their position of dominance and its resulting privileges and, secondarily, from a no-growth economy. There are no easy answers to actualizing the principles and ideals of American democracy, but workable solutions must be found.

Given this background and review, what is the evidence that there is a changing mood in the black population?

SURVEYS OF BLACK ATTITUDES

Just as white attitudes are assessed by survey research methods, research centers, opinion pollsters, and other groups or individuals, so are black attitudes. *Newsweek* magazine's assessments of attitudes, obtained by public opinion surveys, will be reported first, followed by data from the University of Michigan's Survey Research Center (acquired in preparing the Kerner Commission Report), and data from an individual black researcher. Structurally, these three assessments of the changing mood in the black population follow the same pattern as the earlier analysis on the changing mood in the white population.

There were shifts of magnitude in the black population from 1963 to 1969, and although those years are not the focus of this book, what happened in that period had an effect on the mood and attitudes since 1969, the immediate concern. Therefore, a flashback to the period 1963–69 is useful in understanding later shifts.

National publications in the sixties displayed great interest in civil concerns, and one such magazine was the New York–based weekly, *Newsweek*. During the six-year period, 1963–69, *Newsweek* conducted three public opinion surveys to assess and report the black mood in America. The first survey was reported in July 1963, the second in October 1965, and the third in June 1969. All three polls selected blacks throughout the country and across the social class spectrum as respondents in an attempt to secure an authentic cross-section of black attitudes.

"Newsweek" Surveys

Newsweek selected Louis Harris, a well-known public opinion pollster, to conduct the 1963 survey. He was assisted by a forty-man task force appointed by *Newsweek,* and together they interviewed more than 1,250 persons for an average of two and one-quarter hours each. These black men and women were chosen carefully as a cross-section of the national black community. Of these, 100 were black leaders who were interviewed in great depth. The survey's editorial comment is titled "Anatomy of a Revolution"[13] and the presentation of data is called "The Negro in America."[14]

Analysis of the collected data revealed seven broad, basic findings:

1. The civil rights protest had the allegiance of vast majorities of blacks, regardless of where they lived and their economic condition or age; the protest was an authentic, deep-seated revolution.

2. The goal of blacks was to end discrimination in all its forms; blacks wanted their rightful share of the American dream, which included a better job, higher pay, a better home, and better educational facilities.

3. Most credit for social gains was overwhelmingly awarded to Martin Luther King, Jr., the NAACP, and John F. Kennedy, in that order.

4. The black revolution was anti–Jim Crow, not anti-white.

5. The revolt was committed to nonviolence, although one black in five felt some violence was inevitable.

6. Dedication to the movement was overwhelming, and so was the

determination to win, whether the winning strategy meant boycotts, demonstrations, or going to jail.

7. Hope was the key word in describing the revolution.

These seven findings present a concise picture of the black mood and its corresponding attitudes in 1963, but elaboration is needed to give the reader a full sense of the time. Why did the movement develop when it did? *Newsweek's* explanation is that it was a revolution of rising expectations, not a revolution of despair. The movement was propelled by the cumulative impetus of black economic gains, advances in education and leadership, and the promise of a better future. Milestones in black progress toward their mood of 1963 were World War II, the desegregation of the armed forces in 1948, the emergence of independent black African nations, and, most of all, the Supreme Court's desegregation decision of 1954. The goal in 1963 was complete equality, nothing less.

The church's role at this stage should not be underestimated; it served as both tactical headquarters and sanctuary. *Newsweek* pointed out that, even in the South, the police rarely interfered with blacks' right of assembly so long as they assembled in their churches. Further, certain ministers played a leadership role in taking their congregations out of the churches and into the streets to demonstrate against discrimination and injustice. Given the religious tradition of most blacks and what they had heard in church about the brotherhood of man, linked to their sense of the moral rightness of black efforts to end discrimination, they felt God was on the side of blacks in this struggle.

A potent weapon used by blacks at this time was the boycott. Two-thirds of blacks with incomes of $5,500 and higher said they were ready to boycott any company that practiced discrimination, and one black in four had already boycotted stores and products because of reports of discrimination by companies. Chief targets of boycotts had been Wonder and Bond breads, Woolworth, Kress, and Grant dime stores, Falstaff Brewing Company, and Coca-Cola.

But even blacks who took the initiative in the civil rights struggle admitted that they could not win the battle for equality without white help. Foremost, blacks felt that eventually the white man would comprehend the injustice of discrimination; until this occurred, black leaders especially felt that their people could get jobs, education, and their civil rights only with the help of a predominantly white Congress, a white president, and a white Supreme Court. Among the people, four blacks in ten felt that for them to utilize public accommodations, a federal law would have to be passed; but in 1963, only one black in ten expected

Congress to pass such a bill. This belief expressed no confidence in Congress, dominated by Southerners who held key committee chairmanships. There was confidence, however, in the president, John F. Kennedy. Even more confidence was expressed in the Supreme Court; two-thirds of the blacks who were polled gave the Supreme Court credit "for their biggest breakthroughs toward equality."[15]

Despite this confidence in the president and the Supreme Court, and in spite of the overall hope, *Newsweek* saw some danger signs in 1963. First, if neither President Kennedy nor the courts could solve black problems, the revolution might shift from nonviolence to violence because of the determination of blacks to be equal. Second, the gravest threat of violence was in Northern and Southern big-city slums, where one black in five believed he would have to use violence to obtain his rights.

Newsweek judged blacks to be effective in mobilizing, marching, and winning some recognition but guilty of great political apathy, even when blacks were encouraged to enter politics. *Newsweek* felt that it was a mistake for blacks to underestimate the force of the vote in America.

In politics, John F. Kennedy and the Democratic party received overwhelming endorsement from blacks. Kennedy outranked the leading contenders of the day by 30 to 1; his contenders were Nelson Rockefeller, George Romney, and Barry Goldwater. Only 4 blacks in 100 felt the Republicans could aid the civil rights struggle in 1963. In 1960, 85 percent of the blacks who were polled had voted for Kennedy, while Nixon received only 11 percent. In retrospect, Dwight D. Eisenhower was considered the president who had done less for blacks than any other president since 1932 (48%—or almost half of those polled), while 73 percent, almost 3 out of 4, felt that Kennedy had done most.

With respect to black leadership, the *Newsweek* poll showed that people who were identified as leaders were locked into a course of action by the aggressiveness of the rank and file. The leaders endorsed the major black goals: economic equality and opportunity and full integration. They also agreed with the philosophy of nonviolence, reliance on court decisions and corrective legislation, and negotiations with white leadership. The leader who towered above all others was Dr. Martin Luther King, Jr., and the most significant organization was the NAACP. Other favorably rated organizations were the Urban League, the Congress of Racial Equality (CORE), and the Student Nonviolent Coordinating Committee (SNCC). There was almost no support for the Black Muslims and their plea for separatism; 41 percent of the rank-

and-file blacks who were polled did not recognize the Muslim cause. *Newsweek's* ranking of leaders by leaders, and of leaders by the rank and file is shown in table 3–1.

TABLE 3–1. WHO ARE THE LEADERS—HOW THEY RATE

| Ratings by Rank and File | | | Ratings by the Leaders | |
Favorable	Poor		Favorable	Poor
88	1	Martin Luther King, Jr.	95	1
80	1	Jackie Robinson	82	2
79	1	James Meredith	81	1
78	1	Medgar Evers	92	1
68	1	Roy Wilkins	92	0
64	*	Thurgood Marshall	94	1
62	2	Ralph Bunche	87	2
60	1	Dick Gregory	80	3
56	3	Harry Belafonte	73	2
55	3	Lena Horne	68	2
53	3	Floyd Patterson	50	9
51	7	Adam Clayton Powell	52	16
40	1	James Baldwin	67	3
15	29	Elijah Muhammad	17	65

* Less than 1 percent

SOURCE: *Newsweek*, 29 July 1963, p. 31.

Looking at these leaders, one wonders: Leaders of what? It is questionable, in retrospect, that actors, comedians, baseball players, and boxers would appear as leaders, except for their contributions of funds and their roles in soliciting funds to assist the civil rights movement. Also in retrospect, one wonders why political figures ranked so low, or were not ranked at all.

What did blacks think of whites in 1963? *Newsweek* concluded that blacks considered whites their greatest burden, but felt that the burden grew lighter every day. Among the rank and file, only 1 black in 4 thought the dominant group sincerely desired that blacks get a better break; 41 percent thought the white man wanted to keep blacks "in their place" and 17 percent said whites simply did not care. Black leaders exhibited more trust in whites than did rank-and-file blacks, but they did not give whites a vote of confidence. Blacks in middle- and upper-income groups also displayed more trust in whites than did blacks in the lower-income groups; 33 percent of middle- and upper-income blacks in the North gave whites a favorable vote, while 45 percent of their equivalents in the South responded favorably.

In spite of some negativism, blacks on the whole were clearly optimistic about the future. Fifty-two percent of them felt that white attitudes toward blacks had improved since 1958, and 73 percent felt that white attitudes would continue to improve in the next five years (to 1968). But blacks put more trust in government and institutions than in individual whites.[16]

Of all whites, Roman Catholic priests who worked daily in black communities were most trusted (55% of blacks). Contrary to rumor, blacks thought well of Jews.

Newsweek pollsters asked blacks what two or three white leaders and organizations they disliked most and trusted least. Although the degree of dislike differed in some cases between black leaders and the rank and file, they agreed on the organizations and persons, as follows (ranked from most disliked and least trusted by the rank and file): Ku Klux Klan, White Citizens Council, Ross Barnett, George C. Wallace, Barry Goldwater, Orval Faubus, American Nazi party, John Birch Society.

Concluding, *Newsweek* said that (1) the black revolution would not stop; it would go on; (2) blacks were losing patience with gradualism; (3) blacks felt their faith in mass protest had produced results and, as a result, blacks were "walking taller" (dignity and respect); (4) violence would remain a constant risk of the revolution and the flashpoint was likeliest in Northern slums; and (5) blacks want freedom, which meant freedom from all the injustices that go with a dark skin.

Looking into the future, *Newsweek* predicted that

> the crisis point will come if and when the irresistible force of Negro protest meets the immovable object of white intractability. In polls for *The Washington Post,* Louis Harris found majorities of white Americans in favor—at least in principle—of taking Federal action to secure the Negro's rights. But the white man's commitment thins in practice. Three in five don't think the Negro is ready to hold a better job or live in a better neighborhood, and nearly three in four feel Negroes are moving faster than whites will accept them. The white man's resistance is particularly strong at the prospect of a Negro moving into the house next door to his; just as deeply the Negro wants the right to move there if he chooses. The combination makes housing potentially the most explosive of all the issues at stake in the Negro revolution.
>
> ... The final question will not be so much what the Negro will settle for—he is united and insistent—as how much the white man

will give him. Negroes think that he will change—that he will start treating them better because of his conscience, because he fears their militancy, or simply because he is an American. But whether or not the white man is willing to open the final door, the Negro will not stop knocking.[17]

In its October 25, 1965, issue *Newsweek* summed up the position of the Negro in America, based on fresh survey data procured by a new Louis Harris poll. Its 1965 survey showed that blacks and whites wanted essentially the same things in life: "a free society, a good job with better prospects, decent homes and schools, a feeling of safety on the streets at night."[18] A continued source of conflict between the races was the difference between desire and attainment of these segments of the American dream by blacks and whites. Whites on the whole felt blacks had those things but blacks felt they did not.

Four out of five whites said they had a high standard of living; 9 out of 10 whites said they shared in the mobility and opportunity which is central to an open society: the opportunity to move, or advance on the job, or find a new job. But barely one-half of the blacks who were polled said their standard of living was high; only 57 percent said they had a chance for job advancement, and 33 1/3 percent doubted their chance of finding a new job, or moving, or being sure their children had a good education. Almost twice as many blacks as whites (69% to 39%) said crime in the streets was a real problem in their lives.[19]

Newsweek's brief report concluded that the basic demands of the black revolt were unchanged and that it was not likely the revolt would be blunted until blacks have their full share of what the dominant group has in America. The interviewers found that the black revolt had further eroded some of the white man's stereotypes about blacks and softened his resistance to change; this meant that whites were changing, but the changes were mixed. For example, the black revolt made many whites uncomfortable, and 30 percent thought blacks were pushing too hard. Most white Southerners and many white Northerners retained long-standing stereotypes of blacks as "loose living, ill-smelling, relentlessly grinning sort(s) who have neither the ability nor the ambition of the white man."[20]

But the overall picture of the Negro in America in late 1965 was of a group making progress. The majority of whites expressed willingness to accept casual contacts with blacks at work, at play, in school, at stores, and at lunch counters. Even in housing, which *Newsweek* considered the most potentially explosive issue in 1963, progress was visible in

terms of shifting white attitudes, In 1963, "51 percent of all whites—
and 46 percent in the North—bridled at the notion of having a Negro
family live next door. Today, only 30 percent in the North and 37 percent in the nation say they would object to having Negro neighbors."[21]

Whereas the 1963 survey was reported in depth, in twenty printed
pages, the 1965 survey was reported in summary form, on half a printed
page. Also, the 1965 survey reported both white and black attitudes. The
difference in space allocation between the 1963 and the 1965 survey is
striking; whether significance can be attached to the difference is a matter of conjecture.

The third major poll was reported in the June 30, 1969, issue of
Newsweek. Even before reading the findings, one is struck by the difference in language: on the 1963 cover, "The *Negro* in America"; on the
1969 cover, "Report from *Black* America" (italics mine). The mood of
America's largest minority group, as assessed by *Newsweek*, was reflected in the language the magazine used: the minority had become
"several shades blacker," as a group, between 1963 and 1969.

In conducting this third major poll, *Newsweek* continued to use its
own staff but combined its efforts with those of Richard M. Scammon
and the Gallup Organization, Inc., replacing Louis Harris, who had conducted the two previous surveys. The black population sample represented a national cross-section which could bear valid comparison with
the two earlier samples, and 977 personal interviews of about 70 minutes
each were conducted by a team of black poll takers. The in-depth report
is twenty printed pages (including p. 12, where *Newsweek* reported on a
subsequent visit to three black men previously profiled), equal to the
space allocated in 1963.

Since the 1965 poll, several traumatic occurrences had unfolded for
the nation, especially for blacks. The murder of Martin Luther King,
Jr., de-emphasis of the war on poverty, emphasis on the war in Vietnam,
riots, and the rebirth of black cultural concerns had affected the mood
of the people. Also, a new display of black political power was illustrated
by the election to public office of Mayors Richard Hatcher in Gary,
Charles Evers in Fayette, Mississippi, and Carl Stokes in Cleveland.
Also visible was white backlash in Minneapolis, Los Angeles, and to a
smaller extent in New York.

Broad, basic findings of the 1969 survey were:
1. The vast majority of American blacks still wanted an equal
   place in an open society where integration is a free option.
2. There was a feeling of progress, especially in the economic

realm, but an equally strong feeling that progress had been too slow.

3. Most blacks still rejected violence as a tactic, but a significant number felt that rioting was justified and that the disorders had advanced black aspirations.
4. Martin Luther King, Jr., was more highly regarded in death than in life, but his nonviolent philosophy had lost ground.
5. Blacks were shedding their illusions about what white America was willing to do for them; increasingly, blacks felt that whites would make concessions only under pressure.
6. Twenty-one percent of the blacks polled were favorably disposed to the idea of a separate nation for blacks within the boundaries of the United States; this feeling resulted from their despair of significant gains under present arrangements.
7. The most alienated group of blacks was the under-30 population in the North.
8. Black leadership was fragmented and many new faces were on the scene, compared with 1963.
9. There was a thrust for a "self-reliant brand of separatism coupled with a concerted drive to capture political and economic control of the ghetto and its institutions."[22]

Underneath these broad findings, what was visible about blacks and the mood of blacks in mid-1969? Richard M. Scammon constructed a demographic profile to find out, and discovered that the profile was full of diversity, but pointed out that white Americans tended to look on blacks as a relatively monolithic group. Two significant aspects of the black profile were the high percentage of black youth (the median age of the black population was 21, compared with a median age of 29 for the white population) and the geographical location of the population (more than half of the black population still lived in the South, despite the mass migrations to the North since World War II). The concentration of blacks in the South had decreased from the density of a generation ago, when three-fourths of this group lived in the South, but the number remained important. North and South, more than half of American blacks resided in the central cities of metropolitan areas. However, only one-fourth of the white population lived in the cities. As blacks had moved into cities, whites had moved out. *Newsweek* pointed out that between 1967 and 1969 the white "escape rate" from central cities had tripled, to an annual average of nearly one-half million.[23]

With respect to income levels, the median family income for blacks increased over the decade 1957–67 at a higher rate than the white median family income. However, blacks still lagged far behind whites. In 1967 the median white family income was $8,274, compared with $5,141 for nonwhites.

Scammon identified what he felt were significant advances for blacks: increases in educational attainment by black youth and better-quality housing. But overall Scammon found that "in jobs, housing, education, and income Blacks still lagged behind Whites—in some areas considerably behind." [24]

The 1969 survey found blacks were "angry—but they still had a dream."[25] The following responses were given by blacks in answer to specific questions about progress toward equality and social justice: (1) by 63 percent to 21 percent, blacks felt they could win equality without violence; (2) by 74 percent to 16 percent they favored integration; and (3) 70 percent said blacks had made progress since 1964; an almost equal number believed that progress would continue in the next five years. But there were regional differences in response patterns: Southerners were more hopeful than Northerners, Northerners more militant than Southerners, and young Northern blacks were angriest of all. The poorest blacks were most conservative of all. However, a feeling of grievance and willingness to act on issues was characteristic of blacks with higher income and education.

There were small but real increases in alienation and despair. Twenty percent of blacks wanted a separate black nation inside the United States, 1 in 7 did not consider America worth fighting for in a world war, and 25 percent felt blacks should arm themselves. The priorities listed by blacks were jobs (51%), education (39%), and housing (36%).

On the increase was the feeling that the pace of progress was too slow (59%, up 16 points from 1966); only 22 percent of blacks were satisfied with the pace of progress. Also increasing was the separatist streak —stronger than in the two previous *Newsweek* polls, and possibly the strongest since Marcus Garvey's back-to-Africa movement in the 1920s. Black self-esteem was also increasing; in fact, the term *black* was found to have gained wide usage, especially among urban Northerners, the young, and the relatively affluent. "Natural" hair styles and Afro clothes also had growing appeal.

In 1969 blacks were less trusting in the good faith and good will of whites, but groups and institutions, such as the Supreme Court, which still seemed to care about the black plight received a vote of confidence.

The anti-poverty program of the federal government also received supportive votes. Jews were rated favorably by 2 to 1, and higher than the non-Jewish white population; thus majority black sentiment was not like the anti-Semitic rhetoric of some ghetto militants. But Congress, trade unions, college students, state governments, and the mass media had diminished esteem in the eyes of the blacks polled. Lowest ratings were given to police and to President Richard Nixon. Sixty-eight percent of blacks polled felt that what blacks had gained so far could be attributed to black action, not to white charity.

For blacks in 1969 political affiliation remained Democratic (76%), but only 62 percent felt that the party would do the most for blacks. Twenty-four percent doubted that it made much difference what political party won in America.

The 1969 survey revealed continuities in respect to patterns expressed by blacks. Martin Luther King, Jr., continued to be respected in death. Eighty-two percent of blacks polled believed a conspiracy was involved in his death, and 67 percent did not believe a full and honest investigation of the circumstances had been made. The NAACP continued to be a respected organization, as did the Urban League, but their ratings fell 21 and 10 points respectively.

In terms of leadership, new faces, new voices, and new styles were identifiable. No one person could lay claim to King's national following. Some black leaders thought it was good that monolithic Negro leadership no longer existed. In addition to the black mayors, Hatcher, Evers, and Stokes, the following names were cited in terms of more narrowly defined leadership roles in 1969, as leaders of certain sectors of the black population or leaders of key organizations: Ralph David Abernathy, Julian Bond, Roy Innis, Price Cobbs, Ernest Chambers, Harry Edwards, William Clay, Alvin Poussaint, Nathan Hare, Hosea Williams, Elma Lewis, James Foreman, George Wiley, and Jesse Jackson. Still leaders, but no longer regarded as highly as in the past, were Bayard Rustin and Whitney Young, Jr. Perhaps the most commonly agreed upon point among the emerging leaders was an emphasis on local autonomy—"community control"—in one form or another.

The new turn in black leadership reflected both the complexity and the diversity of problems and issues facing blacks at the end of the sixties and the schism in the black community over strategies appropriate to achieving commonly agreed upon ends. Regarding the former, *Newsweek* made this observation:

American Negroes have got just about all they are going to get for the time being from the courts and the Congress. But the landmark court rulings and legislation of the 1960's have accomplished only so much—and the task of making a decent place for blacks in American society has proved far more complex than was first realized.[26]

In reference to the black community's divisiveness, *Newsweek* noted:

> As the new leaders describe it, the black separatist movement represents far more than just docile resignation to the facts of American life. The young Negro leaders see in separatism a chance to develop a cultural identity, consciousness of being black and a continuity with the past.
> Separatism: "A sense of nationhood for black Americans. This doesn't imply necessarily a territorial entity."[27]

Even some black leaders who did not accept the notion of separatism expressed the conviction that the capitalist system offered no avenue for black hopes of economic betterment. Some black leaders also had lost faith in American political processes.

There were continuing regional differences in black life. In 1969 Jonathan Rodgers, writing for *Newsweek,* described key facets of Northern urban ghetto life as "hustler, preacher, panther." He said hustlers and numbers runners were as active as they had been prior to the civil rights movement. Rodgers also said "the hustler has always been the most admired man in ghetto areas because he is the only black man 'making it' who lives there."[28] Churches in the ghetto were filled, but mostly with old people. The Black Panthers were growing in numbers, almost exclusively among the young, and were carrying on a free breakfast program that fed 500 children a day. They were also constantly battling the police, who accelerated their raids on alleged Panther headquarters as Panther influence seemed to grow.

Joseph B. Cumming, Jr., also writing for *Newsweek,* assessed the South as characterized by "changes deep and subtle." He had watched the Southern black movement in the early sixties and witnessed cataclysmic efforts to change the entrenched Southern system of discrimination and segregation. Returning to the South in 1969, he initially had the feeling that "everything had happened; nothing had changed."[29] But looking deeper, he saw real changes in the number of blacks who were registered to vote, the number of black officeholders, and the number of black children in integrated classes.

Symbolic changes were evident, too; the buildings which SNCC had used for its revolutionary efforts in 1964 and 1965, had been recycled. In Jackson, Mississippi, SNCC's old headquarters had become a restaurant; in Greenwood, Mississippi, its old offices had become the home of Delta Opportunities Corporation, which was working out job-training and economic-development schemes for blacks leaving agricultural work. The aim of blacks in the South, generally, was to consolidate gains made in the earlier sixties and to continue to work for black unity among the social classes. Cumming also found a slowing of migration to the North and the return of some young blacks to the South.

He detected a subtle change in the nature of Southern racism: the volume of white protest was lower, and ideological arguments against integration were waning, but whites still blocked black progress wherever they could. And when blacks moved into better parts of town, whites moved away if they could afford to. When black children moved into public schools, white parents who could afford it withdrew their children and sent them to private schools.

Cumming summed up his return to the South as follows:

> Wherever local blacks have something going they can call a movement, the power structure shows respect. Wherever Negro voter registration is large, demagoguery is muted. Wherever schools are significantly integrated, future generations will be more politically aware and less susceptible to the old myths of fear and hatred. The Second Reconstruction will work if the Federal government does not lose its nerve—especially in renewing the 1965 Voting Rights Act, which is scheduled to expire in August 1970. Despite all the subtle alignments that the white South has devised to keep the Negro poor, dependent, uneducated and politically powerless, a deep and subtle change of climate has taken place that will not be undone.[30]

Ghetto blacks under 30 years old were different enough from the rest of black America in 1969 to rate a page of separate coverage. Characterizing them as "the tough new breed," *Newsweek* said these young men and women of the North probably are the most militant generation yet in Negro America.[31] Despite their anger and toughness, it was remarkable that three-fourths of them still aspired to the traditional goals. However, their faith in the old strategies for achieving those ends had diminished and their trust in the white man's intentions had "curdled."

A capsule view of *Newsweek's* polls of how black attitudes changed from 1966 to 1969 may be obtained from table 3–2. Blank spaces in the 1966 column indicate that the question was not asked that year.

TABLE 3–2. SHIFTING BLACK ATTITUDES

Issue	Substance of Question	Yes Responses 1966	Yes Responses 1969
Police	Local police are harmful to black rights	33%	46%
Violence	Those who say they would join a riot	15	11
"	Blacks who believe riots have helped more than hurt in their struggle		40
"	Blacks can win rights without violence		63
"	There will be more riots in the future		64
"	Riots are justified		31
Vietnam War	Blacks should oppose the war in Vietnam because they have less freedom to fight for	35	56
Whites	Whites are either hostile or indifferent	54	69
"	Whites really mean well		20
"	White attitudes have gotten better in the last five years (1964–1969)		54
"	Expect whites to improve over the next five years		61
"	Reason alone has been the factor for any gains	51	46
"	Black action, not white charity, has been the factor for any gains		68
Federal Government	The federal government is helpful to black rights	74 (LBJ)	25 (Nixon)
"	The Democratic party will do the most for blacks		62
"	Blacks who consider themselves Democrats		76
Draft laws	Draft laws are unfair to blacks	25	47

Source: *Newsweek*, 30 June 1969, pp. 19–22.

Survey Research Center's Findings

The Survey Research Center at the University of Michigan has assembled data on black as well as white attitudes. Howard Schuman and Shirley Hatchett, staff members at the center, published findings on black attitudes in *Black Racial Attitudes: Trends and Complexities* (1974). Their book draws on three sample surveys: (1) interviews with 2,809 black respondents in fifteen American cities during the first three months of 1968, (2) a Detroit Area Study, conducted from April 24 to July 31, 1968, and (3) another Detroit Area Study, carried out from April 15 to September 26, 1971. The first survey sampled fifteen cities and the second and third focused on Detroit only. Schuman and Hatchett limited their conclusions to Detroit but point out that Detroit is not atypical of most major Northern cities.[32]

The Detroit Area Study of 1971 repeated a set of thirteen questions which had been asked in the Detroit Area Study of 1968, including six questions which had been asked in the first survey. Therefore a comparison between the 1971 study and either or both of the earlier studies provides evidence of changes in attitudes and beliefs over a three-year period, 1968–71. Schuman and Hatchett present strong evidence (below) that black attitudes changed between 1968 and 1971, but they acknowledge that their conclusions are limited by the number and range of the questions they asked.

A. Perceptions of White Attitudes and Discrimination

1. *(Progress)* Some people say that over the last 10 or 15 years, there has been a lot of progress in getting rid of racial discrimination. Others say there hasn't been much real change for most (Negroes) over that time.* Which do you agree with most?

2. *(Keep Down)* On the whole, do you think most white people in Detroit want to see (Negroes) get a better break, or do they want to keep (Negroes) down, or don't they care one way or the other?

3. *(Trust)* Do you personally feel that you can trust most white people, some white people, or none at all?

---

*In printed form, "Negro" is the term used in these questions. However, the word is placed in parentheses in all questions because the interviewers had been instructed to use the terms, "black," "Negro," or "colored" as preferred by the respondent, insofar as the respondent indicated a preference. Thus the parentheses are used to show this variability. See the explanation by Schuman and Hatchett in their footnote 9, page 13, of *Black Racial Attitudes: Trends and Complexities*.

4. *(Clerks)* Do you think (Negro) customers who shop in the big downtown stores are treated as politely as white customers, or are they treated less politely?

5. *(Jobs)* How many places in Detroit do you think will hire a white person before they will hire a (Negro) even though they have the same qualifications ... many, some, or just a few places?

6. *(Teachers)* Do you think (Negro) teachers take more of an interest in teaching (Negro) students than white teachers do?

B. Actions and Policies

7. *(Neighborhood)* Would you personally prefer to live in a neighborhood with all (Negroes), mostly (Negroes), mostly whites, or a neighborhood that's mixed half and half?

8. *(Best Means)* As you see it, what's the best way for (Negroes) to try to gain their rights—use laws and persuasion, use non-violent protest, or be ready to use violence?

9. *(Second Means)* [Asked of those not answering violence on #8] If (law and persuasion/non-violent protest) doesn't work, then do you think (Negroes) should be ready to use violence?

10. *(Principals)* Some people say there should be (Negro) principals in schools with mostly (Negro) students because (Negroes) should have the most say in running inner city schools. Would you agree with that or not?

11. *(Fight for U.S.)* If our country got into a big World War today, would you personally feel the United States is worth fighting for?

C. Other Questions

12. *(Riot)* This next question has to do with the effects of the riot in Detroit four years ago in July, 1967. Do you think that because of that disturbance there are more whites in favor of equal rights for (Negroes), fewer whites in favor, or that the riot didn't make much difference?

13. *(Entertainers)* On another subject (related to how you spend your spare time), could you tell me who two or three of your favorite actors or entertainers are? [Coded for race of each entertainer mentioned][33]

Schuman and Hatchett report that

> nine of the eleven directional questions ... show shifts in the direc-
> tion of greater alienation from white society, greater black con-
> sciousness, greater militancy. Six of these shifts are significant
> beyond the .05 level, with two showing chi square values (23.1 for
> item 2 and 26.0 for item 9) far beyond the probability of chance oc-
> currence. Thus it seems safe to conclude that Black attitudes
> changed in *some* important ways over the three-year period. More-
> over, the average (mean and median) change of +6 percent for
> those eleven items taken as a whole is not slight in absolute terms for
> such a short period. Over ten years, for example, it would lead to a
> 20 percent shift in black attitudes on this set of items—no small
> change for America if attitudes count for anything.[34]

One of the largest shifts in black attitudes on individual items was
with respect to question 2 on the fundamental nature of black–white relations. In 1968 about 43 percent of Detroit blacks believed that most
whites "want to see Negroes get a better break," but this had dropped to
28 percent in 1971, while the percentage believing that most whites
"want to keep Negroes down" rose from 23 to 41 percent during the
same period.[35]

In responding to item 4, blacks said they felt Negro customers were
treated less politely than white customers; 12 percent more black respondents felt this way in 1971 than in 1968. Schuman and Hatchett interpret this response as increasing skepticism of white behavior.[36]

The authors reported only a small difference or borderline significance on item 8, concerned with the best means for Negroes to try to
gain their rights; but item 9, a more "latent" question on the readiness
to use violence to secure black rights, showed a much more marked
change. Whereas in 1968 only 23 percent of the black population was
willing to consider violence if other means failed, by 1971 that figure
had risen to 44 percent. Shuman and Hatchett interpret the two items to
mean that few blacks (about 11%) were ready to advocate violence in
1971, but a much larger proportion (44%) no longer rejected violence as
an ultimately necessary strategy.[37]

The data indicated that blacks in 1971 were not more likely to
claim that white teachers lack interest in black students (item 6), nor
was there any visible increase in the wish to make race the criterion for
selection of school principals (item 10).

With respect to item 7, there was a significant increase in the desire
of blacks to live mainly or wholly in black neighborhoods.[38] The authors

interpret this response as suggesting an increase in "black consciousness," as expressed in personal preferences for association with other blacks and as opposed to an increase in black power, which would have been expressed if blacks were willing to discriminate publicly against whites (which they did not do), as in the school principal question.

On item 13 there was no evidence of a shift in attitudes between 1968 and 1971 on favorite actors or entertainers. The authors say, "If implicit preference for black entertainers represents a manifestation of cultural 'black consciousness', then there is no evidence ... of an increase in this cultural emphasis between 1968 and 1971."[39] They are correct in saying there was no significant *increase*; however, when one looks at their table 1 (p. 10), it is apparent that blacks expressed a distinct *preference* for black entertainers in 1968 (67.2%) and 1971 (69.1%). Therefore, the data show that the preference existed in 1968 and continued into 1971, even though there was no significant increase.

Answering item 11, 85.8 percent of black respondents said they would be willing to fight for the United States (1968) if the country got into a world war. In 1971 90.9 percent indicated a willingness to fight.[40] The authors found this response surprising in light of the social climate in 1971 of growing disillusionment with the war in Vietnam. They said they would have expected increased black resistance to military service, but that did not occur.

Item 12 showed one of the largest attitude shifts. In 1968 the majority of Detroit blacks felt the 1967 Detroit riot had stimulated white sympathies, but in 1971 a significantly larger proportion of blacks believed the riot had reduced white support. The authors' interpretation is that "if the urban riot is conceived of as a form of protest, Blacks increasingly look back on it as unsuccessful in terms of its effects on white attitudes."[41]

Item 1, related to the perception of progress in eliminating racial discrimination, showed only a small, nonsignificant difference (+4.5), which the authors found difficult to interpret.

Schuman and Hatchett were careful to express the limitations of their findings in terms of generalizability. Equal care is given to explaining methodological problems in evaluating changes and to explaining and analyzing the effects of the race of the interviewer on responses. Within these limitations, the authors conclude that black attitudes in fifteen American cities changed between 1968 and 1971, and that the most important shift was in perceptions of whites. In 1971, more blacks perceived "most whites" to be hostile and oppressive—more than in 1968.

As a result of this altered perception, it seemed that in 1971 more blacks were willing to believe that extreme measures, including violence, might be needed to achieve equal rights. The authors concluded that blacks had a less benign, though possibly more realistic, view of whites in 1971 than in 1968.[42]

Other conclusions were that beliefs about the pervasiveness of job discrimination had not changed significantly. There was also an increased suspicion of white intentions. However, it did not seem to involve rejection of the nation as a whole, if this was measured by willingness to fight for the country in a major war. The authors said that it was incorrect to view the black population as rapidly becoming of one mind in hostility toward whites, or as monolithic on any other issue.

In chapter 5, "Demographic and Socioeconomic Factors," an important finding was the relationship between alienation scores and age and education. Consistent with all recent studies since the mid-'60s, Schuman and Hatchett found that younger blacks were considerably more alienated from white society than older blacks; in magnitude, this was the strongest background correlate of black racial attitudes. Not as strong but more complex, and unexpected by the researchers, was the finding for education. Alienation was highest among the least and the most educated respondents, although a curvilinear relationship appeared only among persons 21 to 35 years of age.[43] Their figure 4, however, makes it clear that all black respondents were, at minimum, moderately alienated since even the lowest responses fell midway (between 3 and 4) on a 6-point scale of alienation by education and age and with respondents up to 69 years old.[44]

Discussing the alienation index and other attitudes, beliefs, and actions in chapter 6, the authors indicated that the strongest correlates of the alienation index from the three surveys were other items which dealt with expectations of open hostility from whites. Almost as strong was the belief that blacks could not expect a fair chance in America, either as individuals "working to achieve" or as citizens dealing with such societal representatives as the police or politicians. Thus it was concluded that black alienation, as represented by high scores on the alienation index, occurs at the personal level of primary group relationships as well as at the wider level of citizen-to-society relationships in daily life. Other conclusions were distrust of the possibilities for interracial friendships in daily life and for fair treatment of blacks in major structures of the larger society, such as occupations and the political area. Also, alienation spilled into spheres described as not manifestly racial, such as rejection of traditional religious practices and involvement. But racial issues did not so pervade black consciousness that they were associated with all other social and political issues.[45]

What do these findings suggest for the future, specifically the remaining years of the 1970s? Schuman and Hatchett suggest that there is good reason to speculate that black disillusionment with whites will increase, primarily because black alienation has its greatest hold on the young. Also, they suggest that traditional white prejudice will decline further, and explain that if this seems contradictory, it is "no more so than the fact that black optimism survived so many long years of the most intense bigotry on the part of the majority of the white population."[46]

Going beyond the young, Schuman and Hatchett say that black alienation is more complex and has a wider base than white liberalism. The association of black alienation with education is not simple; black alienation can be seen clearly among both the least and the most educated blacks, whereas white liberalism is clearly associated with higher schooling. Also, blacks have direct and continuing experiences and grievances which support alienation. For example, reports of hiring and promotion discrimination reach their peak not among the young but among those in their middle years.[47] Thus personal experiences create alienation even in middle-aged, highly educated blacks who might not be ideologically alienated. Black alienation in the seventies is composed partly of "overall group ideology, partly of roles and careers, and partly of individual attitude."[48]

Briefly, the authors base the preceding conclusions on

> our own belief . . . that a sea-change occurred in black attitudes in the mid-60's, and that the urban riots which reached their peak in 1967 and 1968 were both an effect and a substantial further cause of this change. After the signs and symbols of progress during the 1950's and early 1960's the riots *crystallized* the belief among many blacks that progress was too slight and their status in American society still basically frustrating . . . .
>
> This change in black views may well be as fundamental as the transformation in white views that began in the 1940's (if not before) and has been traced in a number of trend studies. Whites began to become relatively more liberal in racial attitudes at that early date, and have continued this movement over the past three decades, though of course with a long way to go still from the black perspective. Now it appears that black views may have embarked

upon an almost equally important shift and movement, one represented by the title of our main index, Alienation from White Society.[49]

Finally, Schuman and Hatchett point out that they have surveyed black racial *attitudes* and *beliefs* (recall Myrdal's discussion of beliefs), not behavior or even behavioral intention.[50] But attitudes and beliefs, collectively, constitute a mood, and that mood has changed since 1969.

From these data we fail to get a sense of the degree of alienation, if any, between the black lower class and classes of blacks above them (intragroup hostilities). We also fail to get a sense of common bonds of interest or concerns, if any, between middle-class persons of both races.

THE KERNER REPORT ON BLACK ATTITUDES

As stated earlier, the Kerner Commission Report pictured America as one nation, divided, and moving toward two societies—separate and unequal. In its analysis, this commission found that civil disorders were not merely a problem of the racial ghetto or the city; instead, the disorders were "symptoms of social ills that have become endemic in our society and now affect every American—black or white, businessman or factory worker, suburban commuter or slum dweller."[51] Thus it can be said that these social ills were felt most deeply by urban blacks, who, being powerless to solve their problems, were pushed to the point of engaging in civil disorders, commonly called "riots."

These civil disorders can be an indicator of the changing mood in the black population, although the disturbances for the most part occurred prior to 1969. Elements of the black population have resorted to this extreme manifestation of frustration, powerlessness, hostility, and resentment from time to time. The periods 1900–1910 and 1917–1921 were such times.[52] A bloody riot occurred in Detroit in June 1943. Twenty years later, in 1963, the "modern" series of serious disorders began, and flared up periodically through 1968.

But outbursts of this kind have not been the typical, ongoing, or dominant behavior pattern of blacks in America. The dominant pattern has been to respond to intense bigotry by pushing for change through legal action (court suits and new laws), through appeals to the national government through the chief executive, and through continued appeals to the conscience of the American people. When portions of the black minority change from their dominant pattern of working through established mechanisms to effect peaceful social change to a pattern of sporadic violent disorders, it is an indication that the black mood has changed, at least in the centers where disorders occur and, usually, among the lower classes.

The Report of the National Advisory Commission on Civil Disorders explained the meaning of civil disorders in 1967, which included black attitudes (affective) and reasons (cognitive). The report said:

> By 1967, whites could point to the demise of slavery, the decline of illiteracy among Negroes, amendments and civil rights legislation and the growing size of the Negro middle class. Whites would call it Negro progress from slavery to freedom toward equality.
>
> Negroes could point to the doctrine of white supremacy, its widespread acceptance, its persistence after emancipation, and its influence on the definition of the place of Negroes in American life. They could point to their long fight for full citizenship, when they had active opposition from most of the white population and little or no support from the government. They could see progress toward equality accompanied by bitter resistance. Perhaps most of all, they could feel the persistent, pervasive racism that kept them in inferior segregated schools, restricted them to ghettos, barred them from fair employment, provided double standards in courts of justice, inflicted bodily harm on their children, and blighted their lives with a sense of hopelessness and despair.
>
> In all of this and in the context of professed ideals, Negroes would find more retrogression than progress, more rejection than acceptance....
>
> Over the years the character of Negro protest has changed. Originally it was a white liberal and Negro upper class movement aimed at securing the constitutional rights of Negroes through propaganda, lawsuits, and legislation. In recent years the emphasis in tactics shifted first to direct action and then among the most militant—to rhetoric of "Black Power." The role of white liberals declined as Negroes came to direct the struggle. At the same time the Negro protest movement became more of a mass movement, with increasing participation from the working classes. As these changes were occurring, and while substantial progress was being made to secure constitutional rights for the Negroes, the goals of the movement were broadened. Protest groups now demand special efforts to overcome the Negro's poverty and cultural deprivation—conditions that cannot be erased simply by ensuring constitutional rights.
>
> The central thrust of Negro protest in the current period has aimed at the inclusion of Negroes in American society on a basis of

full equality rather than at a fundamental transformation of American institutions. There have been elements calling for a revolutionary overthrow of the American social system or for a complete withdrawal of Negroes from American society. But these solutions have
had little popular support. Negro protest, for the most part, has
been firmly rooted in the basic values of American society, seeking
not their destruction but their fulfillment.[53]

To sum up, this prestigious commission found a changing mood in
the black population—but prior to 1969. The new mood was one of
"pushing and straining" for full equality and justice, and for basic, expressed values in the American Creed, rather than revolutionary overthrow of the system. The urban uprisings represented an extreme reaction after pushing and straining did not result in solutions to economic
and other acute problems of the black lower class in the cities. It is most
important to focus on the process of pushing and straining as indicative
of the philosophy of the black minority to exert concerted action so as to
change patterns of discrimination and segregation. The notion that concerted action by blacks is essential to the enhancement of black status in
America is found throughout part IX of Myrdal's *An American Dilemma*.[54]

ALPHONSO PINKNEY ON BLACK ATTITUDES

Alphonso Pinkney has written two editions of *Black Americans,* the
first in 1969 and the second in 1975. In the preface to the second edition
he stated that

> since the First Edition of *Black Americans* in 1969 little change in
> the status of black people relative to whites in the United States has
> come about, but in the time between that edition and the present one
> many changes have occurred in the mind and mood of black Ameri-
> cans. Chief among these has been the ascendancy of nationalist sen-
> timent in the black community.[55]

Pinkney's eighth chapter, "The Black Revolt and Its Consequences," covered the mid-1950s to 1972; in time coverage, it overlap-
ped the ninth chapter, "The Rise of Black Nationalism and the Future,"
which extended to 1975. It was in these chapters that Pinkney, a black
American, described black attitudes as he saw them change, develop,
and shift over time.

After the Supreme Court decision of May 1954, Pinkney found that
black attitudes were positive, anticipating the beginning of a new era in

black-white relations.[56] By 1955 he saw signs of growing unrest, based upon identification with African colonies' becoming free. He also perceived disillusionment after Emmett Till was lynched in Mississippi and those who were responsible for his murder were not apprehended. By the end of 1955, after the Rosa Parks incident in Montgomery, Alabama, Pinkney saw attitudes and demonstrations of solidarity among blacks in opposition to long-standing practices of segregation and discrimination. That solidarity crystallized in nonviolent resistance, which became the "official" means of dealing with the South's caste system.[57] Pinkney followed Louis Lomax in calling this nonviolent resistance the "birth of what might be called the black revolt" in modern times.

The nonviolent resistance movement spread across the South, but white opposition to social change in black-white relations hardened. The hardening process was called "massive resistance" in the Deep South, and it was effective in slowing the pace of desegregation of public education. Established patterns, offensive to blacks, such as the continuous failure of all-white juries to convict whites in cases of lynching blacks, did not change.

In 1960 the nonviolent resistance movement adopted a different strategy because of the determined resistance of whites to obeying the law where blacks were concerned. Black college students in North Carolina started a sit-in movement, asking to be served at public lunch counters. This movement grew rapidly and economic boycotts were developed against stores which retained segregated practices. The sit-in concept expanded to other areas, such as churches and segregated beaches, and to other tactics, such as freedom rides. This change in strategy and acceleration and increase in the number of areas under attack for established patterns of discrimination and segregation were a result of the change in black attitudes. Blacks were not willing to wait forever for equality and justice, and that attitude was reflected in behavior which sought to effect social change in black-white relations. Nonviolent behavior was characteristic of black efforts until 1963, when, in Birmingham, Alabama, blacks retaliated against white segregationists who bombed black property. These bombings followed more than a month of police brutality, led by "Bull" Connor against blacks. Blacks could take the suffering and degradation no more; they abandoned the nonviolent approach and fought back with bottles, sticks, and stones and burned a nine-block area of the city. Black behavior reflected a change in black attitudes, which had become "No more; enough is enough."

The Civil Rights Act of 1964 and the Voting Rights Act of 1965 resulted in large measure from the sustained, collective efforts of blacks and their white allies to gain a larger measure of equality and justice. These acts primarily benefited Southern blacks; blacks in urban areas in other sections of the country were little affected by the nonviolent efforts of their countrymen from 1955 to 1965. Since the quality of black life remained relatively unchanged in urban areas, black urban people were more than ordinarily receptive to the idea of black power.

Blacks looked upon this concept differently than did whites, who seemed frightened or offended by the concept. Whites felt that the concept implied reverse racism, black supremacy, or black violence.[58] Blacks felt that the concept implied increased political and economic power for themselves, enhanced self-image, development of more militant young black leadership, and strong resistance to police brutality.[59] However, blacks were not unanimous in their acceptance of black power. Most notably, Martin Luther King, Jr., Bayard Rustin, and moderate leaders of civil rights organizations, such as the NAACP and the Urban League, rejected and opposed the concept; their reasons were somewhat different, but the effect was the same—rejection. The more militant organizations, such as CORE and SNCC, were the chief proponents of the concept.

In like manner, whites were not unanimous in their rejection of black power as a viable concept. Students at Oberlin College held an intercollegiate conference in November 1966 to "eliminate the emotionalism which clouds the debate on Black Power and to try to point out the basic issues involved."[60] In August 1967 the National Student Association resolved to support the implementation of this concept by any means necessary. In September 1967 the delegates at the National Conference for New Politics in Chicago voted to support all resolutions of the Newark Black Power Conference and to support black control of institutions in black communities.[61]

Pinkney's viewpoint is that the civil rights movement, through 1965, was basically reformist—directed to securing rights that were guaranteed to citizens in the Constitution and establishing the principle of legal equality as public policy. Also, the civil rights movement sought to establish the responsibility of the federal government to protect the constitutional rights of citizens. He felt that, to a degree, these goals had been achieved, or at least accepted as a matter of principle.[62]

But the black-power movement sought to go beyond social reform to political, economic, and social control by blacks over the institutions responsible to them. The black-power movement sought to address the problems facing black people in urban communities, especially urban slums. In this sense, Pinkney saw the black-power movement as an extension of the civil rights movement and, in fact, as a black liberation movement. He also saw this movement as a transition between the civil rights and black nationalist movements, with all three movements representing shifts in black attitudes over the twenty-year period, 1955–75.

Nationalists, generally speaking, feel that integration is neither likely nor desirable and that the massive problems faced by blacks require more radical measures for solution than moderate blacks recommend.[63] Blacks need to be independent from white control over basic social institutions. (Again, black nationalist movements are not new in the United States; contemporary forms are part of the recurring pattern. Black nationalism reasserts itself when blacks feel that equality and justice never will be extended to them as members of the American mainstream. The Garvey movement was the most obvious example of the phenomenon.) Organizations with a nationalist focus, which have operated since 1966, are the Black Panther party (focus of revolutionary nationalism), the Congress of African People (focus on cultural nationalism), and the Nation of Islam (combined focus on religious, cultural, economic, and educational nationalism).[64] The Nation of Islam is the most prosperous of the various nationalist organizations and the oldest of those organizations. The Honorable Elijah Muhammad headed this organization from 1934 to his death in February 1975. His son, Wallace D. Muhammad, now leads the Nation, which is undergoing drastic philosophic changes.[65]

Pinkney sums up the black situation this way. When Richard Nixon was elected president in November 1968, white Americans were worn out with black rebellions, student demonstrations, and the revolutionary rhetoric which had been part of the antiwar movement. In line with what he had promised the American people in his campaign, Nixon and his administration moved to repress blacks and all other people whom they perceived as radicals. They achieved the goal of repression, and the plight of blacks again became one of survival. Thus the black community appears to have withdrawn temporarily from activism.[66]

Pinkney predicts that (1) the present state of relative inactivity in the black movement is probably temporary; (2) given the complex nature of American society and the aversion of Americans to fundamental social change, the likelihood is that, at best, blacks can expect to attain some improved degree of parity with other groups in the society in the future; (3) in spite of the spread of black nationalist ideology, most blacks at present are more interested in entering the mainstream of American society than in destroying its structure; (4) in the future, black Americans will make greater demands on the society and resistance by white Americans to those demands will intensify; (5) employment projections will not be promising; and (6) black pupils will experience greater segregation in education as *de facto* segregation keeps pace with segregated housing. It is in conventional politics that the greatest changes are likely for blacks. Blacks are likely to participate in all elections in greater numbers and as a result will elect a greater number of blacks to city, state, and national offices, but this will not significantly alter the status of the black minority in America.[67]

In conclusion, Pinkney describes the United States as basically a reformist society where social change comes slowly, especially in black-white relations. Because he says, this society is more concerned with order and stability than with human rights, a typical approach to social problems is to permit them to go unattended in the hope that they will somehow vanish. Whenever problems reach crisis proportions, attempts are made to deal with them without changing the institutions which are responsible for creating them, and this is especially true in black-white relations.

> Whether the racial crisis in the United States deteriorates or improves depends on the willingness of white Americans, especially those in positions of power, to face the problems with candor and to deal with them boldly. The demand by black Americans for equality is in no sense unreasonable; indeed, it is long overdue. And this demand will likely intensify with time. The mood and power of black Americans at the present time are such that this demand cannot long be ignored. The longer the delay, the greater the physical and social destruction which is likely to result; domestic tranquility depends on racial justice. Afro-Americans are aware of their oppression and it is unlikely that an aroused black community will long permit its inhabitants to remain an oppressed colony in a rich nation.[68]

SUMMARY OF SHIFTING BLACK ATTITUDES

The survey data reported by *Newsweek,* by Schuman and Hatchett, the report of the Kerner Commission, and the research of Pinkney all show a changing mood in the black population. This changing mood dates back to 1954, when the *Brown* decision struck down the legality of "separate but equal" as the conceptual and operational framework for black-white relations, and to 1955, when blacks took the initiative to end long-standing practices of segregation and discrimination in the South. Black initiatives under the civil rights banner reached their peak in the years 1963 to 1965. From 1965 to 1968 there was a diversified mood among blacks, embracing–

1. nonviolent civil rights activities to gain equality and justice
2. black power to gain economic, political and psychological control over institutions in black communities especially
3. black nationalist movements.

Urban uprisings, or "riots," reached their peak in 1967 and 1968; these disorders represented utmost dissatisfaction with the pace and quality of fundamental change for blacks in cities. From 1969 to 1976 black attitudes have reflected increased disillusionment with whites, based on the almost complete halt in black progress since the inauguration of Nixon as president in 1969. Blacks feel that Nixon, and his successor, Ford, responded to the white "backlash" and to white neoconservatism, but also that these chief executives set public policies which will tilt the future course of American society in a neoconservative direction.

Summing up broad views obtained from opinion polls and survey research, Schuman and Hatchett feel that in the years ahead traditional white prejudice against blacks will continue to decline but black disillusionment with whites will increase.

Pinkney feels that blacks will make greater demands on the society and whites will intensify their resistance to those demands.

There is general agreement among *Newsweek,* Schuman and Hatchett, the Kerner Commission, and Pinkney that, despite the complexities of black attitudes and the varying ideologies in the black minority, most blacks are still more interested in entering the mainstream of American society as equal citizens than in trying to destroy its structure.

IS BLACK PROGRESS REAL OR A DELUSION?

The changing moods in the black and the white populations have a major common thread: perception of black progress, or lack of it, in relation to the standard attained by the white population. Many blacks feel that their group's rate of progress is too slow and that the content of black progress is lacking in quality and quantity. Many whites feel that the rate of black progress is too fast and that the content of that progress is above their own possibilities because of federal intervention on behalf

of blacks (by affirmative action programs, for example). The perceptions are different, reflecting once again Ralph Barton Perry's "egocentric predicament," but the result is the same: feelings of negativism engendered by beliefs.

These feelings are reinforced by articles and speeches from white
and black intellectuals. One such article was "Black Progress and Liberal Rhetoric" by Ben J. Wattenberg and Richard M. Scammon in
Commentary (April 1973), and portions of the article were reprinted in
the *Washington Star* (April 29, 1973, p. E3). A speech responding to
this article, and similar ideas, was given by Robert B. Hill of the National Urban League's Research Department at the annual conference
of the league on July 24, 1973, in Washington, D.C.—titled "Benign
Neglect Revisited: The Illusion of Black Progress." Dr. Hill addressed
the question of black progress and related issues such as the "conspiracy of silence."

Wattenberg and Scammon held that from 1961 to 1973 a remarkable development had taken place in America: so many blacks had
moved into the middle class that it could be said that a majority of
blacks were in that class—a slender majority, but a majority nevertheless. They also held that the data of black advancement had been kept
secret by liberals—a strategy they said was mistaken and might prove to
be counterproductive, a hindrance to the continued progress of American blacks. Wattenberg and Scammon used data from the Census
Bureau to support their claim of "enormous black progress."

Hill attacked the idea that *"enormous* progress" had been made by
black Americans in the last decade. He explained that blacks had made
steady progress during the 1960s but the economic situation had deteriorated since 1969. Hill attacked also their definition of "middle class"
and presented evidence that President Nixon had been informed of the
"facts" about black progress by his advisor, Daniel P. Moynihan. This
meant there was no "conspiracy of silence" about black progress. Hill
used data from the Census Bureau to support his arguments, as well as
data compiled by the National Urban League's Research Department.

If we accept the premise that the Wattenberg and Scammon presentation is representative of the viewpoint of many whites and that the
Hill presentation is representative of the viewpoint of many blacks, we
can see why white and black perceptions of the same situation differ
vastly. But who is right? Is black progress real or a delusion? Is the glass
half full or half empty?

Writing in 1971, Herman P. Miller, in the second edition of *Rich*

Man, Poor Man, made this pithy statement: "[The] complicated pattern or progress mixed with retrogression makes it hazardous to generalize about the social and economic conditions of Negroes in America."[69] Miller explained that

> the plight of the Negro in America is well known. Thousands of surveys have established that Negroes lag behind whites in health, education, employment, income, housing, and most other aspects of life. It has also been established that these conditions are getting worse, not better, in the poorest slum areas.
>
> These facts, grim and foreboding, have been widely publicized throughout the world. There is, however, another aspect of Negro life which has received much less attention, but which shows great progress and hope for the future. A close examination of recent statistical evidence shows that despite the deterioration of social and economic conditions of Negroes in the very worst slums, the Negro population has experienced a marked improvement in many important aspects of life in recent years. Today for the first time Negroes are moving into the middle- and upper-income groups in substantial numbers.[70]

Note the language of the writers. Wattenberg and Scammon say *"enormous* progress" has been made by blacks; Hill says *"steady"* progress was made during the 1960s, and Miller says *"marked improvement [has occurred] in many important aspects of life."* The language differences are not merely semantic variations. Words shape attitudes and beliefs, and though most Americans read or listen to the words, they do not study the accompanying tables to authenticate, refute, or qualify the words. Furthermore, words, and the intellectuals who use them, help to shape the course of public policy. Thus the use of words is not to be regarded lightly.

While Miller's book was published in 1971, most of his charts use data through 1968 or 1969, which show black progress during the civil rights struggle and the Kennedy and Johnson years. Looking at key indicators of progress, or lack of it, Miller made short, lucid explanations of his findings, and they are therefore quoted directly.

A. *Unemployment:* Unemployment is a sensitive indicator of economic change. As a rule of thumb, the unemployment rate of Negroes is about twice that of whites, regardless of the age or sex of the group that is compared or the general economic climate at the time of the comparison. The 2:1 ratio is particularly stable for adult men and women. Among teen-agers, however, there has been a growing disparity between the rates for whites and Negroes since the recession of 1957–1958. In 1969, nearly one-fourth of Negro teen-agers were unemployed, as compared with about 11 percent for the whites.

The fact that unemployment rates have dropped sharply—and that they have dropped proportionately as much for Negroes as for whites during the economic expansion of the sixties—is a sign of progress. It must also be noted, however, that the unemployment rate for Negroes at the height of prosperity is greater than the rate for whites during any of the past three recessions. The high rate of youth unemployment is particularly distressing not only because of the immediate frustrations and hardships it causes for the youngsters and their families, but also because it undermines training programs and the attempts to prevent school dropouts. If one-fourth of Negro youths are still unable to find jobs after nine years of continuous prosperity, they have a right to join the chorus when Bayard Rustin asks: "What is this foolishness about training? You can't train any segment of the population unless there's a demand for their work."

In contrast to the favorable trends in the data for the nation, the census conducted in Watts shortly after the riots of 1965 showed that in this ghetto unemployment rates in that peak year were nearly as high as they had been in the recession year of 1960.

B. *Occupational change:*

There were some rather striking changes in the occupational distribution of nonwhite men and women between 1960 and 1968. Among men, the most significant change was a drop in the proportion employed as farm workers (from 14 to 7 percent) and as laborers (from 23 to 18 percent). At the same time, the proportion employed as professional workers and as craftsmen increased rather sharply. The increase in professional and technical employment among nonwhite men translates into about 200,000 additional Negro families that have their feet firmly on the bottom round of the middle class ladder. These are the families that can make the break from Harlem to Long Island and from the District of Columbia to Bethesda. These are the new faces now appearing as TV announcers, government officials, and business executives. . . .

Despite the signs of progress, the most striking fact about the occupational distribution of nonwhite men remains their very heavy concentration in low-paid jobs. *Nearly 40% of Negro men still work as laborers, janitors, porters, busboys, and in similar service jobs.*

The progress for women has been much more striking than that for men. Cleaning up white people's homes is still a common type of job among Negro women. About 20 percent do this kind of work. Although the proportion has dropped sharply since 1960, it is still very high, especially when one considers that an additional 10 percent do the same kind of work as domestics (chambermaids, charwomen, janitors, etc.) but are employed by hotels, restaurants, hospitals, and similar service establishments rather than by housewives. *Thus, in 1969, after several years of progress, conservatively 30 percent of the Negro women are doing unskilled and menial housework in one form or another.*

Yet there has been a sharp increase in the number of Negro women employed in white-collar jobs. The proportion has risen from 19 to 24 percent for the three job categories—professional, clerical, and sales.

C. *Income:*

Income is an important measure of success in our society. Although Negro family income remains low in comparison with the rest of the population, the income of both Negroes and whites is at an all-time high and the gap between the two groups has narrowed. In 1968 Negro family income was only 60 percent of white income; yet, three years earlier it was 54 percent and a decade earlier (1958) it was only about 50 percent....

For the country as a whole, the average income of Negro husband-wife families was 72 percent of the white average in 1968, and in the North and West it was 85 percent of the white average. Particularly significant is the fact that the incomes of young Negro families in the North and West are nearly the same as those of young white families. This represents a marked change from the situation a decade ago, when the income gap between young Negro families and white families outside of the South was 25 percent. The clear implication of these figures is that the incomes of young Negro couples in the northern and western states are responding favorably to the efforts that have been made in recent years to improve their education, training, and job opportunities. These are the groups that would be most likely to show the greatest improvement because many of them have recently completed their education or training at improved schools and are better prepared to compete for jobs.

The figures shown above pertain to the relative income gap, which has narrowed. But what about the absolute gap—the dollar gap? This gap between whites and non-whites has widened since 1947. In that year, white families averaged $4,900 and non-whites $2,500. The whites made $2,400 more. By 1968, the incomes of both groups had risen markedly, but so had the dollar gap. Family income in 1968 averaged $8,900 for whites and $5,600 for nonwhites. The whites made $3,300 more. Thus we find that although nonwhites gained relatively more income than whites between 1947 and 1968, the absolute gains were greater for whites.

Perhaps as significant as the gap between the incomes of the two groups is the actual amount of income received by nonwhite families. In 1968, one-fifth of the nonwhite families received more than $10,000 a year —more than double the proportion with incomes that high just eight years earlier, taking into account the changes in the cost of living. Conversely, the proportion of nonwhite families with incomes under $3,000 was cut by 50 percent from 1960 to 1968.

D. *Education:* Increases in educational attainment in recent years, as measured by years of school completed, have been made by both whites and Negroes, with the increases made by young adult Negro men being especially dramatic. In 1966, only half of Negro men 25 to 29 years old were high school graduates, but in 1969, 60 percent of the Negro men of this age had at least completed high school. The percentage of Negro men who have completed college has also increased in the recent past. In 1966, only 5 percent of Negro men 25 to 34 years old had completed college, as compared with 8 percent of the Negro men of this age in 1969.

Even with these gains in educational attainment by young Negro men, there is still a large gap between the level of education of these men as compared with that of white men of the same age. Although 60 percent of the Negro men 25 to 29 years old have completed at least four years of high school, 78 percent of the white men of this age are at least high school graduates. And 20 percent of white men 25 to 34 years old have completed four years of college or more, as compared with 8 percent of the Negro men of this age.

In the past few years, there have been significant increases in the school enrollment of Negroes at the noncompulsory attendance ages. Among those below the compulsory attendance age—children 3 and 4 years old—the percentage enrolled in nursery school and kindergarten increased from 10 percent in 1964 to 19 percent in 1968. In fact, Negro children 3 and 4 years old are more likely to be enrolled in school than are the white children of this age. This early enrollment in the preprimary education of young Negro children holds promise of a further narrowing of the gap in educational attainment between Negroes and whites. The Head Start projects with their nursery school and kindergarten programs or preprimary education, which began in 1965, must be given credit for a part of this increase in the enrollment of 3- and 4-year-olds.

Among those over the compulsory attendance age, there have also been substantial gains in the percentage enrolled in school. The percentage of 18- and 19-year-old Negroes enrolled in school increased from 36 percent in 1964 to 45 percent in 1968, and the percentage of 20- to 24-year-old Negroes enrolled increased from 8 percent to 12 percent during the same period.

The number of Negroes in college has also increased rapidly. . . . In 1968, there were 434,000 Negroes enrolled in college—6 percent of total college enrollment—an increase of 85 percent over the 234,000 Negroes enrolled in college in 1964.

E. *Increase in*
   "broken" families: One measure of family instability is the proportion of families headed by women. This is admittedly a very crude measure. Some women have family responsibilities thrust upon them because of widowhood and others have husbands who are away in the armed forces or are otherwise away from home involuntarily. Nevertheless, a very important reason why women head families is because of divorce or separation, and a sharp increase over time in the proportion of female-headed families may be regarded as symptomatic of a family problem. The figures below suggest that family instability has increased among nonwhites during the years 1950–1969. There has been no change in the proportion of white families headed by women since 1950. In contrast, the proportion of nonwhite families headed by women has increased from 18 percent in 1950 to 27 percent in 1969. Despite the rise in family income in recent years and the improvement in the occupational distribution of nonwhite men, there is no evidence of a corresponding improvement in family stability.

F. *Deterioration*
   in the worst
   slum areas: But in the poorest neighborhoods, all of these social indicators (average incomes, incidence of poverty, number of broken families) showed deterioration. In Hough, one of the worst of the poor neighborhoods, the incidence of poverty increased, and the

male unemployment rate remained virtually unchanged. A similar study made in various neighborhoods in South Los Angeles after the riot in Watts . . . showed much the same pattern.

There can be little question that despite the general improvement in the conditions of life for Negroes nationally, conditions have grown worse in places like Hough and Watts. As Negro families succeed, they tend to move out of these economically and socially depressed areas to better neighborhoods where they and their children have the opportunity to lead a better life. They leave behind the least educated and the most deprived—unwed mothers, deserted wives, the physically and mentally handicapped, and the aged. As a result there is a concentration of misery in the very hearts of our largest cities. It is precisely in such places that riots take place and it is here that more action is needed in massive doses to accelerate a narrowing of the gap in social and economic status between whites and Negroes. [71]

Miller's "marked improvement" and Hill's "steady improvement" seem to be the more objective statements about black progress through the sixties—rather than "enormous improvement." It must be remembered that this progress was made because of activist initiatives by blacks, assistance of liberal whites, and judicial, executive, and legislative actions at the federal level.

What has happened to this progress in the decade of the seventies? Using the Bureau of the Census publication, *The Social and Economic Status of the Black Population in the United States 1974,* and following the categories on the preceding pages, we find a mixed picture. In education and in the number of elected black officials there is continued progress for blacks; in fact, there is greater progress in the number of blacks elected to public office than in any other category. Regression is evident in the unemployment figures, income, housing, increase in broken families, health care and insurance, and deterioration in the worst slum areas.

Elected Officials and Voting

In the 1970s the increase in the number of black elected officials represents the greatest continuing progress for blacks. In May 1975 there were 3,503 black elected officials in forty-five states and the District of Columbia, an increase of 88 percent (1,643) over the preceding four years. The largest increase was in the South, where 53 percent of the black population resides. Fifty-five percent of all elected black officials are in the South, including 44 percent of black state legislators and executives and 61 percent of black mayors.[72]

Figure 3–1 shows the increase in black elected officials from 1969 to 1975. These gains can be attributed to actualization of the right to vote as guaranteed by the Fifteenth Amendment to the Constitution. The abstract guarantee had little meaning for blacks in most Southern states until the civil rights movements of the mid-1960s and the national reaction to them stimulated passage of the Voting Rights Act of 1965,

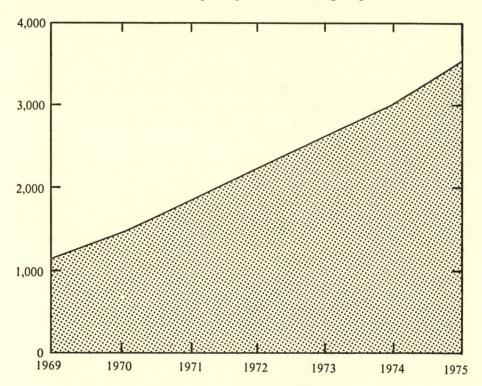

SOURCE: Joint Center for Political Studies, Washington, D.C., 1975.

FIGURE 3–1. BLACK ELECTED OFFICIALS IN THE UNITED STATES, 1969 TO 1975

the Voter Education Project, and other measures. The Voting Rights Act gave meaning to the theoretical right to vote, and when blacks were able to vote they cast their ballots for qualified black candidates.

In 1975 the states with the largest number of black officeholders were Illinois and Louisiana. Two lieutenant governors are black. Alabama, Georgia, and South Carolina have more black members in the state legislatures than at any time since Reconstruction. This is unquestionably a sign of progress for blacks, and for America as well, because not only do blacks vote for blacks, whites vote for blacks, too.

There were 135 black mayors in 1975, an increase of 67 percent from 1971, and only 29 black mayors in 1968. Most of these mayors headed small towns and predominantly black communities, but some of them preside over the large cities of Atlanta, Cincinnati, Dayton, Detroit, Gary, Los Angeles, and Newark.

It is clear that there is marked and continuing progress for blacks in the increased numbers of black elected officials. Yet blacks still account for less than 1 percent of all elected officials in America.[73] Blacks still have a far way to go to attain parity.

In terms of voting, blacks were not maintaining their achievements in registering and participation into 1975 (the Census Bureau first collected data on registration in 1966). Registration rates for blacks in 1974 were at the lowest level reported for any of the last five general elections.[74] The registration rate for blacks living in the South was not statistically different in 1974 than in 1970, but there was a steep decline in the North and West, where the rate dipped from 65 percent in 1970 to 54 percent in 1974.[75] Only about one-third of the potential black electorate reported that they voted in November 1974.[76]

This information should jolt black people into action, so that they continue to register and vote as they did in the 1960s. Otherwise, the potential black strength in influencing public officials who make public policy is lost. Further, the black population will be perceived as a "paper tiger," and correctly so, by the major political parties. Where blacks have been most overtly discriminated against—the South—they continue to register and vote, and the results are apparent. But in the North and West, where discrimination is more subtle and covert, blacks are not maintaining their interest in participating in the political system. This should be perceived as both a political and an educational problem. There should be increased attention on educating the adult populace on the necessity to register and vote and on the political process of getting them to the polls at each election.

Education

After elected officials, education is the next area of continued progress for blacks in the seventies. There are marked gains in school enrollment of blacks and in higher retention rates, and the combination has resulted in higher education attainment levels.[77] These marked gains provide evidence that young blacks are taking advantage of increased educational opportunity and reflect the continued belief of black people that education is valuable.

Enrollment figures are particularly striking for college-age blacks (18 to 24) and for very young black children (under 5). From 1970 to 1974 there was a 56 percent growth in college enrollment of blacks, compared with a 15 percent increase for whites. This is positive for blacks, but the proportion of blacks in college was still below that of whites, 18 percent compared with 25 percent. The figures suggest that black youth have equal or higher educational aspirations than their white counterparts. However, it remains true that a smaller proportion of blacks than whites is enrolled in higher education, and the pool of black graduates is much smaller than the pool of white college graduates —for well-known historical reasons. The proportion of black college graduates in 1973 was less than the proportion of white graduates in 1960. Again, blacks have a long way to go to attain parity.

Figure 3–2 shows comparative high school completion rates for blacks and whites and males and females in 1960, 1965, 1970, and 1974. Its message is clear. Graduation rates of black males and females have climbed in that fourteen-year period but blacks still are below whites in terms of high school completion, and black males have the lowest rate of all. Since high school graduation is required for entry into most occupations, and since it is one of the minimums specified for college or post-secondary attendance, further effort must be exerted to keep black youth in school through graduation and extra efforts must be taken with young black males.

Procuring a job in direct relation to one's qualifications—a job that pays a living wage (or more) and offers probabilities of moving up the career ladder—is central to success and happiness in American society, as it actually operates. Also, the kind and quality of employment which is available to parents directly affects the ability of their offspring to participate in higher education (a costly process) and the type of higher educational institution they will be able to enter. Unemployment also is a sensitive indicator of economic change, as Herman P. Miller pointed out.

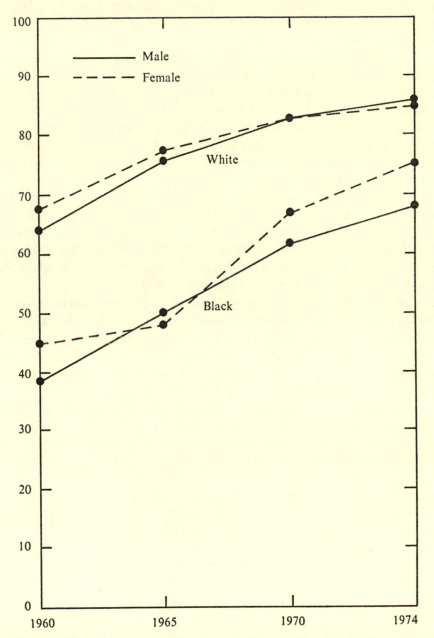

SOURCE: U.S. Department of Commerce, Social and Economic Statistics Administration, Bureau of the Census, *The Social and Economic Status of the Black Population in the U.S., 1974*, p. 91.

FIGURE 3–2. PERCENT OF PERSONS 20 TO 24 YEARS OLD WHO COMPLETED FOUR YEARS OF HIGH SCHOOL OR MORE, BY SEX: 1960, 1965, 1970, and 1974

Unemployment

In 1974 there was a downturn in the economy, so the unemployment rate increased for blacks and whites until October 1975. Unemployment reached 13.7 percent for blacks and 7.6 percent for whites in the first quarter of 1975. The jobless rate for black teenagers was 39.8 percent for the first quarter of 1975; the rate for white teenagers was about 18.0 percent.[78] The figures speak for themselves—the unemployment rate for blacks was about double that for whites, and the rate for black youth was nearly 40 percent.

The 2:1 black-to-white unemployment ratio cannot be blamed only on this downturn in the economy. Unemployment rates for blacks have held at about double those for whites since 1960, except for a narrowing to 1.8 in 1970 and 1971 (see figure 3–3). Since 1969, black unemployment has not fallen below 8.2 percent (1970), but the white unemployment rate has been as low as 4.3 percent (1973).

It overwhelms one to read the figures on unemployment among black teenagers. In 1973 the unemployment rate for blacks of both sexes, 16 to 19 years of age, was 31.4 percent, versus 12.6 percent for comparable whites.[79] Even in 1968, one of the years of black progress, the nonwhite teenage jobless rate was 25 percent but the rate for whites was 11 percent.[80]

In its *Quarterly Economic Report on the Black Worker* (May 1975) the Research Department of the National Urban League presented highlights of its findings on unemployment in the first quarter of 1975. Using a "hidden unemployment index," the Urban League calculated the unofficial unemployment rate for blacks as 25.8 percent in the first quarter of 1975, up from 21.1 percent in the last quarter of 1974. A record 2.9 million blacks were unemployed, according to the hidden unemployment index, and blacks accounted for almost all (47/49) of the increase in unemployment in the nation during the latter half of the first quarter of 1975. Particularly hard hit were black poverty-area workers, young black Vietnam veterans, and two-parent black families. Industries with particularly high unemployment rates for blacks were automobile, construction, apparel, textiles, and food processing. Among black workers in government, the sharpest rise was among federal workers, particularly postal workers. Thus the picture shown by Urban League figures and the hidden unemployment index is even worse than that shown by the Census Bureau's figures.[81]

It is a truism that in any economic downturn all groups in a society are affected negatively. But blacks are affected first because they have

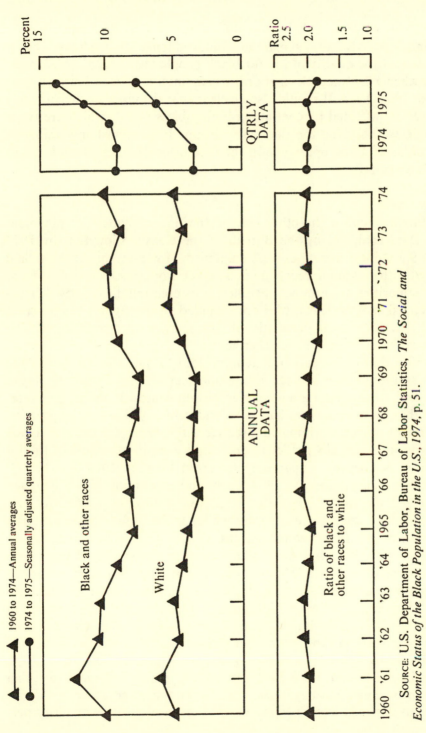

Percent

15

10

5

0

QTRLY
DATA

1975

1974

'74

'73

'72

'71

1970

'69

'68

'67

'66

1965

'64

'63

'62

'61

1960

Black and other races

White

ANNUAL
DATA

Ratio

2.5

2.0

1.5

1.0

Ratio of black and
other races to white

1960 to 1974—Annual averages

1974 to 1975—Seasonally adjusted quarterly averages

Source: U.S. Department of Labor, Bureau of Labor Statistics, *The Social and
Economic Status of the Black Population in the U.S., 1974*, p. 51.

FIGURE 3–3. UNEMPLOYMENT RATES, 1960 TO 1975

no seniority to protect their jobs; they were the last hired and they are the first fired. Also, they remain unemployed longer than whites. Thus it is clear that the quality of life for black people has to be affected negatively when a 2:1 unemployment ratio is maintained over a fourteen-year period, 1960–1974. It should also be clear that the mood of such a group is adversely affected by continuing high jobless rates—which are twice as high as those for the dominant group. It is almost impossible to remain hopeful and optimistic in the face of continuing unemployment of this magnitude.

Employment

Employment is the other side of the unemployment/employment coin. Data compiled by the Bureau of the Census show that by 1974 about 9.3 million nonwhites were employed. However, this figure should be used with caution in reporting upon black workers because blacks and other minorities are grouped together, thus creating distortions. For example, Asian Americans, who are included in the figure, could create distortions in certain occupational areas, such as "professional and technical" and "medical and other health."

With that qualification, it is important to note that in the decade 1964–74 there was a greater occupational upgrading among employed black and other races than among employed whites. It should be understood that these minorities had been underemployed over a long period because of societally imposed practices, for example, limiting black males to low-level GS grades in civil service positions. Most of the increase in occupational upgrading occurred between 1964 and 1970.[82] But despite this progress, in 1974 blacks and other minorities still lagged far behind whites in high-status, high-paying jobs. Also, minority persons of color were more likely than whites to be employed involuntarily at part-time jobs for economic reasons.

Examination of figures on the occupations of employed black men and women in the decade 1964–1974 makes it clear that there was much occupational upgrading among blacks and other nonwhites; and occupational upgrading represents progress.[83] For example, the percent of black and other nonwhite males employed in white-collar jobs rose from 16 to 24 percent in those years, but the greatest gain was between 1964 and 1970 (16% to 22%), with only a 2 percent increase from 1970 to 1974. In 1964 there were 58 percent black males and males of other races in blue-collar occupations; that figure increased to 60 percent in 1970 but declined to 57 percent in 1974. However, these minority persons are most identifiable in the subgroup "non-farm laborers," within the blue-collar category. Nevertheless, when compared with the white population, where in 1974 42 percent of the males were employed in white-collar jobs and 46 percent in blue-collar jobs (with "operatives, except transport" and "mechanics and repairers" being the largest subgroups), blacks still have a long way to go to achieve parity.

The percent of black and other nonwhite females employed in white-collar jobs rose from 22 to 42 in the 1964–74 decade, with concentration in the "clerical workers" subgrouping. Again, the largest percent of increase was between 1964 and 1970, from 22 to 36 percent. In 1964 there were 15 percent black females and females of other races in blue-collar occupations; that percentage increased to 19 in 1970 and to 20 in 1974. Proportions of service workers (minorities) declined from 56 percent in 1964 to 37 percent in 1974; proportions of farm workers (minorities) declined from 6 to 1 percent in that decade. There was progress in the decade, but parity was not achieved.

The U.S. Commission on Civil Rights summed up the situation with respect to equal employment opportunity:

> During the last decade some progress has been made toward achieving the Nation's objective of equal employment opportunity. The laws and Executive orders cited in this report have contributed to this end. Nevertheless, the rate of progress has been inadequate and major problems of systemic discrimination continue to affect adversely minorities and women.
>
> The Federal effort to end this discrimination has not been equal to the task. It has been seriously hampered by lack of overall leadership and direction, deficiencies in existing laws, and the assignment of authority to a number of agencies which have issued inconsistent policies, and developed independent and uncoordinated compliance programs. Attempts by the Congress and agency officials to rectify the problems which beset this enforcement program and prevent it from effectively assisting the classes adversely affected by discrimination have been largely unsuccessful.[84]

Income

The corollary of employment is income. From the data compiled by the Bureau of the Census it can be seen that in the period 1969–73 the median income of black families in constant 1973 dollars did not grow. An appreciable increase had been evident from 1964 to 1968: 32 percent. In 1973 black families had a median income of $7,270, compared with a median income of $12,600 for white families.[85]

The 1974 data show that "the average income level of black families (after adjustment for increase in prices), declined over the 1973 average."[86] The decline for black families was statistically significant at the 1.6 level, which was not statistically different from a similar decrease for white families. Because of the rising rate of unemployment, however, there was an apparent increase of 79,000 blacks in poverty according to the Census Bureau. The number of whites in poverty also rose.[87]

The Bureau of Labor Statistics estimated that a family of four needed $9,200 in the fall of 1974 to maintain its *lower* standard of living. But because prices continued to rise through 1975, even people who were employed found their incomes eroded by the inflationary spiral, and people who were employed on two jobs, underemployed, unemployed, or in poverty were comparatively worse off. The median income in 1974 was estimated by the Census Bureau to be $7,800 for black families and $13,400 for white families.[88] Thus if $9,200 was needed for a family of four to maintain a lower-level standard of living and the median income of black families was $7,800 in 1974, the figures speak for themselves. The median income of black families was not adequate to maintain a lower-level standard of living, even if the family had only four persons, and many black families are larger than that.

In *The Social and Economic Status of the Black Population* (1973) there is evidence that

> the overall income position of black families relative to white families, as measured by the income ratio, has declined within recent years. The ratio of median family income of blacks to whites has moved downward from 0.61 in 1969 to 0.58 in 1973, after a rise during the period 1964 to 1969–70. Another measure of income comparability, the index of income overlap, also showed that there was no further narrowing of the income differences between black and white families in the 1970's.[89]

Historically, black women have often been employed and the salaries of husband and wife combined to produce a total family income. In the white family, historically, the husband has been the sole wage earner, although this has changed in recent years. In 1972, at each income level (except under $3,000) the average number of earners per family was higher for blacks than for whites (see table 3–3). In fact, in the in-

TABLE 3–3. SUMMARY MEASURES OF FAMILY CHARACTERISTICS, BY TOTAL MONEY INCOME, 1972

Selected Characteristics	Total	Total family income						
		Under $3,000	$3,000 to $4,999	$5,000 to $6,999	$7,000 to $9,999	$10,000 to $14,999	$15,000 to $24,000	$25,000 and over
NEGRO								
Mean family income....................................	$8,667	$1,852	$3,941	$5,884	$8,353	$12,183	$18,108	$33,807
Average Number of: Related children per family with children..............................	2.58	2.38	2.87	2.82	2.69	2.50	2.21	2.30
Earners per family................................	1.53	0.67	1.09	1.44	1.73	2.04	2.38	2.89
Ratio of nonearners to earners....................................	1.52	4.04	2.59	1.90	1.39	1.11	0.76	0.71
Median age of head..............................	42.0	40.0	42.2	42.3	40.8	42.6	42.9	45.9
Median school years completed..........................	10.6	8.9	9.3	10.2	10.9	12.1	12.3	12.8
WHITE								
Mean family income....................................	$13,103	$1,702	$4,010	$5,983	$8,475	$12,272	$18,666	$35,733
Average number of: Related children per family with children..............................	2.14	2.00	2.13	2.12	2.12	2.14	2.13	2.10
Earners per family................................	1.66	0.69	0.88	1.20	1.49	1.75	2.17	2.33
Ratio of nonearners to earners....................................	1.06	2.97	2.19	1.54	1.20	1.03	0.74	0.65
Median age of head..............................	45.7	54.7	57.6	47.8	43.1	42.1	45.4	49.3
Median school years completed..........................	12.4	9.1	9.0	10.7	12.1	12.4	12.7	14.2

SOURCE: U. S. Department of Commerce, Social and Economic Statistics Administration, Bureau of the Census, *The Social and Economic Status of the Black Population in the U.S., 1973*, p. 21.

come range of $10,000 and above it took *more than two earners* to bring in the money: 2.04 in the income bracket $10,000–$14,999; 2.38 in the income bracket $15,000–$24,999 and 2.89 in the bracket $25,000 and over. Also, as a general rule the earners in the black family had more people to support than in the white family. For both black families and white families, an increase in income could be seen with increased education of the family head.

While education increases income, education does not make the incomes of blacks and whites equal, according to a study by Robert P. Althauser and Sydney S. Spivack. Published as *The Unequal Elites* (1975), their study revealed that black college graduates may complete more advanced education than whites but they earn $1,000 to $2,000 less annual income. Generally, they found that whites and blacks with equal resources are paid different amounts (whites earn more) in both the public and private sectors. Their data suggested that the long-standing and widely held belief that increasing the qualifications of blacks, especially their level of education, would ameliorate racial discrimination, is false.[90]

There are regional variations in the family income of black families. In young black families (whose head is under 35) in the North and West, with husband and wife employed all year long, the mean family income (black to white) was .98 in 1972. Note that to achieve this ratio meant that the young black wife had to work fifty or fifty-two weeks a year alongside her husband (see table 3–4). This represents parity to some (Wattenberg and Scammon), despite the fact that more black than white wives had to work all year long to earn the money (52% black versus 36% white in 1970) outside the South.

In the South in 1972, these young black families (head under 35) had made substantial progress in improving their income status relative to white income. The black-to-white ratio had become .90 in mean family income in 1972, with the black wife working all year round (50%, compared with 42% for whites). This ratio was .87 in 1973.[91]

The regional variations show that in the North, West, and South, in young families (head under 35) with both mates employed year around, the income gap between black families and white families has been greatly reduced. However, in the North and West these black families were only 6.2 percent of the 5.3 million black families in America in March 1973, a very small proportion.[92] This is progress, and no secret should be made of it, but it should not be trumpeted as if the millennium has been reached. None of the census figures reflect the economic decline of 1974, not even the most recently published data.[93]

Most troubling is the proportion of low-income black families. About 28 percent of all black families were below the low-income level in 1973, compared with about 7 percent of white families. The number of poor black families was about the same in 1974. But low-income black persons constituted 31 percent of the black population; this was more than three times the 9 percent figure for the white population.[94]

Between 1969 and 1973 the number of low-income black families increased, and families headed by women, black and white, were more likely to be poor than families headed by men. Higher poverty rates

TABLE 3–4. EARNINGS IN 1972 OF HUSBAND AND WIFE FOR FAMILIES IN WHICH BOTH HUSBAND AND WIFE HAD EARNINGS, BY AGE OF HEAD AND REGION

Race and earnings of husband and wife and work experience of wife	Total			Husband under 35 years old		
	United States	North and West	South	United States	North and West	South
NEGRO						
Mean family income	$12,387	$14,052	$10,872	$11,589	$12,551	$10,770
Mean earnings of husband	7,349	8,366	6,425	7,218	7,577	6,913
Mean earnings of wife	4,014	4,723	3,370	3,906	4,473	3,423
Earnings as a percent of family income	32	34	31	34	36	32
Wife worked 50 to 52 weeks	$5,299	$6,192	$4,487	$5,608	$6,345	$4,927
Earnings as a percent of family income	43	44	41	48	51	46
WHITE						
Mean family income	$15,432	$15,986	$14,231	$12,480	$12,743	$11,981
Mean earnings of husband	9,996	10,358	9,212	8,466	8,648	8,120
Mean earnings of wife	3,932	4,023	3,737	3,531	3,581	3,434
Earnings as a percent of family income	26	25	26	28	28	29
Wife worked 50 to 52 weeks	$5,601	$5,751	$5,276	$5,526	$5,630	$5,327
Earnings as a percent of family income	36	36	37	44	44	44
RATIO: NEGRO TO WHITE						
Mean family income	0.80	0.88	0.76	0.93	0.98	0.90
Mean earnings of husband	0.74	0.81	0.70	0.85	0.88	0.85
Mean earnings of wife	1.02	1.17	0.90	1.11	1.25	1.00
Wife worked 50 to 52 weeks	0.95	1.08	0.85	1.01	1.13	0.92

SOURCE: U.S. Department of Commerce, Social and Economic Statistics Administration, Bureau of the Census, *The Social and Economic Status of the Black Population in the U.S., 1973*, p. 27.

were related to the sex of the family head, large family size, no earners in the family, a nonworking head, and a head lacking a high school diploma. Black families had more of these characteristics than white families. About 54 percent of black families that had four or more children were below the low-income level in 1972, compared with 16 percent for white families of this size.[95]

Robert B. Hill, using data collected by the Census Bureau and published as *Current Population Reports,* made the following observations about the black poor:

> Between 1962 and 1969, the black poor dropped from 12 million to 7.1 million persons. But by 1972, 600,000 more blacks (or 7.7 million) became poor while the white poor declined by 500,000 (from 16.7 to 16.2 million).
>
> It should be noted, however, that most of the black poor are poor and despite the fact that they work. Sixty-two percent of poor black families have wage or salary earnings, compared to 53 percent of poor white families. The economic situation is so acute for these families that some of them also have to rely on public assistance to supplement their earnings. But despite the fact that 53 percent of the poor black families receive public assistance, only 36 percent of their total income comes from that source.[96]

This means that many black and white wage earners are employed for less than living wages, which points out the continuing discrepancy between philosophy and actuality in America. The traditional work ethic philosophy has espoused the notion that people should work as hard as they can and that their hard work will pay off for them, resulting in at least material adequacy. (However, the reality is that the minimum wage is less than adequate to provide a modest living for a family of four, especially in urban areas like Washington, D.C.) So unless full employment becomes a reality—and it must be accompanied by a realistic minimum wage level and/or cost ceilings—income will continue to be less than adequate for many working people, black and white.

Housing

Since the kind and quality of housing one is able to procure and retain is related directly to income, the housing status of blacks is reasonably predictable, given the preceding discussion on income and employment. Between 1960 and 1970 homeownership and occupancy increased somewhat for blacks, but the rate of growth was minimal. In the central cities the homeownership rate was 31 percent in 1960 and 35 percent in 1970—a 4 percent growth in the ten-year period, which included the greatest civil rights efforts of the twentieth century. The homeownership rate for blacks was higher in the suburbs, but the rate of growth was minimal there as well, from 52 percent in 1960 to 54 percent in 1970. The greatest change can be found in nonmetropolitan areas—from 45 percent in 1960 to 52 percent in 1970: a 7 percent gain. But in 1970 thrcc times as many blacks as whites occupied "substandard" dwellings —23 percent of the 6.2 million black-occupied housing units.[97]

Black households were underrepresented in the 1973 housing inventory, with about 6 percent of new housing units occupied by blacks, compared with 10 percent of all occupied units in 1970. Homeownership rates increased slightly for whites from 1970 to 1973, but equivalent rates for blacks remained close to the 1970 rates.[98]

Also related to income are household expenditures. Black homes have fewer major appliances, on the average, than do white households. Blacks usually own a refrigerator and kitchen range (both necessities) and a black-and-white television set. Whites have these appliances, as well as a clothes washer, dryer, dishwasher, home freezer, color and black-and-white television sets, and air conditioning. Blacks were less likely than whites to own an automobile in 1973 (57% black, 84% white), and the models blacks owned were older than those of whites. Thirty-six percent of white families, compared with 18 percent of black families, owned two or more automobiles in 1973.[99]

Health

The life expectancy of blacks remains below that of whites. For blacks born in 1973, the average life expectancy is 70.1 years for females and 61.9 years for malcs. This average life expectancy is up somewhat; for blacks who were born in 1971, the average life expectancy for females was 69.3 years and 61.2 years for males. Compared with the dominant population, the 1973 figures for whites were 76.1 years for females and 68.4 years for males.[100]

Infant mortality rates have declined for blacks and whites for the past three decades, but in 1972 the rates for blacks and other minorities were 75 percent higher than the rate for whites, 29.0 and 16.3 respectively. Suicide among black females and other female minorities increased from 3.0 to 3.9 percent between 1965 and 1971.[101]

Increase in "Broken" Families

Census data show an increase in "broken" families in the black population. From 1965 to 1970 the proportion of black families with a husband and wife declined from 73 to 68 percent; this trend continued into 1975, when the percentage dropped to 61. The percentage of black families headed by a female, with no spouse present, moved from 28 to 35 percent, and has been near the 35 percent level from 1972 to 1975. Nine percent of white families were headed by women in 1970 and 11 percent in 1975.[102] Sometimes such black and white families are one-parent but stable; often they are poor, when headed by a woman only.

The decline in two-parent black families is troublesome, since that kind of family structure is held to be valuable in the larger society and since the income level of two-parent families is almost sure to be larger and more adequate. Further, if the decline continues, it probably will portend less stability for black families in the future. Minor children and elderly adults may suffer most if this decline continues, for it is those at the extremes of the age spectrum who usually need families most. Further, the extended family was historically the institution on which most blacks could depend for life-long support—emotional, financial, and other. At the same time, however, the data show that 61 percent of black families are not broken; so a majority—in fact, almost two-thirds—of black families are still together. The picture is troubling but not pathological. Given the nature of the social system under which blacks live and the ongoing problems of getting a job and supporting a family, it is easy to explain black-white differences in family structure. Societal assistance for all American families needs to be studied.

Separation and/or divorce rates are still escalating in America. In the larger society, the divorce rate is one in three, and growing. There is more divorce among upper socioeconomic groups, as well as more delay in marriage on the part of the young, more single-parent families, and more variety in living arrangements (e.g., "shacking").[103]

The black population certainly has not escaped societal changes. In 1974 a greater proportion of black female family heads was either divorced or single than in 1970.[104] This group was increasing most rapidly among black female heads, and the women tended to be younger in 1974 than in 1970. About 70 percent of the black female family heads had children to support in 1974, whereas 67 percent had the same responsibility in 1970. Some 3.2 million black children in 1974, compared with some 2.6 million in 1970, were in families headed by females only.[105] Many female-headed black families receive Aid to Families with Dependent Children (AFDC), commonly called "welfare."

The society seems to be going through a period of change which both reflects and affects basic attitudes toward conformity with traditional behavior. The change is pervasive, and affects the family as a social institution most directly.

To return to the central question: "Is black progress real or a delusion?" and its corollary, "Is the glass half full or half empty?" The evidence shows that black progress is real in the areas of elected officials and education. Black progress was real in employment and income during the decade of the 1960s, but the overall condition has deteriorated since 1969. The glass is both—half full and half empty—and evaporation is occurring in the decade of the 1970s.

However, even in time of progress the economic and social conditions of blacks in urban slums did not improve, nor was there ever a real change in the unemployment rate of blacks compared with the unemployment rate of whites. Even when unemployment rates dropped markedly, and dropped proportionally as much for blacks as for whites, the ratio remained roughly 2:1 for adults. So, realistically speaking, black progress was authentic for blacks outside urban slums in the 1960s, especially in the North, West, and South. This progress was most marked among young families (family head under 35 years old), with both husband and wife working fifty to fifty-two weeks every year.

This progress did not just happen. It was a response to court decisions, black initiatives in direct action, legislative enactments, presidential enforcement of laws and executive orders, and the cooperative efforts of non-blacks—the result of cumulative efforts (of Myrdal's principle of cumulation and reciprocal reinforcement) from many sectors. There were strong countervailing efforts from other sectors, such as "Bull" Connor and others, but the society refused to allow these forces to prevail.

These cumulative and reciprocally reinforcing efforts were made in an expanding economy; so more jobs were available for blacks and other minorities—as well as women—to fill without displacing whites. The efforts were also made in a changing world, where nonwhite nations struggled for their freedom and independence from colonial powers or entrenched elite power structures. Therefore economic and international factors must never be overlooked in assessing the progress of the black minority in the United States in the decade of the 1960s.

Retrogression has befallen blacks in the seventies, and is most pronounced in unemployment rates. Since lack of employment is tied to every aspect of life—housing, food, clothing, education, health care—the quality of black life is regressing. Thus the progress was real but it is not permanent. This lack of permanence in black progress is a key to understanding pessimistic black feeling and behavior; what was so hard won can be, and usually is, very easily and quickly lost. Again, viewed in historical perspective, black status in the 1970s is like regression, or reversion to type, in America. Temporary gains led to heightened expectations of attaining equality and justice in this time, but in the black subculture those gains always are accompanied by insecurity and fear of losing what has been won because the historical experience of the black group shows that, almost invariably, great losses follow great gains. Therefore, no significant difference occurs with respect to the economic and social status of the black minority in America.

This is where we find ourselves today—at a point of no significant difference with respect to equality and justice in income, employment, housing, and health. Programs which made some difference in educational opportunity, such as the Committee on Legal Education Opportunity (CLEO), are rapidly being phased out. This means that in education, one of the areas in which blacks have made progress in the 1970s, the fight for equality of opportunity must continue unabated at every level. A ray of hope is in exercise of the franchise. New strategies are needed to attack long-standing problems, together with committed, incorruptible leaders who will show people the way to move ahead.

Black people have been led through several phases in the fifteen years from 1960 to 1975. From "We Shall Overcome" (Martin Luther King, Jr.) to "Burn, Baby, Burn" (Watts) to "Black Power" and "Kill Honky" (Stokely Carmichael) to "All Power to the People" (Black Panthers) to "I Am Somebody" and "Green Power" (Rev. Jesse Jackson), blacks have struggled to maintain psychic balance while wrestling against the odds. Blacks who were educated, intelligent, highly motivated, had the right contacts, or were fortunate enough to be in the right place at the right time progressed during this period; gains were real for this group. For blacks who were unfortunate enough to be ill-educated, average or low in intelligence, lacking motivation and contacts, or not strategically located, life changed not at all, unless it changed for the worst.

Substantiating the latter point is a telecast presented by NBC on June 29, 1975, in the Washington, D.C., metropolitan area. Titled *A Country Called Watts,* the program, narrated by Tom Pettit and Gail Christian, interviewed residents of Watts ten years after the burning of that community in 1965 to see what tangible progress had been made in the ten-year period. Residents said that the federal programs had "dried up," that the community had had beautiful government promises but the federal government had reneged on funds. They felt the federal government had made giant steps, which soon faltered; three years after the riot the government gave up on programs for Watts, saying that the effort cost too much money and the payoff came too slowly. By 1968, federal emphasis had shifted to the war in Vietnam. The commentators said that by 1969 the federal government was spending as much in one week in Vietnam as was spent totally in Watts; they also quoted Sargent Shriver as saying he had sent domestic antipoverty programs to President Lyndon Johnson but that he had never heard from the president. Watts residents reported that in 1975 some state-level programs were operating in their community, but not federal programs.

When asked to relate current problems, community residents and narrators spelled out the following: (1) in the job situation, unemployment and poverty; (2) a growing number of fatherless homes, but strong mothers; (3) inadequate housing: HUD owned hundreds of boarded up homes; and the community center, also owned by HUD, could not meet the housing codes; (4) poor education: low standards, inadequate teaching, unmotivated students; (5) a nonfunctional shopping center had been built, but never had tenants; and (6) an inadequate hospital and a high mortality rate for babies. The narrators closed this program by stating that Watts is not unique; it is typical of what has happened to poverty programs in American cities.[106]

That same day, June 29, 1975, the ABC network presented a telecast in the Washington, D.C., metropolitan area about Oakland, California, titled *A Tale of Two Cities*. Excerpts from the report of the Kerner Commission were given at the beginning and at the end of this program, which concluded that Oakland had become characterized by *de facto* apartheid. Rod McLeish, commentator, felt after his visit to Oakland that whites did not want to associate with blacks in any way as equals and that blacks were beginning to feel the same way about whites. McLeish stated his opinion that whites in Oakland had *not* changed very much over the last twenty years but that blacks *had* changed. For example, most blacks were "down on capitalism" because of their experiences under the system, although not every local black community leader had given up. As the title of the program indicates, Oakland had become two cities, one black and one white, despite the upward mobility of a few highly successful, middle-class blacks. McLeish concluded the program with this succinct comment, "This is America— a tale of two countries." The linkage was with the Kerner Commission Report, which stated that America was moving toward two societies, separate and unequal; and Oakland had become two cities characterized by *de facto* apartheid in 1975. "This is America—a tale of two countries."[107]

CHANGING TONE OF THREE BLACK-ORIENTED PERIODICALS

Paralleling the examination of a changing tone in three white intellectually oriented periodicals, we will examine a changing tone in three black intellectually oriented periodicals—though no claim is made that the two sets of periodicals are equally influential on the general public, the national power structure, or their own ethnic groups.

Black intellectual journals have been extremely important for expressing the various ideological currents in the raging sea of black thought during the 1960s and '70s. The dynamic of a changing mood in three black journals, *Black World (Negro Digest),* * *Freedomways,* and *The Black Scholar,* is evident in the historical periods which reflect the ideological transformations. After the period of civil rights (1963–66), there was a movement to black nationalism and black power (1966–68), and then to pan-Africanism and black internationalist power (1969–71). The period from 1972 to the present has been one of increased ideological debate and conflict over Marxist-Leninist ideology.

Black World was published on a monthly basis, as *The Black Scholar* presently is, and *Freedomways* is published as a quarterly. *Black World* is examined first because it offers the most complete and consistent evidence of a changing mood. *Freedomways* shows a similar trend but reflects a difference in the degree of change. *Black Scholar,* which did not begin publication until 1969, began on a militant note and has continued this emphasis.

Articles published in *Negro Digest* in the early '60s contained strong commitments to the civil rights movement and the goal of full equality in an integrated society. The commitment to integration can be seen in the number of articles specifically devoted to the civil rights movement. In addition, *Negro Digest,* (as it was then called) often printed articles by white authors, which allowed self-examination and admission of guilt but which also, on occasion, allowed white Americans to gently criticize black Americans for their shortcomings.

In spite of the hopefulness the civil rights movement seemed to inspire, an undercurrent of pessimism occasionally surfaced along with the optimism. A number of articles, even in the early sixties, warned of the limits of protest and the dangers of white backlash. The changing mood in *Black World* seemed to be a struggle for dominance between warring ideologies. The poles of the discussion seemed to be present in a 1963

---

*In May 1970, *Negro Digest* became *Black World*. *Black World* was defunct as of May 1976.

article titled "Integration or Black Nationalism, Which Route Will Negroes Choose?" Its author, Richard Thorne, asserted that civil rights and black nationalism were the two main approaches to the solution of the black American's problems at that time. According to Thorne, the very term *civil rights* implied, by definition, its own objective, which was acquisition of those lawful rights denied to the Negro. For Thorne, the civil rights approach was limited at best. The black nationalist approach, by contrast, included much more; it took in values, attitudes, self-image, and history and interpreted or constructed them to the advantage of black people.

The emphasis this early article placed on control and manipulation of black history and culture allows one to understand the flowering of this idea into the cultural, nationalist ideas of Maulana Ron Karenga, the attempt to develop a black aesthetic, and the demand for black-studies curricula on traditionally white campuses. Although both ideological extremes seemed to be present at the same time in *Black World,* there was a demonstrable contrast in the tone of articles published in the early and in the late sixties. That contrast can be shown in a sampling of articles published in *Negro Digest* during the periods of commitment to the civil rights movement (1963–66), black power and nationalism (1966–69), pan-Africanism (1969–73), and the movement to the left (1973 to the present).

In January 1964 the lead article, titled "Prospects for '64 in the Civil Rights Struggle," offered short statements from each major leader of the civil rights movement. The tone of their statements was generally optimistic:

Martin Luther King, Jr.: "The thrust of the Negro toward full emancipation will *increase* rather than *decrease.* . . . I do not foresee any widespread turning of the Negro to violence."[108]

Roy Wilkins: "The outlook for substantial Civil Rights gains in 1964 is, as of this writing, more promising than ever before."[109]

Whitney Young: "My own contacts with top government and business officials lead me to believe that overt acts of discrimination will diminish if not disappear."[110]

James Farmer: "The revolution will not be fully com-
                         pleted in 1964, but it will be moved a
                         full measure forward."[111]

John Lewis: "In 1964, the Negro movement will
                         become the people's movement, a
                         movement for all the hungry, all the
                         poor, all the voteless."[112]

In another 1964 article, titled "The Techniques of Winning Freedom Now," Wyatt T. Walker claimed that the entire nation would come
to feel the brunt of nonviolent forces demanding "Freedom Now!"
Walker was a co-worker with Martin Luther King; his article was basically a defense of nonviolence as a technique in the civil rights struggle.

In 1965, *Negro Digest* continued to publish articles that were supportive of the civil rights movement. In the January issue the lead article, "Individual Responsibility and the Negro Image," was written by
John H. Johnson, president of the Johnson Publishing Company. He
wrote, "We stand today at a forking point in the American experience.
We are in the middle of a non-violent social revolution that goes to the
heart of our meaning as a people." He urged every individual to assume
"personal responsibility for race relations in America."[113] He was
strongly supportive of the work done by such organizations as the Urban
League in interpreting the Negro to the white man and the white man to
the Negro.

In other articles that same year, a number of writers offered support or strategies for the movement. The April issue included an article
titled "Why Direct Action Must Not Cease" by Robert F. Drinan, S.J.,
dean of the Boston College Law School. Drinan urged blacks to continue
their protest activities. In his view, nonviolent protest had to continue so
that whites would not be allowed to forget what blacks had suffered in
their quest for first-class citizenship. In addition to carrying President
Johnson's Thanksgiving message on voting rights, the June 1965 issue
included another article on civil rights by Judge Raymond Pace Alexander. In "The Five Civil Rights Groups Should Merge Forces," Judge
Alexander suggested that CORE, SNCC, SCLC, the NAACP, and the
Urban League unite on a program of action to secure those rights still
denied the Negro. Judge Alexander saw no fundamental doctrinal issues
separating these organizations and felt that there would be greater
power in a union of all the forces working in this field.

By 1966 discontent with the tactics of the civil rights movement and with the pace and quality of change began to surface more and more often in articles in *Negro Digest*. The attack was not at first on the movement itself but on the nonviolent approach of the movement. In the January 1966 issue, Nathan Hare suggested that nonviolence as a protest style might be on its way out. The signs to which he pointed included the riots in Watts and the emergence in the Deep South of groups like the Deacons for Defense and Justice. Hare also reported that he had been informed by a SNCC leader that "his group was dropping nonviolence for the most part because Negroes in southern localities where they are being killed by whites no longer want to hear non-violent ideology."[114] The unnamed SNCC worker explained that the impatience with nonviolence on the part of blacks in the South was one of the main reasons why Dr. King was at that time moving his campaign to the North. Hare acknowledged that there had been "some conspicuous gains"; it was his view, however, that the Negro had "not progressed—in spite of propaganda to the contrary—in the manner that he must if he is to obtain equality in the next one thousand years."[115] With regard to nonviolence, Hare suggested that Negroes were "coming to see the curious contrast between non-violence for them and the customarily unpunished killing of Negroes, including army majors in uniform, by white southerners."[116] He concluded that the switch from nonviolence was only dimly in sight but it "was occurring—and would become more extreme in the future . . . . "[117]

Nathan Hare's words proved to be portentous, for it was in the summer of 1966 that Stokely Carmichael began to use the controversial slogan "black power." The national press presented the slogan and the advocates of black power in such a way that they frightened much of the white public and polarized much of the black community. At the height of the discussion of the implications of the new militancy, *Negro Digest* conducted a symposium on the subject. The results were published in the November 1966 issue under the title "The Meaning and Measure of Black Power." The editor posed the following questions for the participants in the symposium:

1. Is the Civil Rights movement at the crossroads?—And, if so, what are the practical alternatives to it?
2. What is your own reaction to the term, "Black Power," and why do you feel the national press and the white public reacted as they did to the term?[118]

While all the participants agreed that the civil rights movement was indeed at the crossroads, one of them went so far as to say that the movement was dead. The civil rights movement had resulted in improved conditions for some members of the black middle class but, as another participant pointed out, conditions in the black ghettos of large cities and in the Southern backwoods had worsened steadily. With regard to black power, the symposium participants seemed to agree that it was an idea whose time had come. The concept of black power, as defined by John Oliver Killens, called on black people to write their own history and create their own myths and legends while unifying themselves along psychological, political, economic, and cultural lines. As for the future, efforts to liberate black people would be led by blacks. Blacks, in Sterling Stuckey's view, would have to make their own decisions, elect their own representatives, and lead and support their own movement.

In the pages of *Negro Digest,* 1966 was a transitional year. Between 1966 and 1969, black intellectuals seemed engaged in a search for new directions and a new ideology. In *Negro Digest,* much of the discussion of new directions centered on the concept of nationalism. But some black intellectuals, who were less inclined to accept a black nationalist posture, emphasized the need for a broader political perspective. The Vietnam War and its negative influence on American attitudes toward domestic problems had begun to alarm a number of civil rights groups and activists during this period. Dr. Martin Luther King, Jr., in the June 1967 issue of *Negro Digest,* charged that the war had demolished the hopes engendered by the Great Society programs. While America was engaged in an expensive war, the domestic welfare of blacks was neglected. When it came to fighting the war, blacks were considered full citizens, but they still remained second-class citizens at home.

Nationalism, defined in the narrowest way, refers to nation-state creation or to feelings about a land base. Movements toward a return to Africa or toward securing territory in the United States are usually labeled "nationalist movements." In the wider sense in which the term was used in the sixties, it included values, attitudes, and self-image. By 1967 the word *nationalism* was beginning to appear quite frequently in the pages of *Negro Digest.*

In June of 1967 Clemmont E. Vontress, in his article "There Is Too Much Apathy on the Negro Campus," alleged that black students were apathetic and were not committed to civil rights. He claimed they were more involved in trying to acquire clothes, cars, and degrees and only superficially supported the black struggle by their Afro hair styles and attendance at speeches by black activists such as Stokely Carmichael. Vontress believed that since black colleges trained some two-thirds of black students, the leadership for the black struggle should come from these institutions. However, students who were striving for black suburbia and middle-class status were fearful of the risks involved in activism. Black professors, Vontress claimed, were responsible for such views by their own life styles and apolitical lectures. Vontress pointed out that Nathan Hare was an exception and, because of his radical position, could lose his position at Howard University.

Attention was also given to the plight of black students on white campuses. Peter Bailey's "New Image of the Ivy League" (July 1967), in contrast to Vontress, reports on the growing black consciousness and commitment of black students in Ivy League schools. He discussed a conference held in 1966 of intercollegiate Ivy League black student groups, where students attended workshops conducted by various civil rights leaders who stressed that black students should be linked to the black masses. In the August issue Richard C. Tolbert asserted, in "A New Brand of Nationalism," that the word *nationalism* could apply to "the desire for nationality group unity; and it can exist when a multiplicity of nationality groups share the same country." Also in August of that year, John A. Williams, in "Race, War and Politics," gave a historical analysis of American racism and pointed out that other minorities also were victims, as well as blacks. He emphasized that the wars the United States engaged in were, in many ways, racist. From this historical analysis he drew the conclusion that since many of the revolutionary wars at that time were waged by nonwhites, and were sometimes connected with the Communist bloc, there was the possibility of a dangerous conflict. He cited the American attitude toward China as the most obvious example of this potentially explosive situation, but added that United States fears of China included not only fear of communism but Chinese possession of the atomic bomb. In this article Williams, using a broader historical perspective, attempted to point out, as King had, the relationship between American racial policies at home and abroad.

Considerable attention was also paid to black colleges during 1967. In "The Place of the Black College in the Human Rights Struggle" (September 1967), Charles V. Hamilton proposed that the black college should be revolutionary in its purposes, procedures, and goals—"legitimate" in relation to the distinctive ethos of blackness, rather than in relation to a larger white, anachronistic middle class. He proposed a black college that would "quickly understand that Western technology was not the criterion of greatness."[119]

For black students on white campuses, S. E. Anderson emphasized the importance of education, communication, and cooperation. His essay, "Toward Racial Relevancy: Militancy and Black Students," warned that black students on white campuses must avoid the dangers of overintellectualizing and romanticizing the civil rights struggle.

The Detroit rebellion, in the summer of 1967, had a profound impact on the ideological development of the black movement. The November issue of *Negro Digest* was a special issue, focusing on Detroit, and the key issue was the emergence of a new black leadership. Several activists and thinkers in Detroit contributed articles, each supporting some form of black nationalism. Hoyt Fuller, the editor of *Negro Digest,* gave a report of the evolution of black leadership in Detroit. Reverend Albert Cleage, Milton Henry, and Richard Henry were presented as examples of the new black leadership. (Cleage was the innovator of the Black Nationalist Christian Movement and Richard and Milton Henry [brothers] had worked with Malcolm X and later started the Malcolm X Society in Detroit, which was the forerunner of the Republic of New Africa.) In December 1967, Peter Bailey, in an essay titled "What Afro-American Nationalism Means to Me," wrote "African-American nationalism rejects extreme group defeating individualism; instead, it stresses collective group action as the best means for promoting progress and security."[120] Nationalist ideas in the late sixties began to have a strong influence on writing and thinking about art and aesthetics, politics, history, and education. The emphasis was on black standards and black goals and objectives.

There was considerable recognition by 1968 that a change was in the making. Clifford Darden, author of an article titled "The Post-Malcolm Movement," which appeared in the June 1968 issue of *Negro Digest*, wrote:

> If anyone originally doubted the prospects for success of the Old Civil Rights Movement, his initial suspicions have certainly materialized in the events of the last two years. The revolutions in the Black ghetto, the waning influence and effectiveness of the old-guard Negro spokesmen and the increasing anti-Black mood of Congress—all of these events have signalled the end of an era.[121]

After acknowledging the demise of the civil rights approach, Darden issued a call for new leaders to guide the movement, leaders who could serve as skilled power brokers and negotiate black Americans' continued progress. Darden was especially critical of the Negro middle class (NMC), whose goal for so long had been integration or assimilation into white society. He looked with hope toward the "expanding numbers of Black collegians, who—unlike the present NMC—had been reared under two ideological phases of the movement for Black equality."[122] The two "ideological phases" to which Darden alluded were the integration-assimilationist phase and the new "black power," or nationalist, phase which he saw coming into its own.

However, during the rising tide of nationalist sentiments difficulties emerged in achieving national unity. The July 1968 *Negro Digest* had an article by Betty De Ramus, a Detroit community organizer, who in "Detroit Revisited" said that one year after the rebellion the new black leadership, the Federation for Self-Determination, had fallen apart. In another article in this issue, Robert L. Zangrando, a white liberal, criticized Kenneth Clark, a noted black social scientist, for his opposition to black power. Zangrando insisted on a careful evaluation of the concept of black power and accused Clark of a narrow view in his wholesale dismissal of the movement. Clark believed that integration was the only path for black people and that black-power advocates were antiwhite. Zangrando stressed that open discussion of various views was necessary, and felt that Clark's position as a scholar should enable him to accept various strategies in the black struggle.* Richard Tolbert, in his article "Needed: A Compatible Ideology (August 1968)," gives a historical analysis of the two political trends—assimilation and nationalism—and shows that the black-power versus black-and-white-unite debate was merely the recurrence of this theme. He stressed the importance of developing the black community and thought assimilation was an attack on this effort.

One of the most significant presentations of the ideological trends in the black movement in 1968 was S. E. Anderson's "The Fragmented Movement." Anderson identified five major tendencies in the movement: integrationists, city-statesmen, back to Africa, black nation, and revolutionary nationalism. He accepted revolutionary nationalism as the correct ideology because it sought to revolutionize the United States from a black perspective. The back-to-Africa movement, though nation-

---

*Clark, as a member of the board of trustees at Antioch College, opposed the ideas of black studies programs and separate dorms for blacks.

alist, was merely escapist, and while Anderson distinguished two forms
of this tendency—that is, a physical return and a cultural return (cultural nationalism)—he felt they both overlooked the political reality
that black people are in the United States and must fight here.

The black nation (Republic of New Africa) adherents' demand for
six states in the South did not face the fact that only by changing the
total system in the United States could black people find liberation. Anderson characterized the leadership of the RNA as romantic and out of
touch with the real problems, and he opposed integrationists and city-
statesmen because both wanted assimilation within the present system.
Thus Anderson's presentation was not merely a call for nationalism but
a more definitive and refined conceptualization of it.

In 1969 the developing disaffection with the civil rights movement
and the growing emphasis on the ethos of blackness, black power, and
black nationalism found expression in the feature article for the January
issue, the cover of which announced "We Have Become a Black Nation." The article is excerpted from the book *The Black Messiah* by the
Reverend Albert B. Cleage, Jr., pastor of Detroit's Shrine of the Black
Madonna. According to Cleage, the black nation was "as real as if it
had a capital, a Congress and a president."[123] Cleage believed that the
unity he described came from blacks' commitment to "one purpose,"
and that purpose was freedom for black people. The push for freedom
which Cleage described was not a movement toward integration into a
white world, for Cleage saw that world as an enemy world from which
blacks had been systematically excluded and which they now despised
and rejected. He pointed out that there were some black people who
would rather avoid the violence and conflict which he believed to be inevitable. In his view, however, the "good old days" when it was possible
to be a "comfortable Uncle Tom" were gone forever. Cleage concluded
that in the period of becoming a black nation, the black church could
play a significant role in strengthening and unifying black people for the
struggle ahead.

The growing emphasis on black nationalism and black power had
serious implications for every aspect of black life. Black education in
1969 was one of the most important areas of concern. In the wake of the
violence that followed the death of Dr. Martin Luther King, Jr., on
April 4, 1968, black students on predominantly white campuses began to
present demands to college and univeristy administrators. The students
asked for more black students and professors, more black courses, and
all-black dormitories. The March issue of *Negro Digest,* labeled part II

of *Toward a Dark University,* featured articles and symposium positions by Nathan Hare, Vincent Harding, Benjamin E. Mays, James R. Lawson, Gerald McWorter, Roscoe C. Brown, and others. This issue attempted to respond to the new militancy of black students on white campuses and to raise questions about the role of education in historically black institutions. In "New Creations or Familiar Death," Vincent Harding charged that the activities of Northern white universities caused a critical "brain drain" at black schools in the South. He made a number of suggestions designed to make it possible for black and white institutions to serve, rather than destroy, each other. Other articles in this issue defended black students' demands for separate black programs and examined the role of education in the struggle for black liberation.

The growth of pan-African consciousness in 1969 was reflected in "Black World" by William Barrow (May 1969). This title foreshadowed the change of the journal's title a year later, and the article reflected the pan-African scope it was to cover. Barrow pointed out that racist America, and the Western world in general, was on the decline. At the same time, Asia (China), Africa, and the nonwhite world were rising. The proposition of W. E. B. DuBois that the color line was to be the question of the twentieth century became a glaring reality. The growing consciousness of black people of their common problem throughout the world was demonstrated in the response of Africans in America to the murder of Lumumba and Nkrumah's invitation to DuBois to work in Ghana. These developments strongly supported the notion of a black world.

In June 1969, Attalie Markholt attacked white liberalism in the article "White Incubus." He felt that white liberals began with the racist assumption that it was tragic to be black. White liberals possessed, with arrogance, paternalism on the one hand and a sense of conscience and morality on the other, and these attitudes, Markholt asserted, were inseparable from their white "superiority."

Articles in the *Negro Digest* in 1969 continually stressed the importance of identifying with Africa and people of African descent whereever they may be. Lindsay Barret's "Should Black Americans be Involved in African Affairs?" (August) suggested that the exploitation of Africans in America was part of the world colonial experience and, as such, black Americans shared a common experience with Africans in Africa. The common ethnic identity and experience indicated that blacks in the United States should be involved in African affairs as long as they had a political frame of reference consistent with African liberation. The October issue carried a report by the editor of *Negro Digest,* Hoyt Fuller, on the significance of the Algiers Cultural Festival. Fuller was particularly pleased with the way in which Stokely Carmichael and Eldridge Cleaver attempted to reconcile their differences. (In the past, their differences had led to polemics and Carmichael's resignation from the Panther party.) Fuller felt this reconciliation and its larger implications—that ideological differences can be resolved—pointed to a greater unity in the African world.

Near the end of 1969, *Negro Digest* conducted a symposium in which participants were asked to take "the measure and meaning of the sixties" and to suggest "what lies ahead for black Americans." The following picture emerged from the points of view expressed by the seventeen symposium participants: from nonwhite protest and hopes of integration, black people seemed to have moved to self-defense, violence, black pride, and hopes of black power. There was also a large expansion of interest in identifying with the larger Third World community. Participants seemed to see a need for a clear ideology that would eradicate confusion, provide unity, and allow blacks to move with confidence toward a clearly defined goal. Based on the sixties, A. B. Spellman deduced ten trends for the seventies:

1. We can expect greater military preparation on the pigs' part and frequent violent conflicts with them.
2. We can expect new, subtle forms of cooptation of articulate black people. The communication and education industries are already moving in this direction. I expect Black Studies, especially on white campuses, to turn into a monster in the 1970's. I think that in 1980 we will find dozens of colleges turning out hundreds of black-talking *bourgies* with Ph.D.'s in Malcolm X and John Coltrane. What a horror! Revolutionary institutions like Malcom X University in Durham will prove to be the relevant education centers.
3. Community control of public school education will continue to be a national issue.
4. Coalition politics with white people will prove, for the umpteenth time, to be a very dead end.
5. Large numbers of black individuals, particularly men, will continue to intermarry and so define themselves out of the struggle.
6. There will be a further decline of large national organizations and an increase in the number of local programs designed to meet the specific needs of a given community. It will be the unified efforts by these local programs acting in concert that will

produce the synthesis that we need to move to a revolutionary
stage.

7. This decline in large national organizations and increase in local
programs will produce a different kind of leader: one with little
national charisma but with a functional local constituency.

8. There will be a radical revival of interest in local politics, as
black and white people struggle for control of municipal governments.

9. Pan-Africanism, around the writings and speeches of Osagyefo,
Nkrumah and Malcolm, will be the dominant ideology.

10. Black people will think of something to do that no one, black or
white, ever had the slightest notion that they would do. Of this I
am certain.[124]

Of these ten trends, two stand out as dominant in the mid-seventies. The
eighth, interest in local politics, and the ninth, the ideology of pan-
Africanism, are highly visible elements in black communities at the
present time.

The emphasis on blackness is especially apparent in art, and much
of the search for a "black aesthetic" took place in the pages of *Negro
Digest*. That search seemed to involve, first of all, an attack on the ways
in which white critics dealt with literature by blacks. In August 1967,
Darwin Turner offered a critical appraisal of Robert Bone's *The Negro
Novel in America,* a book which, according to Turner, brought Bone the
"exalted reputation as the Great White Father of Negro Literature."[125]
In July 1969, Sarah Webster Fabio's "A Black Paper" responded to
David Littlejohn's *Black on White: A Critical Survey of Writing by
American Negroes.*

While some black artists and intellectuals attacked the presumptions and errors of white critics, others addressed themselves to the task
of breaking white literary icons. Two of the more important iconoclasts
in the *Negro Digest* were Addison Gayle and Carolyn F. Gerald. In
"Black Literature and the White Aesthetic," Gayle suggested that the
vehicle for the cultural and social symbols of inferiority under which
blacks have labored in this country can be traced to distortion of the Pla-
tonic ideal. He pointed out, however, that the use of a "white aesthetic"
to stifle and strangle the cultures of other nations was not to be attributed to Plato but, instead, to his "hereditary brothers far from the Ae-
gean."[126] Hinton R. Helper, a nineteenth-century intellectual, is one of
those "hereditary brothers." In the preface to *Nojoque: A Question for
a Continent,* Helper frankly states that he intends "to write the negro

[sic] out of America."[127] According to Gayle, the headings of the two major chapters of this book reveal the whole symbolic apparatus of the white aesthetic handed down from Plato to America. The heading of one chapter is "Black: A Thing of Ugliness, Disease"; another is "White: A Thing of Life, Health, and Beauty." Carolyn F. Gerald offered a solution to the problem Addison Gayle described in her paper "The Black Writer and His Role" (January 1969). Her major premise was that the writer is the guardian of those myths and images that a people use to explain themselves. The task of the black writer, in her view, is the desecration and smashing of idols, the turning inside out of symbols,[128] especially those idols, symbols, and images which polarize black and white and impute negative values to blackness.

While the destruction of white literary idols may have been a necessary first step, it was still necessary to find standards to replace those rejected by black artists. The January 1968 issue of *Negro Digest* contained an article which made a strong contribution to the new thinking about the black aesthetic. According to Maulana Ron Karenga, black art must expose the enemy, praise the people, and support the revolution. He continued by saying that "all art that does not discuss and contribute to the revolution is invalid."[129] The notion that art can be an important revolutionary force helps to explain why a number of those who came to prominence in *Negro Digest* as artists became significant political thinkers in the seventies.

In January 1970 James and Grace Boggs wrote "Uprooting Racists and Racism." This essay later appeared in the book *Racism and the Class Struggle,* by the same authors. The Boggses, considered leading theoreticians on the black movement, influenced many black activists. In this article which began by criticizing the Kerner Commission Report, the authors pointed out that while the commission identified white racism as the basis for conflict, it proceeded to analyze blacks, not whites. It did not see racism as institutionalized and systematized. The Boggses, influenced by Marxism-Leninism, supported the notion that racism grows out of capitalism. However, they also asserted that all whites benefit from racism and then traced the process of capitalist accumulation and production to show how racism became institutionalized. They concluded that the United States is economically overdeveloped but politically underdeveloped, and that those who want to achieve a black revolution must give politics top priority.

In May 1970, *Negro Digest* became *Black World*. This titular change involved recognition of the fact that black intellectuals had moved from the discussion of integration to the exploration of a separate and distinctive black "world." The comments of the editor in the May issue were of particular importance as a description of this shift of focus. He stated that the scope of the journal would widen to include discussions of events in Africa as well as in the United States, and emphasized the common experience of colonialism and enslavement for all black people. The issue of freedom for blacks in America could no longer be separated from the issue of political and economic liberation of the entire Third World community. The editor implemented this idea in August by adding a special section, "Toward Pan Africanism." Several articles appeared, dealing with various parts of the black world, the Caribbean, DuBois, black power, and a statement on pan-Africanism.

Also in the May issue was an article titled "Where Is the Black Revolution?" by Keorapetse Kgositsile. Kgositsile argued that there would be no "black revolution" until blacks learn to defeat the subtle and not-so-subtle ways in which America acts to contain and exploit blacks' efforts toward self-liberation. In "Black Americans and the Modern Political Struggle," Charles V. Hamilton pointed out that "black power" in the sixties, with its emphasis on unity and black organization, was also present in many forms in the nineteenth century and in the early part of this century, while the debate between the black proponents of Marxism and black nationalism raises points "similar in nature to arguments advanced in the 1930's."[130] Black people, then, should not have to ask the same questions all over again as they move into the seventies. Hamilton urged blacks to move to a new level, "occasioned by new times and new needs and possibilities."[131]

In 1970 the A. Philip Randolph Institute acquired space in the *New York Times* and printed an appeal to blacks for their support of Israel in the Middle East conflict. Many who supported the appeal were prominent black leaders, generally considered at best liberal (if not moderate) in their political outlook. The *Black World*, in October 1970, published a response to the appeal and reprinted the appeal. Hoyt Fuller, editor of *Black World*, engaged in the debate as well. James Logan, leader of a group known as A.F.R.I.C.A., pointed out how the supporters of the appeal were primarily members of such organizations as the NAACP, Urban League, and the A. Philip Randolph Institute, who received large sums of money from Jews. Fuller, in a more personal commentary, showed the connection between Bayard Rustin's support of Israel (Rustin heads the A. Philip Randolph Institute) and his anti-black-studies and anti-black-power position. Fuller, like Logan, uncovered the fact that the money used by the Institute did not come from the black community and, consequently, the views and philosophy of the institute were not formulated according to the interests of the black community. Fuller further showed that a substantial element of the Jewish intellectual establishment opposed black studies and programs that aided black people. Yet historically the government and some blacks had sought out Jews to be leaders and experts on black affairs. Fuller then named Daniel J. Boorstin and Norman Podhoretz as those who opposed black interests and who, because of their authoritative positions, could negatively influence policy.

Debates and polemics continued in *Black World* during 1971. In the January, March, and May 1971 issues, Harold Cruse played the role of social critic and intellectual historian as excerpts from his forthcoming book appeared in the journal. (See table 3–5 for the Cruse–Mayfield debate.)

In the January 1971 *Black World,* Cruse attacked *The Black Scholar's* first issue on culture. Cruse implied that no relevant discussion took place on culture and that articles by Africans, such as President Sékou Touré of Guinea's "Dialectical Approach by Africans," were of no use to black Americans. In the May 1971 issue of *Black World,* Robert Chrisman, editor of *The Black Scholar,* attacked Cruse's position. (Chrisman had earlier criticized Cruse in the first issue of *The Black Scholar* [November 1969].) Chrisman emphasized the wealth of knowledge to be gained from Third World thinkers. He pointed out that, in contrast to Euro-American Marxists, these thinkers had been able to make Marxism-Leninism fit their specific conditions. Cruse had criticized the Marxist-Leninist approach of some black intellectuals, but Chrisman called for open intellectual exchange and felt that a Marxist-Leninist perspective contributed to the clarification of issues facing blacks. Both *The Black Scholar* and *Black World,* in his view, could be the vehicles for the discussion and refinement of the needed ideology.

In the July 1972 issue was a special article which paid tribute to Kwame Nkrumah, and articles appeared by veteran pan-Africans C. L. R. James and Stokely Carmichael, who had alleged he was Nkrumahist.

The October 1972 issue contained a number of articles which examined "the black political situation in the seventies." In an article titled "The New Black Political Culture," Ronald Walters saw the black political convention in Gary, Indiana, and the Washington-based thrust for African liberation as two of the most important political developments in the seventies. According to Walters, the change from the civil rights approach to black self-determination through electoral politics and through African liberation represented the maturation of the black political culture within the framework of a new set of political problems.

In "Urban Conduit-Colonialism and Public Policy," Charles V. Hamilton saw money for the cities as an important political and economic issue in the seventies. Although blacks were inheriting political control of many cities, they were doing so at a time when cities were running out of financial resources. And while much of the income from taxable property was no longer available to city governments, considerable amounts of money from the public sector came into the black community in the form of welfare and other public assistance payments. Hamilton alleged that blacks were merely conduits in a conduit-colonial system that used blacks to transfer public capital from one segment of the economy to another. That money which comes into the black community from the public sector is paid out to "absentee landlords, to exploitative merchants, to credit gougers and loan sharks." [132] In Hamilton's view, the black political agenda in the seventies must address itself to stopping the operation of this conduit.

In "African States and the Politics of Economic Freedom," Olu Akaraogun argued that "the disillusionment with mere political independence which pervades African States today stems from the fact that African leaders are not in a position to influence the direction of their economies."[133] Akaraogun described the ways in which European and American foreign interests have continued to control the economy of African countries. He suggested that black Americans could be substantially helpful in providing international political support and technical assistance to African countries.

The changing mood in the white world was not neglected by *Black World* in 1973. In March, James McGinnis in "Crisis and Contradictions in Black Studies" expressed the views that 1968–70 was a period of vast recruitment of black students to white universities and black studies were on the upswing. Much of this was due to the death of Martin Luther King, Jr. But in 1973 conservatism had replaced liberalism, and there were cuts in black student recruitment and black studies programs. In the same issue, James P. Comer, in "Nixon Policies and the Black Future in America," reflected on the conservatism of Nixon. While the Kennedy and Johnson administrations stood for affirmative action, Nixon was anti-busing and permitted Moynihan's "benign neglect" policy to prevail. During the Nixon administration no special efforts were made to aid minorities. Indeed, many blacks had forecast this possibility and voted against Nixon both times that he ran for election as president.

In 1972, the October issue of *Black World* was devoted to an examination of "the black political situation in the seventies." Since 1972 was an election year, the articles in the October issue offered a discussion of black politics in America. In 1973, the October issue focused on "the political situation in the black world." It featured an interview with President Mwalima Julius Nyerere of Tanzania, who was asked what role black Americans might play in the future development of Africa. President Nyerere replied that black Americans could "provide skills, and attitudes, and an experience" which could reduce the domination and exploitation of Africa by white Western powers.[134]

The question of blacks and their relationship to a land base was continued in another article titled "African-American Nationalism" by Ronald Walters. Walters believed that "Black Nationalism in the past had been defined so narrowly as to make it dysfunctional as an operational code for the masses of Black people."[135] While the tradition of separatist movements seeking a land base—whether in Africa or in territory within the United States—is very much a part of black nationalism, Walters was much more interested in the "landless" variety. He indicated that the "peculiar situation of Black people in America generated a mature nationalism based upon the fact of Race and Color." Walters chose to define nationalism not only as a struggle over land but also as a struggle over resources and justice. All black people who struggle to secure those things which are indicators of social and personal status in a materialistic and status-conscious society are thereby involved in "nationalist" behavior.

In "The Death Walk against Afrika," Don L. Lee returned to the question of land. The land which for him is all important is Africa. Lee asserts that the black American's ties to Africa are "historical, emotional, spiritual, cultural, political, economic and biological."[136] In his view, blacks must strive to internationalize their movements; each individual must become "the international Black man," working for Africa wherever he is. He offered a list of suggestions about what blacks in this country could do to become involved in the development of Africa.

The economic crisis and ideological changes in the black movement led to much debate over Marxism-Leninism as an ideological alternative. Earl Ofarri's "Black Labor: Powerful Force for Liberation" showed the relationship between capitalist development and the central role of black labor in the black movement. He pointed out that some groups (e.g., the Black Workers' Congress) point the way for black workers and the black struggle in general.

In May 1974, Hoyt Fuller's "On Black Studies and the Critics" defended the validity of black studies against the prevailing notion that they were dead. He exposed Martin Kilson, Bayard Rustin, and Thomas Sowell as black spokesmen who, in their actions against black nationalism, reflected the interests of the white and Jewish intellectual circles.

The October 1974 issue, like that of October 1973, was devoted to "the political situation in the black world." The lead article issue was "The Little Rock National Black Convention," part 1 of Harold Cruse's "Black Politics Series." In this essay Cruse raised important questions about the course of black politics in the present and future. His observations were based on an assessment of the past. For Cruse, the shift to the demand for black power was a crucial turning point in the sixties. The black-power slogan "signaled a turning inward, a reversal of self-motivated aims in the direction of 'black economic and political control' of black communities."[137] By 1974, according to Cruse, black militancy ceased to be "synonymous with 'racial integration' and is now wedded to the psychology of 'Black separatism' of varying persuasions."[138] Cruse strongly suggested that black-power politics reached a dead end and that no one had appeared who could lead the black movement "beyond the methodology of intuitive pragmatics in pursuit of 'Liberation' to organizational competition in national politics."[139] Because the Little Rock convention failed in this regard, Cruse viewed it as an unfortunate political retreat.

In the same issue, Haki R. Madhubuti (Don L. Lee) deplored the emergence of Marxist-Leninist influence in the black movement. It was Madhubuti's opinion, in an essay titled "Enemy from the White Left, White Right and In-Between," that blacks are in the midst of an ideological conflict that could lead to clarity or destruction. The struggle for national liberation must be directed by a theory of national liberation, and in Madhubuti's view that theory should be drawn from the historical experience of the people involved in the struggle. The problem in the black movement, as he saw it, was the constant battle over white supremacist-imperialist ideology, for whether it is Communist or capitalist ideology, it still reflects the needs and the historical experience of whites. Madhubuti warned that the language of the left, of the black Marxists of the seventies, was beginning to seep into the black nationalist–pan-Africanist movement and rendering that movement ineffective. A similar attack on Marxism-Leninism was made by Kalamuya Salaam in "Tell No Lies, Claim No Easy Victories."

The lead article in November 1974 was "Toward Ideological Clarity," by Amiri Baraka (Leroi Jones). It was a short version of a position paper in which Baraka put forth some of the main themes of an ideology for black liberation and black consciousness in the 1970s. The essay reflected Baraka's movement from a pan-African nationalist position to a position influenced by Marxist–Leninist–Mao Tse-tung thought.

In May 1975, Ladun Anise, in "The Tyranny of a Purist Ideology," analyzed the Sixth Pan-African Congress and concluded that the lack of unity manifested in Dar es Salaam, Tanzania, was due to the purist approach of the "Marxists" in attendance, who would not accept a pluralistic attempt at black unity. One of those to whom Anise referred indirectly was Amiri Baraka, chairman of the Congress of African People. In the July 1975 issue, Baraka's "Why I Changed My Ideology: Black Nationalism and Socialist Revolution" told why he moved to the left. Proclaiming adherence to Marxism-Leninism, or more precisely to Marxism–Leninism–Mao Tse-tung thought, Baraka pointed out the limitations of black nationalism and the historical connection between capitalism and racism, that is, class and race.

This move by Baraka was in opposition to his earlier cultural nationalism, at least in form, and provoked criticism of him by former allies in the cultural-nationalist camp. Yet Baraka's criticism was directed not only against capitalists and narrow nationalists but also against the Communist party in the United States, as well as collaborationists with capitalism. This position resulted from his support for the Chinese in the Sino-Soviet conflict. Baraka also called for black involvement in the national elections of 1976, but independent of the two major parties. His political activity in the National Black Assembly was attacked by a black elected official who did not want communist participation in the assembly. This state representative, Hannah Atkins (D. Oklahoma), later resigned from the assembly. The debate between Baraka and Atkins appeared as part of the October issue of *Black World,* which again was a special issue devoted to "the political situation in the Black World."

The emergence of *Freedomways* in 1961 was the direct result of the intensification of the civil rights struggle during the post–World War II period. The founding editors, Shirley Graham and Esther Jackson, Afro-American women who had been very active in the struggle (and married to prominent political activists W. E. B. DuBois and James Jackson), were determined to create a medium which would reflect and analyze this movement and its link with the African, Caribbean, and Latin American struggles. Whereas a shift to a broader focus was made in *Negro Digest/Black World, Freedomways* always had a pan-African or Third World focus. In fact, the first issue had articles by Africans and African Americans—by Ceza Nabaraoui on Guinea, Kwame Nkrumah and W. E. B. DuBois, John H. Clarke on his visit to Cuba, and Shirley Graham on her trip to China. Indeed, even in its early years *Freedomways* examined the black world and the struggles of people of African descent.

While the fall 1962 issue was devoted to the theme of an emerging Africa, the winter 1963 issue focused on the emancipation centennial. The editors pointed out that, 100 years after the Emancipation Proclamation, blacks still were not free. And in the fall 1963 issue attention was given to the death of W. E. B. DuBois, who had substantially contributed to the magazine, as well as to the March on Washington on the one hand and the Organization of African Unity on the other, both of which were significant events in 1963. In winter 1964 a special issue on the Southern freedom movement appeared with articles by various activists in the South, including Reverend Shuttlesworth and Haywood Burns, as well as contributing editors of *Freedomways*. Of special importance was Gloria Richardson's "Focus on Cambridge." In this article Mrs. Richardson (at that time chairman of the Cambridge Nonviolent Action Committee) emphatically announced that "the black revolt is now ready to go into a new phase." She further stated that

> no longer are we primarily interested in public accommodations. The "bread and butter" issues have come to the fore. A one-point program will become more and more obsolete as the months wear on. The attack now has to be directed toward the economic and political structure of a community if any real progress is to be made and if tokenism is to be eliminated. The leadership within the movement is moving toward this and the people are moving with them.[140]

Mrs. Richardson pointed to another development in the civil rights struggle, which she described as a propensity toward violence. The civil rights movement had already passed through two distinct phases: the nonviolent action phase, which was symbolized by the Montgomery bus boycott, and the direct action phase, which was symbolized by the student sit-ins. By 1963 it seemed especially difficult to maintain the nonviolent aspect of the movement.

In the fall issue for 1965, John H. O'Dell, associate managing edi-

tor and a frequent contributor to *Freedomways,* reported that "the Freedom Movement had now reached the most decisive moment in our
history, more rife with possibilities for major advances or serious
retrogression than any period since the overthrow of the first
Reconstruction."[141] The "point of no return," in his view, was "the
struggle to complete the restoration of full political-governmental power
to the black community in the South."[142] In "The Threshold of a New
Reconstruction," O'Dell attempted a searchingly critical appraisal of
the accomplishments of the freedom movement while making note of
new problems that were surfacing in 1965. According to O'Dell, "the
overall concrete achievement ... of the Freedom Movement had been
the dismantling of the public forms of segregation and the winning of
the passage of new legislation which reaffirmed the 'equal rights' principle under the Constitution." [143] The important fact about the accomplishments of the freedom movement to that date was that they
*"represented an accumulation of quantitative changes which had pre-
pared the conditions for a qualitative change in the habits, mores, customs, thought-patterns and material circumstances of southern life,
making possible the final uprooting of the relics of the slave society ... "[144]*

Also in the fall issue for 1965 were articles by Robert S. Browne,
"The Freedom Movement and the War in Vietnam," and Jose Malcolm,
"Notes on the Dominican Crisis," on United States imperialist aggres-
sion against nonwhite people.

The winter 1966 issue included a statement by the Student Nonviolent Coordinating Committee (SNCC) on America's involvement in
Vietnam that accused the United States of deception in the alleged purpose of the war—the freedom of the Vietnamese people. The struggle by
blacks in the South had shown that the United States was not for freedom. The murder of civil rights activists such as Samuel L. Younge, Jr.,
and the murder of Vietnamese by the United States government reflected that both at home and internationally the United States had no
regard for the law.

Also in 1966, *Freedomways'* authors continued to stress the need
for political power, and Mississippi seemed to be an important testing
ground for many of the new ideas about the potential strength of the
black vote. The spring and summer issues for 1966 contained an article
in two parts by Lawrence Guyot and Michael Thelwell, "The Politics of
Necessity and Survival in Mississippi," and the authors stated the following:

The movement for Negro rights in Mississippi indicates very bluntly that we cannot look to the Office of the Presidency, the Democratic or Republican Parties as presently constituted, the redemptive force of love, public moral outrage, the northern liberal establishment, nor even to the Congress with its "Great Society" legislation. We are not saying that these institutions and groups are necessarily hostile or can be of no practical assistance to the Mississippi Negro in his struggle for survival and political freedom. This is not so. But it is true that the political and legal rights of the Negroes of Mississippi even when guaranteed by the Constitution and enforced by civilized morality, will continue to be subject to the self-interests of these institutions unless reinforced by political power.[145]

The authors supported their conclusions through an examination of the historical record of "Mississippi's illegal actions against its Negro population and the national record of tolerance and indifference to these policies."

In winter 1967, *Freedomways'* editorials spoke against the ouster of Adam Clayton Powell from the House of Representatives. Pointing out the significant legislation in education and civil rights for which he had been responsible, they also criticized his faults and inconsistencies. Another editorial welcomed Dr. Alpheous Hunter, who had returned from Africa after the reactionary overthrow of Kwame Nkrumah. (The spring 1966 issue covered the coup, which is significant, especially in terms of the previously mentioned pan-African commitment of *Freedomways*. Its founding co-editor, Shirley Graham, had gone to Ghana with her husband and remained there after his death, until the coup.)

It is important to note that *Freedomways* had a large editorial board and there was a commonality among many of the contributors to the journal. This commonality resulted from three historical ties: a common struggle for the liberation of all people of African descent, a common quest for democracy and peace, and a common interest in socialism. These ties existed even prior to the post–World War II period. Consequently, when Martin Luther King, Jr. was killed in 1968, an editorial was written not only in tribute to his efforts in civil rights but for peace and the poor as well. This tribute consisted of an editorial, "Farewell to 'A Drum Major of Justice and Peace', " and the printing of King's address honoring W. E. B. DuBois.

In the winter 1969 issue Ernest Kaiser critiqued Harold Cruse in "The Crisis of the Negro Intellectual." This article first reviewed all previous comments on Cruse's book of the same title (this approach was important as a reflection of the cross-current of intellectual exchange in black intellectual journals). Kaiser pointed out that Cruse broke with the left and Marxism and he existed in an ideological void. Unable to attack the capitalist system and its vile racism, Cruse attacked Marxists and even blacks themselves. Without understanding the political economy of capitalism, Cruse called for cultural nationalism, thus idealistically emphasizing the cultural superstructure over the socioeconomic basis of capitalism and racism.

Also in 1969, *Freedomways* documented the growth of concern for the problems of the poor on the part of a major civil rights organization, SCLC. In an article titled "Charleston's Legacy to the Poor People's Campaign," John H. O'Dell asserted that the Charleston hospital strike forged unity between the community-organizing techniques developed during the civil rights era of the freedom movement and the working-class organizational techniques developed by the labor movement. The organization involved in that strike was the Southern Christian Leadership Conference (SCLC), founded by Dr. Martin Luther King, Jr.

SCLC began in 1963 to move from a primary concern for the civil rights of all blacks to specific concerns of particular groups of black workers. That year the organization became involved in a limited way with the grievances of Negro steelworkers in Atlanta and active participation with striking workers at the Scripto Pen Company in that city a couple of years later. In 1965 SCLC aided garbage workers in Memphis, Atlanta, and St. Petersburg. What was significant in all this was that the "process of an emerging multiethnic social force representing the most exploited among the workers of our country was leaving its impact upon and profoundly influencing the program and strategic direction of SCLC, as the primary mass-action organization of the Freedom Movement."[146]

The fall 1969 issue of *Freedomways* broadened its discussion of national minorities with a special on the American Indian and the Mexican American.

In the first-quarter issue of 1970, Ernest Kaiser presented the first of a two-part article, "In Defense of the People's Black and White History and Culture." Kaiser, in view of the demand for black studies, made a comprehensive analysis of American intellectual culture. He showed that the intellectual establishment was hostile to all progressive social philosophies. In the next issue he exposed reactionary black thinkers who opposed black studies. Kaiser supported the changing mood of black students and felt their demands for black studies would produce a wealth of material on black history.* He accused Roy Wilkins, Bayard Rustin, Kenneth Clark, Martin Kilson, Andrew Brimmer, and even John Hope Franklin of obstructing the progressive demands of black students for black studies.

In an article published in 1970, John O'Dell suggested that the freedom movement or the black revolution, as it is sometimes called, is really the "motor and generator" for a broad spectrum of movements demanding the progressive reformation of American life. O'Dell continued what had been a serious and provocative commentary on the entire decade in an article titled "The Contours of the 'Black Revolution' in the 1970's." Reflecting on the freedom movement in the '70s, O'Dell pointed out that it "mirrors one of the major contradictions in American life and poses fundamental questions about the institutional structure of American society and the capacity of the present structure to solve problems of long standing existence."[147] While the movement had been directed primarily at racism rather than capitalism, O'Dell saw the possibility of a radical shift of focus. He expects that in the seventies the black revolution will no longer be black in an isolated sense but will become "a broadly based revolution of social emancipation and national regeneration drawing into its involvement a cross-section of ethnic groups and socio-economic classes, whose interests are tied to the kind of fundamental changes which our interest requires."[148]

Freedomways' coverage of education also suggested an evolutionary pattern. In 1964 an article by Jean Carey Bond, "The New York School Crisis: Integration for What?" was strongly supportive of the attempt to integrate the New York public schools. In 1968, however, *Freedomways* published a special issue describing the "crisis in education and the changing Afro-American community." This issue offered a number of articles which suggested that its authors were more concerned with relevant than with merely integrated education. In "Educational Values and Community Power" and "Lessons of the 201 Complex in Harlem," Milton Galamison and Charles E. Wilson discussed the explosive issue of community control of public school education. In "Education in the Black Community," Charles V. Hamilton suggested that black parents were most concerned about the entire set of values that a school communicates; the emphasis is no longer solely on the acquisition of verbal and mathematical skills.

In "New Directions in Education—1970," Rae Bands expressed

---

*Kaiser is on the staff of the Schomberg Collection, one of the largest black libraries.

concern over the alleged failure of compensatory education. She deplored the emergence of what she called "scientific racism," the attempt of "racist" sociologists, biologists, and psychologists to prove that blacks are genetically inferior and therefore can reach only a low level of educational achievement. After describing in detail the studies which support these views, she concluded that education for the black community must provide skills "to effectively increase the life changes of Blacks."[149]

Finally, in 1971, Dorothy Burnham attacked the validity of Arthur Jensen's article "How Much Can We Boost IQ and Scholastic Achievement?" In "Jensenism: The New Pseudoscience of Racism," Burnham deplored the fact that two years after the publication of the Jensen article "Head Start and other compensatory programs had been scuttled, funds for education at every level had been cut, welfare and medical programs had gone by the board, contributions of the federal government to the health and welfare programs of the beleaguered cities had been drastically cut."[150] In Burnham's view, a "totally false theory had been used as part of the program to deprive the disadvantaged of their right to education."[151]

In the early and mid-1970s *Freedomways* responded to various forms of racism and to the socioeconomic system of capitalism which buttressed racism. Whereas *Freedomways* in the 1960s emphasized the importance of SCLC in the fight for the poor, in the 1970s Jesse Jackson (formerly of SCLC) and his People United to Save Humanity (PUSH) gained considerable recognition. Two articles by Jackson, "Three Challenges to Organized Labor" (Fourth Quarter 1972), and "Confronting Monopoly and Keeping the Movement Moving" (First Quarter 1974), were of significance. PUSH was characterized by Jackson as a "civil economics" rather than a civil rights organization. However a more leftist and Marxist-Leninist presentation was Clarence J. Munford's "Travels in the Soviet Union—Manchild in the Land of Lenin." Munford, who has also written considerably in the *Black Scholar,* showed how the Soviet Union made the transition to socialism and thus eradicated the ills of capitalism (i.e., sexism, national oppression, poverty, and ignorance). His tour of Soviet Central Asia was of particular significance inasmuch as the nonwhite citizens of the Soviet Union did not wear the yoke of racism as a result of the socialist revolution led by Lenin.

There is much to suggest that *Freedomways* was beginning to respond in the seventies to attacks from white ultraconservatives over various forms of institutionalized racism. In addition to attacks on education, Arlene Bennet in "Eugenics and Institutionalized Racism" (1974) pointed to the potential dangers to blacks from influential whites who fear the "accumulation of bad or undesirable genes in a given population."[152] Those who fear "dysgenic threats" would therefore advocate sterlization of groups of people, namely blacks. Dr. Bennet also pointed to the danger involved in unethical research on human beings. The most likely subjects for this kind of experimentation are, for the most part, "the inner city Blacks and Hispanics who fill the hospital wards, make up the majority of prisoners, and fill the city public schools."[153]

Also in this issue (Second Quarter 1974) was a fact sheet explaining the circumstances of the trial of the North Carolina activist Reverend Ben Chavis. *Freedomways* thus showed firm support of political activists who faced political repression. In the last quarter of 1974 the editorial "Crisis of '74—Tasks of '75" pointed out that the inflation, taxes, unemployment, and political corruption of the Nixon administration were expressions of a developing depression which primarily hit the working class.

Declaring that the United States was moving backward, the editors pointed out that the two major political parties were instruments of the ruling class and protected the profits of this class. *Freedomways* consequently expressed the leftward direction of the movement. This should not be seen as a shift of focus, however, since many who were associated with the magazine from the start were part of the left even before World War II.

Reading *Freedomways* over a ten-year period answers important questions about the evolution of the freedom movement. The decade of the seventies has not completely revealed the forms the struggle will take, but John H. O'Dell and other thoughtful writers for *Freedomways* have begun to define the direction of the changes, even though the forms and occasions remain unclear.

By 1969 the transition to a conservative stance on black issues had begun in white intellectual journals, while black intellectuals had moved, even earlier, to a discussion of black nationalism. *The Black Scholar* makes it apparent that black intellectuals in the seventies seem to concern themselves first and foremost with fashioning an ideology to support and direct the liberation of the African world community.

In November 1969 *The Black Scholar* began publication with an issue devoted to "the culture of revolution," which made cultural revolution a priority on black intellectual's agenda. According to Guinea's president, Sékou Touré, control of culture can lead to domination or liberation. Interest in an African culture that would unite African people all over the world was reflected in Nathan Hare's "Report on the Pan-African Cultural Festival." In "A Black Value System," Imamu Baraka discussed the seven points in the Ujaama value system. Further emphasis was placed on Africa in Stokely Carmichael's essay "Pan-Africanism: Land and Power." Robert Chrisman, evaluating Harold Cruse's *The Crisis of the Negro Intellectual,* pointed out that Cruse was too personal, vague, and general in his book.

The general direction of *The Black Scholar* was a reflection of a sizable section of the black movement toward pan-Africanism. The February 1971 issue was the first of two in that year that focused on pan-Africanism. As Nkrumah's Ghana had substantially influenced *Freedomways* in the 1960s, Tanzania and Guinea influenced many young Afro-American activists in the 1970s. This February issue carried Julius Nyerere's (president of Tanzania) "African Socialism: Ujaama in Practice." In addition, this issue carried one of the many contributions by Shirley Graham, "The Liberation of Africa: Power, Peace and Justice." In fact, *The Black Scholar* was instrumental in persuading the State Department to allow Mrs. Graham's visits to this country, after her stay in African and Communist countries.

One of the most significant issues in 1971 was the March pan-African issue, which strongly indicated the ideological bent among black intellectuals at that time. The most significant articles were those by Charles V. Hamilton, S. E. Anderson, and Imamu Baraka. In "Pan-Africanism and the Black Struggle," Charles Hamilton asserted that the "Black struggle in the United States at this historical stage . . . must engage and deal with such . . . issues of survival as jobs, housing, education, community control of important decision making institutions."[154] He stressed that black Americans have a vital international role to play as well: "to utilize the resources of land, economics and ideology to maximize Black political power in this country in order to influence (reverse, neutralize) Western intervention in revolutionary developing Africa. This can only be done," he continued, "from within the United States, and it can only be done by an economically and politically powerful force within this country."[155]

In "Revolutionary Black Nationalism Is Pan-African," S. E. Anderson insisted that

we must begin to perceive revolutionary black nationalism as an interlocking stage in the world wide (Bandung) struggle against racism, imperialism, and capitalism. More precisely, Afro-Americans must institutionalize revolutionary Black nationalism not as a narrow and chauvinistic way of life, but rather a way of life that affirms its belief and faith in the Pan-African liberation Movement and a way of life that is flexible in the day to day growth of the domestic and international aspects of the struggle.[156]

In the "Pan-African Party and the Black Nation," Baraka called for the formation of a political institution which would move to fulfill and express the needs of black people wherever they are. This institution would first take the form of a political party, necessary as a preliminary organizing vehicle. Ultimately, Baraka envisioned, this political institution would evolve toward a nation, at which point it would be most effective in fulfilling and expressing the needs of blacks everywhere.

Also in this first issue was President Touré of Guinea's contribution, an article titled "The Permanent Revolution," which was to be one of many by him in *The Black Scholar*.

Editor Nathan Hare, in an editorial, sought to give content to the concept of pan-Africanism. Hare stated that the important struggle was a race struggle, as opposed to a class struggle. He did not accept racial chauvinism and Negritude, but called for the making of a new and revolutionary culture.

The Black Scholar's aim was to voice the broad interest of the black community and not just the interests of intellectuals. Therefore the special April–May 1971 issue focused on black prisoners. Of special note was an article by Angela Davis, "The Soledad Brothers," written while she was incarcerated as a political prisoner. The articles reflected a changing mood and attitude toward prisoners as victims of the system.

The section "Young Black Writers" in the September 1971 issue was the result of an essay contest in which there were three winners. The first prize went to Adolph Reed, Jr.'s "Pan-Africanism: Ideology for Liberation?" which was an assessment of the pan-African movement. It accused some pan-Africanists of being romantic and not realistic in dealing with the problem of blacks in the United States.

In the January 1972 issue, "The Black Colony: The African Struggle" focused on the African continent. An article by Sékou Touré was a further elaboration on culture and the role of the leadership of the movement. But of particular note was the article "Harvard's Investments in Southern Africa" by the Pan-African Liberation Committee. This article brought into bold relief the role of Harvard's investments in Portuguese imperialism in Africa. Through a detailed analysis of these investments the conclusion was reached that Harvard should divest itself of the stock.

By 1972 a new ideological center in the intellectual discussion was apparent and that center was Marxist-Leninist in influence. Certainly Marxist-Leninist ideas were not new to black intellectuals, for a number of them had strongly identified with communism in the thirties and forties. The recurrence of this ideological emphasis in the seventies is significant inasmuch as both the national liberation movements and the world socialist system, in their opposition to imperialism, challenged bourgeois ideology and offered an ideological alternative for the black struggle. In February 1972, Robert Allen suggested, in an article titled "A Historical Synthesis: Black Liberation and World Revolution," that the domestic struggle by blacks against racism was intricately linked with the world struggle against imperialism. Allen continued: "If we admit that racism and cultural chauvinism are ideological and institutional components of imperialism, as I have tried to show, then it follows that their ultimate destruction will require the overthrow of imperialism."[157]

The impact of Marxist-Leninist ideology on the pan-African movement has led to the recognition of class divisions within the movement and the realization that racism is rooted in capitalist relations of production. Throughout 1972, articles written under a Marxist influence continued to appear.

The May 1972 issue included an article by Carl Bloice, "The Black Worker's Future under American Capitalism," which pointed out the nature of capitalist exploitation and the socioeconomic status of blacks. The leftward slant of this article was duplicated by two on Marxism-Leninism in the September 1972 issue. Earl Ofari, in "Marxism-Leninism: The Key to Black Liberation," gave a historical analysis of a Marxist-Leninist view on the national question and pointed to the limits of reforms and nationalism. He emphasized that each must be a step toward proletarian consciousness and that reforms must be seen as tactics that intensify the class struggle. Tony Thomas's "Black Nationalism and Confused Marxists" criticized the position of such groups as the Black Panthers (Eldridge Cleaver) and even Earl Ofari for not understanding Marxism-Leninism and the correct position on the national question. Thomas called for examination of the program of Malcolm X as a means to moving from nationalism to socialism by means of a black political party. Thomas, a member of the Trotskyist Socialist Workers Party, alleged that a Leninist position on the national question meant individual support of all nationalism. Thomas believed that nationalist sentiments of the black community should be channeled into a black political party which would be independent of both major parties.*

In 1973 *The Black Scholar* continued its discussion of pan-Africanism. At the same time, however, more and more articles written from a leftist perspective also appeared. An article in the February 1973 issue, by Robert Chrisman and Robert L. Allen, offered a flowing report based on a trip to Cuba. In "The Cuban Revolution: Lessons for the Third World," the editors offered Cuba as a shining example of "a revolutionary society which, by its example, is giving hope to oppressed peoples throughout the world."[158] In the same issue, Stokely Carmichael attempted to debate Marxist-Leninists with his own interpretation of the relationship between Marxism and Nkrumahism.

The July–August issue of *The Black Scholar* centered on "the pan-African debate." This issue, as reported in the editorial, was published in response to the growing ideological contradictions within the black movement. The debate was considered by the editors as crucial and not merely academic. Since some 100,000 people were active in the African Liberation Day march that preceding May, the crucial ideological content of future demonstrations could possibly emerge from such a debate. Robert Chrisman's opening article, "Aspects of Pan-Africanism," gave a historical survey of pan-Africanism and then engaged in criticism of Henry Winston's *Strategy for a Black Agenda: A Critique of New Theories of Liberation in the United States and Africa,* a third of which was devoted to pan-Africanism. Winston, chairman of the Communist Party U.S.A., had put forth the notion that pan-Africanism could remain progressive only if it remained anti-imperialist. Chrisman agreed with this but disagreed with Winston's analysis of black national consciousness (termed *neo-pan-Africanism* by Winston) and his criticism of various black leaders such as Carmichael, Baraka, Innis, Foreman, and Boggs. Chrisman's criticism focused on what he thought was Winston's limited understanding of the relationship between racism and capitalism, the formation of national black consciousness, Third World struggles, and the significance of Mao's concept of cultural revolution. Chrisman demonstrated that the leftward motion of the pan-African movement had created a new ideological exchange between various elements that had Marxist-Leninist sentiments.

---

*For a criticism of Tony Thomas's article see "Letters to *The Black Scholar*" (Donald Andrews), *The Black Scholar* (January 1973), pp. 59–60.

Numerous articles in this issue approached pan-Africanism from the left, yet most of the authors were influenced by Marxism-Leninism rather than being Marxist-Leninists *per se*. The exception was C. J. Munford's "The Fallacy of Lumpen Ideology." This article attempted to rectify any mistaken view that his previous article, "Social Structure and Black Revolution" (November–December 1972), which appeared next to Eldridge Cleaver's "On Lumpen Ideology," had anything in common with Cleaver's work. Munford exposed Cleaver's "lumpen as vanguard" thesis as a means to attack the international Communist and worker movement. Munford showed Cleaver's ideology as an eclectic mixture of "populist egalitarianism, anti-technologism, and demo-fascism,"[159] while Munford's world view was Marxist-Leninist. Munford showed how Cleaver's analysis of class relations was fallacious and how Cleaver's antiworking-class views and hatred for the working class led to his operating as an agent of monopoly capital. Munford not only criticized Cleaver but reevaluated his first article by pointing out its basic pitfalls and attributing these errors to his lack of consistent study of the classics and science of Marxism-Leninism.

The April 1974 issue had several articles dealing with the forthcoming Sixth Pan-African Congress and African liberation in general. The Sixth Pan-African Congress was of importance since it would be the first congress since the 1945 Manchester meeting. The response to the conference, as well as documents from it, appeared in the July–August 1974 issue. David Lawrence Horne gave a positive evaluation to the conference while Earl Ofari was critical and his perspective was more on the left. The speeches of Julius K. Nyerere and Sékou Touré were reproduced, and Touré in particular made a class analysis of pan-Africanism, calling for class struggle and, as well, condemning Negritude. Touré emphasized that revolutionary pan-Africanism must give impetus to the world revolutionary process.

Besides the Sixth Pan-African Conference, there was an important ideological conference in May, sponsored by the African Liberation Support Committee. Indeed, since the attention of the latter conference was on the ideological direction of the black movement, it was considered extremely important to many black political activists. Phil Hutchins' "Report on the ALSC National Conference" in this issue summarized this conference.* The pan-African movement by this point had taken a definite leftward swing, and an ideological battle was fought

---

*Hutchins was formerly the chairman of SNCC, following H. Rap Brown.

over whether race or class was at the heart of black oppression. Hutchins favored the ideological posture of the chief organizer of the ALSC, Owusu Sadaukai, and that of the Youth Organization for Black Unity (YOBU), whose members were close associates of Sadaukai, such as Nelson Johnson, Mark Smith, and Ron Washington. YOBU, through the early newspaper *African World* and work on ALSC, had argued that pan-Africanism must fight both capitalism and racism. Amiri Baraka, Stokely Carmichael, and others took positions, but Hutchins reported that the position of Sadaukai seemed to be the major thrust of ALSC. Of significance is the fact that those who followed the political line of Sadaukai were opposed to both the Communist Party U.S.A. and its antecedents, the Young Workers Liberation League and the Trotskyist Socialist Workers Party.

This leftward swing did not go unanswered by right-wing nationalists in the pages of *The Black Scholar*. In September 1974 Haki Madhubuti (Don L. Lee) wrote an article, "The Latest Purge: The Attack on Black Nationalism and Pan-Afrikanism by the New Left, the Sons and Daughters of the Old Left." Madhubuti saw the black struggle as a struggle against the white race and emphasized that whites were attacking black nationalism through the white left by infiltrating the ALSC and Baraka's Congress of African People and, consequently, coopting the black nationalist movement. Madhubuti held that Marxism was just another European ideology suited to the needs of white people and that white people, from antiquity, have been racist. This article intensified the ideological debate on class and race, and several articles appeared in a later issue, both in opposition to and support of Madhubuti.

Table 3–5 gives additional indications of the intellectual exchange in the three black intellectual journals. It is not exhaustive but it includes selective representations of articles which were important in the discussion of key issues. Articles appear in the table by subject rather than chronologically. The issues under discussion were either traditional exchanges or contemporaneous problems which reflected a changing mood. Table 3–5 is found on page 179.

SUMMARY AND CONCLUSIONS

It seems apparent that while some whites have been becoming more conservative, some blacks have been becoming more radical. Disappointment with the degree of change in the system, as well as recognition of the various contradictions in the system, led to a desire among some intellectuals to change the system itself. Black intellectuals who today espouse Marxist-Leninist ideas are relatively few, but their number and intensity seem to be growing. Other influential black intellectuals have gone on record in opposition to Marxist-Leninist views. *The New York Times* of February 11, 1975, for example, carried an article about Nathan Hare's resignation in protest of the Marxist emphasis he saw developing in *The Black Scholar*.* It is difficult, therefore, to know how much weight to place on what seems to be a developing trend among a small band of black intellectuals. There is such a trend, however, and those ideas are getting a hearing in black publications which have an articulate audience.

It may be said that the role of black intellectual journals has been as a forum for the exchange of ideas on the various issues in the black struggle. For the most part, articles that had the greatest influence were those that addressed the most immediate problems and sometimes the most controversial questions. Authors of these articles in black intellectual journals were not ivory-tower scholars but intellectual activists who were, both practically and theoretically, involved in the black struggle for equality and justice in this era. The weight of their influence over the rest of the black academic community is very difficult to assess quantitatively and qualitatively at this time, although an educated guess would assess it as small. One can be less tentative about their influence, direct or indirect, upon the black community in general; it is minuscule. Nevertheless, it seems obvious that the current ideological debate is a reflection of a change in the mood of some black intellectual activists.

---

*See the January 1976 issue of *Black World* for a more recent article by Nathan Hare on his views of the black struggle.

TABLE 3–5. INTELLECTUAL EXCHANGE IN THE THREE BLACK INTELLECTUAL JOURNALS

Subject	Author and Journal	Topic of Article
Education	E. Fannie Granton *Negro Digest* (June 1967)	In "New School of African Thought" Granton reported on Gaston Neal's school, which began in October 1966 and was designed for black cultural development. Stokely Carmichael, Sterling Brown, Owen Dodson, and A. B. Spellman were present for the opening.
Education and black studies on the white campus	Ronald Williams *Negro Digest* (January 1970)	In a review of *Black Studies in the University,* Williams outlined the varying positions of some influential black thinkers. Harold Cruse felt that integration hampered black cultural development and encouraged blacks to adopt a cultural-nationalist philosophy. Further, he emphasized the need for blacks to establish their own journals, periodicals, and theaters. Black and white cooperation would eventually emerge, according to Cruse, out of cultural pluralism. Ron Karenga called for a change in the frame of reference for blacks. Cultural self-determination, he asserted, would be the basis for black liberation.* Gerald McWorter (Abdul Hakimu Ibn Alkalimat) and Nathan Hare pointed to the ills of the educational system in 1969 but only broadly defined new alternatives. Martin Kilson opposed the idea that black people, because of their oppression, will be cleansed of all evils and stressed that the black issue must be viewed historically.
Africanization and education	Preston Wilcox *Freedomways* (Fall 1968)	In "Africanization: The New Input to Black Education" Wilcox stated that education for blacks must be part of a cultural revolution and tied to Africa. He felt the learning process should emphasize ethnic and private values rather than the broader public values, which tend to be color blind. Instead of promoting Americanism, therefore, black education should promote black group interest.
Future of black studies	Robert Allen *The Black Scholar* (September 1974)	In "Politics of the Attack on Black Studies" Allen pointed out that black studies and the demand for changes in education by black students was part of the militant black student movement of the 1960s. Those in the struggle recognized not

* Karenga is the creator of the Kawaida doctrine, a black value system, and the Kwanza ceremony. Kwanza is a substitution for "White" Christmas, and blacks celebrate the seven principles of Kawaida. Amiri Baraka supported this value system at this time. See "A Black Value System," *The Black Scholar,* (Nov. 1969).

Subject	Author and Journal	Topic of Article
		only the exclusion of black students and scholars from American higher education but the exclusion of the total black experience in America. Pressure by students led to the establishment of numerous black studies programs, but by 1972 such programs decreased because of attacks from the academic establishment.
Black studies and affirmative action	Sidney Walton *The Black Scholar* (September 1974)	Walton, in "Black Studies and Affirmative Action," urged black educators to recognize the importance of career and vocational training in black studies. It is the responsibility of black educators, according to Walton, to prepare students to qualify for jobs opened up by affirmative action programs and to give a black commitment to education. But he pointed out that black educators in white schools are underrepresented and are not able to offer, in white-controlled institutions, courses designed to meet the community needs of blacks.
Imperialism and black liberation	People's College *The Black Scholar* (September 1974)	"Imperialism and Black Liberation" is a summary of recent developments in the African Liberation Support Committee toward an anti-imperialist posture. People's College is in Nashville, Tennessee, and is an anti-imperialist collective of workers and students headed by Abdul Alkalimat (Gerald McWorter). This article also offers an outline of a study guide for understanding the relationship between black liberation and imperialism, drawing from various leftist sources.
Dr. Kwame Nkrumah and pan-Africanism	*Black World* (July 1972) (All three journals printed articles dealing with Kwame Nkrumah because of his prominence in the pan-African and the socialist movements.)	*Black World* produced a special issue on the death of Dr. Nkrumah. Among the many articles were "Kwame Nkrumah: Founder of African Emancipation" by C. L. R. James; "Nkrumah and Beyond" by Rududzo Murapa; "Nkrumah: The Great Internationalist" by the Committee for Political Development; and "A Message from Stokely Carmichael" (Carmichael was a supposed follower of Nkrumahism).
Dr. Kwame Nkrumah and pan-Africanism	*The Black Scholar* (May 1972)	This issue of *The Black Scholar* carried articles supposedly written by Nkrumah. "On the Ghana Coup" was thought to be a letter to Kofi Busia, who took power after Nkrumah was overthrown but in turn was overthrown in January 1972. This letter was said to have appeared in a Ghana newspaper in February 1972. The article was

Subject	Author and Journal	Topic of Article
		printed as a tribute to the memory of Nkrumah, but its authenticity was questionable and it was alleged that Nkrumah had not tried to write it and was not interested in writing such a letter.
Dr. Kwame Nkrumah and pan-Africanism	*Freedomways* (Second & Third Quarters, 1966)	Several articles appeared in *Freedomways* in 1966 in response to the coup in February. Two editors of *Freedomways*, Shirley Graham and Alpheous Hunter, were active participants in Nkrumah's Ghana. In the second quarter Christine Johnson wrote "Letter on the Coup" and in the third quarter Shirley Graham wrote "What Happened in Ghana: The Inside Story."
Harold Cruse ideological debate	Julian Mayfield *Negro Digest* (June 1968)	In "Crisis or Crusade" Mayfield pointed out that Cruse was carrying out a personal grudge against several black intellectuals and artists rather than offering an intellectual/social critique. This assertion of Mayfield's was important because Cruse's book, *Crisis of the Negro Intellectual*, was considered a tremendous work by many. Mayfield pointed out that the focus of the book was very narrow since it centered around the black activists in the Communist party in Harlem during the 1940s and '50s.
Harold Cruse ideological debate	Harold Cruse *Negro Digest* (November 1968)	Cruse responded to Mayfield in "Harold Cruse Looks Back on Black Art and Politics in Harlem." He asserted that Mayfield was not an original thinker and implied that this was a typical characteristic of those in the Communist black left, who merely rubber-stamp proposals of the party. Cruse's major theme was that the party allowed white nationalism within its ranks but not black nationalism. The article was very subjective and Cruse attacked many different people who had contact with Mayfield.
Harold Cruse ideological debate	Julian Mayfield *Negro Digest* (November 1968)	In "Childe Harold" Mayfield responded to Cruse and depicted him as a pathetic figure and an ultrablack nationalist. He called Cruse myopic because he could not see beyond New York during the war period. Cruse, Mayfield thought, missed the aim of the recent movement, which was to struggle against U.S. imperialism.
Harold Cruse ideological debate	Harold Cruse *Black World* (January, March, May 1971)	In *Black World* in January, March, and May 1971 Cruse had articles titled "Outlines in Black and White," which were excerpts from a forthcoming work. In January he attacked the first issue of *The Black Scholar* for having no relevance to black Americans. In his opinion, the differ-

Subject	Author and Journal	Topic of Article
		ences between the African and the Afro-American needed a totally different approach.
Commentary intellectuals	Ernest Kaiser *Freedomways* (First Quarter 1970)	Kaiser, in the article "In Defense of People's Black and White Culture" pointed out that a number of *Commentary* intellectuals were not only racist but were against the masses. Irving Howe, in "The New York Intellectual" (*Commentary*, Oct. 1968), attacked most leftists of the '30s and defended turncoats from the left. Howe criticized *Commentary*, Sidney Hook, and Irving Kristol for their light criticism of McCarthyism. Daniel Bell attacked Howe and his magazine *Dissent* for criticism of *Commentary*. Alfred Kogins (*Commentary*, Feb. 1970) discussed social criticism without ideology. Robert Heilbroner (*Commentary*, Dec. 1969) tried to prove that there was no future for socialism. Kaiser's aim in this article was to show how many establishment intellectuals had antiprogressive ideas and were antisocialist. His article was historically valuable because it analyzed the mood of white intellectuals as not merely a racial phenomenon.
Haki Madhubuti: race/class debate	Ronald Walters *The Black Scholar* (October 1974)	Walters supported Haki and attacked the Marxist-materialistic position that material reality determines consciousness. The movement toward Marxism was mistakenly seen by Walters as a means to become white. (Walters had been responsible for the exclusion of whites from the African Heritage Studies Association Conference earlier in April.)
Haki Madhubuti: race/class debate	S. E. Anderson *The Black Scholar* (October 1974)	Anderson opposed Haki and pointed out that the scientific world outlook of Marxism-Leninism is not white or black, like any other science. He felt Haki's position was a fetter on the world revolutionary process.
Haki Madhubuti: race/class debate	Mark Smith *The Black Scholar* (January–February 1975)	Smith opposed Haki. In probably the most thorough response to Haki's position, Smith criticized Haki for being anti-Marxist, narrowly nationalist, and ascientific. He also defended Marx and Engels from the accusation that they were racist, and stated that they provided the alternative to racism and the ideology necessary for black liberation.
Haki Madhubuti: race/class debate	Preston Wilcox *The Black Scholar* (March 1975)	Wilcox supported Haki, and saw Marxism-Leninism as a white ideology. He believed that racism was more than the ideological property of capitalism.

IV

THE CHANGING TONE
OF THE FEDERAL GOVERNMENT SINCE 1969

The preamble to the Constitution of the United States imposes a moral and political duty on the federal government to provide for the general welfare of its citizenry. The equal protection clause of the Fourteenth Amendment imposes upon the federal government the obligation to see that the constitutional rights of citizens are not abridged or diluted by policies and programs of the several states and their local communities. Thus blacks and other persons who have been deprived of their constitutional rights have legitimately appealed to the federal government for relief from this discriminatory status; or, to put it another way, blacks and other minorities have been compelled to seek assistance from the federal government to remedy inequities forced upon them by state laws, local ordinances, and other means. Due to the long history of nonfeasance of state and local governments in providing and making services available to black persons and those of other minority status, the federal government was the only means for redress of grievances. Therefore, a compelling-interest argument has been made charging the national government with protecting the rights and liberties of blacks by virtue of the Fourteenth Amendment.

The federal government, to state a truism, is composed of three branches: judicial, executive, legislative—equal in power and responsibility and designed to check and balance each other. This organizational form was intended to prevent despotism and achieve balance in a system designated as a political and social democracy. Neither the separation of powers nor the equality of power in each of these three branches has always worked as well in practice as in theory. From time to time it has appeared that one branch has in fact exercised ascendancy over the others; for example, Congress has had to delegate some of its legislative power to certain regulatory agencies which are regarded as quasi-legislative. Another example is when a strong president, as head of his political party, has controlled Congress very effectively, especially when he and the majority of congressmen are of the same party.

The reverse also holds. There have been eras in American history when one or more branches of the federal government seemed to abdicate their responsibilities to the citizenry and another branch stepped into the vacuum to shore up the promises and responsibilities of national government in this democratic system. It was the judicial branch of the federal government which found itself in this position of stepping into the void in the late 1940s and early 1950s with respect to the protection of the civil liberties and equal rights of citizens.

The courts took the lead in reasserting civil liberties after the Joseph McCarthy period. Also, the Supreme Court rendered landmark decisions outlawing white primaries and restrictive covenants in housing. As is well known, in 1954 this court rendered its decision that separate-but-equal was not equality in education. By these and other actions, it was the judicial branch of the federal government which took a leadership role in protecting civil liberties and equal rights of citizens in the decade following the end of World War II. This branch of the government continued to make decisions in that same direction up to 1969; but decisions have begun to take on a different tone in the decade of the seventies. The judiciary in the seventies is not unlike the executive and legislative branches in the seventies.

It is the feeling of blacks, other minorities, and the poor that the government, through each of the three major branches, has in the 1970s altered and reduced its forcefulness in supporting the minorities' struggle for full equality. Consequently these groups are now experiencing a reactionary change from that begun in the mid-fifties through the 1960s. This current, changing mood of the government has been described as one of "benign neglect," for the government—without a great deal of fanfare—has reduced its activities, which might have sustained or fostered enhancement of the rights and liberties of underprivileged groups.

JUDICIAL BRANCH

The following discussion will examine the changing mood of the judiciary through the mechanism of the United States Supreme Court, the highest tribunal of the land. The Supreme Court (hereafter referred to as the court) should not be looked upon as merely a court, for its broad discretion in deciding constitutional matters which affect the American populace makes the court a very important entity in the political process.[1]

This examination is a contextual analysis which will first look at the Warren court's equalitarian humanistic approach to constitutional issues. After that, decisions of the strict-constructionist Burger court will be presented to show the change in the court's view in various areas.

In his book *The Warren Court,* John P. Frank states the background of the court prior to Warren:

> Warren came to the Supreme Court at the nadir of its fortunes. Chief Justice Stone, who had served in that capacity from 1941 to 1946, was a very great justice, but far less successful in the special duties of a chief. Chief Justice Vinson, who followed him, was a man of splendid character and great dedication to his country, but had no particular talent for the business of being Chief Justice of the United States. The Court's opinion output had been a downward spiral so that, for example, in the year 1950, the Court had decided fewer cases than in any year since 1850.[2]

With the appointment of Warren as chief justice, the court became the most effective force for the protection and promotion of political, economic, and civil liberties. Cases decided during the Warren era reveal a radical shift to libertarianism as the court began a social revolution to remedy the residue of suppression resulting from McCarthyism. In doing so, the court became the viable force in addressing the constitutional rights of black people and other minorities.

In its dealings, the Warren court completed a revolution in American history which had begun during the Roosevelt New Deal. The court substantially and logically extended the constitutional guarantees of the individual, and in the meantime developed a dialogue of activism which in effect broadened the concepts of individual rights and liberties in the Bill of Rights.

From 1953 to 1969, the constituency of the court consisted variously of the chief justice and Associate Justices Black, Brennan, Douglas, Goldberg, Fortas, and Marshall, who formed the liberal activist bloc, with Justices Clark, Harlan, Stewart, and White voting as conservative strict constructionists.[3]

Chief Justice Earl Warren, governor of California at the time of the decision to incarcerate Japanese Americans in prison camps during World War II, had no history of being a liberal. In fact, President Eisenhower appointed Warren to the court because of his perceived conservative nature. At the Republican convention in 1952, Earl Warren sought his party's nomination for the presidency, and won the California delegation's first ballot. The other major candidates were Dwight D. Eisenhower and Senator Robert A. Taft of Ohio. Warren was eliminated from consideration, and the Republicans nominated General Eisenhower after many delegates revolted against the supporters of Senator Taft, who appeared to control the convention committees.

It was felt by many that the convention's weight was thrown to Eisenhower when California's Senator Nixon indicated he would seek the office of vice president on a ticket with Eisenhower. This move was a primary cause of Warren's being eliminated. Senator Nixon was presented as a fighter against Communist infiltration in the civil service. As a result of this maneuver, Nixon and Warren never became close friends. One year later Eisenhower became president, Chief Justice Vinson died, and Warren became Eisenhower's first choice to succeed Vinson.[4]

The justice who had served on the court the longest number of years was Hugo Black. In 1942 Black had dissented from the majority in *Betts* v. *Brady,* holding that the state has no obligation to appoint an attorney for one who is too poor to obtain one of his own.[5] In the years which followed, Black reiterated his dissent whenever the Sixth Amendment right to counsel arose before the court. In 1963, the issue was at bar in the case of *Gideon* v. *Wainwright,* and this time Justice Black spoke for the majority in overruling *Betts,* holding that one who is too poor to retain counsel cannot be afforded a fair trial unless counsel is provided for him.[6] Black strengthened his liberal stance from the late 1950s to the 1960s, which could not have been predicted when he was appointed to the court in 1937. Who would have thought a former Alabama Ku Klux Klan member would have such an impact on constitutional guarantees affecting equal representation, free speech, and desegregation?

Throughout William O. Douglas's thirty-six and one-half years on the court he consistently and emphatically supported individual rights and liberties. Douglas wrote with speed and meticulous accuracy. In addition to his courtroom work, he wrote over twenty books.

President Kennedy's 1962 appointment of a Jewish member, Arthur Goldberg, to the court represented a consistent commitment to the liberal majority and the side that supported judicial restraint. Again, in 1967, the liberal forces were strengthened by President Johnson's appointment of Thurgood Marshall, who was the first black ever to serve in this judicial position.

Justice John Harlan was the persistent spokesman for the more conservative judicial hands-off policy. As he assumed the role of chief dissenter, Harlan was often joined by the conservative Eisenhower appointees Potter Stewart and Charles E. Whittaker. The unpredictable "swing" vote came from Byron White, though he most often agreed with the Warren dissenters. Also on this side was Tom Clark, a long-time appointee of President Truman.

Warren, after being on the court less than a year, and his liberal court on May 17, 1954, unanimously announced the "most momentous opinion of American life after World War II." [7] The case was *Brown v. Board of Education of Topeka, Kansas,* where the court held that "in the field of education the separate but equal doctrine has no place."[8] Warren, in delivering the decision of the court, asserted that separate educational facilities are inherently unequal and are thus unconstitutional, for the practice clearly denies equal protection of the law. Warren referred to various studies by educators, psychologists, and sociologists to support his theory that segregated schools have a detrimental effect on black children since they perpetrate a sense of inferiority that has an adverse effect on a child's motivation to learn.

As a result of the decision, the court experienced very unpleasant repercussions. In defiance of the mandate, ninety-six Southern senators and representatives issued "a declaration attacking the Supreme Court and pledging themselves to use all lawful means to bring about a reversal of its decision, which, they asserted, was 'contrary to the Constitution' and to prevent the use of force in its implementations." Other criticism of the court charged it with aiding communism, invading states' rights, and basing the decision not on law but on sociological studies. In addition, school boards across the country refused to obey the court's mandate to desegregate. One year after the 1954 *Brown* decision, the court fashioned guidelines for implementing school desegregation on *Brown II.* The decision compelled the termination of dual school systems "with all deliberate speed" and called for the establishment of unitary systems "at once."[9]

To reaffirm and preserve the integrity of the *Brown* decisions, a unanimous court voted in *Cooper v. Aaron* (1958) not to postpone the Little Rock, Arkansas, desegregation plan, as proposed by state action. The court emphasized that even though the states are primarily responsible for public education, they must exercise [this] activity consistently with federal constitutional requirements as they apply to "state action," so that the officials are restrained from any attempt to nullify the court's order to desegregate public schools.[10] Subsequent decisions solidified the equalitarian court as state school authorities continued to ignore the court's mandate.

In 1964 the court stated in *Griffin* v. *County School Board, Prince Edward County, Virginia,* that "the time for more deliberate speed has run out."[11] Later, in 1968, the court emphasized in *Green* v. *County School Board of New Kent County, Virginia* that "the burden on a school board today is to come forward with a plan that promises realistically to work, and promises realistically to work now."[12]

The Warren court's activism in support of civil rights and liberties became an explosive political issue in the 1968 presidential campaign. GOP candidate Richard Nixon promised to replace the legal maxim of "justice in our time" and to restore "law and order" by changing the Supreme Court's personnel.[13] When Nixon won the election, he gained the opportunity to fulfill his aspiration, as well as his campaign promise to restructure the court, beginning in 1969, when Chief Justice Warren retired. Congress confirmed Nixon's nomination for the position, Chief Justice Warren Burger. Previously, Justice Fortas had been named a replacement for Warren, but opposition from Southern Democrats and right-wing Republicans, along with the disclosure that Fortas had accepted a fee from Louis Wolfson's foundation, forced Fortas to retire from the court. He was replaced by Burger's close friend from his home state of Minnesota, Harry Blackmun, after congressional rejection of two more conservative Nixon nominees, Clement Haynsworth and G. Harrold Carswell.[14]

Again, in September 1971, after several congressional rejections, Justices Lewis Powell and William Rehnquist came to the court at the retirement of Justices Black and Harlan. This gave the president a sufficiently strong hold on the court to perpetuate his conservative policies.[15] The fate of the Warren court's liberalism rested on Justices Marshall, Brennan, and Douglas.

The 1970 court term marked the beginning of the Burger court with a workload of cases, over 50 percent of which were in the areas of race, criminal procedure, First Amendment freedoms, and the election process.[16] With Burger and the new conservative court, minority groups began to experience limitations on the Warren court's liberal constitutional doctrines, as in the 1971 court term, which is a prime example.

In the school desegregation cases the court unanimously added the use of busing, concomitant with other devices, to eliminate the dual systems of state-supported elementary and secondary schools in the South.

In *Swann* v. *Charlotte-Mecklenburg Board of Education* (1971), Chief Justice Burger, speaking for the court, supported the use of busing as a tool for fulfillment of the state's constitutional obligation to desegregate public schools.[17] However, the court went further, stating that time and travel distance must be considered to assure they will not impose on the health or the process of educating the children being transported. Such a consideration, which is left to school boards, has operated as a mechanism to reject busing to achieve quality and integrated school systems. Justice Burger gave a narrow interpretation of the law on the controversial issue of busing and left determination of a remedy to the discretion of the lower federal courts.

One week after the court announced the *Swann* decision, it decided *James* v. *Valtierra* (1971). The subject of the case was low-rent housing, which indirectly related to school desegregation. A sharply divided court sustained a state constitutional provision that made it imperative for a majority of the electorate to vote approval of all proposals for low-income housing projects. Since most white voters in the middle- and high-income brackets do not want low-income housing in their neighborhoods, they will not vote in favor of such proposals. Thus the decision has an adverse effect on people with low incomes, and perpetuates *de facto* housing patterns and segregated schools.

> When *Valtierra* and *Swann* are reviewed together the following conclusion is evident: Even though the Burger Court handed down a unanimous and seemingly sweeping pronouncement in favor of the rapid termination of dual school districts, it underwent at least one important method for eliminating a dual school system (de jure and de facto) by permitting voters to prevent the construction of public housing in white areas—all in the name of reflecting a "devotion to democracy."[18]

However, four months later Chief Justice Burger announced in *Winston-Salem/Forsyth County Board of Education* v. *Scott* (1971) that *Swann* must not be interpreted as requiring school authorities to impose fixed racial balances or quotas in their desegregation plans.[19] Such seesaw action by the court has kept the purpose and function of busing in continuous controversy. Subsequent cases evidence the court's refusal to construe the holding of the desegregation cases. The court's only action has been to repeat the previous language.

Criminal procedure is another area in which the Burger court's impact through case law has deviated from the liberal court's mandate.

The Warren court's decision in *Miranda* v. *Arizona* (1966) required the accused to be informed of their rights and precluded the government's use of statements that had been illegally obtained.[20] But in *Harris* v. *New York* (1971), Chief Justice Burger, in writing the majority opinion, held that an illegally obtained confession could be used to impeach the accused's testimony.[21]

In *McKeiver* v. *Pennsylvania* (1971) the court ignored the plight of Southern youngsters who, without a jury trial, had been adjudged "juvenile delinquents" when they participated in civil rights protest, and it refused to impose jury trials and other constitutional protections in the stages of prosecution. The case essentially restated the state courts' doctrine of *in parens patriae* (guardian over persons under disability).[22] Such action had been retracted by the Warren court in *In re Gault* (1967).[23]

Justice Powell, in writing *San Antonio Independent School District* v. *Rodriguez* (1973), stated that education is not one of the fundamental rights guaranteed by the Fourteenth Amendment.[24]

Justice Brennan delivered the decision of the court in its first decision on school desegregation in the North, *Keyes* v. *School District No. 1, Denver, Colorado* (1973). Here the court did little but state: "We emphasize that the differentiating factor between dejure segregation and so called defacto segregation is purpose or intent to segregate."[25] However aggrieved, parties must prove segregated schools exist by intent, for there was no mandating for such.

Also notable with respect to school desegregation is Chief Justice Burger's opinion in *Milliken* v. *Bradley* (1974). The court refused to impose a statewide multidistrict remedy of desegregation on a finding of single-district *de jure* segregation in the absence of findings that the other districts or the state had committed acts that fostered segregation which had a "cross district" effect.[26]

Another example of the residue of the Warren court's activism was the unanimous opinion in *Griggs* v. *Duke Power Company* (1971). Chief Justice Burger ruled on the matter of employment practices (pre-employment testing and the seniority system) that appeared neutral on its face but in effect operated as a barrier to blacks seeking employment and upgrading. The court held that such practices are prohibited if there is no direct relationship with the job to be performed, despite the employer's lack of discriminatory intent.[27]

In 1975 the court readdressed employment discrimination in *Albemarle Paper Company* v. *Moody* (1975).[28] The respondents, black employees, sought injunctive relief against the company's seniority system, employment testing, and back pay policies, which allegedly discriminated against blacks (after nine years in lower federal courts). Justice Stewart, acting for the court, refused to invalidate all use of testing and remanded the case to the district court to decide the relief to be granted.

Public law, which encompasses cases brought by environmental, consumer, and civil rights organizations, has been critically affected by Justice White's opinion in *Alyeska Pipeline Service Company* v. *Wilderness Society* (1975).[29] The court refused to allow recovery of attorney fees for services rendered in the *Wilderness Society's* suit to bar construction of a pipeline by Alyeska.

The management of judicial review has also undergone significant changes which have adversely affected the interests of black people. (That which affects the allocation of the court's time and its disposition or nondisposition to intervene is part of the "management" of the court.) Limitations on standing, appeals, and class actions have reduced the ability of the court to come to the aid of black people seeking to redress policies and practices. Kenneth S. Tollett states the following on the changing management of the court:

> The managerial mind-set of the Chief Justice and some of his associates casts a shadow not only over the reliability of the court as an institution to redress the grievances and the violations of the rights of Blacks but also over the viability of the Court if Burger's Study Group on the caseload of the Supreme Court's recommendations for a National Court of Appeals are instituted. However, if the reliability of the Court is so suspect, then its viability may be a question of less concern.[30]

In essence, the holdings of the Burger court have been twofold: they have reaffirmed the traditional values and principles in the law and have declined to expand the law in civil and individual rights, criminal procedure and education, and other spheres.[31] The court has steadfastly reinforced state autonomy, placed limitations on accessibility to the court, and moved from strict scrutiny where suspect classifications are involved. With clearness of thought and style, the court has applied the ancient Fourteenth Amendment equal-protection concept, which adheres to the intent of Congress in construing a statute.

The court, in addition, has used the commerce power to protect the economic interests of big business. The impact of the Burger court on big business has been exemplified in cases which have in effect narrowed government regulatory laws, favored labor management (as opposed to unions), and defeated the majority of private suits for government enforcement against price fixing and environmental hazards.[32]

After four years of rarely disagreeing with his "Minnesota twin," Chief Justice Burger, Justice Blackmun has increasingly voted and spoken for the court in such a way which has excepted him from the conservative majority bloc. Even though Blackmun has begun to take an independent course, it is too soon to predict whether he has transformed enough to align himself with the liberal forces.

Due to physical illness, the long and outstanding career of a defender of free speech, Justice William O. Douglas, ended with his retirement on November 12, 1975. This left a vacancy on the court and gave President Ford the opportunity to choose the man to fill it. Little more than two weeks after Justice Douglas's retirement, President Ford nominated Judge John Paul Stevens as successor. At the time of his nomination, Stevens sat as a member of the United States Court of Appeals for the Seventh Circuit, which encompasses Chicago, Illinois. Unlike the slow-moving, controversial confirmations of the Nixon appointees, the Senate moved with assiduous speed, confirming this associate justice in less than one month. Not only was President Ford's choice one of the briefest nomination–confirmation–swearing in proceedings in recent times, the Congress voted unanimously, 98–0, to confirm him.

To date, Justice Stevens, the 101st justice of the court, has not been labeled either conservative or liberal. In view of the increasing number of critical issues facing the court, his vote will indicate what impact he will have on the court.

With the retirement of Justice Douglas the liberal force on the court was reduced to two, Justices Marshall and Brennan. Also under consideration is the viability of Justice Marshall, due to poor physical health. The concern of blacks and other minorities is that the retirement of another liberal will give the president the opportunity to appoint another justice, and it is reasonable to assume that future appointments will be closely attuned to the president's ideological position.

From the viewpoint of disadvantaged citizens, it is clear that the Burger court has rendered more conservative decisions than the Warren court. For some fifteen years the Warren court decided tough cases in favor of individual rights and was generally characterized by judicial activism. But the Burger court, thus far, usually renders judgments on the side of constituted authority and is characterized by judicial restraint.

This shift in the judiciary represents a changing mood. However, the future could be bleaker, with respect to the changing mood of the court, if it continues its disposition and nondisposition to intervene and not to intervene in matters previously presented in this book. Also, the composition of the court will affect the course of future decisions.

EXECUTIVE BRANCH

The president is the key figure in engineering the federal government's involvement in social reform. Robert M. Solow and Eli Ginzburg concluded that "no one else is likely to be able to fashion the required public consensus on goals and to get and maintain the required Congressional support—especially on those occasions when the situation calls for major reforms on several fronts."[33] Similarly, the U.S. Civil Rights Commission concluded in its report for 1970 that responsibility for the success or failure of civil rights enforcement lay primarily with the occupant of the Oval Office.[34] Both Presidents Kennedy and Johnson embraced the opportunity to marshal the resources of the nation to bring about social reform. Both men held an "activist" view of the presidency, believing that it was their role to serve as the prime mover in governmental action.

Richard Nixon also expressed a belief in the "activist" view of the office. In an interview in 1968, he observed that the president "must articulate the nation's values, define its goals and marshal its will." He predicted that "under a Nixon Administration, the Presidency will be deeply involved in the entire sweep of America's public concerns."[35] Once in office, President Nixon demonstrated that his conception of the nation's goals and the nature of the federal government's involvement in social problems differed sharply from that of his predecessors. Gerald Ford continued Nixon's domestic policies, although in a somewhat acrimonious manner. The survey of presidential political philosophies which follows reflects how the attitude of the federal executive toward social change underwent a marked shift after 1969.

John F. Kennedy's first State of the Union message made clear his commitment to the vigorous involvement of the federal government in social reform. Although he acknowledged the constraints imposed by fiscal considerations, he asserted that "we will do what must be done." The new president reproved the country with the observation that "our national household is cluttered with unfinished and neglected tasks." Kennedy then outlined a domestic program that included programs to aid housing, education, and health care for the aged. He referred to civil rights as an issue which "disturbs the national conscience" and sullies the image of the United States in the eyes of newly independent nations.[36]

In February 1962 and again in June 1963, Kennedy addressed the nation on civil rights, identifying himself and the executive branch with the goals of the movement. But despite the unassailable commitment and vigor of the Kennedy administration, its record of substantive achievement was meager. The narrowness of his electoral victory, the intransigence of a conservative Congress, and the brevity of Kennedy's tenure in office limited the amount that he could accomplish. Kennedy's assassination elevated to the presidency a man who was able to wield the powers of that office to achieve social reforms with far greater effectiveness.

In a passage from one of his famous civil rights speeches, Lyndon B. Johnson revealed the alacrity with which he used the powers of the executive branch to effect social change. After relating his experience as a young man in Texas teaching poor Mexican Americans, Johnson said: "It never occurred to me in my fondest dreams that I might have the chance to help the sons and daughters of those students, and to help people like them all over this country. But now I do have that chance. And I'll let you in on a secret—I mean to use it."[37]

It would be difficult to imagine a chief executive subscribing to an activist view of the presidency more fully than did Lyndon Baines Johnson. In his first State of the Union message, which he delivered on January 8, 1964, Johnson unveiled a legislative program of staggering proportions. Heading the list was his expectation that the 89th Congress would do more to advance the cause of civil rights "than the last 100 sessions combined." He also announced his intention to wage an "unconditional war on poverty." Among his other proposals were enactment of legislation to provide medical care for the aged, assistance for mass transit systems, support for teacher training programs, and expansion of the food stamp program. Johnson challenged the Congress to build "more homes, more schools, more libraries and more hospitals than any single session of Congress in the history of our Republic." The president pointed out that he expected his proposals to be enacted forthwith: "All this and more can and must be done. It can be done by this summer."[38]

Johnson moved quickly to allay the fears of those who doubted his commitment to civil rights because of his Southern background. In a message delivered to Congress four days after Kennedy's death, he contended that the time for deliberation had passed. His very first priority was passage of the pending civil rights bill.[39]

During the last half of his administration, the war in Vietnam, urban rioting, and the white backlash shattered the community of support that had developed for Johnson's domestic programs. Yet the president persevered in his advocacy of the Great Society. Although he conceded that the demands of the war made it impossible to fund the antipoverty program at the level he had hoped, Johnson maintained that it would have been cruelly inconsistent to abandon poor Americans in order to support the Asian war effort. He argued that the wherewithal to conduct the war should not be exacted from "those who are most in need."[40]

In response to urban rioting, Johnson proposed to aid local law enforcement agencies to "deal promptly with disorder," but he also maintained that "despair and frustrated hopes in the cities" could be dispelled "only by attacking the causes of violence and only where there is civil order founded on justice." The president renewed his pledge to "rebuild our cities" by sponsoring construction of new housing and providing jobs for the hard-core unemployed.[41]

Johnson also responded to charges made by conservatives that the government was doing too much for the poor and that the administration of Great Society programs was less than efficient. The president conceded that there were "some failures" among his programs. He called for the improvement and reorganization of some agencies. But at the same time he insisted that the government should not slacken its effort until it had "broken the back of poverty."[42]

By 1968 the divisiveness and rancor evoked by the war had consumed Johnson's "finite stock of political capital and led to his departure from office."[43] At a farewell reception, Johnson concluded that the social advances made during his administration were "infinitesimal" compared to what he felt needed to be done in the future. According to the president, the quality of American life would depend upon how the nation responded to its poor. He warned:

> If we turn a deaf ear to them, or if we try to patronize them, or if we simply try to suppress their impatience and deny its causes then we are not going to solve anything. All we are going to do is compound our trouble.[44]

Like his predecessor, Richard Nixon, when he assumed the presidency, held the belief that the chief executive "must take an activist view of his office."[45] Yet the point of departure for the activism of Richard Nixon was far different from that of Lyndon Johnson. Rather than bringing the plight of the underprivileged to the attention of the nation, Nixon maintained that "no generation has ever enjoyed higher incomes, better health and nutrition, longer life expectancy or greater mobility in their lives than we do today."[46]

The sense of urgency to rectify social inequities that characterized the Kennedy and Johnson administrations seemed entirely lacking in Nixon's administration. Nixon seemed to suggest that the federal government had attempted to do far more to aid the disadvantaged than it should have.

The Nixon administration's policy of delay and retreat on school desegregation was one indication that the mood of the chief of the executive branch toward social reform had changed drastically. On July 3, 1969, it was announced that cutting off federal funds would no longer be relied upon to ensure compliance with desegregation guidelines. Instead, the government's primary weapon would be litigation initiated by the Justice Department. The U.S. Civil Rights Commission complained that the shift in policy would greatly weaken the effectiveness of the administration's efforts to achieve desegregation. According to *Congressional Quarterly,* the new Nixon policy was a "major factor" in the refusal of forty Southern school districts to carry out previously agreed upon plans for desegregation.[47]

In August 1969, Robert Finch, secretary of the Department of Health, Education, and Welfare, made the unprecedented move of interceding to ask the courts to postpone a deadline for desegregation. Several lawyers for the Justice Department were so disgruntled by Finch's action that they resigned in protest. *Congressional Quarterly* concluded that in his first year as president, Nixon had "severed the longtime alliance of the federal government with civil rights advocates in school desegregation cases."[48]

In February 1970 the administration demanded the resignation of Leon E. Panetta, director of the Office of Civil Rights for HEW. Panetta attributed his dismissal primarily to Nixon's displeasure over his attempts to enforce school desegregation. Collaborating with Peter Gall, Panetta recorded his experience at HEW in a volume titled *Bring Us Together: The Nixon Team and the Civil Rights Retreat.* He charged that during the first fifteen months of his presidency, Nixon "lowered the priorities for social programs that benefited the poor black and poor white communities." The former administration official considered the president's desegregation policy to be "the grossest kind of insult and threat to the minority community."[49]

In March 1970, President Nixon outlined his position on desegregation. He insisted that he was not "backing away" from the intent of the *Brown* decision of 1954, but he also contended that the implementation of that decision required an "area of flexibility." Nixon noted his administration's opposition to busing pupils "beyond normal geographic school zones." Another tenet of the Nixon policy was that the government should confine itself to removing instances of *de jure* segregation. The president explained that although *de facto* segregation was "undesirable," it was "not generally held to violate the Constitution" and consequently he would make no effort to combat it.[50]

In June of that same year the resignation of the commissioner of education, James E. Allen, was demanded. The preceding April Allen had publicly vowed to eliminate both *de jure* and *de facto* segregation.

In August, Justice Department lawyers argued before the Supreme Court against the use of busing to achieve racial balance. In April 1971 the court ruled that busing was an acceptable tool to achieve integration, but Nixon insisted that the decision made reference only to instances of *de jure* segregation. Countering the thrust of the decision, Nixon proposed a moratorium on new busing orders and instructed the attorney general to intervene whenever the lower courts exceeded what he interpreted to be the constitutional requirement for desegregation. In October 1972, Nixon pledged to secure a halt to court-ordered busing, either through legislation or a new amendment to the Constitution. He asserted that finding a means to halt busing was "a matter of highest priority."[51]

Similarly, Nixon's position on open housing reflected a clear change in mood from the previous administration. The president maintained that he would push for open housing "only to the extent that the law requires." Even more explicitly, he stated: "I can assure you that it is not the policy of this government to use the power of the Federal Government . . . for forced integration of the suburbs."[52]

The general thrust of the administration toward social reform as it related specifically to blacks was epitomized by Daniel Patrick Moynihan's much publicized memorandum of March 1970 in which he suggested ways by which the administration could improve its relationship with the black community. Moynihan recommended that Nixon call a meeting to improve communications between officials who dealt with blacks, that research on crime be intensified, and that an appeal be made to the "silent black majority." The greatest amount of controversy was caused by his recommendation that "the issue of race could benefit from a period of 'benign neglect'."[53] Predictably, the reaction of civil rights supporters was hostile. A statement, issued jointly by several organizations and leaders, charged that the administration had launched a "calculated, aggressive and systematic effort . . . to wipe out all the civil rights gains made in the 1950's and 1960's."[54]

It was not only in regard to policies relating to black Americans that the president appeared to be attempting to reverse advances that were made by the previous administration. Twice, in 1972 alone, Nixon vetoed what he termed "inflated appropriations" for HEW. Incongruously, he professed in his veto message that his administration was "second to none" in its "concern and clear accomplishments" in regard to areas falling under the purview of HEW.[55]

Nixon also vetoed the Rehabilitation Act of 1972 (H.R. 8795) and the Public Works and Economic Development Act Amendments (H.R. 16071). In addition, the president attempted to bring about the dissolution of the Office of Economic Opportunity by halting the funds necessary for its functioning. According to Nixon, the functions of OEO would be carried out with greater facility if they were transferred to other departments.[56]

The president's domestic policies were consistent with his aim to bring about a "new federalism, in which power, fund and responsibility will flow from Washington to the states and the people."[57] The implications of the "new federalism" were ominous for the poor and disadvantaged. Ginzburg and Solow decried the absurdity of expecting that "state and local governments will look out solicitously for the interests of the designated beneficiaries of federally financed programs."[58]

Vernon E. Jordan, executive director of the National Urban League, observed that in view of blacks' historical reliance upon the federal government to relieve the injustices perpetrated by state and local authorities, the new federalism appeared to be like "hiring the wolf to guard the sheep." Jordan was very sensitive to the impact of federal programs on aid to the disadvantaged. Before a National Press Club audience in 1973, he lambasted cutbacks in federal support for employment, housing, education, and health care. Jordan observed that Nixon appeared to be making an effort to "destroy the social reforms of the 1960's."[59] Although the Watergate scandal proved to be Nixon's undoing, his policies continued without any substantive alteration under the direction of the man he had personally chosen to be his successor.

During an interview on the occasion of the first anniversary of his presidency, Gerald Ford observed that the policies of his administration did not differ significantly from those of his predecessor.[60] Despite the heavy losses suffered by the Republicans in the 1974 elections, the president perceived no mandate for a return to the social activism of the Kennedy and Johnson years. On the contrary, he concluded that the election results reflected an "urgent demand for fiscal restraint."[61]

In his first State of the Union message, which was delivered on January 15, 1975, Ford charged that in the past the federal government had been "self-indulgent" in granting "ever-increasing levels of government benefits." He pledged that the only new spending programs that would escape his veto were those designed to spur the development of new energy sources.[62] In his first year in office, Ford vetoed thirty-five bills. Among them was the Rehabilitation Act (H.R. 14275), and in his veto message the president explained that although the bill was "certainly worthy" in its intent, he would not affix his signature to it partly because of the adverse effect it might have on the economy.[63] Another of Ford's vetoes blocked an appropriation bill that provided $2.9 billion in aid to education. The veto was condemned by the National Education Association as a "national disgrace."[64] The president also vetoed subsidies for middle-income housing.

The Ford policy on busing to achieve desegregation was almost identical to the Nixon policy. When asked for his reaction to appeals for federal assistance to quell violent opposition to busing from Mayor Kevin White of Boston in October 1974, the president made the gratuitous observation that he had "consistently opposed forced busing."[65] The U.S. Civil Rights Commission charged that Ford's remarks contributed to the resistance of the residents of South Boston to the busing plan which had been ordered by a federal court.[66] One year later, the president met with Senator John Tower of Texas to discuss alternatives for preventing the use of busing to achieve desegregation.

Another means of assessing presidential attitudes in documenting a changing tone of the executive branch of government is to look at the budget recommendations of each president as originally submitted to Congress, because fiscal resources ought to be related to desired policies, goals, and objectives. During the early 1960s, the growth of the federal budget was kept to a minimum. Between 1961 and 1965 it grew by only $5.2 million, with the major increases in space, income management (Social Security), and physical resources (highways and water). In the second half of the decade, government expenditures increased rapidly in response to the demands of the war in Vietnam and Great Society programs. The first budget presented by President Johnson reflected his desire to build the Great Society; he placed emphasis on expenditures for health, education, and welfare programs and downplayed defense spending. Johnson also made note of the need to keep the budget from getting out of control.

In presenting his budget for fiscal year 1966, Johnson was aware that some legislators did not believe it possible to finance both "guns and butter." Addressing himself to that problem, he maintained that government expenditures ought to reflect a substantial commitment to the Great Society and noted that until defense spending declined, expenditures would necessarily increase markedly.

The effect of the war was more clearly evident in Johnson's proposed budget for 1967, when the war added $10.5 billion to the budget. In his presentation to Congress the President included tables which indicated what the government's expenditure could have been had it not been for the drain of the war. Still, Johnson maintained that the government could and should provide guns and butter, by proceeding with Great Society programs at a more moderate level of funding and by enacting new taxes. Conservatives in Congress were unmoved by his admonitions against abandoning the war on poverty in order to pursue the war in Vietnam.

As part of his budget request for fiscal year 1968 the president asked for a 6 percent surcharge on corporate and individual income taxes. Having failed to get it, he went back to Congress with a request for a 10 percent surcharge and warned that failure to enact the tax would result in a $29 billion budget deficit. Congress responded by passing an appropriations bill that required executive agencies to spend $9.1 billion less than the president had requested in his budget. Congress exempted war expenditures and other "uncontrollable" budget items from its restrictions. The following year, Congress enacted the tax surcharge, with the proviso that there had to be a $6 billion reduction in federal spending.[67]

During the Johnson administration, defense expenditures increased from $52 billion to $81 billion—an increase of about $29 billion. During the same period, expenditures for education and manpower increased from $1.5 billion to $6.5 billion; for health, from $1.3 billion to $11.6 billion; and for community development and housing, from $288 million in 1965 to $1.9 billion in 1969.

Just before leaving office, President Johnson submitted a budget for the 1970 fiscal year in which he proposed a modest increase in defense spending, as well as increased expenditures for urban aid and education and substantial increments for health and welfare. After his inauguration, President Nixon undertook his own study of the budget and in April he announced his priorities. In accord with the new president's wishes, Congress trimmed the budget that Johnson had proposed by $5.8 billion.

The budget for fiscal year 1971 was the first for which Nixon was completely responsible. Reflecting the priorities that were to characterize the first four years of his administration, Nixon proposed $14.4 billion in new expenditures and cut $11.5 billion from some programs that were already extant. He cut $5.2 billion from the defense budget and $400 million from the space program. Of the $14.4 billion in increased expenditures in the 1971 budget, $10 billion were mandated by "uncontrollable" items, such as Social Security, Medicare, and Medicaid. Since these increases were required by law, the president was not responsible for them. According to an analysis of the budget by the Brookings Institution, Nixon's budget presented "a major initiative" in the field of income maintenance through his family assistance plan. His goals in housing were termed "somewhat smaller, but still ambitious." In his housing proposals, Nixon put major emphasis on rural development. Also, according to the Brookings analysis, water pollution was a major concern (the president slated $4 billion to fight water pollution at the rate of $1 billion per year for four years). Revenue sharing was another priority item, although it only received an initial allocation of $300 million.

On the other side of the ledger, the Brookings report concluded that Nixon had decided "against any additional large sums for the major education and health programs." In fact, the education budget for 1971 was less than it was in 1969 or 1970. According to the report, "almost all" assistance to educational institutions was cut back by President Nixon in the 1971 budget.[68]

In his budget message Nixon pledged to bring the economy back under control by "reducing," "restructuring," and "terminating" many of the "overcommitments of the past," and apparently education was one of the items on which the ax fell hardest.[69]

An examination of Nixon's allocations for the Department of Health, Education, and Welfare sheds some light on the nature of his commitment to domestic programs. Nixon allocated $64.8 billion to the department, an increase of about $7 billion over the amount that was allocated for it the previous year. At first glance, that appears to indicate a strong commitment on the part of the president to HEW programs, but analysis reveals that of the $7 billion in increased allocations, $6.3 billion were mandated by increases in Social Security, Medicare, and Medicaid benefits over which the president had little if any control.

The president termed his budget for 1972 a "full employment" budget, which is to say that spending was scheduled for the same level that corresponded with a full-employment economy. The president listed five categories of spending that would be his priorities for the year: revenue sharing, human needs (health care, civil rights, crime prevention), foreign aid, the environment (ecology, housing, community development), and reorganization and reform of the government.

Of the funds allocated for revenue sharing, $5 billion were to be issued as general grants and an additional $11.1 billion were to be expended in urban and rural community development, education, manpower training, law enforcement, and transportation. Nixon took particular pride in the fact that in 1971 and in 1972 he had proposed spending more to meet "human needs" than for defense.[70] In fact, 42 percent of the budget was spent on human resources in 1971 and only 34 percent was allocated for defense. For the fiscal year 1973, Nixon noted that fully 45 percent of his budget was to be spent for human resources while only 31.8 percent was to be used for defense purposes. However, an analysis of the budget by *Congressional Quarterly* questioned whether the relative increases in human resources spending were true reflections of Nixon's priorities. *Congressional Quarterly* concluded that

> the relative uncontrollability of most of the human resources expenditures showed that the shift taking place in proportionate spending for human resources and defense since fiscal 1968 was due primarily to the inexorable growth in commitments under human resources programs, some of long standing and not to initiatives of the Nixon Administration, although the administration claimed credit for the change.[71]

Further, it was noted in the *Congressional Quarterly* analysis that nearly 71 percent of the budget went for "uncontrollable" items. Of the remaining funds over which the administration had some discretion, nearly two-thirds were allocated for defense purposes. In addition, of the $110.8 billion allocated for human resources in the budget for 1973, uncontrollable items accounted for $91.4 billion (Social Security, unemployment compensation, veterans' benefits, Medicaid, etc.).

In a radio address on the budget for 1974, Nixon again pointed out that, under his administration, "instead of spending one-third of our budget on human resources and nearly half of our budget on defense as we were doing in 1969—we have exactly reversed those priorities." At the same time the president warned of "some very sharp reductions in some very familiar programs." Specifically, he referred to federal aid to hospital construction, urban renewal, and aid to schools near federal facilities.[72]

The budget for fiscal year 1975 revealed apparent shifts in priorities. *Congressional Quarterly* observed that although the president certainly did not become a champion of social activism, neither did he continue the attacks on existing programs that had characterized his previous budget messages. Instead, the president appeared to be motivated by an attempt to pull the economy out of recession. One clear shift in policy was the addition of 22,200 civilian employees to the federal payroll. The budget also recommended an additional $34.2 billion in pay and benefits for employees. Frederick V. Malek, assistant director of the Office of Management and Budget, was quoted as saying that the president was committed to avoiding recession: "If it means busting the budget, then he will bust the budget rather than keep people out of jobs." But with the exception of that apparent shift, *Congressional Quarterly* reported that Nixon's recommendations "continued budgetary trends begun during previous administrations or previous Nixon years."[73] The familiar themes of restraining the activity of the federal government and increased state, local, and individual responsibilities were sounded once again.

Gerald Ford transmitted his first budget message to Congress on February 3, 1975, for fiscal year 1976 and outlined the five areas that were the priorities of his administration.

> Tax reductions and aid to the unemployed to stimulate economic recovery
>
> New energy programs
>
> Increased defense spending
>
> A year-long moratorium on all new federal spending programs other than those related to energy development
>
> A 5 percent ceiling on pay raises for federal employees and all individuals who received benefits from the government that were tied to changes in consumer prices

The basic themes that were sounded in Nixon's last budget were repeated by President Ford. Although he proposed new outlays for defense spending, Ford boasted that in his budget the proportion of money spent on defense would be less than that spent on human resources and revenue sharing. As Nixon had done in the 1975 budget, Ford expressed increased concern for the plight of the unemployed but, at the same time, clamped down on new federal spending.[74]

Presidential use of the veto provides still another indication of the priorities of the chief executive. Presidents Kennedy and Johnson made only sparing use of the veto in comparison to Nixon and Ford. The Democratic presidents each rejected thirteen public bills during their administrations. Neither of them had a veto overridden by Congress, which was controlled by their party. Nixon vetoed twenty-eight public bills during his first term, four of which were overridden. Ford vetoed twenty-four public bills during his first five months in office and four of them were overridden. Kennedy and Johnson appeared to use the veto on a case-by-case basis, while the Republican presidents appeared to use the veto as a policy-making instrument for retrenchment of federal involvement in social reform.

Most of the bills vetoed by Kennedy had few long-range policy implications. Three of the five bills he vetoed during his first year in office dealt with the District of Columbia. During the period 1963 to 1965, President Johnson vetoed only four public bills, none of which dealt with social reform.[75]

Beginning in 1966, the rising costs of the war in Vietnam were reflected in Johnson's use of the veto. The first bill (H.R. 2035) that he vetoed in that year was intended to increase the payments for "star route postal contracts." The president termed the measure "inflationary." In 1967 he vetoed a bill (H.R. 6926) that would have increased life insurance coverage for federal employees, because the bill called for expenditures that exceeded his budget request by $48 million.

Johnson's veto of a crime bill for the District of Columbia during the same year revealed his concern for the protection of civil liberties. The omnibus crime bill (H.R. 5688) would have made it easier for Washington police to exact legally binding confessions from defendants and would have given the police the right to hold persons in custody for up to four hours without charging them with a crime. Johnson objected to the draconian measures which would be legalized by the bill and suggested that a more appropriate way to fight crime would be by improving the administration of the police department. He noted that he had been urged to veto the bill by civil rights groups and the District of Columbia Bar Association.[76]

In no instance during the Kennedy and Johnson administrations was the veto used to curtail new social reform legislation. Nixon and Ford were to break with that trend and make vigorous use of the veto as a means of shaping public policy. During his first four years as president, Richard Nixon issued more than twice as many vetoes of public bills as were issued during the eight years of the Kennedy and Johnson administrations. Generally, Nixon's vetoes were motivated by his dual policy goals of attenuating the federal government's involvement in social reform and limiting the growth of the federal budget. His first veto blocked a $19.7 billion appropriation for the Office of Economic Opportunity and the Department of Labor and Health, Education, and Welfare. That appropriation exceeded his budget request by $1.1 billion. He was particularly unhappy with the part of the bill that provided aid to education in impacted areas. In vetoing the bill, Nixon stated that it would have required "excessive" increases in federal spending.

The president also blocked Congress's appropriations for the Department of Housing and Urban Development, the Veterans Administration, the National Aeronautics and Space Administration, and other agencies. This bill (H.R. 17548) provided $541 million over the amount that he had requested. Similarly, a bill (H.R. 17089) that would have adjusted the pay scales of federal blue-collar workers to make them comparable to those in private industry was checked by a Nixon veto.

One of the president's most controversial acts was his veto of the two-year extension of the Office of Economic Opportunity in 1972 (S. 2007). Nixon charged that the OEO extension bill was an indication of Congress's "fiscal irresponsibility." Some $2.1 billion of that OEO appropriation were to be used to support child-care centers. Nixon attacked the program on the grounds that it was too expensive and that it would serve to weaken the family structure.

Nixon was successful in blocking these various bills, but his vetoes were overridden on four occasions during his first term. For example, his attempt to veto the $2.79 billion appropriation for continued implementation of the Hill-Burton Hospital Construction Act (H.R. 11102) was thwarted. Similarly, his veto of the $4.4 billion appropriation for the Office of Education (H.R. 16916) was overridden, as were his vetoes of a bill to increase pension benefits for retired railroad employees (H.R. 15927) and the Federal Water Pollution Control Act (S. 2770).

To ensure that his vetoes could not be circumvented, the president

made use of the pocket veto.* Nixon's pocket veto of the Vocational Rehabilitation Bill (H.R. 8395) prevented an almost inevitable override.
The Rehabilitation Bill, which would have provided vocational rehabilitation services for the handicapped, was passed overwhelmingly by the
House and the Senate; nevertheless, the president complained that the
appropriation exceeded his budget request. He also charged that the
commissions that would have been established by the bill to study the
problems experienced by the handicapped with housing, employment,
and transportation would "waste the taxpayer's dollars."

Among the bills pocket-vetoed by Nixon during his first term were
the following:

> H.R. 16654, a revised appropriation bill for the Departments of
> Labor and HEW, which was enacted after Nixon vetoed S. 2007
> H.R. 56, which would have established a data bank for information
> related to environmental concerns
> H.R. 16071, which would have extended the Public Works and
> Economic Development Act of 1965 through 1974
> S. 4018, which would have supported the construction and repair of
> public works on rivers and harbors
> H.R. 10880, which would have provided $450 million for the ex-
> pansion of health care for veterans
> H.R. 14424, which would have established a National Institute for
> the Aging
> H.R. 15657, which would have established a fifteen-member coun-
> cil as a federal lobby for the aged.[77]

Nixon's overwhelming electoral victory in 1972 did not slacken his
use of the veto. Among the bills which met with presidential disapproval
in 1973 were the following:

> H.R. 3298, which would have extended federal aid to rural com-
> munities for construction of water and sewer lines
> H.R. 7935, which would have raised the minimum wage in two
> stages, first to $2.00 and then to $2.20
> S. 504, or Emergency Medical Services.[78]

---

*The pocket veto is an indirect veto of a legislative bill by a president who retains the bill
unsigned on his desk until after Congress has adjourned, either for the year or for a
specified period. When Congress is in session a bill becomes law without the president's
signature if he fails to act on it within ten days, excluding Sundays, from the time it
reaches him. However, if Congress adjourns within that ten-day period, the bill is dead
without the formal veto of the president.

Despite his troubles stemming from the Watergate investigations, President Nixon managed to issue, and make stick, two vetoes in 1974, before being forced to resign. In March, Nixon vetoed the Emergency Energy Bill (S. 2589), and on August 8, the day before his resignation became effective, he vetoed an appropriation bill for the Department of Agriculture and the Environmental Protection Agency.[79]

Gerald R. Ford proved to be a worthy successor to Nixon in his use of the veto. On August 13, just four days after taking the oath of office, Ford vetoed a bill that would have upgraded deputy U.S. marshals and thus entitled them to a pay raise. Ford felt that the bill would have created pay inequities vis-à-vis other federal law enforcement personnel.

By January 9, 1975, Ford had vetoed twelve additional bills and pocket-vetoed eleven others. On July 25, 1975, he vetoed the first appropriations bill that was presented to him that year. It would have provided $7.9 billion for education. Ford maintained that that figure was "too much to ask the American people—and our economy—to bear."[80] The bill was the thirty-fifth that the president had vetoed since taking office. Some leading newspapers labeled Ford's administrative actions "government by veto."

A president's choice of vice president is yet another indication of attitudes toward social reform. Kennedy chose Lyndon Johnson, who, although a Southerner, had engineered the Senate's passage of the 1957 and 1960 civil rights acts. Johnson chose Hubert Humphrey to be his vice president. A liberal, Humphrey had distinguished himself by his advocacy of a strong civil rights plank in the 1948 Democratic national platform. He had been instrumental in the passage of the Civil Rights Act of 1964.

Nixon, on the other hand, chose as his running mate Spiro Agnew, who as governor of Maryland had established himself as an advocate of "law and order" through his publicized but patronizing admonition to the state's black leadership following the civil disorders of 1968. While governor, Agnew had ordered that 227 black student protestors be jailed for their part in a demonstration at Bowie State College.

Agnew played an integral part in reaching Nixon's goal of limiting the federal government's involvement in social reform. While the president, ensconced in the trappings and dignity of his office, enunciated his political philosophy of "new federalism," Agnew attempted to discredit the segment of the intellectual community that had shaped the social policies of the sixties and that could have mounted the most articulate protest against the erosion of the federal government's commitment to the disadvantaged. Identifying them as an "assaulting elite," Agnew asserted that such intellectuals could be found in all the institutions which contributed to the molding of public opinion. He charged that "they are for the most part, articulate and possessed of that smugness which comes only when one is dogmatically certain of one's essential rightness."[81]

In a controversial speech delivered in New Orleans in October 1969, Agnew lambasted liberal dissidents. He stated: "A spirit of national masochism prevails, encouraged by an effete corps of impudent snobs who characterize themselves as intellectuals."[82] While social programs were constrained by Nixon from the White House, the vice president took to the hustings to launch a visceral attack on the advocates of such programs.

After Agnew's departure from office, Nixon selected Gerald R. Ford to be his second vice president. The *Congressional Quarterly* noted that prior to becoming vice president, Ford had had a record of "consistent conservatism."[83] As House minority leader, Ford had been an unremitting critic of Lyndon Johnson's Great Society programs.

After becoming chief executive, Ford chose Nelson Rockefeller, a liberal, to serve as vice president. The incongruous combination of a conservative president and a liberal vice president eventually became untenable. In November 1975 Rockefeller let it be known that he would not serve as Ford's vice president after the completion of his term.

It should also be noted that a president's choice of cabinet heads indicates his attitudes for or against policies of social reform. Obvious examples are Nixon's choice of John Mitchell as attorney general, compared with Kennedy's choice of his brother, Robert F. Kennedy, as attorney general. One has only to recall recent history to remember the diverse actions and behaviors of the two attorneys general, reflecting presidential valuations of the chief executives who selected and retained them in this key position.

A final indicator of executive attitude and changing tone is executive impoundment of appropriated funds—when the president refuses to spend funds voted by Congress for specific programs. The practice has been used intermittently by presidents, beginning with Thomas Jefferson, but only rarely and only for specific projects. Not until Franklin D. Roosevelt's New Deal did impoundment as a tool of policy reach notable proportions.

Post–World War II examples of impoundment include President Truman's refusal to spend the entire amount of funds allocated for the air force (1949) and his ignoring of a rider in an omnibus appropriations act which provided for a loan to Spain. In 1959 President Eisenhower approved impoundment of funds for a Nike-Zeus antiballistic system.

In 1961 the Kennedy administration requested $200 million for development of the B-70 bomber. Congress went beyond the president's request, by not only authorizing the expenditure but adding $180 million to the amount requested. Robert S. McNamara, secretary of defense, refused to spend the funds. In fact, during both the Kennedy and the Johnson administrations, as Congress authorized funds for new weapons systems that were opposed by the secretary of defense, the administration in most cases simply refused to develop the systems. In 1965 President Johnson impounded funds for small watershed projects because he objected to the use of congressional stipulations, which required that an administration first get approval from the appropriate congressional committee before it could proceed with carrying out a program.

These examples show how a president can thwart the intent of Congress; but why is impoundment a problem? The Constitution made no mention of impoundment when it assigned executive power to the president and legislative power to Congress. Therefore arguments about the use of impoundment revolve around whether the president has the authority, under the Constitution or under the provisions of certain statutes, to impound and whether impoundment constitutes a breach of the separation-of-powers concept that underlies the national government. Much recent impoundment has been felt to be extralegal or at least of questionable legal status because it appears that some presidents have acted outside their authority, but it has not been stopped by Congress.

The president has general authority to withhold expenditures under certain circumstances. For example, the economy acts of 1932 and 1933 and the Reorganization Act of 1939 granted the president authority to effect savings through reduction of personnel, the salaries of public officials, and consolidation of executive agencies. In 1964 the Civil Rights Act conferred on the president the obligation to withhold funds from federally financed programs which discriminate on the basis of race, color, or national origin. The Highway Beautification Act of 1965 provides for the termination of federal highway funds to states which do not enact billboard control legislation.

Congress also has empowered the president to reduce expenditures under the terms of ceilings it has set. Further, certain statutes grant the president general authority to oversee the "health" of the economy, which means the president can withhold expenditures if he deems such action in the best interests of economic well-being. Presidents have used the congressional setting of a debt limit as a reason for withholding funds. In 1957, for example, to bring a budget under the debt-limit ceiling, President Eisenhower cut defense spending funds; but after the debt ceiling was revised, he released the funds.

Presidents have also justified impoundment by citing Article II, sections 2 and 3 of the Constitution. Section 2 makes the president the commander in chief of the army and navy of the United States, and section 3 states that "the Executive shall take care that the laws be faithfully executed." But it is not clear from the language of the Constitution whether the president is *required* to spend funds appropriated by Congress or whether he can make personal and independent decisions about the use of federal monies.

The impounding during the two Nixon administrations was, in general, quite different from that of previous presidents. Nixon increased the scope as well as the amount of funds impounded and justified his actions in a manner quite unlike that of most presidents. He claimed an inherent right to impound, reinterpreted statutes to justify impoundment, and refused to give impoundment figures to the Congress except when required by law. When he provided figures, he sought to conceal the real extent of impoundment by placing certain funds in categories of another name, which is substantively the same as impounding. So unprecedented was his use of this device that Congress was moved to do what it had never before done: write legislation which would subject impoundment to congressional scrutiny.

The question of impoundment reached a new height as President Nixon ended his first term in 1972. Congressmen charged Nixon was impounding funds to assert his own plans and policies for the federal government, over the priorities of Congress; his actions reached above and beyond the measures required to avoid further inflation (which was the justification President Nixon used). In fact, according to Representative Joseph L. Evins (D., Tennessee) in a report on January 15, 1973, the Nixon administration impounded $12 billion in funds appropriated by Congress. This included $6 billion in sewage treatment funds that had been voted by Congress over Nixon's veto. Three areas in which Nixon impounded funds illustrate the manner in which his actions differed from those of other presidents.

From 1972 to 1974 the Nixon administration impounded funds for the Rural Environmental Assistance Program, Farmers Home Administration disaster loans, the Rural Electrification Administration loan program, and rural water and sewer grants, all of which were important agricultural programs.[84] Terminating the Rural Environmental Assistance Program, the Department of Agriculture justified its action by noting that the legislation *authorized* the program but did not *require* that the department carry out the program.[85] Going further, the department stated that neither the substantive legislation nor the appropriation bill required that the full amount be spent but merely authorized execution of the program—a most unusual interpretation of the law.[86] FHA disaster loans were reserved to help the president adhere to his $250 billion budget limit and to reduce inflationary pressures in the economy. Like the Rural Environmental Assistance Program, rural water and sewer grants were terminated because the legislation authorized but did not require the secretary of agriculture to carry out the program.[87] Justification for the termination of Rural Electrification Administration loans was as follows:

> What I have found is that when I first voted for REA, eighty per-
> cent of the loans went for the purpose of rural development and get-
> ting electricity to farms. Now eighty percent of this two percent
> money goes for country clubs and dilettantes, for example, and oth-
> ers who can afford living in the country. I am not for two percent
> money for people who can afford five percent of seven.[88]

In a reflection of its changing mood, Congress reacted strongly to the administration's action. The House Committee on Agriculture rewrote legislation for the Rural Electrification Assistance Program and inserted mandatory language, providing that the secretary of agriculture "shall" carry out the REA program and would make payments "in an aggregate amount equal to the sums appropriated therefore."[89]

Reacting to the termination of REA loans, the Senate rebuffed the president's contention that 2 percent monies were being given to those who could afford higher rates. The Senate reported that fewer than 10 percent of the loans that had been issued were exclusively 2 percent monies. Most loans were a combination of 2 percent money and monies from the Rural Utilities Cooperative Finance Corporation, a private credit cooperative that offered loans at 5 percent interest. The Senate then passed a bill "authorizing and directing" the loan administrator to approve loans in the amount determined necessary or appropriated by the Congress.[90] The House version also contained mandatory language but provided a "special rate" of 2 percent for some loans and a "standard rate" of 5 percent for most borrowers.[91] The secretary of agriculture agreed to carry out the program if the mandatory language was removed from the bill, which the conference committee agreed to do.

Congress rewrote legislation mandating expenditure of funds for the rural water and sewer grants, but was unable to muster enough votes to override a presidential veto. As a general approach to impoundment of agriculture funds, the Senate added an amendment to the 1973 agriculture appropriations bill, stating that monies appropriated by the bill "shall be made available for expenditure except as specifically provided by law," thereby making provision for statutes such as the Anti-Deficiency Act.[92]

A second category of impoundments covered funds for various environmental programs. In 1972 the amendments to the Federal Water Pollution Control Act became law when the House and Senate overrode a presidential veto. The President then instructed the Environmental Protection Agency to spend less than half of the amount set in the statutory ceilings. Instead of spending $5 billion in 1973 and $6 billion in 1974, the head of the EPA was instructed to spend $2 billion and $3 billion respectively.[93] Legislators who had worked out the provisions of the bill in a conference committee maintained that the language made it clear that the president was not required to spend the full amount provided for each year but could spend any amount up to the amount provided. Legislative reaction to this impoundment was similar to the reaction to the agriculture impoundments. Senator Muskie, sponsor of the Senate bill, remarked that impounding the funds showed a lack of administrative commitment to controlling water pollution. The bill had been written to provide discretionary leeway for enforcement, and to ignore this discretionary language was, in effect, to make an excuse for not following through on a commitment. The Senator said he could write stronger, mandatory language, and in the future he would.[94]

The Nixon administration made an even greater departure from previous practice when it withheld funds for community development. In March 1971 testimony before the Senate Banking, Housing, and Urban Affairs Committee, the secretary of housing and urban development reported that funds were being withheld from urban programs in anticipation of passage of the revenue-sharing program.[95] Impoundment in anticipation of other legislation was a new twist in the use of that tool—as if to say: If you want housing, it would be advisable to pass revenue sharing. The reaction of Congress was again to require that housing and other funds be spent.[96]

Besides creating more and different justifications for impoundment, the Nixon administration had been reluctant to reveal to the Congress the total amount it had placed in reserve funds. In October 1972 a debt-limit bill was enacted which required transmission of an impoundment report to the Congress. The bill called for prompt reporting,[97] but by January 6, 1973, no report had been made. The Senate then passed an amendment requiring that the desired information be transmitted by February 10, 1973.[98] A report from the Office of Management and Budget was transmitted on January 29 which stated that there were budgetary reserves in the amount of $8.7 billion.[99] However, that report omitted $9 billion which was held in categories other than reserve funds.[100]

Of the amounts impounded, the largest item was $6 billion in water pollution control monies—$3 billion each for fiscal years 1973 and 1974.[101] The report also omitted $441 million in contract authority or different types of housing programs; $382.8 million in proposed recisions for manpower services, health services, food and drug programs, and education programs; $1.9 billion withheld from the departments of Labor and Health, Education, and Welfare; and $300 million from the FHA disaster loan program.[102]

The Nixon administration then used this report to indicate that its impoundings were smaller than those of past presidents. In an article for the *New York Times,* Secretary Weinberger wrote the following:

> Here are the facts: as of Jan. 29 of this year, 3.5 percent of the total unified budget was being impounded. That compares with 7.8 percent on June 30, 1961, under President Kennedy, 6.1 percent in 1962, 4 percent in 1963; 3.5 percent in 1963 under President Johnson's first budget, 4.7 percent in 1965, 6.5 percent in 1966, 6.7 percent in 1967, and 5.5 percent in 1968.[103]

However, when the $9 billion which was omitted from the impoundment figure is added, the percentage becomes at least double that given in the *Times*. In addition, some of the funds that were withheld were permanently withdrawn, primarily welfare expenditures. Of a total $17.7 billion impounded as of January 29, 1973, 2.4 percent were Defense Department funds, 15.6 percent were from agriculture, and 19.2 percent were from the Department of Housing and Urban Development. Of the reserved funds, which would no longer be available by the end of 1973, only .4 percent were from defense; 72.6 percent of the agriculture funds would lapse; and 99.3 percent of the HUD funds would not be available for expenditure.[104]

The distribution of funds impounded by type of expenditure in 1973 was consistent with the distribution of the previous two years. In 1971, of a total $12.7 billion impounded, the aggregate for welfare categories was twice that of defense, although the defense category had the largest departmental total. In that year, 11 percent of the funds reserved were for defense expenditures, followed closely by the Department of Health, Education, and Welfare, which accounted for 10.3 percent of the funds. Aggregating expenditures into defense, welfare, agriculture, and transportation leaves the defense percentage unchanged, welfare becomes 12 percent of the total, and agriculture and transportation constitute 4 and 3.5 percent of the total respectively. Comparing defense reserves with all other large categories of reserved funds shows that the latter accounted for twice the reserves in the defense area.[105]

As of January 25, 1972, when a total of $10.5 billion was reserved, 22 percent of all reserved funds were from the defense area, while 74 percent were from agriculture, welfare, and transportation. An enormous 65 percent of the funds were from the Department of Transportation alone.[106] Examination of the differences in percentage totals between these aggregate categories of expenditure lends credence to Nixon critics who charge that he used impounding to rearrange the program priorities set by former Congresses and continued by the sitting Congress.

Since Roosevelt's terms in office, every president has impounded funds. Many of the most controversial instances occurred in defense spending, where the president justified the withholding of funds by reference to his powers as commander in chief. The Constitution does not make clear the extent of the president's powers as commander in chief, but it makes clear the fact that he shares authority with the Congress. Article I, section 8 declares to Congress the authority to

> Lay and collect taxes to provide for the common defense . . .
> Raise and support armies . . .
> Provide and maintain a Navy . . .
> Make rules for the government and regulation of the land and naval forces . . .
> Make all laws which shall be necessary and proper for carrying into execution the foregoing powers[107]

If it is not clear to what extent the president's authority as commander in chief extends to authority over levels of expenditure, it is also not clear that he *cannot* use it in that manner.

Presidents Johnson and Nixon broadened that authority to include actions taken in the interest of dampening inflationary pressures in the economy. This is a step beyond actions presidents had previously taken. Rather than affecting the level of expenditure in a particular area, this definition opens the door for a broad range of policy-making decisions. Relying on economic justifications is much less effective than relying on the authority of being commander in chief because it can more easily be argued that the executive shares expertise in the economic area with the Congress, that more information is available to all decision-making parties. In defense matters the executive can claim that his decision is based on classified information to which very few others should be privy, a plausible if not a legal argument.

In addition to claiming broad powers to impound, based on economic justifications, Nixon significantly altered the impoundment argument by claiming inherent constitutional authority, as well as by refusing to indicate to Congress how much had been impounded and by refusing to spend appropriated monies even when bills were passed over his veto. When impounding, no previous president had claimed an inherent right to reserve funds, nor refused to transmit to Congress information concerning the amounts withheld. Nixon was the first to hide billions in the White House basement, as it were.

In the absence of definitive statutory guidelines to cover all situations where impounding might be necessary, and without an equally definitive ruling by the Supreme Court on the extent to which constitutionally delegated powers affect a president's authority to impound, the question of who has the power to determine levels of expenditure must be settled in the political arena.

The fall 1975 issue of *Congressional Quarterly Guide to Current American Government* pointed out that:

> Former President Nixon's attempt to block federal programs he opposed by refusing to spend money Congress has appropriated is still causing grief on Capitol Hill.

> Ironically, the agent of the present trouble is a law Congress passed near the end of the Nixon presidency to make sure he no longer would be able to thwart the will of Congress by impounding funds. [Title X of the Congressional Budget and Impoundment Control Act of 1974 (PL 93–344)].

Concerns about the law range from complaints that it is smothering both the executive and legislative branches on paperwork, to warnings that it may signal the beginning of an unhealthy erosion of presidential power.

As of mid-April, about half of the total $26.8-billion in fiscal year 1975 funds that President Ford sought to withhold under the law had been released. Approximately $11-billion was let go by the administration either voluntarily or as a result of court action. The rest had been made available for spending as a result of the law.[108]

Whether one examines the political philosophies or economic policies of the last four presidents or their uses of the veto and impoundment, the same conclusion will be reached. Clearly, the Nixon presidency represented a sharp break with the social reform efforts that characterized the administrations of Presidents Kennedy and Johnson. As political scientist Louis W. Koenig has pointed out, the office of the presidency "has made no enduring and unqualified commitment to either the advantaged or the disadvantaged."[109]

Unlike Kennedy, who vigorously enforced existing civil rights laws and advocated the passage of new social reform measures, or Johnson, who worked to bring about the passage of sweeping new civil rights acts and led the country into an "unconditional war on poverty," Nixon (with the one exception of his family assistance plan) called a halt to new measures for social reform and, through budgetary cuts, impoundment, and the veto, sought to limit those programs already in existence or those which were put forth by Congress.

Attempting to bring about a "new federalism" through revenue sharing, Nixon advocated that state and local governments be entrusted with the responsibility for social reform—the very same political units that the disadvantaged held most immediately responsible for their plight. Gerald R. Ford, Nixon's personally chosen successor, made no substantial changes in the domestic policies of his predecessor.

LEGISLATIVE BRANCH

It would be foolhardy to attempt to make broad generalizations about the mood of an institution as intricate as the Congress of the United States. In his recent study, titled *Congressional Power: Congress and Social Change,* Gary Orfield of the Brookings Institution came to the following conclusion:

The diffusion of power and the diversity of political viewpoints within Congress make it easy to support a wide range of interpretations of Congressional authority. Within an institution where great influence over the same issue may rest in one house with a reactionary Southern planter, and in the other with a very liberal New York lawyer, a casual observer can easily become confused about Congress' position. It often is far easier to examine issues apparently supporting the thesis of dominance by a progressive presidency than it is to sort out the net effect of the ebbs and flows of power within the complex overlapping policy systems that make up Congress. The sorting out of real policy influence is further complicated by the frequent Congressional practice of disguising real changes as "technical" alterations, or accomplishing change between the executive branch and powerful members of Congress.[110]

Orfield also points out that Congress is "inherently neither liberal nor conservative"; rather, its political posture is shaped by "the times," "delayed responses of the seniority system," and the "tides of public opinion." He also warns that when examining the legislature, one should keep in mind that the "real obstacles" to social reform lie not so much in the halls of Congress as in "society as a whole."[111]

Nevertheless, it appears that, following the unprecedented volume of social reform legislation which was produced by the first session of the 89th Congress, support for social legislation waned considerably. That was true despite the fact that after 1969 the legislative branch appeared to be more committed to social reform than the executive branch.

According to the Congressional Quarterly Service, during the first two years of his administration President Kennedy's relations with Congress were "far from ideal,"[112] despite the fact that the Democrats enjoyed a majority in both the House (263 to 174) and the Senate (64 to 36). The inability of the Democratic majority to enact much of the president's program can be attributed in part to the removal of Vice President Lyndon Johnson from the position of majority leader in the Senate and to the death of Sam Rayburn, who had served as Speaker of the House for seventeen years. Those masters of the legislative process were succeeded by Mike Mansfield (D., Montana) and John McCormack (D., Massachusetts) respectively. Although the latter two men were highly respected, some members of Congress felt that they lacked the drive and know-how of their predecessors.[113]

Another obstacle for the Kennedy legislative program was the House Rules Committee, which was chaired by conservative Howard W.

Smith (D., Virginia). To prevent the Rules Committee from bottleneck-
ing important New Frontier legislation, shortly after taking office Kennedy pushed to have the committee membership expanded from twelve
to fifteen so that additional liberal Democrats could be appointed to it.
The successful fight to enlarge the membership of the committee was
the last major accomplishment in Speaker Rayburn's career. He died
eleven months later of cancer.

In 1962 Kennedy campaigned vigorously to increase the Democratic majorities in Congress. He maintained that the elections would
give the country a choice between "anchoring down" with the Republicans or "sailing" with the Democrats.[114] As a result of the 1962
elections, the Democrats lost four seats in the House and picked up four
in the Senate.

The record of the 88th Congress on domestic legislation was mixed.
It enacted increases in the minimum wage and Social Security benefits,
aid to depressed areas, a manpower retraining program, and a $4.9 bil-
lion omnibus housing bill. In addition, the 88th Congress submitted to
the states a constitutional amendment banning the poll tax. On the other
hand, Congress rejected legislation that would have established a Department of Urban Affairs, at least in part because the administration
let it be known that Robert Weaver, a black man, was slated to become
head of the department. Congress also rejected aid to education, a mass
transportation bill, and a program to combat unemployment among
youth. In addition, it blocked a program that would have provided medical care for the aged. Congress took no action on the Civil Rights bill
which was submitted by the president in February 1963.

Following Kennedy's assassination and under the heavy-handed but
skillful prodding of President Johnson, Congress bestirred itself during
the final months of the 88th session. By the end of the session Congress
had enacted much of the program that Kennedy had put forth during his
three years in office, including aid to mass transit, a food stamp program, expansion of the National Defense Education Act, legal aid for
indigents, and extension of aid to hospital construction. Perhaps the two
most far-reaching pieces of legislation passed by the 88th Congress were
the Civil Rights Act of 1964 and the Economic Opportunity Act of
1964, which became the basis for the War on Poverty.

The Republicans suffered a crushing defeat in the 1964 elections.
In the 89th Congress the Democrats had an overwhelming majority of
295 to 140 in the House and 68 to 32 in the Senate. Democratic legislation was produced in a "seemingly endless stream." To prevent their

programs from being blocked by the Rules Committee, House Democrats revised House procedures to make it possible, under certain conditions, for the Speaker to bypass the committee and bring legislation to the floor. During the first session of the 89th Congress, the conservative coalition of Republicans and Southern Democrats was successful in blocking legislation only 25 percent of the time, compared with 67 percent in 1963 and a formidible 74 percent in 1961.

Among the acts passed by the first session of the 89th Congress were the Voting Rights Act of 1965, a $7.8 billion housing assistance bill, establishment of the Department of Housing and Urban Development, aid to higher education, a doubling of the initial appropriation for the War on Poverty, and $1 billion in aid for Appalachia. Particularly significant was passage of a medical bill, because such a measure had been a plank in the Democratic platform for two decades.

Yet by the second session of the 89th Congress the escalation of the war in Vietnam and the development of the white backlash impaired the effectiveness of advocates of social reform legislation. Beginning in 1966, some Republicans and Southern Democrats advanced the view that it was impossible for the country to have both "guns and butter." They adamantly maintained that the "guns" had to come first. Consequently, while the defense budget was passed almost without alteration, vigorous attacks were launched on domestic programs. Nevertheless, the second session of the 89th Congress enacted legislation that established a Department of Transportation, the Teacher Corps, an increase in the minimum wage, and the Model Cities program. Among the casualties of the incipient white backlash was Johnson's open housing bill. Perhaps the initiation of efforts to remove Harlem representative Adam Clayton Powell, Jr., from his position as chairman of the House Education and Labor Committee could be interpreted as another indication of the souring mood of the Congress. One of several criticisms made of Powell was that he had openly advocated black power.

In the 1966 elections the Republican party reasserted itself, reflecting a national shift toward the right. Democrats lost forty-seven seats in the House and three seats in the Senate, although they maintained substantial majorities in both houses. In the House, Democrats outnumbered Republicans 248 to 187, and in the Senate 64 to 36.

Conservatives in the 90th Congress charged that Great Society programs were inflationary, that they could not be supported while the war was going on, and that they made the federal government appear to be rewarding urban rioters. In 1967, funding for the war effort again passed with little difficulty. In contrast, funds requested by the president for antipoverty programs, Model Cities, and the Teacher Corps were cut back sharply. Congress rejected proposals for rural development and highway beautification. Adam Clayton Powell was denied his seat in the House. The *Congressional Quarterly* observed that during its second session the 90th Congress was in "a conservative mood." Yet the Congress passed an increased appropriation for some Great Society programs that had previously been subjected to harsh criticism; among them were the Teacher Corps, Model Cities, and the antipoverty program. The ambivalence of the second session was demonstrated by its passage of an open housing bill, to which was attached an "anti-riot" provision.

In 1968 Richard Nixon became the first newly elected president in over a century whose party did not elect a majority in either house of Congress. In the 91st Congress the Democrats held a majority of 57 to 43 in the Senate and 247 to 188 in the House. Although the first session of the 91st Congress was the sixth longest in the history of the nation, its legislative output was the smallest in thirty-six years. Despite the steady increase in conservative power in the Congress, by comparison with the new president the legislature appeared to be progressive. During the first session it rejected the nomination of Clement Haynsworth to the Supreme Court, increased appropriations for education, and food stamps; it also cut the administration's defense budget. In addition, Congress increased Social Security benefits and passed a Housing and Urban Development Act. The antipoverty program was extended despite an effort to turn the administration of the program over to the states.

During the second session the Congress authorized $25 billion in aid to education and extended the 1965 Voting Rights Act for an additional five years. Much of this was done despite presidential vetoes. While the Congress mounted a moderate defense of the major programs of the Great Society, it failed to take any domestic initiatives such as those that characterized Congress during the Johnson years.

In the elections of 1970, Democrats lost two seats in the Senate but gained nine in the House. As a result of the elections, 55 Democrats and 45 Republicans were sent to the Senate and 256 Democrats and 180 Republicans were seated in the House. According to a survey conducted by *Congressional Quarterly,* the election results produced "no clear trend on national issues." Of some importance, however, was the fact that Vietnam and civil rights were no longer significant issues. The electorate appeared to be more concerned with economic issues, such as inflation and unemployment. In 1971 the Congress, in a major initiative, enacted a $6.3 billion appropriation for the Office of Economic Opportunity, which included a provision for federally supported child-care centers; but the legislature could not muster enough support to override a presidential veto of the measure.[115]

In 1971 the conservative coalition of Republicans and Southern Democrats made its best showing since 1957. The conservative coalition defeated Northern Democrats on 83 percent of the votes in which they were in opposition. Also in 1971, liberal Democrat Edward Kennedy was replaced as Senate majority whip by the more conservative Robert Byrd of West Virginia. The growing strength of the conservative coalition had been most evident over the issue of busing, and as busing became increasingly a tool for desegregation in the North, some Northern Democrats who had previously been staunch supporters of integration and busing became vehement opponents. The conservative coalition has been more successful in securing antibusing measures in the House than in the Senate.

The elections of 1974 saw a repudiation of Richard Nixon, but despite the much heralded election of many new liberal members of Congress, the *Washington Post* concluded that the difference between the newly elected liberals and their more conservative counterparts was primarily one of style, not substance.[116] In effect, then, the growing strength of the conservative coalition in Congress had continued unabated since the second session of the 89th Congress. In fact, that session, and the one that preceded it, appear to have been legislative aberrations. After a brief period of social enlightenment during the early years of the Johnson administration, the Congress had resumed a moderately conservative stance on issues of social reform. A look at two broad areas of concern to minorities, civil rights and antipoverty legislation, will clarify this congressional resumption of moderate conservatism.

Civil Rights

Examination of the histories of civil rights and antipoverty legislation brings the erosion of congressional social commitment into sharp relief. It also underscores the importance of congressional committees and key congressmen in furthering or impeding the passage of such legislation.

The passage of the Voting Rights Act of 1965 was a watershed in congressional social activism. The act, a product of bipartisan cooperation, had the support of Senate Majority Leader Mike Mansfield (D., Montana) as well as Minority Leader Everett McKinley Dirksen (R., Illinois). Attorney General Nicholas Katzenbach and Deputy Attorney General Ramsey Clark were also instrumental in the formulation and passage of the bill. In the Senate, the bill was managed by Philip A. Hart (D., Michigan) and in the House by Emanuel Celler (D., New York). As a result of concerted action, the bill passed the House by an overwhelming vote of 328 to 74 and the Senate by 79 to 18. The Voting Rights Act was the last piece of civil rights legislation to be passed in undiluted form.

During the same session of Congress, an unsuccessful effort was made to strengthen Title VII of the Civil Rights Act of 1964 by granting the Equal Economic Opportunity Commission (EEOC) the authority to issue cease and desist orders against employers they found guilty of discriminatory hiring practices. The bill (H.R. 10065) would also have extended Title VII coverage to organizations with as few as eight employees. Although the House Education and Labor Committee, which was chaired by Adam Clayton Powell, Jr. (D., New York), reported the bill out in August 1965, action by the full House was postponed until the next session of Congress. Already, some of the drive had gone out of congressional civil rights efforts.[117]

In April 1966 the House passed H.R. 10065 by a vote of 300 to 93. The measure had received the endorsement of President Johnson and the AFL-CIO, as well as that of participants in a White House conference on civil rights which was held in June. But that was not enough to budge the Senate, which failed to take any action on the bill.

In 1967 the bill fared even worse. Neither the House Education and Labor Committee nor the Senate Labor and Public Welfare Committee even reported out H.R. 10065. In that year, Adam Clayton Powell, Jr. was ousted from Congress by his colleagues and replaced as chairman of the Education and Labor Committee by Carl D. Perkins (D., Kentucky). The Senate committee was chaired by Ralph W. Yarborough (D., Texas).

Again, in 1968, Congress failed to provide the EEOC with enforcement powers. Although the Senate Labor and Public Welfare Committee reported out a bill, no action was taken on it by the full Senate, primarily because Minority Leader Everett Dirksen vowed to mount a filibuster. Dirksen termed the bill "one of the most offensive pieces of legislation that could come before Congress."[118] In the House, the bill did not emerge from committee.

In 1969 Dirksen made known his hostility to the EEOC during congressional hearings that were held in March. During those hearings the minority leader charged Clifford Alexander, head of the EEOC, with "punitive harassment of employers."[119] Further, Dirksen threatened to have Alexander removed from his position unless he refrained from overseeing employment practices with such assiduity. Shortly thereafter, Alexander tendered his resignation and was succeeded by William H. Brown III. The departing official denounced the Nixon administration for having failed to support him during his tenure in office.

President Nixon was opposed to granting direct enforcement powers to the EEOC, a policy which had been advocated by Alexander and some civil rights advocates. Through Attorney General Kleindienst and William Brown, the president proposed a compromise bill that would have required the commission to go through federal courts to obtain cease and desist orders, instead of granting it the authority to issue such orders directly. Both the Nixon compromise and the stronger bill were considered in House and Senate committees in 1969, but no further action was taken.

In 1970 the Senate Labor and Public Welfare Committee reported out a bill which granted the EEOC direct enforcement powers. The full Senate resisted efforts, led by Senator Peter H. Dominick (R., Colorado), to have the administration's compromise bill accepted as an alternative. On October 1, 1970, the full Senate passed the bill (S. 2453) by a vote of 47 to 24 and then referred it to the House for final action. There it and a similar bill (which had been reported out of the Education and Labor Committee) were blocked from further consideration by the Rules Committee, which was chaired by Representative William M. Colmer (D., Mississippi).

In June 1971 the House Education and Labor Committee reported out a bill which also gave the EEOC direct enforcement powers. It had been urged to do so by the Commission on Civil Rights, the NAACP, and the AFL-CIO. The direct powers bill was rejected by the full House, which instead adopted the administration-backed compromise bill by a vote of 200 to 195. Clarence Mitchell, director of the Washington bureau of the NAACP, termed the House action a "slap in the face" for civil rights.[120] In October the Senate committee, chaired by Harrison A. Williams, Jr. (D., New Jersey), reported out both bills that had been passed by the full House and a stronger one granting direct powers.

Only the latter received the committee's endorsement. Neither bill was voted on in 1971.

In 1972 Congress finally passed the Equal Employment Opportunity Act, which empowered the EEOC to seek remedies for discrimination by employers through bringing suit in federal courts. The bill also extended the coverage of Title VII of the 1964 Civil Rights Act to organizations with as few as fifteen employees. This act, which had been fought over for six years, was both a victory and a defeat for civil rights supporters. Liberal senators such as Jacob Javits (R., New York) and Harrison Williams had been unable to convince a majority of their colleagues to extend coverage to organizations with as few as eight employees or to grant the EEOC direct enforcement powers. The time-consuming court procedure mandated by Congress was at least partly responsible for the accumulation of a backlog of 97,761 discrimination cases by the end of 1974.[121]

Other civil rights bills proposed during the late sixties similarly failed to win the wholehearted support of Congress. An open housing bill was proposed by President Johnson in 1966 but failed to gain passage until 1968, after the assassination of Martin Luther King, Jr., and then only in a watered-down form, with an anti-riot provision attached. Busing to achieve school desegregation was perhaps the most volatile issue raised during the period. It brought out latent hostility and racial antagonism even in some Northern areas that formerly were thought to have been bastions of liberal sentiment.

In 1970 opponents of busing were able to muster a voting majority in the House for the first time. Their strength has been growing since that time, as demonstrated by the regularity with which the House has attached amendments to HEW appropriations bills preventing the department from requiring busing as a remedy for segregation. In 1971 a move to delete such a proviso from the HEW appropriation for fiscal 1972 was defeated by a vote of 149 to 206. In 1972 the House endorsed a Nixon proposal to make busing a tool of last resort by a vote of 283 to 103.[122] An amendment to the Elementary and Secondary Education Act of 1974, which prohibited busing beyond the school next closest to a student's home, was passed in the House by a vote of 293 to 117.[123]

The antibusing measures that have been passed by the House have been consistently toned down by the Senate. However, observing the defection of a number of Northern liberal senators in 1975, Robert B. McKay of the Aspen Institute for Humanistic Studies suggested that the passage of stronger antibusing legislation could be in the offing.[124]

Antipoverty Legislation

Paralleling the apparent shift from commitment to civil rights is the waning support for the antipoverty program as it was envisioned during the Johnson administration. A sizable number of conservative legislators have seemed more intent upon waging war on the antipoverty program than on poverty itself.

The antipoverty program was brought into existence by the passage of the Economic Opportunity Act of 1964. The Office of Economic Opportunity (OEO) was established in order to effect its provisions. Congress amended the 1964 act to grant governors the power to keep some OEO programs out of their states. Another amendment required Job Corps enrollees to sign affidavits disavowing any connection with organizations advocating the overthrow of the government.

In 1965 Republicans mounted an unsuccessful campaign to replace the War on Poverty with their own Opportunity Crusade, which would have been administered through government agencies other than the OEO, which some conservatives wanted scuttled. Congress also decided in 1965 that no more than 45,000 persons could be enrolled in the Job Corps. In addition, the establishment of codes of conduct for enrollees was mandated. Congress also put a $15,000 ceiling on the salaries of local antipoverty officials.

In 1967 Congress reduced enrollee expenditures for the Job Corps from $7,500 to $6,900, and restricted legal-service lawyers from taking certain criminal cases. It also proscribed the participation of community action employees in "unlawful demonstrations."[125]

The reelection of Richard Nixon cast a pall on the future of the program. Upon assuming office in 1969, Nixon asked Congress not to extend the Job Corps for more than one additional year, at the end of which the White House Domestic Council would have devised a plan for its revision. On his own initiative, the president shut down fifty-nine Job Corps centers.

It soon became apparent that the White House plan was to dismantle OEO by transferring its programs to other governmental agencies. In 1971 Congress attempted to shore up the agency against further inroads by the administration by granting it a two-year extension and banning additional program transfers. Congress also created an extensive child-care program under OEO auspices. The president vetoed the legislators' efforts and they could not muster the votes to override. Congress was obliged to tailor a new bill to satisfy the objections of the administration. In the bill that finally gained passage, the child-care provision was de-

leted, the president was given greater control over the legal-services program, and OEO was laid bare for further diminution at the hands of the
president.

By August 1974, President Ford was able to report that the Community Action Program was the only remnant of the War on Poverty
remaining under the purview of OEO and that he saw no need for the
continuance of even that program.[126] On January 4, 1975, President
Ford signed a bill which abolished OEO and replaced it with the Community Services Administration.[127]

As was noted at the outset of this discussion, Congress is not a
monolith, and it has not been consistent in its attitude toward social reform. The extension of the Voting Rights Act in 1970 and again in 1975
represents instances in which the liberal element prevailed. From the
viewpoint of minorities, Congress has been more progressive in the
seventies than has the executive branch under the Nixon and Ford administrations. In general, however, Congress has been less supportive of
social reform since 1969 than it was in the mid-1960s.

Eternal vigilance and readiness for action must be maintained by
the electorate; this is true for individuals and for groups. In fact, it is
usually organized groups which can be counted on to monitor activities
in Congress and to take appropriate action. For example, late in 1975 it
was Senate Bill 1 which posed a new threat to freedom. Many legal experts held that if this bill was passed, it would kill the Bill of Rights and
possibly pave the way for a police state in America. The October 1975
issue of *Grapevine,* published by the Joint Strategy and Action Committee, Inc., was devoted to an analysis of this bill, which was "a 753-page
attempt to codify, revise and reform the entire U.S. criminal code."[128] It
summarized the civil liberties implications of Senate Bill 1 as follows:

> (1) the bill "would redefine criminality in such a way as to endanger
> the lives and liberties of thousands of people and groups which at-
> tempt to work for justice and social change or to air legitimate
> grievances;" ... "the definitions are so vague that almost any kind
> of civil rights, peace protest or labor action could be considered
> criminal activity under this section and all of the participants in
> such organizing or action sent to jail;" (2) the trend toward secrecy
> in government and its immunity from public accountability would
> be fortified by several sections which redefine 'national defense in-
> formation' to include just about anything the government decides it
> wants to keep from the public and provide criminal sanctions

against anyone who discloses such information; (3) freedom of the press would also be limited under Section 1114; (4) electronic surveillance without a court order would be increased; (5) there would be more immunity from prosecution for government officials on the grounds that the conduct charged "was required or authorized by law to carry out the defendant's authority." Thus this would insulate officials from the prohibitions of criminal law, divorcing personal responsibility from official action, and setting a lower standard of conduct for every federal employee from the President downward; (6) sanction of police entrapment activities; (7) codification of the recent Supreme Court rulings on obscenity; (8) a rejection of the Brown Commission's recommendations to establish effective national control of handguns; (9) a reaffirmation of the 'use immunity' law allowing indeterminate sentences to supersede the Fifth Amendment privilege against self-incrimination; (10) lengthen mandatory maximum sentences and longer minimum sentences before a prisoner is eligible for parole; (11) imprisonment and stiff fines for the personal use of marijuana; (12) in the case of American Indians, the federal government will almost totally preempt the tribal government's jurisdiction within reservation boundaries.[129]

The Joint Strategy and Action Committee, upon the advice of legal scholars, suggested that this bill was "inherently unamendable and should be recommitted for a complete overhaul and re-drafting." The committee quoted Norval Morris, dean of the University of Chicago Law School, who feared that in the case of S. 1 "politicians have used grave problems of criminality and violence in the country as mechanisms for the passage of legislation that is largely irrelevant to dealing with those problems."[130]

What was done about S. 1? The committee urged a public outcry against it in the form of writing senators, Judiciary Committee members, and the bill's sponsors about those sections deemed most obnoxious and asking that they work to amend the bill or vote against it. Also, local newspapers were contacted and urged to run stories and editorials on the dangers of this bill. Further, educational outreach programs were conducted in churches and in communities on the implications of this legislation. The serious implications of S. 1 let us know that civil liberties cannot be taken for granted in America, nor can the intent of Congress. S. 1 did not get out of committee. To be further considered, the bill would have to be reintroduced.

SUMMARY AND CONCLUSIONS

The changing tone of the federal government's three branches has been toward conservatism since 1969. But to be less supportive of social reforms that aim at actualizing the American Creed is to be guilty of eroding one's commitment to those segments of the American citizenry that have not yet realized the promises of the American dream.

It is most important to note that most of the gains for minorities and the poor have resulted from federal insistence upon equal protection. These groups have never been able to rely upon state governments, local governments, private industry, or voluntary individual or group efforts for consistency or steadfastness for equal protection of the laws, equal rights, or equal opportunity. A reading of the history of race and intergroup relations in the United States will document this failure beyond doubt. Thus a wavering stance of the federal government is perceived by minorities and the poor as devastating to their life chances and as reneging on constitutional guarantees. These guarantees can be thought of as form; and form is empty without substance. Substance comes from enlightened leadership and from laws passed and enforced. The federal government must live up to its role of seeing that all citizens receive equal protection. The federal government must be held accountable for the *substance* of constitutional guarantees, as well as the *form*. Without both, there is no American democracy.

Myrdal pointed out that if the forces to improve Negro status are removed, Negro status reverts to its former plane (as discussed earlier). Laws and social practices for equality and justice are forces to improve Negro status. If these are removed, whether by conscious design or in the name of expediency or political hysteria, the effect is the same: blacks as a group are hurt, and slowed and impeded in their quest for equality and justice.

Responsible, determined, dedicated leadership is needed at all levels of government, but especially at the national level. The federal system dictates that common affairs, that is, questions that affect the country as a whole, are the appropriate business of the central authority. The continuing American dilemma is such a "common" affair. The national government will err grievously if it abdicates its proper role in solving racial and economic questions which affect America as a whole, and which affect international opinion about this country.

All Americans would do well to remember the words of Justice Frankfurter, who said: "On the few tragic occasions in the history of the Nation, North and South, when law was forcibly resisted or systematically evaded, it has signalled the breakdown of Constitutional processes of government on which ultimately rest the liberties of all."[131] Let us look upon these words as words to the wise and modify our collective behavior in observing the American Creed.

V

THE CHANGING MOOD AND EDUCATION

EDUCATIONAL POLICY QUESTIONS

Emerging from the changing mood in America, and at the same time contributing to it, is a growing body of social science literature which says, one way or another, that (a) schooling makes little or no difference in the lives of individuals and minority groups or (b) the rate of return from long years of formal study is increasingly low and therefore, especially in higher education, is not worth the price. There is an assault on policies and programs, including those in education, that are designed to help blacks, other minorities, and the poor. The assault also can be seen in an attack on the meanings of the concepts of equality and justice. These concepts are the rubric under which blacks and their allies have fought and achieved such legislation as the Civil Rights Act of 1964, the Voting Rights Act of 1965, the Elementary and Secondary Education Act of 1965 (amended in 1974), the Higher Education Act of 1965 (with amendments in 1972), and affirmative action policies. These attacks are perceived negatively by blacks and other minority persons and are interpreted as part of an eroding commitment by the dominant society and its policy makers.

Such social science literature can be said to have begun with publication of the Coleman Report data in 1966. It seemed to reach a zenith in 1972, but it continues even today. The 1972 zenith saw the publication of Jencks' widely cited book, *Inequality,* the Mosteller and Moynihan work, *On Equality of Educational Opportunity,* and a flood of journal articles (especially in influential intellectual journals) concerning the whole question of equality, with special reference to equality of educational opportunity. Both books used as their data base the 1966 Coleman materials and, although they reinterpreted his findings, they did not come to very different conclusions.

Today, specifically with respect to educational policy, there is an attack on the worth of public schooling. The attack can be seen in arguments which say (a) schools don't help much and (b) even if schools help, they cost more than they are worth, or they are repressive institutions. The latter portion of this argument is reflected in such statements as (a) the rate of return is down for persons with higher education degrees; therefore young people would do well not to go to college, and (b) Title I (ESEA) and other compensatory programs have shown some results, but the cost is too great in proportion to the results obtained. At bottom, this is the cost/benefit business model applied to the educational enterprise. It suggests that the attack on educational inequities has not resulted in gains large enough to be worth the monies spent; in other words, sufficient "profits" were not realized from the expenditures. Therefore, as a matter of policy it would be well not to allocate societal resources to attack academic retardation or to give increased access to higher educational institutions because the gains and the results are too modest in terms of the achievement of the young, and because educators have failed to overcome the academic achievement problems of minority-group children and youths.

Pushed far enough, this viewpoint questions whether there is a continuing obligation on the part of society to provide publicly supported schooling, at least in formal, institutionalized school settings. Various "deschooling" proposals attest to the reality of this statement. In like manner, one of the points made by the Supreme Court majority in the *Rodriguez* decision concerning school finance in Texas was that no *right to education* is implied under the equal protection clause of the Fourteenth Amendment. Certainly all informed persons know that this is true in a literal or strict interpretation of the Constitution; nevertheless, the battle for free public schooling took so long and was so hard fought that most citizens felt the *principle* of a right to publicly supported education had been clearly established, beyond a reasonable doubt, through need, longevity, and custom.

It was in 1642 that Massachusetts took the leadership role in requiring parents and masters to see that the children under their control were educated and in levying fines on all adults who failed to meet this requirement. In 1647 Massachusetts required towns to establish schools. But the movement toward universal free elementary education was not complete in the United States until 1918, when Mississippi enacted a compulsory attendance law—the last state's commitment to the idea of compulsory attendance to ensure universal elementary education. The movement took 276 years to come to fruition. (Yet Mississippi was the first state to repeal its compulsory attendance laws after the *Brown* decision of 1954.)

American society has subscribed to the concept of universal free schooling at the high school level for only about 100 years. It was not until the 1870s that a series of judicial decisions in the state courts of Michigan, Illinois, and other states laid a sound legal basis for the public secondary school. The most famous of these are the *Kalamazoo* decision of the Michigan Supreme Court in 1874 and the 1878 Illinois decision in *Richard* v. *Raymond*.[1]

In a nation that has celebrated a bicentennial of freedom from tyranny and oppression, it would be inspiring to see a similar commitment to freedom for continued opportunity, including the opportunity to be educated at public expense for as long as is necessary to develop individual capabilities to the utmost. Yet the Burger court's viewpoint, and that of leading elite intellectuals, makes one shudder. We must realize what the ultimate and negative consequences could be for educational policy if these views continue to be pushed—with the prospect of an increasingly conservative court and with public opinion shaped by emotive dialogue about forced busing and the declining value of education.

Also with respect to educational policy, the societal question is constantly raised: Should the courts shape educational policies and practices by virtue of their decisions? This suggests that the courts are not the appropriate societal agent or institution for making policy decisions and that such decisions are undesirable. Yet neither the executive nor the legislative branch of government at the federal or any state level has taken a leadership role in education which could be depended upon to promote equal educational opportunity for minorities and the poor. It is easy to criticize the judicial branch for what it has done, but who criticizes the other two branches, and the states and cities, for what they have *not* done in the way of enhancing equality in education?

Directly related to criticism of the courts in this respect is the school busing controversy. Because busing is a means or tactic endorsed by the courts as one way of achieving equal access to educational opportunity, busing and the courts have come under direct, sustained attack. For example, white ethnics in Boston mounted and sustained direct, personal, and often physical attacks against the people who were bused (black children), the people who were thought to favor busing (Senator Ted Kennedy), and the property itself (the buses and school buildings in question). The educational situation deteriorated so badly at South Boston High School under these attacks and counterattacks that the school was placed in federal receivership and the local school board stripped of much of its authority in December 1975.

At the intellectual and policy-making levels, the influential people are affected by the research and public statements of James S. Coleman, the well-known sociologist. Coleman presented a paper, "Recent Trends in School Integration," at the meeting of the American Education Research Association in Washington, D.C. in April 1975, that concluded that school integration did not enhance the achievements of black children and that the courts should not be instruments of social policy. After this delivery to an academic/intellectual audience, Coleman granted interviews to the *Boston Globe* (May 18), the *Los Angeles Times* (May 29), the *Chicago Sun-Times,* and the *National Observer* (June 7), in which he explicitly opposed federal court orders requiring extensive urban school desegregation. Coleman argued that a large proportion of school segregation by race and social class is attributable to individual actions and that the courts should not interfere with them. He also said desegregation seemed to cause "white flight" from cities. In terms of policy recommendations, Coleman advocated racial intermarriage. This series of interviews gave Coleman great publicity throughout the nation.

By the end of July 1975, Coleman's language had changed. "Trends in School *Integration"* became "Trends in School *Segregation, 1968–73"* (italics mine; the latter is referred to as Coleman II in the literature). Excerpts and interpretations appeared in such publications as *Current* (July/August 1975) and *Phi Delta Kappan.*[2]

In 1975 Coleman held that large-city school-desegregation efforts had resulted in increased segregation because whites had fled from those cities. As a result, continued efforts at the reduction of segregation require the controversial policy of busing. Two alternative policy implications can be drawn from this state of affairs: (1) metropolitan-wide school desegregation through the courts, with busing across district boundaries, or (2) reducing school segregation that results from residential segregation by reducing residential segregation, which is especially difficult and, in itself, requires such policies as busing, which spark great resistance. Under the second alternative, local communities would decide how much segregation they want to eliminate from their school systems and the means for such elimination. The courts would restrict their decisions to educational remedies which would correct segregation resulting from deliberate actions of states and school officials. There would not be court-ordered busing, for example, to reduce school segregation caused by voluntary residential patterns.

In the *Phi Delta Kappan,* Coleman raised the question of individual rights. He cited the historical practice of allowing each family to choose a school for its children by choosing its place of residence ("except in the dual systems of the South") and held that this is a right that many Americans will not easily relinquish. Since the educational policy of busing eliminates one's right to choose his child's school through choice of residence, some parents will fight the policy. For instance, white ethnics in Boston (and others) will continue to flee, and whites with sufficient economic resources will move to more affluent suburbs or choose private schooling. (We will return to the exception of the "dual systems of the South.")

Therefore, Coleman proposed his own solution to the problem of busing as a tactic to desegregate schools. He suggested that there should be, as a matter of educational policy, the "right of each child in a metropolitan area to attend any school in that area, so long as the school to which he chose to go had no higher proportion of his race than his neighborhood school."[3] Such a right would have to be granted at the state level because no school district is permitted to give its children the right to attend school in another district. Also, Coleman pointed out, there would have to be a capacity limitation for each school so that no school would be required to resort to split or double shifts because it is a popular school. Such a policy, he said, would necessitate a state transfer of funds to follow the child across school district lines; this would not be easy to do, but it is within the power of the state.

This is "freedom of choice," but with a new wrinkle: it is possible to choose a school outside one's school district provided the state grants the right to cross school district lines and transfers corresponding funds. The solution may appear benign and rational, but it is directly contradictory to the findings of the U.S. Civil Rights Commission on freedom-of-choice options as viable educational policy. In volume 2 of the three-part series, *Twenty Years after Brown,* finding 5 on equality of educational opportunity says " 'freedom of choice' has proved a totally ineffective method of school desegregation."[4] Yet this was Coleman's recommendation for educational policy in October 1975. He pointed out that, in his opinion, new research shows that the achievement benefit in schools that were integrated by court-ordered (forced) busing are not so substantial as to demand school desegregation, whatever the other consequences may be.

Also, worthy of note, is the cursory way Coleman passed over the forced segregation that blacks had to endure so long. In citing the historical practice of allowing each family to choose a school for its children by choosing its residence, he noted parenthetically: "except in the dual systems of the South." But he did not explain that this exception represented forced segregation, societally imposed upon blacks by public policy. It is this system of forced segregation in all its aspects, which caused the patterns of residential, school, and other forms of segregation. Thus the necessity for the *Brown* decision, and all other decisions which flowed from it, came from the system of segregation which was for so long *forced* upon black people, which was properly referred to as *de jure* in the South. It was highly visible and easily verifiable; so the societal desegregation policies were aimed at the Southern states originally, as Coleman pointed out.[5]

What few Northerners and intellectuals point out is that the alleged *de facto* Northern practices were *de jure* in intent and effect. *De facto* means exercising power as if such power is legally constituted, and the *de facto* real estate practices in the North were just as deadly in intent and effect as the *de jure* real estate practices in the South. These *de facto* practices, considered totally, became a system of *forced* segregation in the North although that system was not a part of state law. And the covert, more subtle Northern practices are harder to attack than were the overt Southern laws. Thus blacks and other minorities have suffered from forced segregation, North and South. The emotional appeal of forced busing as a term is not lost on us, but in intellectual honesty it should be described in the context of forced segregation, North and South, over an extended period of time.

With respect to the effect of social science literature on educational policy, the concept of "equality of opportunity" has been translated into "equality of results," so far as the shaping of educational policy is concerned. There are very pointed references to a "paucity" of results from the extension and enlargement of educational opportunity for blacks since the 1954 *Brown* decision—or, to put it another way, to the continuing black-white disparity in achievement test scores and school grades. This is explained in terms of black deficits:

1. Blacks are held to be deficient in native intelligence, and this is said to be a genetic difference, not correctable by schooling.
2. Blacks are deemed deficient in family structure and organization —too many families are headed by women in a society where it is deemed right and good that families be headed by men—and this represents a pathological state.

3. Blacks are supposedly deficient in environmental conditions and culture; this makes the group deprived and disadvantaged.

Conditions 2 and 3 are held to be correctable by schooling, but the process costs too much and takes too long; therefore the societal benefits are not worth the societal costs. Thus the overall conclusion in terms of educational policy is that schooling will not help blacks much because of blacks' deficits. This is "blaming the victim" *par excellence.*

There are also policy questions at the level of higher education which are traceable to the alleged results of schooling and black-white disparity in results, as well as male-female disparity, and much of the attack on affirmative action plans and programs is related to these questions. With respect to promotion and employment in faculty positions in institutions of higher education, minority groups and women hear such arguments as: Should persons who are *minimally qualified* or *less qualified* be given *preferential treatment* in hiring or promotion over those who are *more qualified?* These are the new code words that are used to justify the continuation of policies and practices which for so long have given preference to persons who turn out to be white and male. They suggest that blacks, other minorities, and women must of necessity be less qualified than white males. Other code words, used in an effort to maintain the status quo with respect to employment and promotion practices, are *reverse discrimination* and *quotas.*

In fact, current social literature relates the question of meritocracy to the notion of equality and to alleged disparities in educational results. John Gardner's question of the early sixties, "Can we be equal and excellent, too?" is being replaced in the seventies by the suggestion that we cannot be equal *and* meritocratic; so merit is to be preferred over equality. Therefore the argument becomes: Higher education faculty should be employed on merit; persons who are minimally or less qualified should not be given preferential treatment over persons who are more qualified. Each individual should get into the arena and compete.

Social science literature argues that group identity is not a viable base for public policy. Group identification, it is said, has nothing to do with individual qualifications, and it is individuals who are employed. Further, the historical experience of a group is not a viable base for public policy. Past injustices are deplorable, but nothing can be done about that; "no society can hope to undertake to redress the grievances of all the descendants of victims in the past."[6] Those who are alive today are not responsible for the enslavement of blacks or the degradation of women and should not, therefore, be expected to bear the burden of redress. From such arguments as the above, we can deduce the following:

1. The arguments are made in the self-interest of those who have the most of what there is to have.
2. The revival of Social Darwinism in modern language: the most meritorious are the most qualified and the "fittest"; thus the "survival of the fittest" and the notion that those who come out on top are there only because they deserve to be, since they have won out in the competition of life.
3. The revival of laissez-faire, classical liberal notions from Adam Smith's ideas of economic competition and the natural regulation of processes.
4. The notion of the social contract and its violation: government is intervening too much in the lives of people and therefore is violating the social contract by abandoning its proper role.

The argument against the relevance of group identification to public policy formulation ignores the history of the United States and the history of the world. Unfortunately, group membership has been all too relevant to the determination of qualifications, in a negative sense. What we ask is that it be made relevant in a positive sense, to help underprivileged persons overcome the effects of negative, forcibly imposed social policies.

Nowhere in American history do we see that the agricultural skills of blacks were tested before they were snatched from their homelands and brought to work out their lives on American soil. Nor is there any evidence of open competition between whites and blacks to assure that the best-qualified humans would become slaves. Thus we conclude that group membership, not individual qualifications, determined who became a slave and who did not. This was public policy in America. In like manner, the Indians were "removed" to reservations, and kept there, because of their group membership or identification, in spite of what they may or may not have done individually.

Looking at the world community, could one say that group membership was irrelevant to the 6 million Jews who were exterminated by the Nazis? No matter how young they were (babies and children), or how intelligent (scholars), or how productive (businessmen), they were exterminated because they were Jewish, not because of their individual deeds. Further, because of this "holocaust" and the prolonged group suffering of the Jewish people, most of the international community supported the establishment of the state of Israel in 1948 as a homeland to

which Jewish persons could go if they chose to do so. Thus in one sense
the creation and support of the state of Israel was an affirmative action
by the international community to relieve the suffering of a group of
people.

Thus group identification has been a key feature of both domestic
and international public policy. Such public policy can be negative or
positive in terms of the group in question—a national society or a world
community.

With respect to another question, the term *merit* means the quality
or fact of deserving, especially deserving well. It can also mean reward,
recompense, or, sometimes, punishment received or deserved. Therefore
when social scientists say they believe in the merit principle, this can be
translated into (a) reward, (b) recompense, or (c) punishment, received
or deserved. When we apply the notion of merit to the condition of
minorities and women in America, it is important to remember that social policy, practices, customs, and traditions in this country have created ways of thinking, acting, and feeling about people which interfere
with operation of the merit principle (getting what is deserved or
earned) in daily living.

For example, social policy in America has kept blacks separated in
many ways over a long period of time. The 1896 *Plessy* decision guaranteed this; that is, *Plessy* shaped public policy. Thus educational arrangements, employment practices, housing policies, customs, and traditions,
kept blacks unequal. The inequality resulted in an alleged inferiority—
sometimes real and sometimes only perceived. It is therefore the case in
daily living that, more often than would be expected by chance, when a
black Ph.D. (for example) is competing with a white Ph.D. for the same
job, the black is perceived as inferior by the employer (beholder); so the
white gets the job, regardless of merit. The same principle applies to
women; social policy, practices, customs, and traditions have operated to
keep them unequal to men, and stereotypes and labeling have been effective devices to create an image of inferiority in the eye of the potential employer (the beholder).

The facts of blackness or femaleness are accidents of birth and
fixed conditions. Therefore when one is perceived as inferior, based on
the differential visibility of a fixed condition for which one is not responsible, one seeks social change in a society which purports to be democratic and committed to principles of equality and justice. The social
change that is being sought by affirmative action programs is change in
the form of recompense for past inequities. Again, recompense is one of

the meanings of *merit*; it is something that "makes up for," that "is given in compensation for." Qualified blacks and women are asking recompense for what they suffered in the years upon years when they were excluded from equality of opportunity.

In this sense, recompense is not "reverse discrimination" but, rather, a reversal of discrimination. The difference is real, not semantic, in terms of social policy. Many blacks and women feel that they became the scapegoats for the society's economic problems in the 1960s and early 1970s. Their position in society along some indicators, especially expressed attitudes and unemployment, showed this deterioration. But instead of being placed where it belonged, on the vagaries of the economic system, the blame was placed on the victims—blacks and women. Equality in employment practices of necessity excluded some men from jobs that would have been theirs (the zero-sum concept) under unequal employment practices, which had so long prevailed.

Eternal tension is possible in actualization of the abstract concepts of equality, liberty, and justice. A gain in equality for some people may mean a reduction in liberty for other people. How the tensions are resolved depends on the values and commitments of people in power. Tensions are apparent today in societal questions about race relations, ethnicity, equality of educational opportunity, busing, IQ, affirmative action, meritocracy, quotas, open admission to colleges, and the division of wealth and power. Much of the elitist social science literature since 1966, intentionally or unintentionally, has been undercutting the major means by which blacks, other minorities, and women have sought to gain equality and justice in America. Thus elitist social science literature, in a period of increasing conservatism, assisted in skewing public policy in a negative direction, into a downward spiral, regarding the aspirations of underprivileged persons. Educational policy is one aspect of such public policy.

Whatever the shortcomings of education as a means of survival and social mobility, education has been a major means by which underprivileged persons have been able to prepare themselves to survive and live in America. Today, formal schooling is under siege. If public policy turns away from societal support for schooling, or if schooling continues to be seriously undercut, what will blacks and other underprivileged persons do to prepare themselves to live, and live well, in a society that is increasingly technological, complex, and costly—with not enough jobs for all the people who want and need them? What can these groups do in ignorance—or even innocence—in a society that is increasingly sophisticated and manipulative? The attacks focus on the shortcomings of public schooling and on the validity of public policies designed to strengthen and enlarge the public educational system. But the attackers do not make realistic recommendations for a public policy to shore up or to create new societal institutions to replace education as a means that can be used by the underprivileged to survive and live well.

This state of affairs makes blacks wonder if the assault on education is the 1977 version of the age-old "mandate" not to educate blacks, because education makes them dissatisfied with their lot. If this is the case, the strategy is the same; just the words are different. Instead of coming in wolf's clothing, the wolf is coming in sheep's clothing, bleating that "schools cannot help much."

In terms of policy, blacks can see highly unfavorable evaluations of federally funded programs such as Title I (ESEA), Head Start, and Follow Through. The difficulties of refunding previously passed legislation are clearly related to those negative evaluations and to alleged nonpermanent results. There is some unwillingness to pass new laws designed to help the black and the poor, as well as unwillingness to enforce laws already on the books. Because foundation funds are drying up, aid to students in higher education is not nearly as plentiful as it was in the mid-sixties. Mergers of public black colleges into state university systems are suspect. Therefore key questions for blacks and other minority persons are how to reverse the conditions of the social climate in America and what should these groups be doing to enhance their self-interest as part of the public interest, as well as to influence all facets of public policy.

MYRDAL ON EDUCATION

In analyzing the American scene, Gunnar Myrdal began with the role of education in American democratic thought and life. He said:

> Education has always been the great hope for both individual and society. In the American Creed it has been the main ground upon which "equality of opportunity for the individual" and "free outlet for ability" could be based. Education has also been considered as the best way—and the way most compatible with American individualistic ideals—to improve society.[7]

But just what is this education to which Myrdal assigns such a lofty role?

Formal education, according to Emile Durkheim, is "a methodical socialization of the young generation." By "methodical socialization" he makes a distinction between the formal socialization, that is, organized schooling, and the informal socialization which is educative, taking place both in and out of school, but which tends to be more spontaneous and unmethodical—at least not as systematic and consistent as school learning is intended to be.

In all societies, the school exists as a social institution to induct the young into the culture. It is expected to pass on to the young generation all those cultural elements which have promise of contributing to the advancement of mankind. These cultural elements, or organized learnings, are usually arranged as "subjects," for example, mathematics, history. The school is also expected to teach the young the processes through which one acquires, organizes, interrelates, and interprets the data of his experience. The entirety of this process is called formal education.

Young people spend a large portion of their waking hours from age 6 to 18 in the formal process of schooling. Because this society has considered formal schooling so crucial to the enhancement of the life-chances of the young, it has instituted compulsory attendance laws. This means that the child's right to be schooled cannot be abridged by his parents or other persons. Compulsory attendance laws are buttressed by child labor laws, and both are designed to prevent exploitation of the child through enforced remunerative work. The twelve years of school attendance, commonly expected and provided free of direct charge to students and their parents by the public, mean that students are placed in formal educational situations where their attitudes and beliefs can be influenced and shaped by teachers and other school personnel. At the same time, their attitudes and beliefs are constantly influenced and shaped by their families, peers, and the larger society, especially television and radio. This means that the young are in a constant socialization process, which is both methodical and unmethodical. The question is how to use the methodical process to acculturate them more closely with those cultural elements which have greatest promise of contributing to the advancement of American ideals and to solving the American dilemma in race relations.

For the young people who go on to higher education, the methodical formal educational processes continue to operate, from about age 18 to age 22 as undergraduates, and perhaps until age 30 for graduate students. Beyond age 30, we find, the concept of life-long learning is in vogue, and the societal suggestion is that many mature adults should return to formal schooling to learn new skills, attitudes, and roles to cope with the challenges of the swift social change that is evident throughout American society. Thus the expectation is that formal education will involve larger numbers of people for longer periods of time, all through the life span. This means that it will be possible to influence more mature adults at various times in their lives on cultural elements which have greatest promise of contributing to the advancement of American ideals and to solving race problems.

Informal education is no less important than formal schooling. Indeed, it is possible that everyone learns more through the collectivity of informal, out-of-school experiences than in the processes of formal schooling. Further, in-school and out-of-school learning influence each other. When Myrdal talks about education, he is referring to these formal and informal societal arrangements.

Continuing with his assessment of education in American thought and life, Myrdal pointed out eleven diverse features:

1. Research and discussion of education were prolific in America.
2. Pedagogy anticipated the trend to environmentalism in the social sciences and was foremost in expressing belief in the changeability of people.
3. Pragmatism, the major American contribution to philosophy, displayed signs of having been formulated in a culture where education was awarded a prominent role.
4. Americans were leaders in pedagogical thinking, requiring that education relate to the society in which the individual lives; as a result, America has seen more innovative and experimental redirection of schools than any other country.
5. Society's duty to provide public education was established when this nation was young; as a result, America spends more money and provides its young with more schooling than any other country in the world.
6. America has succeeded to some degree in making real the commitment that the entire educational range would be open for the brightest and hardest working youths, apart from the ability of their families to pay for advanced education.
7. Education has always been a primary means of social mobility.
8. The American zest for education has always focused on opportunity for the individual.
9. The stress on enforcing a basic minimum standard of education for all young people has been less than the zeal for education;

there is great disparity in minimum standards of education.

10. These disparities are evident between Negro and white schooling policies and plans, but they are also evident in various regions of the country, cities, and rural districts within a state.

11. A change in American attitudes is under way with respect to raising substandard education to levels of greater equality. Myrdal saw this change as tied in with proposals for federal aid to education and he believed that the Negroes' chance for realizing more equality in education was related directly to this movement for greater federal aid.

Regarding the Negro and education, Myrdal felt that Negroes had accepted the American faith in education and were anxious to learn. In fact, many Negroes exhibited almost religious faith in education as a means to improve themselves and their social status because learning through participation in other institutions, such as business and government, was closed to them. Also, many Negroes hoped that education would help their children escape the drudgery which had befallen them. Myrdal felt that the faith of Negroes in education had been justified to a large extent because education was one of the factors or forces which had helped them achieve a somewhat permanent advance in their condition.[8]

Myrdal found other paradoxes with respect to education in America (other than black-white and regional differences) in the generally high esteem accorded education in the abstract. These were:

a. The generally low status and pay accorded teachers, considering the importance accorded education;

b. Undercurrents of anti-intellectualism and a lack of prestige for learning, compared with the importance attached to education;

c. The feeling that education is produced by elementary and secondary schools and finishes with graduation;

d. Absence of the notion that education is a process of life-long learning and that much of it depends on the individual's exertion;

e. The passivity of students in the process of attaining knowledge;

f. The tendency of teachers to teach too much, which results in "spoon feeding" the young;

g. Passive mass education through the radio, press, popular magazines, and movies. (Today, of course, television would be added to these agencies of passive education.)

Assessing Negro education within the general framework of education in America, Myrdal's key points were:

1. Negroes' statutory right to public education has remained unassailable, even in the South, where it is probable that face-saving was necessary because of the American Creed. Without it, and without the influence of the Negro school and college, the Negro would have been driven back to slavery, for all intents and purposes, in the reactionary periods.
2. The persistent support of Northern philanthropy was a key factor in maintaining Negro education in reactionary periods.
3. The implications of classical versus vocational education as appropriate to Negroes are important in terms of the motives of the whites in power as well as in terms of the attitudes of Negroes themselves.

Assessing white attitudes toward Negro education, Myrdal was explicit: the conflicts of valuation between whites and Negroes in regard to Negro education, the interests involved, and the theories that express them determine the forms of Negro education.[9] Myrdal held that the American Creed prescribes that Negro children should have as much educational opportunity as anyone else in the same community and that Negroes should receive the kind of education which would make them good and equal citizens in a democracy which values culture.

Looking at poor whites, Myrdal stressed the economic implications of retaining the caste system. Poorer whites are in competition with Negroes for jobs and for social status, so the supremacy of individual poor whites is bound up with Negro ignorance. However, whites of the employing class do not have the same material interest in Negro ignorance; in fact, they can gain if their workers and servants have some education, Myrdal held. Likewise, city living requires more formal education than rural living, and Negroes in cities generally received better education than Negroes in rural areas, South and North.

Myrdal explained that whites generally preferred industrial education for Negroes, rather than a more liberal or classical education. This preference was motivated by an interest to preserve the caste order in which Negroes were expected to be servants, farm laborers, and industrial workers. However, despite this preference, whites have never had the "nerve to make of Negro education an accomplished instrument to keep the Negro in their caste status."[10] So, especially in the South at the time Myrdal was writing, and before, the idea of industrial education for

Negroes was a compromise of Southern white policy makers between their belief in education (stemming from the American Creed) and their self-interest in preserving the caste system of the South. Pedagogical advantages and disadvantages of vocational versus classical education were not discussed. Similarly, no effective industrial training was ever given Negroes in Southern public schools, except in cooking and menial service.[11] Really expensive vocational training, which would have put Negroes into effective competition with whites, was never much more than a slogan. Myrdal acknowledged that "discussion of whether Negroes should have a vocational or a liberal schooling is thus only in part a real issue. Partly it is a cover for the more general problem as to what extent Negroes should have much education at all.[12]

Myrdal felt that the attitudes of whites were of greatest importance for the growth of Negro education, for whites had all the power.[13] But he felt that Negroes had influence on the growth of Negro education because whites were divided among themselves and in their own consciences. Unfortunately, however, he felt that Negroes were divided in the same ways.

In examining Negro attitudes, Myrdal felt that, at bottom, all Negroes felt they had the same right as whites to equal opportunities for education. The American Creed gives Negroes the opportunity to express this belief and to press whites for concessions to make Negro education "more equal." Further, it was the stress on education in American culture which made the Negro protest most respectable, since much of it was couched in terms of educational equality. However, Myrdal found some intragroup schism among Negroes. A few upper-class Negroes expressed the caste-like views of whites with respect to equality of educational opportunity for what these Negroes called "common" Negroes and with respect to the content of instruction for them. It was felt that some kind of vocational training, or working with the hands, was the most appropriate instruction for "common" Negroes.

With respect to whether education should be segregated, Myrdal explained that segregation is motivated by white fear of social equality; it is a precaution against social equality. But segregation is also a necessary means of maintaining the tremendous financial discrimination against Negro schools.[14] Negroes are against segregation to the extent that it means discrimination and is a badge of alleged Negro inferiority. But some Negroes prefer the segregated school if the mixed school involves substandard treatment of Negro students and adults. Other Negroes prefer mixed schools, regardless of temporary human costs, as a matter of principle or as a means of improving race relations. Myrdal quoted W. E. B. DuBois:

> Theoretically, the Negro needs neither segregated schools nor mixed schools. What he needs is Education. What he must remember is that there is no magic, either in mixed schools or in segregated schools. A mixed school with poor and unsympathetic teachers, with hostile opinion, and no teaching concerning black folk, is bad. A segregated school with ignorant placeholders, inadequate equipment, poor salaries, and wretched housing, is equally bad. Other things being equal, the mixed school is the broader, more natural basis for the education of all youth. It gives wider contacts; it inspires greater self-confidence; and suppresses the inferiority complex. But other things seldom are equal, and in that case, Sympathy, Knowledge, and the Truth, outweigh all that the mixed school can offer.[15]

Looking at trends and problems with respect to Negro education, particularly in the South, where most Negroes still lived when Myrdal wrote his book, Myrdal saw:

1. "Scandalously poor," educational facilities for Negroes particularly in many rural regions.
2. There was an upward trend in the level of educational facilities offered Negroes. He saw this trend gaining momentum, aided by the intervention of federal agencies, Northern philanthropy, and the growing force of Southern liberalism.
3. The rising educational level of Southern whites helps them understand the necessity of doing something about Negro education.
4. NAACP strategies should help Negro teachers acquire increases in salaries.
5. Graduate schools in the South should be open to Negroes, based on NAACP efforts.
6. Segregation will increasingly become a financial burden and, as a result, will probably decline on the highest level.

Myrdal's summation was that never since Reconstruction had there been fewer reasons for a defeatist attitude with respect to Negro education in the South.[16]

Myrdal concluded that (1) the main problem is how much education the Negro should have and how much he gets; (2) any type of improved education for Negroes is salutary; (3) there is a tremendous need for new school buildings, new equipment, consolidated schools, and school buses for Negroes followed by; (4) the need to improve the standards of Negro teachers; (5) the federal government should take further financial responsibility for education, but without decreasing local responsibility (Myrdal's "ideal" solution was for the federal government to pay certain basic costs, such as construction costs and basic teachers' salaries, with nondiscrimination a condition for aid);[17] and (6) the main fault with Negro education is its inadequacy and "undernourishment"; however, with the prospect of improvement, direction becomes important. "What is needed is an education which makes the Negro child adaptable to and movable in the American culture at large."[18]

> Even the Negro child who will stay in Southern agriculture will need to use various types of machinery, to follow popular journals in his field, to deal with credit institutions and government agencies, and successfully to take part in organizations. He needs to be able to read, write, and reckon, and to be lifted so high above illiteracy that he actually participates in modern American society. Before all, he needs not to be specialized, but to be changeable, "educable." And *he needs it more than the white child, because life will be more difficult for him.*[19]

A final note was that, for Northern cities and for migratory Negroes everywhere, a program of adult education should be instituted to teach Negroes what they need to know in terms of vocational skills and general literacy.

ANALYSIS OF MYRDAL'S VIEWS ON EDUCATION

Myrdal's feeling was that the rising educational level of Negroes is a tremendously important factor for power relations in the United States. In an important way, education is likely to increase dissatisfaction among Negroes with their imposed caste status and will cause them to take concerted action to change that status. The long-range effect of education on Negroes will be to nourish and strengthen Negro protest, Myrdal said.[20] In like manner, education affects the white population.

Using Myrdal's theory, what can we say about the role of formal and informal education in effectuating social change?

Because Myrdal placed beliefs and valuations in the statics of his system, and because of the unique relationship between them, he put great value on education. Education, by disclosing the discrepancies among individuals' valuations, causes people to act in one direction or another because the desire for consistency is a dynamic factor. Education, then, is a genuine social force, coordinated with all the other forces

—economic, legal, institutional, and physical. Education is a causal factor and can affect other causal factors, in line with the principle of cumulation. Because this is a literate, civilized society, education can bring the facts related to social problems to light and help to change the valuations of people. Education has a powerful potential and plays a vital role in solving the American dilemma.

Analyzing the American scene, Myrdal said that Americans' belief in education is a part of, or an important conclusion to, the American Creed. Education has always been the great hope for the individual and for society. In the American Creed, it has been the primary ground upon which equality of opportunity for the individual and free outlet for ability have been based. Furthermore, education has been considered the best way (compatible with American individualistic ideals) to improve society. When the average American faces a problem or situation he does not know how to solve, he tends to look either to education or to enlightened leadership to help him solve the problem.

Thus three roles can be seen for formal education in America:
1. To give Americans knowledge of how to solve the American dilemma;
2. To promote free and open discussion about social problems in America;
3. To develop intelligent leadership in order to have enlightened persons help in the solution of social problems.

Formal education should capitalize on the fact that Americans believe in their national ability to solve problems and in progress. Americans are, at bottom, moral optimists.

Another legitimate task of education is to correct popular beliefs by subjecting them to rigorous examination in the light of the factual evidence. Despite the fact that there will be psychological resistance to such rigorous examination by people who feel a need to retain their biased beliefs in order to justify their way of life, this educational objective must be achieved. When popular beliefs are exposed as false, illogicalities involving valuations become clear to the people who hold them. For if popular beliefs depend on valuations, as Myrdal has shown, the valuations depend on the beliefs in a rational society. Therefore when the supporting beliefs are shown to be wrong, people will of necessity readjust their value hierarchies and their behavior in order to achieve consistency. This amounts to a channeled and controlled "opinion explosion" because education works on large numbers of people all over the nation.

Since the high-order valuations in American culture have legal and moral sanction, this means that if education is successful, the American Creed will be upheld, moral cynicism will be counteracted, and the low-order valuations (irrationalities or prejudices) will yield to the high-order valuations. This is the way that education, through improved knowledge, may make for better citizens. It is not that facts themselves improve anything or solve the problem; it is that improved knowledge exposes illogicalities and rationalizations for what they are. The rational person, desiring to be consistent, cannot continue to live with his inconsistencies; so he changes for the better. Education reaches so many persons, directly and indirectly, that the change for the better is a perceptible, major change.

One may well ask: On what grounds, or by what authority, does education claim the right to assume this role in American society? Education derives its authority from the core of the democratic tradition (the American Creed), and the moral authority of the teacher lies in the child's right to be informed. In addition, the teacher should be competent to assume this role because of his expert knowledge about democratic values.

A counterresponse could be: But why should changes be undertaken by education? To such a retort it can be pointed out that America's formal educational structure reaches almost every young American for twelve years, and a large percentage of them for more than twelve years. America also subscribes to the theory which requires that education be uniquely suited to teach children and young people to investigate, evaluate, and conclude in line with the core of democratic values. To the extent that the school is effective, it will affect the character, opinions, and habits of the young, which will carry over into adult life and into the communities in which they live. Such an educational method and procedure is in line with the American educational tradition of improving the human material by proper schooling.

Formal Education

Let us look at some of the undertakings of formal education:

1. Social problems should be studied in school, with a view to achieving a common set of values. This might take the form of a social studies "core" that every child takes. This core must be characterized by free and open inquiry and discussion, because communication about all problems is vital.

2. The school should stress the art and attitudes needed for group deliberation.
3. The American Creed should permeate instruction and the school should exemplify the values of the American Creed in its day-to-day operations so that the school is a community-exemplar for the creed.
4. The school's role is that of social critic, holding a mirror to social reality and asking that attitudes be checked against social reality. This role comes from the notion that since people seek consistency, they will not like to be inconsistent in their attitudes and beliefs.
5. The school, as a social critic, does not try to disorganize the child but to make him or her mentally more healthy by being more consistent.
6. Leaders and social scientists will be developed through formal education; such enlightened persons are needed for leadership and to ascertain the facts.

The preceding discussion appears to be aimed in large measure at the white majority in America, since they are the power holders and it is they who must change their attitudes in order to resolve the American dilemma. But what of the Negro minority? What does the American Creed dictate for them, and what is the role of formal education as it relates to the Negro minority?

From the standpoint of the American Creed, the Negro's status in America represents a long lapse in public morals; therefore it will be necessary to marshal the resources of formal and informal education and enlightened leadership to repair it. Since an improvement by any of these resources will improve all the others, because they are interrelated, it is wise to use all the resources rather than any one of them, because the cumulative effect will, of necessity, be large over a period of time.

The American Creed, according to Myrdal, dictates that Negro youth should have as much educational opportunity as any other group. Formal education has a vital role to play in that it will increase the forces for raising the status of the Negro; for example:

1. More formal education means more assimilation of the majority culture, thereby decreasing the dissimilarity of Negroes from other Americans (Myrdal's language).
2. Formal education trains and helps give Negroes an economic

livelihood, so that they are ready to move into new positions when opportunities arise.

3. It is a means of social mobility, and since large numbers of Negroes are in the lower class, education presents the possibility that the entire class will climb in status.
4. Increased formal education will make the Negro more dissatisfied with his lot in America and therefore cause him to exert pressures for change, which are likely to cumulate and spiral.
5. Increased education provides theories and tools with which Negroes can protest against their caste status.
6. Formal education changes the Negro's traditional charade of response patterns, which are outmoded in today's world (e.g., docility and passivity).
7. Formal education provides a means of self-realization for the Negro, thereby enhancing his ego and belief in himself.
8. Leaders are developed through the educational sorting and selecting process.

All these factors also have symbolic significance for both Negroes and whites in that they help dispel the stereotyped ideas that the Negro people are incapable of learning and do not care to better their life conditions. To the extent that false beliefs in Negro inferiority are removed by education, to the extent that the Negro is enabled through education to measure up to norms, to the extent that whites are able to see the degradations they have heaped on Negroes, to that extent will the American Creed, via education, remove the caste status of the Negro in America.

It is clear, as Myrdal said, that the Negro child needs formal education which will make him adaptable to, and movable in, the American culture at large, and he needs it more than the white child because life is more difficult for the Negro in America. This means that Negro youth need career and general education, but one should not be gained at the expense of the other, because career education can provide skill and training for immediate employment, whereas general education is transferable and enables the individual to adapt to changing conditions and careers in a rapidly changing social order.

Many adults—black, white, and others—need systematic adult education in the 1970s—in vocational, civic, academic, social, and consumer matters, as occasioned by the shifting needs of the rapidly changing social order and the inadequacy of their previous schooling. Although the literacy rate of the United States population has increased steadily over time, functional shortcomings are clearly evident. A 1975 study by Norvill Northcutt for the U.S. Office of Education revealed that a large proportion of the adult population is unable to cope with contemporary life situations. These adults lack functional competency, and their needs could be met by formal schooling or through a community development approach which can be labeled a nonformal mechanism for educating people.

Under the community development approach, knowledge is made directly relevant to the needs of people and to social practices. Under tutelage, learning and doing are united as education and action. For example, in a community center a teacher of adults would begin with a common problem, such as installment buying and uses of credit. Working with adults on the elements of this problem and teaching them solutions which they can immediately implement is a beginning which could lead to other types of functional learning as well as contribute to cooperative efforts that are learned by working together in this nonformal educational situation.

It is clear that formal education has a crucial and vital role to play, according to Myrdal's theory, and specific tasks of formal education have been enumerated. But what about informal education in such a theory? It, too, plays a crucial and vital part.

Informal Education

Informal learning takes place when instruction is not carried on by an agency or personnel specifically designated for that purpose. Television, for example, is an important means of informal education for the American people. The assumption that informal learning has a contribution to make in solving the American dilemma probably originated in eighteenth-century French humanitarianism and equalitarianism influences on America, which came through Rousseau, and from the seventeenth-century English liberal influence, which came through Locke, and most recently from the liberal influence of John Dewey and his followers.

These humanistic, equalitarian, liberal influences led many Americans to believe the environment is the chief explanation for human differences and, consequently, an important means of improving mankind. These influences also made Americans feel that much is learned informally in living in a social system and being influenced by all of its institutions and groupings. With a belief in the value of informal education thereby established, it follows that the role of informal education is to complement, supplement, and reinforce formal education's teachings on the ideals of America as expressed in the American Creed and to stress the discrepancy between those ideals and actual practice. Groups and institutions, by making people conscious of the great discrepancy, exert pressure in creating awareness and discomfort because of inconsistency and in adding to the upward force of the cumulative spiral. Informal education, like formal education, contributes to extending the sphere of substantial rationality (to use Mannheim's term) for both whites and Negroes, since both groups often behave in a manner which betrays the dominance of functional rationality (and even irrationality). Both groups appear to view the social system from their position in it, for example, rather than see it as a whole.

Informal education must allow for free and open discussion of social problems and issues so that people may see their rationalizations for what they are and so that it will no longer be possible to compartmentalize reality. The "opinion explosion" is the likely result, but because the pressure on the problem has been positive rather than negative, the explosion is likely to be upward, toward greater realization of the high-order ideals.

Specifically, which institutions and groups, not formally charged with educative responsibility, might be useful informally, and in what ways? Religion as a social force, and the church as the institutionalized agent of religion, could be useful. Churches must themselves support the American Creed by deed, not by word only; such support is a source of strength. Emotionally and cognitively, the church as a social institution can provide the time and place for free and open discussion, but its role should be one of stressing consistency, tolerance, understanding, and interest in social problems. However, the church tends to be conservative.

Labor unions are powerful interest groups that have contact with large numbers of people; they also have educational programs. Their educational programs could do a great deal to make people conscious of the discrepancy between ideals and practices. They could become exemplars of change in the right direction by being more consistent with American ideals and opening their groups to Negroes, thereby providing new economic possibilities and new contacts so that the groups may get to know each other in different kinds of situations. White ethnics, particularly, could be positively affected by the informal educational process in a socially progressive union. Again, however, conservatism in labor unions has to be overcome, and this is hard to do.

The major industries could play a role almost identical to that of labor unions in providing new economic and contact possibilities, so that changes of attitude and modifications of customs are more likely. Also, increased employment opportunities would enhance the process of cumulation for the Negro. Blacks don't see this forthcoming, however, because of the no-growth economy.

The mass media have a vital role in informal education, which they must renew by making the nation aware that the Negro problem is a national one, not a regional issue. The mass media can point out specific problems in employment and housing and the effects of deprivation. Radio and television may contribute to a "new image" of Negroes by using them more often in roles other than that of the stereotyped servant or lower-class buffoon. Their competence is attested to when Negroes are used as announcers and in commercials and when they are employed in decision-making positions. Positive achievements, such as home and community improvements, might be reported in the press and magazines. Radio and television might allow more time for public discussion and debate on the major social issues. Today, game shows dominate daytime television, not issue-oriented programs. Neither television nor radio is fulfilling its potential in affecting positive attitudinal change so far as race relations are concerned.

Negroes, as well as whites, need to participate in the political process every time the opportunity is presented. Representative government depends upon an enlightened electorate participating in the electoral process. Negroes, as part of that enlightened electorate, must use their vote to ensure that elected leaders are the kind of people who will be responsive to the needs of the black and the poor. Blacks, however, have been remiss in their voting behavior in the 1970s. The black population cannot afford the luxury of negligence in this respect, and must remedy its shortcomings. Hard-won voting gains must not be lost through carelessness and nonparticipation.

The American legal system also can be an important force in informal education. Americans' ideals are inscribed in the law, ranging downward from the federal Constitution to the myriad of local laws in the fifty states. The purpose of legislating national ideals is to give them legal sanction, publicity, and prestige in a manner which officially dedicates the nation to moving closer to the ideals, and these laws must be enforced consistently over time. If they are so enforced, a change in behavior will be evident, even if a change in attitude does not occur. For example, enforcement of public accommodation laws has meant that blacks may be housed in hotels and eat in restaurants which were closed to them prior to 1965. Therefore, white *behavior* changed with respect to registering blacks in hotels and serving them in restaurants, whether white *attitudes* changed or not. Thus we see that behavorial change is attainable.

In like manner, the Voting Rights Act of 1965 ensured that eligible black voters in Southern states were able to register to vote, despite the white officials who did not want to allow such registration. The *attitude* of white registrars probably did not change, but their *behavior* changed under the impact of federal law, vigorously enforced.

If national political leaders who give lip service to the American Creed and continually point to it were more consistent in their deeds, so that they were consistent with the creed, they would serve as exemplars in the process of social change. The Kennedy and Johnson years showed that presidential leadership could set the tone for progress in solving racial problems. The Nixon administration showed that presidential leadership could set the tone for a reversal of progress in race relations. Therefore it makes a difference to black people what kind of leadership directs the executive branch of government.

From the preceding discussion it can be seen that informal education can play an outstanding role in resolving the American dilemma. Myrdal has implicit faith in the power of education to solve problems, particularly in America.

STATUS OF EDUCATION

Given this faith in education, as seen by Myrdal, and its possibilities as a social force, what is its status? Even as Myrdal wrote his book, it was apparent that the rising level of education of whites in the South gave a stronger basis and greater willingness for improving Negro education.[21] Myrdal's perception was that Negroes would not receive as much education as they were actually getting in the South if the equalitarian creed were not so active, despite the fact that day-to-day behavior was a compromise.[22] In the North, Myrdal felt, the equalitarian valuation was strong enough to dominate public policy, despite the fact that most white people believed Negroes to be inferior and cared little for their potentialities. Educational facilities were improved for blacks throughout the nation, in large part after 1954.

One of the Southern responses to the *Brown* decision was to build new structures for black schooling and provide better equipment in existing buildings. This program was an early delaying tactic by policy makers who felt that blacks would prefer to remain in their own schools, rather than integrate with white students, if black schools were equal to or better than white. These facilities, overall, still were not equal to those provided for whites, but improvement was made.

Court suits, seeking equal salaries for black and white public school teachers in the late 1930s and early 1940s, were won by black teachers in Norfolk, Newport News, Danville, and Richmond, Virginia, as well as in Little Rock, Arkansas. These cases exerted progressive influence far beyond the communities in which they arose, so that there is no longer a problem of equal salaries for black and white teachers. They receive equal pay, based on equal qualifications. A different societal problem with respect to black and white teachers, however, is the retention of black teachers and principals in communities where public schools are integrated. In *Twenty Years after Brown: Equality of Educational Opportunity,* the U.S. Civil Rights Commission pointed out that

> *the desegregation of dual school systems in the South has often resulted in the displacement or demotion of black school staff.* Further, the number of black staff employed to fill new positions appears to be declining. Few Southern school systems have black administrators, and the number of minority educators also is markedly small in many Northern schools. [p. 89]

Graduate and professional schools have been opened to black students. *De jure* exclusionary policies have been eliminated. *De facto* exclusionary policies exist, however, and financial ability to extend the educational process through higher and professional education is still beyond most black families. Equal opportunity in employment, promotions, and salaries are unrealized goals for black men and women in graduate and professional schools throughout America.

Certification standards of Negro and white teachers have improved. A bachelor's degree is almost a universal requirement for entry into the teaching profession at the elementary or secondary level. Northern philanthropy continues in the form of foundation grants to selected black schools and individuals. However, blacks still get less money than whites, both proportionately and absolutely.

The federal government has increased its contributions to education but it has not assumed the payment of certain basic costs all over the country, as Myrdal suggested. Nondiscrimination is a formal condition for receiving federal aid, but this requirement often breaks down in practice. Enforcement is an increasing problem due to the attitudes and policies of presidents Nixon and Ford since 1969, as well as to perceptions of the prevailing social climate.

The value of vocational versus classical education is again discussed and debated. In 1970s jargon, "vocational" education has become "career" education. There is an element of truth in arguments that career education directly equips one for a job and is a practical kind of education, in which a payoff is immediate and predictable. It is also true that whites are included in the career-education concept. Yet history suggests that the notion smacks of a return to the "vocational" education arguments, so that the concept of career education is somewhat suspect, even as blacks take advantage of it and hope to realize its promises. We are afraid that this is partly—as Myrdal said some thirty years ago—a cover "for the more general problem as to what extent Negroes should have much education at all." His observation is still appropriate: "The lines are blurred because the argument for vocational education is used both by the people who want to have more education for Negroes and by those who want to restrict it."[23] His view, again, was that education should help the Negro child adapt to the larger American culture.

Does the black child need this education in an integrated or in a segregated setting? DuBois put it so well in 1935 that we can hardly improve on his words, cited earlier in this chapter.

For the black population and the total population, formal schooling (usually public) has resulted in higher levels of literacy, higher educational attainment, and higher school enrollment ("persistence"). In turn, these results have made it possible for underprivileged persons to qualify for different, higher-level, more satisfying, and more remunerative positions. The process of cumulation, then, would mean that using education as a means or instrument has been effective for many citizens, to the extent that education can prepare people for adult-level employment. Acquiring education or training, however, is only the first step, and the subsequent steps have not been taken by the society at large.

Campbell's research pointed out that, since 1948, college education has made a difference in the attitudes of the white population. Because large numbers of whites have attended college and been exposed to the ideas and concepts that could make them more willing advocates of equality and justice, college education has had a positive effect on sectors of the dominant group since 1948.

Education has equipped blacks to protest more effectively against injustices and inequality in the American social order. Educated blacks found that more desirable jobs were open to them in the 1960s and, as a result, were able to provide a higher standard of living for themselves and their families. They were also able to make higher educational opportunity a reality for their young in larger numbers than had ever been the case in American history. Young blacks are much more highly educated than their ancestors, thanks to increased educational opportunities. Also, as Myrdal pointed out, the stress on education in American culture helped make the black protest more "respectable."

Yet a black-white disparity is still evident in educational attainment and achievement, due primarily to historic inequities that are being reinstituted and reinforced through negatively oriented educational statements and policies. Also, there is cynicism among many black youth because employment opportunities are closed to them. They become reluctant to achieve in school and meet the academic demands when it seems that this effort will not be rewarded by access to meaningful jobs which pay living wages and offer opportunities to climb the career ladder. For blacks are like all other Americans; we have been socialized to want individual success and the good things of life, while trying to make life better for our descendants than it was for us.

Black public colleges are attacked for their "legitimacy," and busing is a primary question with respect to elementary and secondary school desegregation. But despite these beliefs and societal conditions, black people will make a serious mistake if they underestimate the instrumental value of being educated. Black youth, particularly, may be shortsighted enough to think that schooling is not worth the effort. It is the responsibility of their parents and teachers to guide them through this faulty thinking, despite societal pressure to the contrary.

SUMMARY AND CONCLUSIONS

From the perspective of this black author, there is today an assault on the policies and programs, including those in education, that have been designed to help blacks, other minorities, and the poor. There is also an assault on the meaning of equality and justice as those concepts relate to blacks, other minorities, the poor, and women. There is also an assault on the concept that a proper role of the federal government is to intervene in the lives of individuals and groups so as to move individual and group life in the direction of the American Creed. Also under attack is the belief that compensatory action by society is necessary to reverse discrimination against individuals and groups that has prevailed over extended periods of time—as, for example, the discrimination against blacks since 1619.

In *An American Dilemma* Myrdal pointed out the inestimable value of education as a dynamic, genuine social force which *can* contribute to constructive and permanent social change. Whether education will live up to this promise in the last decades of the twentieth century remains to be seen.

It is clear that better access to public education at all levels has made a measurable difference in the lives of blacks and whites since World War II. Further, social status has risen for many blacks and whites since World War II as a result of higher educational attainment. No doubt the national interest has been served through the development of more productive citizens who are much more capable of making economic, social, and political contributions than were citizens in earlier eras.

However, there are cross-currents in the changing mood and in education. The prolongation of the educational process for increasing numbers of the young is a mixed blessing. Additional degrees and credentials enhance occupational opportunity and the possibility of self-realization; so in this respect the extension of the educational process is positive. But this extension may have negative consequences because such education is increasingly removed from action, and the people who are being educated are removed from action in the process. For example, nothing really meaningful is taught to underprivileged people to help them change their condition, except to escape from the circumstances of whatever ghetto they find themselves in. In a sense, this is exploitation of the lower classes in that the high achievers are taught to escape from the ghetto rather than to help solve the ghetto's many problems. The most promising youth are removed from the situation, much as coal is strip-mined from the earth and the area is left desolate and bare.

For all youth, lower class and middle class, power and the uses of power have not been conceived as appropriate for the typical secondary school or even undergraduate curriculum. Teaching about power has not been conceived as an appropriate part of the school's role, yet this omission leaves a critical gap in knowledge. Also generally missing from the common educational pattern are political and economic education and an understanding of one's community, with a view toward how to improve its functionality and a will to do so. Thus many young adults lack the ability to cope with life as it is because their formal or nonformal teaching has not been geared toward that end. Theirs has been a sterile education, designed for upward mobility. Such realities as the uses of power have to be learned from experience and from other segments of the population, and sources for such learning are usually not available to the poor and the black.

In *The Power Elite* (1959), C. Wright Mills charged that public education, as an institution, had failed abysmally in educating the majority of American youth to be intelligent, active participants in a democracy or to play any meaningful political role. Mills argued that public education in America had become just another mass medium that serves the ends of the power elite, that the schools had become mere occupational and social "elevators," and that political timidity is exhibited at all levels. He explained that the failure of public education had been camouflaged by emphasis on the *spread* of education—that more people are educated for a longer period of time than ever before in the history of any country.[24]

This widespread, readily available form of education, according to Mills, is simply a prescribed, stereotyped training which transmits the attitudes, values, and goals that are deemed desirable for the public by the power elite. This kind of education does not permit most people to achieve a high degree of self-realization or competence according to their particular needs and interests. Neither does it provide them with the knowledge and motivation to act consistently, in such a way that democracy will survive.

Mills believed that this state of affairs could be remedied by (1) development of sensibilities, which are cultural, social, political, and technical awarenesses that emerge from the process of self-development;[25] (2) study of "iron problem-areas," which are the real troubles people face by trying to live in this twentieth-century urban, industrial, internationalized society (these problems are "iron" because they are difficult, complex, and often defy solution); (3) school climates that are characterized by deep and wide debate and free inquiry; (4) reeducation and socialization of American school teachers and administrators; (5) enlarged, meaningful adult education programs; and (6) college and university faculty members who are exemplars of "straightforward conduct, clarified character, and open reasonableness."[26]

Mills doubted that education for youth or for adults is the strategic factor in redirecting American society toward its professed ideals, although he felt that education could be an important tool. Only by forming alliances with organizations which are politically relevant could education be meaningful in effecting real social change.[27]

This writer also feels there is no way that education alone can solve the American dilemma, or even that education can assume the primary responsibility for effecting constructive, permanent, pervasive social change in America. Education—formal, nonformal, and informal—is necessary, but not sufficient, for the greater ends, which are the elimination of economic distress, class competition, racism, and sexism as key factors in the formulation and execution of public policies.

VI

THE CHANGING MOOD AND THE FUTURE

MYRDAL'S PROGNOSTICATIONS FOR THE FUTURE

Nineteen hundred and seventy-six is the future to which Myrdal addressed himself in 1944, thirty-two years ago, when *An American Dilemma* was first published. It will be revealing, then, to look at Myrdal's prognostications in chapter 45, "America Again at the Crossroads," which is divided into ten sections.

The first section, "The Negro Problem and the War," begins with Myrdal's belief that as a result of three great wars in which the United States was engaged, the Negro made great strides toward freedom and opportunity—the Revolutionary War, the Civil War, and World War I. The Revolutionary War is credited with starting a development which ultimately ended slavery in the North and made the import of slaves illegal. The Civil War is cited as giving the Negro emancipation and Reconstruction in the South, although this was soon followed by the restoration of white supremacy. World War I gave the Negro the first real opportunity as a worker in industries of the North, started the great migration from the South, and began the "New Negro" movement. These were major advances for blacks, but each advance was followed by a reaction. Nevertheless, not as much ground was lost as had been won; so each of the three wars helped blacks take a permanent step forward.[1]

Myrdal, who wrote *An American Dilemma* while World War II was in progress, stated that America was again in a life-and-death struggle for liberty and equality and that the American Negro was again looking for signs of what war and victory would mean in terms of increased rights and opportunity. Myrdal stated: "There is bound to be a redefinition of the Negro's status in America as a result of this War."[2] That redefinition of status was positive for blacks.

With President Truman's directive to desegregate the armed forces, with increased opportunities available to black men because of the GI Bill, especially in education and housing, progress was made. Increased dissatisfaction had welled up as a result of exposure to other countries' policies and because of having fought for this country. That experience, coupled with residence in regions of America other than the South, and finally with the *Brown* decision and all that followed from it, helped blacks take another step forward in America.

But reaction has set in again; that is what the changing mood is—a reaction. It is incumbent on the nation to see that the reaction does not continue, and it is equally incumbent on the black population to exert concerted action to stop reversals of progress.

What we deduce from Myrdal's analysis of United States wars and from the experience of living in this society is that blacks have gained most as a result of wars and other crises, and therefore this means, in one sense, that we should not fear crises; we should fear calm, quiet periods, for it is in those times that slippage occurs. Static equilibrium in American society has negative consequences for blacks.

Section two, "Social Trends," begins with two observations: (1) "What we usually call 'social trends' have their main significance for the Negro's status because of what is in white people's minds" and (2) "The important changes in the Negro problem do not consist of, or have close relations with, 'social trends' in the narrower meaning of the term but are made up of changes in people's beliefs and valuations."[3] What Myrdal means is that the problems faced by Negroes are rooted in the minds of white Americans, in the deep belief that blacks are inferior and therefore deserve to be treated in substandard ways—consistently allowed less than the white population, which is believed to be superior. In the language of the Kerner Commission, this is racism, pure and simple. Myrdal's detailed investigation of the American scene confirmed his hypothesis that the decisive struggle for the rights of blacks is waged in the minds of white Americans, and it is there that the changes must occur.

Looking at specifications of social relations, Myrdal found that racial etiquette in the South was gradually loosening. Essentially, the rigidities of the past with respect to "no social equality" were breaking down. This could be noted particularly in the treatment accorded highly educated blacks. Also, increasing numbers of more highly educated whites were more vocal in asking that the "equal" portion of the separate-but-equal doctrine be actualized for Negroes. But a cross-current in these shifts was that separation of the races was in fact increasing, due to the exclusionist policy of whites and the withdrawal of Negroes as a reaction to the segregation and discrimination that had been foisted upon them by whites.

There was an increase in social discrimination in the North, probably engendered by the sudden influx of Southern blacks. Myrdal judged this to be temporary, and less discriminatory, than in the South.

With respect to the administration of justice, there was improvement in the South, with such practices as lynching abolished. The NAACP and the Interracial Commission were of prime importance in improving the administration of justice. In the North there was some strain, but, on the whole, judicial order was upheld.

In politics, the South continued to disfranchise the Negro, and did so until the Voting Rights Act of 1965 was passed and enforced. But attacks on the poll tax were under way, and at last were abolished. The Negro was able to vote in the North, and increasing numbers of Negroes moving North meant that more Negroes, in fact, exercised the right to vote.

With respect to public services, the Negro was discriminated against severely in the South, in blunt opposition to the guarantees of the Constitution. Black schools remained inferior. However, New Deal policies helped blacks get a share of public services, though not their deserved share. Also, New Deal policies brought a new type of white public servant to the South—educated people whose primary interest was not keeping blacks "in their place"[4] but in encouraging and advancing them. In the North, blacks on the whole had access to public services.

In sum, the social trends assisted the rise in status of the Negro; but the same was not true of occupational status. In the South, the plight of blacks was worsening and there were no prospects for improvement. No efforts were made by governmental or private agencies to reeducate Southern blacks who had been displaced from the agricultural system or to create real work for them. In the North, whites monopolized the jobs, but due to the Great Depression there were not enough jobs even for whites. Unemployment mounted in the North and blacks were relegated to the relief rolls. Myrdal pointed out that "the whole country, and particularly the North, was much more generous toward the Negro in doling out relief to him than in allowing him to work and earn his bread by his own labor."[5] The same situation is evident in 1976. There are no governmental or private solutions to the problem of nonemployment of blacks; the economic picture remains "grave," to use Myrdal's term.

Welfare relief continues to be doled out, on the one hand, while blacks are censured for accepting it on the other.

In section three, "The Decay of the Caste Theory," Myrdal points out that the notion of white supremacy is gradually losing force among upper-class and educated whites, although it is maintained among lower-class and uneducated people. Myrdal declared: "The gradual destruction of the popular theory behind race prejudice is the most important of all social trends in the field of interracial relations."[6]

Myrdal held that the trend for explaining group differences (from psychology, education, anthropology, and social science) is toward environmentalism rather than heredity and genetic causes. Thus, by implication, explanations tend to say that the white-power majority group is the cause of the Negro's deficiencies and unhappiness,[7] rather than inherent defects in black people. These ideas are spread by the advance of education.

On the other side, Negro protest was rising, spurred by improvement in education for blacks, so that America never again can regard blacks as a patient, submissive minority.[8] Because blacks and whites are permeated by the values of the American Creed, and want to be rational and good and righteous, positive social change should continue with respect to abolition of caste indices, Myrdal surmised.

Section four, "Negroes in the War Crisis," points out that World War II was an ideological war, fought in defense of democracy. How could America continue undemocratic practices internally, while fighting for democracy externally? Thus the ideology of World War II was a positive factor for blacks in the United States. At the same time, blacks had become better equipped, black organizations had grown in strength, and black leaders had become firmer. So blacks were ready to sustain concerted actions in their own behalf, which were supported by the ideology of World War II, which in turn supplemented the American Creed. Some black voices supported the idea of an international "color war" which would end white imperialism and exploitation worldwide, but they were not the majority. However, a cross-current in the black population was sullen skepticism and even cynicism, said Myrdal.[9] Nevertheless, Myrdal felt that the cause of the American black had supreme logical strength, and blacks were better prepared than ever before in history to fight for their cause.

"The War and the Whites," section five, points out that whites were on their way to relinquishing the caste theory before World War II. But the war stirred whites, and they felt the great cause of human liberties to be at stake. So the world conflict and America's stated stance as the defender of the democratic faith served to accelerate an ideological process in whites which had begun earlier. They were able to see that the caste system is extralegal, sometimes illegal, and always unconstitutional. Further, blacks have the law as their weapon in the caste struggle.[10] Thus Negroes, in the fight for equality, have an ally in the white man's conscience. The white man "does not have the moral stamina to make the Negro's subjugation legal and approved by society."[11]

Section six, "The North Moves toward Equality," noted some measure of civic equality for blacks but ruthless discrimination in private relations, as in seeking a job or a home. Myrdal found a social paradox in the North: almost everyone was against discrimination in general but everyone practiced discrimination in his personal affairs. The cumulation of personal discriminations created the color bar in the North and caused unusually severe unemployment, crowded housing conditions, crime, and vice for blacks.[12] Myrdal felt that the aloof stance of white Northerners could be fought with education. Also, he felt that the North would accept fundamental change if that change were pushed by courageous leadership. Since the North had more power than the South, a redefinition of the Negro's status could be made in the North.

Also, the concentration of responsibility was a positive factor for the Negro, Myrdal thought. With labor relations increasingly planned and regulated by national legislation and administration and by broad union policies, it was possible to prevent general discrimination against blacks. Myrdal felt that blacks "must be given their chance in private enterprise or be supported by public funds."[13] He foresaw that "the trend of unionization, social legislation, and national planning will tend to break down economic discrimination, the only type of discrimination which is both important and strong in the North. Other types of discrimination will then tend to decrease according to the law of cumulative causation."[14]

"Tension in the South," section seven, pointed out that the situation in the South is different from that in the North. The white Southerner commonly did not differentiate between public and private relations; he is traditionally and consistently opposed to Negro equality for its own sake and is more deeply split in moral personality than the white Northerner. The war stirred up this conflict, but Myrdal felt that even if short-run gains for blacks were personally devastating to the Negroes involved, the long-term effect of the opinion crisis in the South would be toward increased equality for the Negro. This has occurred in 1976;

there is increased equality for the Negro in the South.

International aspects of America's crossroads position are discussed in Myrdal's section 8. Myrdal points out that the Negro problem has not only become national in scope, but international implications are evident, after many years of being defined only as a regional, Southern problem. The major international implication is that America needs to demonstrate to the world that blacks can be included and integrated in its democracy. This is increasingly important since most of the world's population are people of color, who see implications for themselves in the Negro's plight as America moves into a position of primacy on the international scene. Myrdal's analysis was that, in the international community, whites were in the second phase of dominating the world, but that colored nations were just entering the first stage, where they would begin to exercise power. Further, "backward"[15] nations would become industrialized at a rapid pace. When colored nations acquire power but still feel the sting of white "superiority" and discrimination, they are likely to be satisfied only with the subjugation of whites. Thus Myrdal held that the time to come to an international understanding on the basis of equality is rapidly running out, and the Negro question in the United States is central to such an understanding.

Section nine, "Making the Peace," explains that Americans in general were concerned about peace when the war would be over. It was apparent that the traditional policy of isolationism was necessarily at an end and that America would be forced to engage in world policies, for better or worse. In fact, America would probably have to take world leadership—assuming its turn in the sequence of "main actors on the world stage."[16]

> America then will have the major responsibility for the manner in which humanity approaches the long era during which the white peoples will have to adjust to shrinkage while the colored are bound to expand in numbers, in level of industrial civilization and in political power. For perhaps several decades, the whites will still hold the lead, and America will be the most powerful white nation.[17]

Thus America will have to be concerned about her international reputation because she will be a leader in a world which is predominantly colored, and the two coastal oceans can no longer ensure her insulation from world problems and affairs. For all the people of color in the world, the treatment of the Negro in America is scandalous and like rubbing salt in their wounds. They see that what happens to the Negro in America could happen to them, because the differential of color carries many negative implications in the minds of white Americans. So if white Americans make international policy, they will be forced to take this into account in formulating domestic policy.

The final section, number ten, is "America's Opportunity." Myrdal argues that the main trend in American history is gradual realization of the American Creed. So, in this sense, the problems of blacks may be characterized as America's incomparably great opportunity for the future, as well as America's greatest failure. Thus America is "free to choose whether the Negro shall remain her liability or become her opportunity."[18] The way the American Negro problem is resolved is fateful for all mankind, not just the United States.

From the viewpoint of social science, Myrdal held that the resolution of the American dilemma calls for social engineering.

> Many things that for a long period have been predominantly a matter of individual adjustment will become more and more determined by political decision and public regulation. We are entering an era where fact-finding and scientific theories of causal relations will be seen as instrumental in planning controlled social change. The peace will bring nothing but problems, one mounting upon another, and consequently, new urgent tasks for social engineering.[19]

He saw that many things which had been considered predominantly a matter of individual adjustment will more and more be determined by political decision and public regulation. Myrdal concluded:

> Behind all outward dissimilarities, behind their contradictory valuations, rationalizations, vested interests, group allegiances and animosities, behind fears and defense constructions, behind the role they play in life and the mask they wear, people are all much alike on a fundamental level. And they are all good people. They want to be rational and just. They all plead to their conscience that they meant well even when things went wrong.
>
> Social study is concerned with explaining why all these potentially and intentionally good people so often make life a hell for themselves and each other when they live together, whether in a family, a community, a nation or a world. The fault is certainly not with becoming organized *per se*. In their formal organizations, as we have seen, people invest their highest ideals. These institutions regularly direct the individual toward more cooperation and justice than he would be inclined to observe as an isolated private person. The fault is, rather, that our structures of organizations are too imper-

fcct, each by itself, and badly integrated into a social whole.

The rationalism and moralism which is the driving force behind social study, whether we admit it or not, is the faith that institutions can be improved and strengthened and that people are good enough to live a happier life. With all we know today, there should be the possibility to build a nation and a world where people's great propensities for sympathy and cooperation would not be so thwarted.

To find the practical formulas for this never-ending reconstruction of society is the supreme task of social science. The world catastrophe places tremendous difficulties in our way and may shake our confidence to the depths. Yet we have today in social science a greater trust in the improvability of man and society than we have ever had since the Enlightenment.[20]

SUMMARY AND CONCLUSIONS

Many of the prognostications for the future, made by Myrdal in 1944, have come to fruition, but today America again stands at the crossroads where formation, execution, and enforcement of public policies, positive for blacks and other minorities, are concerned. Through World War II, the postwar years, and the Korean War, blacks made more strides toward freedom and equality. In large measure due to social intervention at the federal level, inroads were made in reducing the vicious circle of separatism, inequality, and injustice, with their concomitant effects. It became very clear that when all three branches of the federal government move together toward American ideals, there is positive social change in institutional and individual behavior. Also, when the executive branch of government fully supports the judicial branch, there is social change in a positive direction. But when there is a cultural lag in one or more of these branches of the federal government, or when they move in different directions, a slowdown occurs which is negative for blacks and the poor. Further, when blacks and the poor work within the system to change their lot, positive results accrue.

The period of the Vietnam War brought cross-currents, with guns and butter as rivals in priorities and allocation of funds. Domestic programs, designed to help blacks and the poor, were underfunded and shunted into second-class status, compared with war efforts. But at the same time the war efforts created an expanding economy, which provided blacks the greatest material gains they had experienced as a group in this country, through increased access to occupations, on-the-job promotion, and higher income. Black protests, white assistance, and enforcement of civil rights laws enhanced the process of cumulative causation.

Thus the gains of the 1960s are a perfect example of Myrdal's thesis that if positive effects can be put together in a systematic fashion, the gains cumulate and spiral, and black status is changed for the better. In like manner, white behavior can be changed by force of law, even without a change in white attitudes. Further, whites' attitudes changed for the better with enforcement of the laws and enlightened leadership, as increased occupational, educational, political, and social contact changed their perceptions of blacks as people. As the status of blacks is enhanced, the notion of innate group inferiority can be seen for the lie it is. Although in retrospect it is clear that many Americans, black and white, were naively optimistic that the civil rights movement of the 1960s would solve the American dilemma, it now is clear that solving the dilemma will be a long war instead of a short campaign.

The ever-increasing levels of mass education since 1948 have generated more willingness for society to change, based on increased understanding. Opinion polls show that since World War II, college-educated white men and women are more positive in their views than those who did not attend college or than people of the prewar generation who did. Education, moreover, has fueled the black protest; more knowledgeable leaders have been produced, and the sit-in movement began with students from black colleges in the South. The general dissatisfaction with second-class citizenship is most clearly discernible among young urban black males and in the highly educated middle-aged segment of the black population. Higher education has proved to be a key variable in both the dominant group and the black population since World War II.

Increased access to higher education for blacks and the poor has come largely through actions at the federal level, such as the GI Bill for veterans and the Higher Education Act of 1965. However, there is increasing speculation that the period of federal "intervention" in higher education may be drawing to a close. In the future, individual states will make many more decisions about higher education policy.

This means that blacks and the poor must, of necessity, work through their elected officials in state legislatures to influence educational policy at the state level. It also means that blacks and the poor must continue to vote for the election of enlightened officials who are committed to American ideals—at the state, local, and federal levels. There can be no letup on the part of blacks and the poor. To relax almost guarantees that forces for the improvement of black status will be removed and, as a result, black status will revert to its former low plane.

In fact, the reaction has set in. That, again, is what the changing mood is—a reaction. Strong efforts are made to restore the "rightness" of white supremacy; the assault on equality and justice is in full swing. Explanations for the lowly condition of many blacks have moved from an environmental base to a genetic base and include genetic-environmental-motivational explanations for black–white disparities. There is fear among whites, arising from the black revolution. Blacks themselves are divided ideologically and in concerted action for black progress. Also, blacks do not go to the polls in the North and West as they do in the South, which means that blacks are not participating in the political process, as they should be doing.

Most puzzling of all is the economic situation. Myrdal had no answers to this dilemma in 1944, and the society offers no sure answers in 1977. Economic problems, however, are at the root of many ongoing social problems in America.

But even the reaction is characterized by cross-currents; so all is not negative—for example, the election of black officials by whites indicates continuing progress. Also, the newspaper columnist, James Reston, pointed out that American ideals still are found in cities:

> Go where you will in the big towns of the United States today and you will find disintegration, racial segregation, economic disruption and political and moral confusion. But at the same time, you will also find recovery, reconstruction, and a tremendous struggle, against formidable odds, by what amounts to a vast army of people of all classes and races, in private and public works, to be faithful to the ideals of the nation.[21]

Thomas Griffith explained in *Time* (Sept. 1, 1975) that some of America's most conspicuous problems stem from increased awareness of them, rather than from worsening conditions. Today's uncertainties are difficult for people to live with, and this explains some of the pessimism that is so apparent in America, despite gains in the quality of life—for example, health care, increased material goods, and the "ongoing progress of those minority millions who are gradually finding opportunities and an acceptance denied their parents in offices, restaurants, universities."[22] Griffith suggests that "the matter with our times is not so much a question of impossibilities but of complexities that can be faced if only public trust and will are restored."[23] James Reston suggested that maybe the remedy to our problems lies in the quality of our leadership.[24]

On the other hand, an editorial comment in the *New York Times* (Nov. 16, 1975) noted with sadness a fading commitment to civil rights and a general erosion of the movement of the sixties.

> The erosion of the movement of the sixties has been massive. From the principled and sometimes impassioned leadership which developed in the White House from 1962 through 1967, the nation has been reduced to a Presidency which persistently attempts to undermine the authority of the Federal courts to enforce the rights of minority school children and gives aid and comfort to legislators who want to trivialize the Constitution by adding an amendment prohibiting busing.

The editorial ended on this note:

> The sum of all those elements suggests a sharp decrease in the sense that racial injustice in America is still acute and that the eradication of that injustice is important to the entire society. It is clear that that perception has been missing in Washington for the last several years; but the decline in the funding of civil rights organizations demonstrates that to some extent, at least, the country is following Washington's negative leadership. That is bad news for those seriously concerned about the quality of American life.[25]

How can the changing mood be redirected for the benefit of blacks and the poor? It is increasingly clear that positive, enlightened leadership is essential at the national level and that it must be evident in at least two branches of government. The same kind of leadership is needed at state and local levels. It is also increasingly clear that if blacks and other underprivileged persons are to survive, and survive well into the twenty-first century, social engineering and social planning of some kind are a necessity. In a social system which is increasingly technological, scientific, urban-suburban-metropolitan, and complex there is no way that individualism and laissez-faire policies can ensure that the basic needs of people will be met all through their life span and at a reasonable level of decency. This is true for all persons, but especially for the black and the poor. Planning also is necessary to assure environmental usage which will not destroy our planet in our lifetimes. Redirecting the changing mood in a positive way will require social engineering and social planning, consistently over time, on the part of policy makers.

There are other societies where policy makers have provided income allowances and subsidies, health care–delivery systems, housing, child-care programs, transportation systems, and old age assistance programs

—all of which appear to operate at a higher and more humane level than comparable systems in the United States. Their policies and practices provide evidence that it is possible to meet human needs within mixed social and economic systems.

Achievement of the promises of the American dream for all groups depends in large measure on the quality of leadership exercised by the president, the Supreme Court, and the Congress in moving the nation forward instead of backward. Courageous moral leadership is essential. Public trust and will must be restored. Domestic needs must have much higher priority. Above all, it is important to remember that problems which were created by man can be solved by man, if there is the will to do so. The problems described in this book are man-made; therefore the real question is whether we truly intend to meet the human needs and solve the man-made problems.

EPILOGUE

This book has examined the changing mood in America, and the author concludes that there is an eroding commitment to blacks, other minorities, and the poor at this time. The book has focused on the current resurgence of conservatism throughout the nation, which has negatively affected these groups in their quest to gain the American Creed's promises of equality and justice in their own land. The book concentrated on the period since 1969; however, for coherence and continuity it was necessary to make many references to the fifteen years prior to 1969, back to 1954 and the *Brown* decision.

"Eroding commitment" means the retrenchment taken since 1969 by federal power holders and decision makers, as well as various sectors of white society, such as "ethnics" and prestigious white intellectuals, with respect to the policies, programs, and moral/psychological commitments to realize the abstractions inherent in the concepts "equality" and "justice" for blacks, other minorities, and the poor. The efforts at progress made in the 1960s by blacks and their allies have been slowed tremendously in the seventies. In fact, examination of the 1974 census report, *Social and Economic Status of the Black Population,* shows that the only continuing areas of progress are in black elected officials and better access to, and participation in, education.

However, even as this is said, we recognize that the gains of the sixties, rather than the retrenchments of the seventies, probably best represent the "changing mood." As we understand the historical experience of blacks in America, the present decade is in many ways a return to business-as-usual, rather than a change in mood, except in the more precise sense of a change in tone from the late sixties. Nevertheless, we recognize the gains of the sixties as progress, and have examined the present decade as a period of retrenchment, inaction, and retrogression.

The author's viewpoint is that the current state of affairs is injurious to blacks, other minorities, and the poor.

The book acknowledges that no segment of the population exhibits a monolithic viewpoint. Further, there were cross-currents of opinion and decision making in the sixties, during the decade of progress, and, similarly, there are cross-currents in the seventies, during this period of retrogression. Neither decade can be portrayed as a period of immutable progress or retrogression. Yet each decade is identifiable in terms of the predominant direction of social change—toward American ideals or away from them.

We conclude that the changing mood can be redirected—toward realization of the promises of America. To change the mood, the nation needs responsible, committed leadership at all levels of government, but the need is greatest at the federal level and in all three branches of government. The nation must also rededicate itself to its highest values and renew the national will to achieve these ends.

FOOTNOTES

Introduction
1. Richard Bardolph, ed., *The Civil Rights Record: Black Americans and the Law, 1849–1970* (New York: Crowell, 1970), pp. 373–78.
2. Ibid., pp. 378–94.

Chapter I
1. Gunnar Myrdal, *An American Dilemma: The Negro Problem and Modern Democracy* (2 vols.; New York: Harper and Row, 1962),1: lxxii.
2. Ibid., 1: 75–78.
3. Ibid., 2: 1067.
4. Ralph Ellison, *"An American Dilemma:* A Review," in *Shadow and Act* (New York: Random House, 1972), pp. 303–17.
5. Ibid., p. 314.
6. Ibid., pp. 315–16.
7. Stanford M. Lyman, *The Black American in Sociological Thought: A Failure of Perspective* (New York: Putnam, 1972), pp. 99–120.
8. Ibid., p. 110.
9. Ibid., pp. 119–20.

Chapter II
1. Angus Campbell, *White Attitudes toward Black People* (Ann Arbor, Mich.: Institute for Social Research, 1971), p. 19.
2. Ibid., p. 41.
3. Ibid.
4. Ibid., p. 68.
5. Ibid., pp. 68–69.
6. Ibid., pp. 124–25.
7. Ibid., p. 155.
8. Ibid., pp. 155–58.
9. Ibid., pp. 159–62.
10. *Report of the National Advisory Commission on Civil Disorders,* by Otto Kerner. chairman (New York: Bantam Books, 1968), p. 413.
11. Ibid., p. 23.

12. Adapted from Fletcher Knebel, "Mood of America," *Look,* 18 Nov. 1969, p. 72.

13. Campbell, *White Attitudes,* p. 54.

14. *New York Times,* 4 Apr. 1975.

15. Andrew M. Greeley, *Why Can't They Be Like Us? America: White Ethnic Groups* (New York: Dutton, 1971), p. 60.

16. Nathan Glazer and Daniel P. Moynihan, *Beyond the Melting Pot* (Cambridge, Mass.: M.I.T. Press, 1963), p. xliii.

17. See Peter Binzen, *White-Town, U.S.A.* (New York: Random House, 1970), p. 53; Robert Coles, *The Middle Americans: Proud and Uncertain* (Boston: Little, Brown, 1971), pp. 11, 105; Glazer and Moynihan, *Beyond the Melting Pot,* p. xxxvii.

18. Michael Novak, *The Rise of the Unmeltable Ethnics: Politics and Culture in the Seventies* (New York: Macmillan, 1972), p. 22.

19. Coles, *The Middle Americans,* pp. 103–04.

20. *New York Times,* 18 Aug. 1975.

21. Ibid.

22. Ibid.

23. Ibid.

24. Joseph Epstein, "The New Conservatives: Intellectuals in Retreat," in *The New Conservatives: A Critique from the Left,* eds., Lewis Coser and Irving Howe (New York: Quadrangle, 1974), p. 9.

25. Daniel P. Moynihan, ed., *On Understanding Poverty: Perspectives from the Social Sciences* (New York: Basic Books, 1969), pp. 31–32, 62.

26. Christopher Jencks, *Inequality: A Reassessment of the Effect of Family and Schooling in America* (New York: Basic Books, 1972), book jacket.

27. S. M. Miller and Ronnie S. Ratner, "The American Resignation: The New Assault on Equality," *Social Policy* 3 (May/June 1972): p. 15.

28. Irving Howe and Bernard Rosenberg, "Are American Jews Turning Toward the Right?" in *The New Conservatives,* pp. 65–66.

29. Miller and Ratner, "American Resignation," p. 14.

30. Frank Riessman, "Editorial: The New Currency of Old Myths," *Social Policy* 3 (May/June 1972): p. 3.

31. Daniel P. Moynihan, "The Professors and the Poor," *Commentary* (Aug. 1968), p. 23.

32. Ibid., p. 27.

33. Ibid., p. 28.

34. Nathan Glazer, "The Limits of Social Policy," *Commentary* (Sept. 1971), p. 52.

35. Ibid., p. 54.

36. Irving Kristol, "About Equality," *Commentary* (Nov. 1972), p. 43.

37. Roger Starr, "Prison, Politics and the Attica Report," *Commentary* (Mar. 1973), p. 37.

38. James Hitchcock "The Intellectuals and the People," *Commentary* (Mar. 1973), p. 69.

39. Nathan Glazer, "Ethnicity and the Schools," *Commentary* (Sept. 1974), p. 55.

40. Ibid., p. 59.

41. Nathan Glazer and Daniel P. Moynihan, "Why Ethnicity?" *Commentary* (Oct. 1974), p. 34.

42. Hadley Arkes, "The Problem of Kenneth Clark," *Commentary* (Nov. 1974), pp. 42–43.

43. Daniel Bell and Irving Kristol, "What Is the Public Interest?" *The Public Interest,* no. 1 (Fall 1965), p. 5.

44. William O. Stanley, *Education and Social Integration* (New York: Teachers College, Columbia University, 1953), pp. 6–9.

45. James S. Coleman, "Toward Open Schools," *The Public Interest,* no. 9 (Fall 1967), p. 22.

46. Edward C. Banfield, "Welfare: A Crisis without 'Solutions', " *The Public Interest,* no. 16 (Summer 1969), p. 93.

47. Ibid., p. 94.

48. Ibid., p. 101.

49. Ibid.

50. Daniel P. Moynihan, "Toward a National Urban Policy," *The Public Interest,* no. 17 (Fall 1969), pp. 4–5.

51. Edward Harwood, "Youth Unemployment—A Tale of Two Ghettoes," *The Public Interest,* no. 17 (Fall 1969), p. 80.

52. Ibid., p. 87.

53. Daniel P. Moynihan, "The Schism in Black America," *The Public Interest,* no. 27 (Spring 1972), p. 8.

54. David J. Armor, "The Evidence on Busing," *The Public Interest,* no. 28 (Summer 1972), pp. 115–16.

55. Daniel P. Moynihan, "Equalizing Education: In Whose Benefit?" *The Public Interest,* no. 29 (Fall 1972), p. 89.

56. Seymour Martin Lipset, "Social Mobility and Equal Opportunity," *The Public Interest,* no. 25 (Fall 1971), p. 96.

57. Ibid., p. 98.

58. Nathan Keyfitz, "Can Inequality Be Cured?" *The Public Interest,* no. 31 (Spring 1973), p. 99.

59. Eli Ginzberg and Robert M. Solow, "An Introduction to This Special Issue," *The Public Interest,* no. 34 (Winter 1974), p. 6.

60. Charles Kadushin, "Who Are the Elite Intellectuals?" *The Public Interest,* no. 29 (Fall 1972), pp. 116–18.

61. Richard J. Herrnstein, "I.Q.," *Atlantic* (Sept. 1971), p. 44.

62. Ibid., p. 57.

63. Ibid., p. 63.

64. Ibid., p. 64.

65. Faustine C. Jones, "The Inequality Controversy," *Journal of Negro Education* 42 (Fall 1973): 537.

66. Rayford W. Logan, *The Betrayal of the Negro: From Rutherford B. Hayes to Woodrow Wilson* (New York: Collier Books, 1965), p. 382.

67. Ibid., p. 392.

68. Ibid., pp. 382, 392.

69. Clarence J. Karier, Joel Spring, and Paul C. Violas, *Roots of Crisis: American Education in the Twentieth Century* (Chicago: Rand McNally, 1973), p. 107.

70. Ibid., p. 85.

71. Robert K. Merton, *Social Theory and Social Structure* (Riverside, N.J.: Glencoe Press, 1949), p. 423.

72. Ibid.

73. Ibid., p. 424.

Chapter III

1. Lerone Bennett, Jr. *The Negro Mood and Other Essays* (Chicago: Johnson Publishing Company, 1964), p. 19.

2. Ibid., p. 6.
3. Ibid., p. 20.
4. Ibid., p. 21.
5. Ibid., p. 14.
6. Ibid., p. 13.
7. Alphonso Pinkney, *Black Americans* (Englewŏod Cliffs, N.J.: Prentice-Hall, 1975), p. 198.
8. Ibid., p. 199.
9. Martin Luther King, Jr., *Where Do We Go from Here: Chaos or Community?* (New York: Harper and Row, 1967), p. 34.
10. Ibid., p. 3.
11. Bennett, *The Negro Mood*, p. vii; King, *Where Do We Go from Here?* p. 4; Pinkney, *Black Americans*, p. 189.
12. Pinkney, *Black Americans*, p. 196.
13. Elliot Osborn, "Anatomy of a Revolution," *Newsweek*, 29 July 1963, p. 7.
14. "The Negro in America," *Newsweek*, 29 July 1963, pp. 15–34.
15. Ibid., p. 27.
16. Ibid., p. 32.
17. Ibid., p. 34.
18. "The Negro in America '65: Progress," *Newsweek*, 25 October 1965, p. 32.
19. Ibid.
20. Ibid.
21. Ibid.
22. "Report from Black America," *Newsweek*, 30 June 1969, p. 17.
23. Ibid., p. 18.
24. Ibid.
25. Ibid., p. 19.
26. Ibid., p. 25.
27. Ibid., p. 26.
28. Ibid., p. 32.
29. Ibid., p. 34.
30. Ibid., p. 35.
31. Ibid., p. 21.
32. Howard Schuman and Shirley Hatchett, *Black Racial Attitudes: Trends and Complexities* (Ann Arbor: University of Michigan Survey Research Center, 1974), p. 3.
33. Ibid., pp. 5–10.
34. Ibid., p. 13.
35. Ibid.
36. Ibid., p. 15.
37. Ibid.
38. Ibid., pp. 15–16.
39. Ibid., p. 16.
40. Ibid., p. 9.
41. Ibid., p. 17.
42. Ibid., p. 117.
43. Ibid., pp. 74–75.
44. Ibid., p. 75.
45. Ibid., pp. 113–14.
46. Ibid., p. 125.
47. Ibid., pp. 126–27.
48. Ibid., p. 128.

49. Ihid., pp. 124–25.
50. Ibid., p. 18.
51. *Report of the National Advisory Commission on Civil Disorders*, Otto Kerner, chairman (New York: Bantam Books, 1968), p. 410.
52. Rayford W. Logan, *The Betrayal of the Negro*, p. 349.
53. Kerner Report, pp. 235–36.
54. Gunnar Myrdal, *An American Dilemma*, 2:709–924.
55. Pinkney, *Black Americans*, p. xiii.
56. Ibid., p. 177.
57. Ibid., pp. 178–79.
58. Ibid., p. 189.
59. Ibid., pp. 190–91.
60. Ibid., p. 193.
61. Ibid.
62. Ibid., p. 195.
63. Ibid., p. 222.
64. Ibid., pp. 215–18.
65. *Washington Post*, 14 July 1975.
66. Pinkney, *Black Americans*, pp. 218–19.
67. Ibid., pp. 220–22.
68. Ibid., p. 223.
69. Herman P. Miller, *Rich Man, Poor Man* (New York: Crowell, 1971), p. 53.
70. Ibid.
71. Ibid., pp. 68–72, 75–86.
72. U.S. Bureau of the Census, *The Social and Economic Status of the Black Population in the United States, 1974* (Washington: Government Printing Office, 1975), p. 150.
73. Ibid., p. 4.
74. Ibid., p. 144.
75. Ibid.
76. Ibid., p. 5.
77. Ibid., p. 3.
78. Ibid., pp. 1–2.
79. Ibid., p. 65.
80. U.S. Bureau of the Census, *The Social and Economic Status of the Black Population, 1973* (Washington: Government Printing Office, 1974), p. 46.
81. National Urban League Research Department, *Quarterly Economic Report on the Black Worker*, (Washington: Merkle Press, May 1975), p. 1.
82. Bureau of the Census, *1974*, p. 57.
83. Ibid., pp. 73–74.
84. U.S. Commission on Civil Rights, *The Federal Civil Rights Enforcement Effort—1974* (Washington: Government Printing Office, 1975), 5:617.
85. Bureau of the Census, *1973*, p. 1.
86. Bureau of the Census, *1974*, p. 23.
87. Ibid., p. 2.
88. Ibid.
89. Bureau of the Census, *1973*, p. 1.
90. Robert P. Althauser and Sydney S. Spivak, *The Unequal Elites* (New York: John Wiley, 1975), p. 133.
91. Bureau of the Census, *1974*, p. 36.
92. Bureau of the Census, *1973*, p. 23.

93. Bureau of the Census, *1974*, p. 36.

94. Ibid., p. 42.

95. Bureau of the Census, *1973*, p. 34.

96. Robert B. Hill, *The Strengths of Black Families* (New York: Emerson Hall, 1972), p. 6.

97. Bureau of the Census, *1973*, p. 106.

98. Bureau of the Census, *1974*, p. 4.

99. Ibid., p. 139.

100. Ibid., p. 122.

101. Bureau of the Census, *1973*, p. 4.

102. Bureau of the Census, *1974*, p. 106.

103. Bureau of the Census, *Current Population Reports: Special Studies,* Series P-23, No. 52, 1975.

104. Bureau of the Census, *1974*, p. 106.

105. Ibid., pp. 108–9.

106. NBC, *A Country Called Watts*, 29 June 1975.

107. ABC, *A Tale of Two Cities, 29 June 1975 (Rod McLeish).*

108. James Farmer, Martin Luther King, Jr., John Lewis, et al., "Prospects for '64 in the Civil Rights Struggle " *Negro Digest* 13 (January 1964): 8.

109. Ibid.

110. Ibid., p. 11.

111. Ibid., p. 12.

112. Ibid., p. 13.

113. John H. Johnson, "Individual Responsibility and the Negro Image," *Negro Digest* 14 (January 1965): 5.

114. Nathan Hare, "An Epitaph for Nonviolence," *Negro Digest* 15 (January 1966): 15.

115. Ibid.

116. Ibid., p. 18.

117. Ibid., p. 20.

118. Julian Bond, Anita Cornwell, Ronald Fair, et al, "The Meaning and Measure of Black Power," *Negro Digest* 15 (November 1966): 20.

119. Charles V. Hamilton, "The Place of the Black College in the Human Rights Struggle," *Negro Digest* 16 (September 1967): 6.

120. Peter Baily, "What Afro-American Nationalism Means to Me," *Negro Digest* 17 (December 1967): 32.

121. Clifford Darden, "The Post-Malcolm Movement," *Negro Digest* 17 (June 1968):4.

122. Ibid., p. 40.

123. Albert B. Cleage Jr., "We Have Become a Black Nation," *Negro Digest* 18 (January 1969): 31.

124. A. B. Spellman (symposium), "The Measure and Meaning of the Sixties," *Negro Digest* 19 (November 1969): 22–23.

125. Darwin T. Turner, "The Literary Presumption of Mr. Bone," *Negro Digest* 16 (August 1967): 54.

126. Addison Gayle, "Black Literature and the White Aesthetic," *Negro Digest* 18 (July 1969): 37.

127. Ibid., p. 36.

128. Carolyn F. Gerald, "The Black Writer and His Role," *Negro Digest* 18 (January 1969): 47.

129. Ron Karenga, "Ron Karenga and Black Cultural Nationalism," *Negro Digest*

17 (January 1968): 5.

130. Charles V. Hamilton, "Black Americans and the Modern Political Struggle," *Black World* 19 (May 1970): 5–6.

131. Ibid., p. 77.

132. Charles V. Hamilton, "Urban Economics, Conduit-Colonialism and Public Policy," *Black World* 21 (October 1972): 41.

133. Olu Akaraogun, "African States and the Politics of Economic Freedom," *Black World* 21 (October 1972): 80.

134. Courtland Cox and Geri Stark, "Interview with President Nyerere of Tanzania," *Black World* 22 (October 1973): 8.

135. Ronald Walters, "African-American Nationalism," *Black World* 22 (October 1973): 9.

136. Don L. Lee, "Death Walk against Afrika," *Black World* 22 (October 1973): 31.

137. Harold Cruse, "The Little Rock National Black Convention," *Black World* 23 (October 1974): 15.

138. Ibid., p. 13.

139. Ibid., p. 82.

140. Gloria Richardson, "Focus on Cambridge," *Freedomways* 4 (Winter 1964): 32.

141. John H. O'Dell, "The Threshold of a New Reconstruction," *Freedomways* 5 (Fall 1965): 495.

142. Ibid.

143. Ibid., p. 497.

144. Ibid., pp. 497–98.

145. Lawrence Guyot and Michael Thelwell, "The Politics of Survival in Mississippi," *Freedomways* 6 (Spring 1966): 121–22.

146. John H. O'Dell, "Charleston's Legacy to the Poor People's Campaign," *Freedomways* 9 (Winter 1969): 210.

147. John H. O'Dell, "The Contours of the 'Black Revolution' in the 1970's," *Freedomways* 10 (First Quarter 1970): 111.

148. Ibid., p. 112.

149. Rae Banks, "New Directions in Education—1970," *Freedomways* 10 (First Quarter 1970): 14.

150. Dorothy Burnham, "Jensenism: The New Pseudoscience of Racism," *Freedomways* 11 (Second Quarter 1971): 156.

151. Ibid.

152. Arlene Benet, "Eugenics as a part of Institutionalized Racism," *Freedomways* 14 (Second Quarter 1974): 121.

153. Ibid., p. 123.

154. George V. Hamilton, "Pan-Africanism and the Black Struggle," *Black Scholar* 2 (March 1971): 10.

155. Ibid., p. 14.

156. S. E. Anderson, "Revolutionary Black Nationalism Is Pan-African," *Black Scholar* 2 (March 1971): 21–22.

157. Robert Allen, "A Historical Synthesis: Black Liberation and World Revolution," *Black Scholar* 3 (February 1972): 15.

158. Allen and Robert Chrisman, "The Cuban Revolution," *Black Scholar* 4 (February 1973): 14.

159. C. J. Munford, "The Fallacy of Lumpen Ideology," *Black Scholar* 4 (July/August 1973): 48.

Chapter IV

1. Harry Kalvern, "The Supreme Court, 1970 Term–Foreword: Even When a Nation Is at War," *Harvard Law Review* 8 (1971) :3.

2. John P. Frank, *The Warren Court* (New York: Macmillan, 1964),

3. William Swindley, "The Warren Court: Completion of a Constitutional Revolution," *Vanderbilt Law Review* 23 (March 1970) :24.

4. Frank, *The Warren Court,* p. 26.

5. *Betts* v. *Brady,* 316 U.S. 455 (1942).

6. Frank, *The Warren Court,* p. 38.

7. Ibid., p. 27.

8. *Brown* v. *Board of Education of Topeka, Kansas,* 347 U.S. 483 (1954).

9. *Brown* v. *Board of Education of Topeka, Kansas,* 349 U.S. 294 (1955).

10. *Cooper* v. *Aaron,* 358 U.S. 119 (1958).

11. *Griffin* v. *County School Board, Prince Edward County, Virginia,* 377 U.S. 218 (1964).

12. *Green* v. *County School Board of New Kent County, Virginia,* 391 U.S. 430 (1968).

13. Alpheus Mason, "Judicial Activism: Old and New," *Virginia Law Review* 55 (April 1969) : 34.

14. Elizabeth Drew, "Washington: The Nixon Court," *Atlantic,* November 1972, p. 8.

15. Ibid., pp. 8, 10.

16. Kalvern, "The Supreme Court," p. 6.

17. *Swann* v. *Charlotte-Mecklenburg Board of Education,* 402 U.S. 1 (1971).

18. Inez Smith Reid, "The Burger Court and the Civil Rights Movement: The Supreme Court Giveth and the Supreme Court Taketh Away," *Rutgers Camden Law Journal* 3 (Spring 1972) : 424.

19. *Winston-Salem/Forsyth County Board of Education* v. *Scott,* 404 U.S. 912 (1971).

20. *Miranda* v. *Arizona,* 384 U.S. 436 (1966).

21. *Harris* v. *New York,* 401 U.S. 222 (1971).

22. *Mckeiver* v. *Pennsylvania,* 403 U.S. 528 (1971).

23. *In re Gault,* 387 U.S. 1 (1967).

24. *San Antonio Independent School District* v. *Rodriguez,* 411 U.S. 1 (1973).

25. *Keyes* v. *School District No. 1, Denver, Colorado,* 413 U.S. 186 (1973).

26. *Milliken* v. *Bradley,* 4 Pl. U.S. 815 (1974).

27. *Griggs* v. *Duke Power Company,* 401 U.S. 424 (1971).

28. *Albemarle Paper Company* v. *Moody,* 422 U.S. 405 (1975).

29. *Alyeska Pipeline Service Company* v. *Wilderness Society,* 421 U.S. 240 (1975).

30. Kenneth S. Tollett, "The Viability and Reliability of the U.S. Supreme Court as an Institution for Social Change and Progress, Part II," 3 *Black Law Journal* (Spring 1973) : 48.

31. Kalvern, "The Supreme Court," p. 10.

32. *Wall Street Journal,* 1 July 1975.

33. Eli Ginzburg and Robert M. Solow, "Some Lessons of the 1960's," *The Public Interest,* no. 34 (Winter 1974), pp. 212–13.

34. Congressional Quarterly, *Civil Rights Progress Report, 1970* (Washington: Congressional Quarterly, 1971), p. 12.

35. Richard M. Nixon, "The Nature of the Presidency: To Unite America," *Vital Speeches of the Day* 35 (15 October 1968) : 6.

36. John F. Kennedy, "State of the Union: Domestic and Foreign Policies," *Vital Speeches of the Day* 27 (15 February 1961) : 259–60.

37. Lyndon B. Johnson, "The Right to Vote: Equal Standards for All," *Vital Speeches of the Day* 31 (April 1965) : 365–67.

38. Lyndon B. Johnson, "State of the Union: The Months Ahead," *Vital Speeches of the Day* 30 (15 January 1964) : 194.

39. James L. Sundquist, *Politics and Policy: The Eisenhower, Kennedy and Johnson Years* (Washington: The Brookings Institution, 1968), pp. 265–66.

40. Lyndon B. Johnson, "State of the Union: Home and Abroad," *Vital Speeches of the Day* 32 (1 February 1966) : 227.

41. Lyndon B. Johnson, "State of the Union: 1968" *Vital Speeches of the Day* 34 (1 February 1968) : 228–29.

42. Ibid. p. 229.

43. Ginzburg and Solow, "Some Lessons," p. 213.

44. James C. Harvey, *Black Civil Rights during the Johnson Administration* (Jackson: University and College Press of Mississippi, 1973), pp. 221–22.

45. Richard M. Nixon, "Nature of the Presidency," p. 6.

46. Congressional Quarterly, *Nixon: The Fifth Year of His Presidency* (Washington: Congressional Quarterly, 1974), p. 21A.

47. Congressional Quarterly, *Nixon: The First Year of His Presidency* (Washington: Congressional Quarterly, 1970), p. 49.

48. Congressional Quarterly, *Civil Rights,* pp. 50–51.

49. Peter Gall and Leon E. Panetta, *Bring Us Together: The Nixon Team and the Civil Rights Retreat* (New York: Lippincott, 1971), pp. ix–x.

50. Congressional Quarterly, *Nixon : The Second Year of His Presidency* (Washington: Congressional Quarterly, 1971), pp. 133A–136A.

51. Congressional Quarterly, *Nixon : The Fourth Year of His Presidency* (Washington: Congressional Quarterly, 1973), pp. 120A, 140A.

52. C.Q., *Second Year,* p. 164A.

53. C.Q., *Civil Rights,* p. 24.

54. Ibid. Among the organizations that signed the statement were the NAACP, National Conference of Black Elected Officials, and the National Council of Negro Women.

55. C.Q., *Fourth Year,* p. 80A.

56. C.Q., *Fifth Year,* p. 24A.

57. C.Q., *Fourth Year,* p. 5.

58. Ginzburg and Solow, "Some Lessons," p. 218.

59. Vernon E. Jordan, "Blacks and the Nixon Administration: The Next Four Years," *Vital Speeches of the Day* 39 (1 May 1973) : 418–19.

60. *Washington Post,* 6 July 1975.

61. Congressional Quarterly, *The Presidency in 1974* (Washington: Congressional Quarterly, 1975), p. 47A.

62. Gerald R. Ford, "State of the Union Message, 1975," *Vital Speeches of the Day* 41 (1 February 1975) : 227.

63. C.Q., *Presidency, 1974,* p. 59.

64. *Washington Star,* 26 July 1975.

65. C.Q., *Presidency, 1974,* p. 84A.

66. *Washington Post,* 21 July 1975.

67. For a fuller discussion of the federal budget during the 1960s see Congressional Quarterly, *Congress and the Nation, I:1945–1964* (Washington: Congressional Quarterly, 1965), pp. 394–395, and 2:127–40.

68. Carl L. Schultze, *Setting National Priorities: The 1971 Budget* (Washington: The Brookings Institution, 1970), pp. 15–16, 71.

69. C.Q., *Second Year,* pp. 9A–10A.

70. Congressional Quarterly, *Nixon: The Third Year of His Presidency* (Washington: Congressional Quarterly, 1972), p. 11A.

71. C.Q., *Fourth Year,* p. 16.

72. C.Q., *Fifth Year,* p. 12A.

73. C.Q., *Presidency, 1974,* p. 98.

74. C.Q., *Weekly Report* (8 February 1975), p. 284.

75. For a fuller discussion of presidential vetoes during the Kennedy administration see Congressional Quarterly, *Weekly Report* (13 October 1961), p. 1720; (13 July 1962), p. 1190; (20 October 1961), p. 2061; (2 November 1961), pp. 2118–19.

76. For a detailed discussion of vetoes during the last four years of the Johnson administration see Congressional Quarterly, *Congress and the Nation,* 2:92A–96A.

77. Congressional Quarterly, *Congress and the Nation, 3:1969–1972* (Washington: Congressional Quarterly, 1973), pp. 101A–5A.

78. Mike Mansfield, *Summary of Major Achievements* (Washington: U.S. Government Printing Office, 1974), p. 318.

79. C.Q., *Weekly Report* (11 January 1975), pp. 106–7.

80. *Washington Post,* 26 July 1975.

81. John R. Coyne, Jr., *The Impudent Snobs: Agnew vs. the Intellectual Establishment* (New Rochelle, N.Y.: Arlington House, 1972), p. 97.

82. Ibid., p. 248.

83. C.Q., *Presidency, 1974,* p. 88.

84. See U.S. Congress, House of Representatives, *Report No. 93-6,* 93d Congress, 1st sess., *Report No. 93-15,* 93d Congress, 1st sess.; Louis Fisher, *Presidential Spending Power* (Princeton University Press, 1975), p. 175; U.S. Congress, *Report No. 93-21,* 93d Congress, 1st sess., p. 1.

85. U.S. Congress, *Report No. 93-6.*

86. U.S. Congress, *Report No. 93-15.*

87. U.S. Congress, *Report No. 93-21.*

88. Fisher, *Presidential Spending Power,* p. 175. This justification was given by President Nixon in a press conference, 31 January 1973.

89. U.S. Congress, House of Representatives, *Report No. 93-6,* p. 11.

90. U.S. Congress, Senate, *Report No. 93-20,* 93d Congress, 1st sess., pp. 25–26.

91. U.S. Congress, House of Representatives, *Report No. 93-91,* 93d Congress, 1st sess.

92. U.S. Congress, *Congressional Record,* 119, 28 June 1973 (daily ed.).

93. Fisher, *Presidential Spending Power,* p. 178.

94. U.S. Congress, House, *Hearings before the Senate. Select Committee on Presidential Campaign Activities, 1973,* 93d Congress, 1st sess. (1973), p. 411.

95. U.S. Congress, Senate, *Hearings on Withholding of Funds for Housing and Urban Development Programs, Fiscal Year 1971 before the Senate Committee on Banking, Housing & Urban Affairs,* 92d Congress, 1st sess. (1971), p. 159.

96. U.S. Congress, *Congressional Record,* 119, 29 June 1973 (daily ed.).

97. Public Law No. 92-599; 86 Stat. 1325, Title IV.

98. Public Law No. 93-1; 87 Stat. 3.

99. U.S. Congress, Senate, *Report No. 93-4,* 93d Congress, 1st sess.

100. Fisher, *Presidential Spending Power,* p. 192.

101. Ibid.

102. Ibid., pp. 193–95.

103. *New York Times,* 27 March 1973, p. 45. It should be noted that the percentages quoted for other presidents may be inaccurate. For different percentages see *National Journal,* vol. 5 (14 April 1973).

104. Calculations based on figures given in Fisher, *Presidential Spending Power,* pp. 191–95.

105. U.S. Congress, Senate, *Hearings before the Senate Judiciary Subcommittee on Separation of Powers,* 91st Congress, 1st sess. (1971), pp. 164–65.

106. C.Q., *Weekly Report* (26 February 1972), pp. 443–45.

107. U.S. Constitution, Art. I, sec. 8.

108. Congressional Quarterly, *Guide to Current American Government, Fall 1975* (Washington: Congressional Quarterly, 1975), p. 327.

109. Louis W. Koenig, *The Chief Executive* (New York: Harcourt Brace Jovanovich, 1968), p. 295.

110. Gary Orfield, *Congressional Power: Congress and Social Change* (New York: Harcourt Brace Jovanovich, 1975), p. 258.

111. Ibid., p. 10.

112. Congressional Quarterly, *Congress and the Nation,* 1:43.

113. Ibid., p. 50.

114. Ibid., p. 45.

115. For a summary of legislative activity from 1965 to 1969 see Congressional Quarterly, *Congress and the Nation,* 2:1–13 and 3 : 1–20.

116. *Washington Post,* 30 June 1975.

117. C.Q., *Congress and the Nation,* 2:364–65.

118. Ibid., p. 385.

119. C.Q., *Congress and the Nation,* 3:497.

120. Ibid., p. 504.

121. C.Q., *Weekly Report* (28 September 1974), p. 2592.

122. C.Q., *Congress and the Nation,* 3:515.

123. C.Q., *Weekly Report* (28 December 1974), p. 2423.

124. Robert B. McKay, "Court, Congress, and School Desegregation," unpublished paper presented to U.S. Commission on Civil Rights Consultation on School Desegregation, The Courts and Suburban Migration, 8 December 1975.

125. C.Q., *Congress and the Nation,* 2:770.

126. C.Q., *1974,* p. 77A.

127. C.Q., *Weekly Report* (11 January 1975), p. 87.

128. Joint Strategy and Action Committee, "Senate Bill I New Threat to Freedom," *Grapevine* (October 1975), p. 1.

129. Ibid., pp. 2–3.

130. Ibid., p. 3.

131. *Cooper* v. *Aaron,* 358 U.S. 122 (1958).

Chapter V

1. Robert F. Butts and Lawrence A. Cremin, *A History of Education in American Culture* (New York: Holt, 1954), pp. 418–49.

2. Maurice deG. Ford, "School Integration and Busing," *Current,* no. 174 (July/August 1975), pp. 30–35 (reprinted from *The Nation,* 5 July 1975), and James S. Coleman, "Racial Segregation in the Schools: New Research with New Policy Implications," *Phi Delta Kappan* 57 (October 1975): 75–78.

3. Coleman, "Racial Segregation," p. 78.

4. U.S. Civil Rights Commission, *Twenty Years after Brown* (Washington: Government Printing Office, 1974), 2:88.

5. Coleman, "Racial Segregation," p. 75.
6. Sidney Hook, statement presented at fact-finding hearings of Office of Federal Contract Compliance of the Department of Labor, 3 October 1975.
7. Gunnar Myrdal, *An American Dilemma* (New York: Harper & Row, 1969), 2:882.
8. Ibid., 2:884.
9. Ibid., 2:893.
10. Ibid., 2:896.
11. Ibid., 2:896–99.
12. Ibid., 2:899.
13. Ibid., 2:895, 900.
14. Ibid., 2:901.
15. Ibid., 2:902; see also W. E. B. DuBois, "Does the Negro Need Separate Schools?" *Journal of Negro Education* 4 (July 1935):335.
16. Myrdal, *An American Dilemma,* 2:904.
17. Ibid., 2:905.
18. Ibid., 2:906.
19. Ibid.
20. Ibid., 2:879–82.
21. Ibid., 2:903.
22. Ibid., 2:893.
23. Ibid., 2:899.
24. C. Wright Mills, *The Power Elite* (New York: Oxford University Press, 1959), p. 319.
25. ——— *Power, Politics and People* (New York: Oxford University Press, 1963), p. 396; see also Mills, *The Power Elite,* P. 318.
26. Ibid., p. 372.
27. Ibid.

Chapter VI

1. Gunnar Myrdal, *An American Dilemma* (New York: Harper & Row, 1962), 2:997.
2. Ibid.
3. Ibid., p. 998.
4. Ibid., p. 1001.
5. Ibid.
6. Ibid., p. 1003.
7. Ibid.
8. Ibid., p. 1004.
9. Ibid., p. 1006.
10. Ibid., p. 1009.
11. Ibid.
12. Ibid., p. 1010.
13. Ibid., p. 1011.
14. Ibid.
15. Ibid., p. 1017.
16. Ibid., p. 1019.
17. Ibid.
18. Ibid., p. 1022.
19. Ibid., pp. 1022–23.
20. Ibid., pp. 1023–24.

21. *Atlanta Constitution,* 26 November 1975.
22. Thomas Griffith, "The Best of Times–1821? 1961? Today?" *Time,* 1 September 1975, p. 53.
23. Ibid.
24. *Atlanta Constitution,* 14 October 1975.
25. *New York Times,* 16 November 1975.

BIBLIOGRAPHY

Books

Althauser, Robert P., and Spivak, Sydney S. *The Unequal Elites.* New York: John Wiley & Sons, 1975.

Banfield, Edward C. *The Unheavenly City in the Nature and Future of Our Urban Crisis.* Boston: Little, Brown, 1970.

Bardolph, Richard. *The Civil Rights Record: Black Americans and the Law, 1849–1970.* New York: Crowell, 1970.

Bennett, Lerone Jr. *The Negro Mood and Other Essays.* Chicago: Johnson Publishing Co., 1964.

Berlin, Isaiah. *Four Essays on Liberty.* London: Oxford University Press, 1969.

Binzen, Peter. *White-Town, U.S.A.* New York: Random House, 1970.

Butts, Robert Freeman, and Cremin, Lawrence A. *A History of Education in American Culture.* New York: Holt, 1953.

Campbell, Angus. *White Attitudes toward Black People.* Ann Arbor, Mich.: Institute for Social Research, 1971.

Cleage, Albert B., Jr. *The Black Messiah.* New York: Sheed & Ward, 1968.

Coles, Robert. *The Middle Americans: Proud and Uncertain.* Boston: Little, Brown, 1971.

Congressional Quarterly. *Civil Rights Progress Report, 1970.* Washington: Congressional Quarterly, 1975.

———.*Congress and the Nation.* 3 vols. Washington: Congressional Quarterly, 1965, 1969, 1973.

———.*Guide to Current American Government, Fall 1975.* Washington: Congressional Quarterly, 1975.

———.*Nixon: The Fifth Year of His Presidency.* Washington: Congressional Quarterly, 1973.

———.*Nixon: The First Year of His Presidency.* Washington: Congressional Quarterly, 1970.

———.*Nixon: The Fourth Year of His Presidency.* Washington: Congressional Quarterly, 1973.

———.*Nixon: The Second Year of His Presidency.* Washington: Congressional Quarterly, 1971.

———.*Nixon: The Third Year of His Presidency.* Washington: Congressional Quarterly, 1972.

————.*The Presidency in 1974*. Washington: Congressional Quarterly, 1975.
Coser, Lewis A., and Howe, Irving, eds. *The New Conservatives: A Critique from the Left*. New York: Quadrangle, 1974.
Coyne, John R., Jr. *The Impudent Snobs: Agnew vs. the Intellectual Establishment*. New Rochelle, N.Y.: Arlington House, 1972.
Davidson, Edmonia W. *Family and Personal Development in Adult Basic Education: Curriculum Guide and Resource Units*. Washington: National University Extension Association, 1971.
Ellison, Ralph. *Shadow and Act*. New York: Random House, 1964.
Festinger, Leon. *A Theory of Cognitive Dissonance*. Evanston, Ill.: Row & Peterson, 1957.
Fisher, Louis. *Presidential Spending Power*. Princeton, N.J.: Princeton University Press, 1975.
Frank, John P. *The Warren Court*. New York: Macmillan, 1964.
Fried, Marc. *The World of the Urban Working Class*. Cambridge, Mass.: Harvard University Press, 1973.
Gall, Peter, and Panetta, Leon E. *Bring Us Together: The Nixon Team and the Civil Rights Retreat*. New York: J. B. Lippincott Co., 1971.
Glazer, Nathan, and Moynihan, Daniel P. *Beyond the Melting Pot*. Cambridge, Mass.: M.I.T. Press, 1970.
Golden, Harry. *Mr. Kennedy and the Negroes*. New York: World Publishing Co., 1964.
Greeley, Andrew M. *Why Can't They Be like Us? America's White Ethnic Groups*. New York: E. P. Dutton, 1969.
Greer, Colin, ed. *Divided Society: The Ethnic Experience in America*. New York: Basic Books, 1974.
Harvey, James C. *Black Civil Rights During the Johnson Administration*. Jackson: University and College Press of Mississippi, 1973.
————.*Civil Rights During the Kennedy Administration*. Hattiesburg: University and College Press of Mississippi, 1971.
Hatchett, Shirley, and Schuman, Howard. *Black Racial Attitudes: Trends and Complexities*. Ann Arbor: University of Michigan Survey Research Center, 1974.
Herrnstein, Richard J. *I.Q. in the Meritocracy*. Boston: Little, Brown, 1973.
Hill, Robert B. *The Strengths of Black Families*. New York: Emerson Hall, 1972.
Jencks, Christopher. *Inequality: A Reassessment of the Effect of Family and Schooling in America*. New York: Basic Books, 1972.
Karier, Clarence J.; Spring, Joel, and Violas, Paul C. *Roots of Crisis: American Education in the Twentieth Century*. Chicago: Rand McNally, 1973.
King, Martin Luther, Jr. *Where Do We Go from Here: Chaos or Community?* New York: Harper & Row, 1967.
————.*The Trumpet of Conscience*. New York: Harper & Row, 1968.
Koenig, Louis W. *The Chief Executive*. New York: Harcourt, Brace and World, 1968.
Logan, Rayford W. *The Betrayal of the Negro: From Rutherford B. Hayes to Woodrow Wilson*. New York: Collier, 1965.
Lyman, Stanford M. *The Black American in Sociological Thought*. New York: Putnam, 1972.
Merton, Robert K. *Social Theory and Social Structure*. Riverside, N.J.: Glencoe Press, 1949.
Miller, Herman P. *Rich Man, Poor Man*. New York: Crowell, 1971.
Mills, C. Wright. *The Power Elite*. New York: Oxford University Press, 1959.
————.*Power, Politics and People*. New York: Oxford University Press, 1963.
Moynihan, Daniel P., and Mosteller, Frederick, eds. *On Equality of Educational Oppor-

tunity. New York: Random House, 1972.

Moynihan, Daniel P., ed. *On Understanding Poverty: Perspectives from the Social Sciences.* New York: Basic Books, 1969.

Myrdal, Gunnar. *An American Dilemma: The Negro Problem and Modern Democracy.* 2 vols. New York: Harper & Row, 1944, 1962.

Novak, Michael. *The Rise of the Unmeltable Ethnics: Politics and Culture in the Seventies.* New York: Macmillan, 1973.

Orfield, Gary. *Congressional Power: Congress and Social Change.* New York: Harcourt Brace Jovanovich, 1975.

Pfeffer, Leo. *This Honorable Court.* Boston: Beacon Press, 1965.

Pinkney, Alphonso. *Black Americans.* Englewood Cliffs, N.J.: Prentice-Hall, 1975.

Podhoretz, Norman, ed. *The Commentary Reader.* New York: Atheneum, 1966.

Rainwater, Lee, and Yancy, William L. *The Moynihan Report and the Politics of Controversy.* Cambridge, Mass.: MIT Press, 1967.

Report of the National Advisory Commission on Civil Disorders (by Otto Kerner, chairman.) New York: Bantam Books, 1968.

Schultze, Carl L. *Setting National Priorities: The 1971 Budget.* Washington: The Brookings Institution, 1970.

Stanley, William O. *Education and Social Integration.* New York: Teachers College, Columbia University, 1953.

Sundquist, James L. *Politics and Policy: Eisenhower, Kennedy and Johnson Years.* Washington: The Brookings Institution, 1968.

Watson, Bernard C. *Stupidity, Sloth and Public Policy: Social Darwinism Rides Again.* Washington: National Urban Coalition, 1973.

Wolk, Allan. *The Presidency and Black Civil Rights: Eisenhower to Nixon.* Rutherford, N.J.: Farleigh Dickenson University Press, 1971.

Journals and Magazines

Abernathy, Ralph D. "Some International Dimensions of the Peace Movement." *Freedomways* 11 (Third Quarter 1971): 237–40.

Abrams, Elliot, "The Quota Commission." *Commentary* (October 1972), pp. 54–57.

Akaraogun, Olu. "African States and the Politics of Economic Freedom." *Black World* 21 (October 1972): 79–87.

Alexander, Raymond Pace. "The Five Civil Rights Groups Should Merge Forces." *Negro Digest* 14 (June 1965): 3–7.

Allen, Robert. "A Historical Synthesis: Black Liberation and World Revolution." *Black Scholar* 3 (February 1972): 7–23.

Allen, Robert, and Rodney, Walter. "Politics of the Attack on Black Studies." *Black Scholar* 6 (September 1974): 2–7.

Allen, Robert L., and Chrisman, Robert. "The Cuban Revolution: Lessons for the Third World." *Black Scholar* 4 (February 1973): 2–15.

"An Exchange on Equality." *Commentary* (February 1973), pp. 12–33.

"An Exchange on I.Q." *Commentary* (July 1973), p. 4.

"An Exchange on Open Admissions." *Commentary* (May 1973), pp. 4, 24.

Anatomy of a Revolution." *Newsweek,* 29 July 1963, pp. 15–34.

Anderson, S. E. "Revolutionary Black Nationalism Is Pan African." *Black Scholar* 3 (March 1971): 16–23.

———."Toward Racial Relevancy: Military and Black Students." *Negro Digest* 16 (September 1967): 12–17.

Anise, Ladun. "The Tyranny of a Purist Ideology." *Black World* 24 (May 1975): 18–27.

Arkes, Hadley. "The Problem of Kenneth Clark." *Commentary* (November 1974), pp. 37–46.

Armor, David J. "The Evidence on Busing." *The Public Interest*, no. 28 (Summer 1972), pp. 90–126.

Atkins, Hanna. "Why I Resigned." *Black World* 24 (October 1975): 44–46.

Baily, Peter. "New Image of the Ivy League." *Negro Digest* 16 (July 1967): 28–30.

Bailey, Peter B. "What African-American Nationalism Means to Me." *Negro Digest* 17 (December 1967): 31–33.

Banfield, Edward C. "Welfare: A Crisis without 'Solutions.' " *The Public Interest,* no. 16 (Summer 1969), pp. 89–101.

Banfield, Edward C., Glazer, Nathan; Harrington, Michael; et al. "Nixon, the Great Society, and the Future of Social Policy—A Symposium." *Commentary* (May 1973), pp. 1–61.

Baraka, Amiri. "A Black Value System." *Black Scholar* 1 (November 1969): 54–60.

_____."Pan-African Party and the Black Nation." *Black Scholar* 2 (March 1971): 24–33.

_____."Toward Ideological Clarity." *Black World* 24 (November 1974): 24–37.

_____."Why I Changed My Ideology: Black Nationalism and Socialist Revolution." *Black World* 24 (July 1975): 30–42.

Barrett, Linsay. "Should Black Americans Be Involved in African Affairs?" *Negro Digest* 18 (August 1969): 10–17.

Barrow, William. "Black World." *Negro Digest* 18 (May 1969): 4.

Bell, Daniel. "On Meritocracy and Equality." *The Public Interest,* no. 29 (Fall 1972), pp. 29–68.

Bell, Daniel, and Kristol, Irving. "What Is the Public Interest?" *The Public Interest,* no. 1 (Fall 1965), pp. 3–5.

Bloice, Carl. "The Future of Black Workers under American Capitalism." *Black Scholar* 3 (May 1972): 14–22.

Boggs, James, and Boggs, Grace Lee. "Uprooting Racists and Racism in the U.S." *Negro Digest* 19 (January 1970): 20–22.

Bond, Jean Carey. "The New York School Crisis: Integration for What?" *Freedomways* 4 (Spring 1964): 196–202.

Bond, Julian; Cornwell, Anita R.; and Fair, Ronald L. "The Meaning and Measure of Black Power." *Negro Digest* 16 (November 1966): 20–37

"Born Dumb?" *Newsweek,* 31 March 1969, p. 84.

Brimmer, Andrew. "Economic Developments in the Black Community." *The Public Interest,* no. 34 (Winter 1974), pp. 146–63.

Burnham, Dorothy. "Jensenism: The New Pseudo-Science of Racism." *Freedomways* 11 (Second Quarter 1971): 150–57.

"Busing, the Courts, and the Politics of Integration." *Commentary* (July 1972), pp. 6–31.

"Can Negroes Learn the Way Whites Do?" *U.S. News and World Report,* 10 March 1969, pp. 48–51.

Carmichael, Stokely. "A Message from Stokely." *Black World* 21 (July 1972): 25.

_____."Marxism-Leninism and Nkrumahism." *Black Scholar* 4 (February 1973): 41–43.

_____."Pan-Africanism: Land and Power." *Black Scholar* 1 (November 1969): 36–43.

Chrisman, Robert. "Aspects of Pan-Africanism." *Black Scholar* 4 (July/August 1973): 2–8.

_____."The Contradictions of Harold Cruse." *Black World* 22 (May 1971): 90–98.

Cleage, Albert. "The Death of Fear." *Negro Digest* 17 (November 1967): 29–31.

_____."We Have Become a Black Nation." *Negro Digest* 18 (January 1969): 30–38.

Cohen, David K. "Does IQ Matter?" *Commentary* (April 1972), pp. 51–59.

Coleman, James S. "Class Integration—A Fundamental Break with Past." *Saturday Review,* 27 May 1972, pp. 58–59.

_____."Equal Schools or Equal Students." *The Public Interest,* no. 4 (Summer 1966), pp. 70–75.

_____."Racial Segregation in the Schools: New Research with New Policy Implications." *Phi Delta Kappan* 57 (October 1975): 75–78.

_____."Toward Open Schools." *The Public Interest,* no. 9 (Fall 1967), pp. 20–27.

Comer, James P. "Nixon's Policies and the Black Future in America." *Black World* 22 (March 1973): 36–39, 66–69.

"Community Services Agency Replaces OEO." *Congressional Quarterly Weekly Report* 11 January 1975, pp. 87–89.

Cox, Courtland, and Stark, Geri. "Interview with President Nyerere of Tanzania." *Black World* 22 (October 1973): 4–8.

Cruse, Harold. "Harold Cruse Looks Back on Black Art and Politics in Harlem." *Negro Digest* 18 (November 1968): 19–25.

_____."Harlem: Special Place in the Theory of Black Cities." *Black World* 20 (May 1971): 9–40.

_____."Black and White: Outlines of the Next Stage." *Black World* 20 (January 1971): 19–41.

_____."The Little Rock National Black Convention." *Black World* 23 (October 1974): 82–88.

Cunningham, James. "Ron Karenga and Black Cultural Nationalism." *Negro Digest* 17 (January 1968): 4.

Danzig, David. "In Defense of 'Black Power'. " *Commentary* (September 1966), pp. 41–48.

_____."The Meaning of Negro Strategy." *Commentary* (February 1969), pp. 41–46.

Darden, Clifford. "The Post-Malcolm Movement." *Negro Digest* 17 (June 1968): 4–9.

Davidson, Edmonia W. "Education and Black Cities: Demographic Background." *Journal of Negro Education* 42 (Summer 1973): 233–60.

Davis, Angela. "The Soledad Brothers." *Black Scholar,* 2 (April/May 1971): 2–7.

Decter, Midge. "The Negro and the New York Schools." *Commentary* (September 1964), pp. 25–34.

De Ramus, Betty. "Detroit Revisited." *Negro Digest* 17 (July 1968): 10–13.

Deyler, Carl N. "Negro in America: Where Myrdal Went Wrong." *New York Times Magazine,* (7 December 1969,) pp. 64–65.

Drew, Elizabeth. "Washington: The Nixon Court." *Atlantic* (November 1972), pp. 6–17.

Drinan, Robert F. "Why Direct Action Must Not Cease." *Negro Digest* 14 (April 1965): 4–13.

DuBois, Shirley Graham. "Liberation of Africa: Power, Peace and Justice." *Black Scholar* 2 (February 1971): 32–38.

DuBois, W. E. B. "Does the Negro Need Separate Schools?" *Journal of Negro Education* 4 (July 1935): 328–35.

Duncan, Otis Dudley. "After the Riots." *The Public Interest,* no. 9 (Fall 1967), pp. 3–7.

"Education: Action Completed." *Congressional Quarterly Weekly Report,* 28 December 1974, p. 3423.

Effrat, Andrew; Feldman, Roy E.; and Sapolsky, Harvey M. "Inducing Poor Children to Learn." *The Public Interest,* no. 15 (Spring 1969), pp. 106–12.

Elliot, Osborn. "Anatomy of a Revolution." *Newsweek,* 29 July 1963, p. 7.

"Employment Discrimination." *Congressional Quarterly Weekly Report,* 28 September 1974, pp. 2591–92.

Epstein, Joseph. "Dr. Coles among the Poor." *Commentary* (August 1972), pp. 60–63.

"Equality and Justice." *Commentary* (February 1973), pp. 12–34.

Evans, Mari; Gerald, Carolyn; and Karenga, Ron. "Measure and Meaning of the Sixties." *Negro Digest* 19 (November 1969): 4–36.

Fabio, Sarah Webster. "A Black Paper." *Negro Digest* 28 (July 1969): 26–30.

Farmer, James; Lewis, John; King, Martin Luther, Jr.; Wilkins, Roy; and Young, Whitney. "Prospects for '64 in the Civil Rights Struggle." *Negro Digest* 13 (January 1964): 8–9.

Finn, Chester E., Jr., and Lenkowsky, Leslie. "'Serrano' vs. *The People." Commentary* (September 1972), pp. 68–72.

Fleming, Harold C. "The Federal Executive and Civil Rights, 1961–1965." *Daedalus* 94 (Fall 1965): 921–48.

Ford, Gerald. "Budget Message of the President." *Congressional Quarterly Weekly Report,* 33, 11 January 1975: 284–89.

_____."State of the Union Message, 1975." *Vital Speeches of the Day* 41 1 February 1975: 226–29.

Frankel, Charles. "The New Egalitarianism and the Old." *Commentary* (September 1973), pp. 54–61.

Fuller, Hoyt. "Algiers Journal." *Negro Digest* 18 (October 1969): 72–87.

_____."The Alien Message of the Wind." *Black World* 19 (October 1970): 49–50.

_____."New Black Leadership in Detroit." *Negro Digest* 17 (November 1967): 32–35.

_____."On Black Studies and the Critics." *Black World* 23 (May 1974): 88–90.

Galamison, Milton. "Educational Values and Community Power." *Freedomways* 8 (Fall 1968): 311–18.

Galbraith, John Kenneth. "An Agenda for American Liberals." *Commentary* (June 1966), pp. 29–34.

Gayle, Addison. "Black Literature and the White Aesthetic." *Negro Digest* 18 (July 1969): 32–39.

Gerald, Carolyn F. "The Black Writer and His Role." *Negro Digest* 18 (January 1969): 42–47.

Ginzberg, Eli, and Solow, Robert M. "An Introduction to This Special Issue." *The Public Interest,* no. 34 (Winter 1974), pp. 4–13.

_____."Some Lessons of the 1960's." *The Public Interest,* no. 3 (Winter 1974), pp. 4–13.

Glazer, Nathan. "Blacks, Jews and the Intellectuals." *Commentary* (April 1969), 33–39.

_____."Ethnicity and the Schools." *Commentary* (September 1974), pp. 55–59.

_____."Is Busing Necessary?" *Commentary* (March 1972), 39–52.

_____."The Limits of Social Policy." *Commentary* (September 1971), pp. 51–58.

_____."Paradoxes of American Poverty." *The Public Interest,* no. 1 (Fall 1965), pp. 71–81.

Glazer, Nathan, and Moynihan, Daniel P. "Why Ethnicity?" *Commentary* (October 1974), pp. 33–39.

Goodman, Frank. "De Facto School Segregation: A Constitutional and Empirical Analysis." *California Law Review* 60 (March 1972): 275–437.

Granton, Fannie. "New School of Afro-American Thought." *Negro Digest* 16 (June 1967): 8–14.

Griffith, Thomas. "The Best of Times—1821? 1961? Today?" *Time,* 1 September 1975, pp. 52–3.

Gunter, Gerald. "The Supreme Court, 1971 Term–Foreword: In Search of Evolving Doctrine on a Changing Court." *Harvard Law Review* 86 (November 1972): 1–48.

Guthrie, James R. "What the Coleman Reanalysis Didn't Tell Us." *Saturday Review*, 22 July 1972, p. 45.

Guyot, Lawrence, and Thelwell, Michael. "The Politics of Necessity and Survival in Mississippi." *Freedomways* 6 (Spring 1966): 120–32.

Hamilton, Charles V. "Black Americans and the Modern Political Struggle." *Black World* 19 (May 1970): 5–9.

_____."Blacks and the Crisis in Political Participation." *The Public Interest*, no. 34 (Winter 1974), pp. 188–210.

_____."Education in the Black Community." *Freedomways* 8 (Fall 1968): 319-24.

_____."Pan Africanism and the Black Struggle in the U.S." *Black Scholar* 2 (March 1971): 10–15.

_____."The Place of the Black College in the Human Rights Struggle." *Negro Digest* 16 (September 1967): 4–10.

_____."Urban Economics, Conduit Colonialism and Public Policy." *Black World* 21 (October 1972): 40–45.

Harding, Vincent. "Some International Implications of the Black University." *Negro Digest* 27 (March 1968): 32–38.

Hare, Nathan. "An Epitaph for Nonviolence." *Negro Digest* 25 (January 1966): 15–20.

_____."Final Reflections on a 'Negro' College: A Case Study." *Negro Digest* 17 (March 1968): 40–46, 70–76.

_____."Report on the Pan-African Cultural Festival." *Black Scholar* 1 (November 1969): 2–10.

Harwood, Edwin. "Youth Unemployment—A Tale of Two Ghettos." *The Public Interest*, no. 17 (Fall 1966), pp. 78–87.

Herrnstein, Richard J. "I.Q." *Atlantic* (September 1971), pp. 43–64.

_____."On Challenging an Orthodoxy." *Commentary* (April 1973), pp. 52–62.

Himmelfarb, Milton. "Gentlemen and Scholars," *Commentary* (October 1973), pp. 68–71.

_____."Is American Jewry in Crisis?" *Commentary* (March 1969), pp. 33–44.

_____."Sword of the Law." *Commentary* (May 1972), pp. 71–73.

Hitchcock, James. "The Intellectuals and the People." *Commentary* (March 1973), pp. 64–69.

Hook, Sidney. "The War against the Democratic Process." *Atlantic* (February 1969), pp. 45–48.

Horne, David Lawrence. "Pan-African Congress: A Positive Assessment." *Black Scholar* 5 (July/August 1974): 2–11.

Howe, Harold. "Paying for American Education." *Education Digest* 33 (October 1967): 1–4.

Hubbard, Howard. "Five Long Hot Summers and How They Grew." *The Public Interest*, no. 12 (Summer 1968), pp. 3–24.

Hutchings, Phil. "Report on the A.L.S.C. National Conference." *Black Scholar* 5 (July/August 1974): 2–11.

"Impounded Funds: $12.3 Billion Held by Administration." *Congressional Quarterly Weekly Report*, 26 (February 1972): 443–45.

"IQ, Lysenkoism and Liberal Orthodoxy." *Commentary* (July 1973), pp. 4–14.

Jencks, Christopher. "Is the Public School Obsolete?" *The Public Interest*, no. 2 (Winter 1966), pp. 18–27.

_____."Reappraisal of the Most Controversial Educational Document of Our Time: The Coleman Report." *New York Times Magazine*, 10 August 1969, pp. 12–13.

Jensen, Arthur R. "How Much Can We Boost IQ and Scholastic Achievement?" *Harvard Educational Review* 39 (Winter 1969): 1–123.
Johnson, Lyndon B. "President Johnson's Message on Voting Rights." *Negro Digest* 14 (June 1965): 9–16.
_____."The Right to Vote: Equal Standards for All." *Vital Speeches of the Day* 31 (April 1965): 354–57.
_____."State of the Union: 1968." *Vital Speeches of the Day* 34 (1 February 1968): 226–30.
_____."State of the Union: 1969." *Vital Speeches of the Day* 35 (1 February 1969): 228–31.
_____."State of the Union: The Great Society." *Vital Speeches of the Day* 31 (1 April 1965): 194–98.
_____."State of the Union: Home and Abroad." *Vital Speeches of the Day,* 32 (1 February 1966): 226–30.
Jones, Faustine C. "The Inequality Controversy." *Journal of Negro Education* 42 (Fall 1973): 537–49.
Jordan, Vernon E. "Blacks and the Nixon Administration: The Next Four Years." *Vital Speeches of the Day* 39 (1 May 1973): 418–20.
Kadushin, Charles. "Who Are the Elite Intellectuals?" *The Public Interest,* no. 29 (Fall 1972), pp. 109–25.
Kain, John H., and Perskey, Joseph J. "Alternatives to the Gilded Ghetto." *The Public Interest,* no. 14 (Winter 1969), pp. 74–87.
Kalvern, Harry. "The Supreme Court, 1970 Term–Foreword: 'Even When a Nation Is at War." *Harvard Law Review* 85 (November 1971): 3–36.
Karenga, Ron. "Ron Karenga and Black Cultural Nationalism." *Negro Digest* 17 (January 1968): 5–9.
Kennedy, John F. "State of the Union: Domestic and Foreign Policies." *Vital Speeches of the Day* 27 (15 February 1961): 226–30.
Keyfitz, Nathan. "Can Inequality Be Cured?" *The Public Interest,* no. 31 (Spring 1973), pp. 91–101.
Kgositsile, Keorapetse. "Where Is the Black Revolution?" *Black World* 19 (May 1970): 16–19.
Knebel, Fletcher. "Mood of America." *Look,* 18 November 1969, pp. 23–32.
Kristol, Irving. "About Equality." *Commentary* (November 1972), pp. 41–47.
_____."Welfare: The Best of Intentions, the Worst of Results." *Atlantic* (August 1971), pp. 45–47.
Lee, Don L. "The Death Walk against Afrika." *Black World* 22 (October 1973): 28–36.
Lipset, Seymour Martin. "Social Mobility and Equal Opportunity." *The Public Interest* no. 29 (Fall 1972), pp. 90–108.
Long, Norton E. "The City as a Reservation." *The Public Interest,* no. 25 (Fall 1971), pp. 22–38.
Madhubuti, Haki. "Enemy: From the White Left, White Right and In-Between . . . " *Black World* 23 (October 1974): 36–47.
_____."The Latest Purge." *Black Scholar* 6 (September 1974): 43–56.
Marmor, ᵀ. R. "Banfield's 'Heresy' " *Commentary* (July 1972), pp. 86–88.
Mason, Alpheus. "Judicial Activism ᵒⁱ and New." *Virginia Law Review* 55 (April 1969): 385–426.
Mayfield, Julian. "Childe Harold." *Negro Digest* 18 (November 1968): 26–27.
_____."Crisis or Crusade." *Negro Digest* 17 (June 1968): 10–24.
McGinnis, James. "Crisis and Contradiction in Black Studies." *Black World* 22 (March 1973): 27–35.

McWorter, Gerald. "The Nature and Needs of the Black University." *Negro Digest* 17 (March 1968): 4–13.

Miller, S. M., and Ratner, Ronnie S. "The American Resignation: The New Assault on Equality." *Social Policy* (May/June 1972), pp. 5–15.

Moynihan, Daniel P. "The Crises in Welfare." *The Public Interest,* no. 10 (Winter 1968), pp. 3–29.

———."Equalizing Education: In Whose Benefit?" *The Public Interest,* no. 29 (Fall 1972), pp. 69–89.

———."Policy vs. Program in the '70's." *The Public Interest,* no. 20 (Summer 1970), pp. 90–100.

———."The Professionalization of Reform" *The Public Interest,* no. 1 (Fall 1965), pp. 6–16.

———."The Professors and the Poor" *Commentary* (August 1968), pp. 19–29.

———."The Schism in Black America." *The Public Interest,* no. 27 (Spring 1972), pp. 3–14.

———."Toward a National Urban Policy." *The Public Interest,* no. 17 (Fall 1969), pp. 3–20.

Munford, C. J. "The Fallacy of Lumpen Ideology." *Black Scholar* 4 (July/August): 47–51.

National Urban League. "Black Unemployment Reaches Record Level During 4th Quarter, 1974." *Quarterly Economic Report on the Black Worker* (March 1975), p. 1.

Neary, John. "A Scientist's Variations on a Disturbing Racial Theme." *Life,* 12 June 1970, pp. 58c–58d.

"Negro IQ and Heredity." *School and Society,* 96 (2 March 1968): 127–8.

"The Negro in America." *Newsweek,* 24 July 1963, pp. 15–34.

"The Negro in America '65: Progress." *Newsweek,* 25 October 1965, p. 32.

Nixon, Richard M. "The Nature of the Presidency: To Unite America." *Vital Speeches of the Day* 35 (15 October 1968): 6–8.

Normand, Clarence; Pettigrew, Thomas F.; Smith, Marshall S.; and Useem, Elizabeth L. "Busing: A Review of 'The Evidence'." *The Public Interest,* no. 30 (Winter 1973), pp. 88–118.

Nyerere, Julius. "African Socialism: Ujaama in Practice." *Black Scholar* 2 (February 1971): 2–7.

———."Julius K. Nyerere's Speech to the Congress." *Black Scholar* 5 (July/August): 16–22.

Obadele, Imari Abubakari. "The Struggle for Land in Mississippi." *Black World* 22 (February 1973): 66–73.

O'Dell, John H. "Charleston's Legacy to the Poor People's Campaign." *Freedomways* 9 (Summer 1969): 197–211.

———."The Contours of the 'Black Revolution' in the 1970's. *"Freedomways"* 10 (Second Quarter 1970): 104–13.

———."The Threshold of a New Reconstruction." *Freedomways* 5 (Fall 1965): 495–508.

Ofari, Earl. "A Critical Review of the Pan-African Congress." *Black Scholar* 5 (July/August 1974): 12–15.

———."Black Labor: Powerful Force for Liberation." *Black World* 22 (October 1973): 42–47.

———."Marxism-Leninism: The Key to Black Liberation." *Black Scholar* 4 (September 1972): 34–46.

Patterson, Orlando. "The Moral Crisis of the Black America." *The Public Interest,* no.

32 (Summer 1973), pp. 43–69.

Podhoretz, Norman. "A Call to Dubious Battle." *Commentary* (July 1972), pp. 4–5.

_____."Is It Good for the Jews?" *Commentary* (February 1972), pp. 7–14.

_____."My Negro Problem—And Ours." *Commentary* (February 1963), pp. 93–101.

_____."The New Inquisitors." *Commentary* (April 1973), pp. 7–8.

_____."School Integration and Liberal Opinion." *Commentary* (March 1972), p. 7.

"The Pottinger Papers." *Commentary* (May 1972), pp. 10–30.

"The Question of Open Admissions." *Commentary* (May 1973), pp. 4–24.

Raab, Earl. "The Black Revolution and the Jewish Question." *Commentary* (January 1969), pp. 23–24.

_____."Quotas by Any Other Name." *Commentary* (January 1972), pp. 41–45.

Ravitch, Diane. "Community Control Revisited." *Commentary* (February 1972), pp. 69–74.

Reid, Inez Smith. "The Burger Court and the Civil Rights Movement: The Supreme Court Giveth and the Supreme Court Taketh Away." *Rutgers Camden Law Journal* 3 (Spring 1972): 410–40.

Reed, Adolph. "Pan-Africanism: Ideology for Liberation?" *Black Scholar* 3 (September 1971): 2–13.

"Report from Black America." *Newsweek,* 30 June 1969, pp. 17–26, 31–35.

Richardson, Gloria. "Focus on Cambridge." *Freedomways* 4 (Winter 1964): 28–34.

Rustin, Bayard. " 'Black Power' and Coalition Politics." *Commentary* (September 1966), pp. 35–40.

_____. "The Future of the Civil Rights Movement." *Commentary* (February 1965), pp. 25–31.

_____. "Lessons of the Long Hot Summer." *Commentary* (October 1967), pp. 39–45.

_____. "The Watts 'Manifesto' and the McCone Report." *Commentary* (March 1966), pp. 29–36.

Salaam, Kalamu ya. "Tell No Lies, Claim No Easy Victories." *Black World* 23 (October 1974): 18–34.

Scammon, Richard M., and Wattenberg, Ben J. "Black Progress and Liberal Rhetoric." *Commentary* (April 1973), pp. 35–44.

_____. "Report from Black America." *Newsweek,* 30 June 1969, pp. 16–26.

Seabury, Paul. "HEW and the Universities." *Commentary* (Feburary 1972), pp. 38–44.

_____. "The Idea of Merit." *Commentary* (December 1972), pp. 41–45.

Simpkins, Edward. "Black Studies—Here to Stay ?" *Black World* 24 (December 1974): 26–29.

Slawson, John. "Mutual Aid and the Negro." *Commentary* (April 1966), pp. 43–52.

Sowell, Thomas. "Black Excellence: The Case of Dunbar High School." *The Public Interest,* no. 34 (Spring 1972), pp. 3–21.

Starr, Roger. "Prison, Politics and the Attica Report." *Commentary* (March 1973), pp. 31–37.

Swindler, William. "The Warren Court: Completion of a Constitutional Revolution." *Vanderbilt Law Review* 23 (March 1970): 205–48.

Thomas, Tony. "Black Nationalism and Confused Marxists." *Black Scholar* 4 (September 1972): 49–52. '

Thorne, Richard. "Integration or Black Nationalism, Which Route Will Negroes Choose?" *Negro Digest* 12 (August 1963): 36–47.

Tolbert, Richard C. "A New Brand of Nationalism." *Negro Digest* 16 (August 1967): 19–28.

_____. "Needed: A Compatible Ideology." *Negro Digest* 17 (August 1968): 4–12.

Tollett, Kenneth S. "The Viability and Reliability of the United States Supreme Court as an Institution for Social Change and Progress: Part II." *Black Law Journal* 3 (Spring 1973): 5–50.

Touré, Sékou. "Harvard's Investments in Southern Africa." *Black Scholar* 3 (January 1972): 25–31.

_____."The Permanent Revolution." *Black Scholar* 2 (March 1971): 2–9.

_____."Sékou Touré's Speech to the Congress." *Black Scholar* 5 (July/August 1974): 23–29.

Tribe, Laurence. "The Supreme Court 1972 Term–Foreword: Toward a Model of Roles in the Due Process of Life and Law." *Harvard Law Review* 87 (1972): 1–53.

Turner, Darwin. "The Literary Presumptions of Mr. Bone." *Negro Digest,* 16 (August 1967): 54–65.

Turner, James. "Blacks in the Cities Land and Self-Determination." *Black Scholar* 1 (April 1970): 9–13.

_____."Black Nationalism: The Inevitable Response." *Black World* 22 (January 1971): 4–13.

Vontress, Clemmont E. "There Is too Much Apathy on the Negro Campus." *Negro Digest* 16 (June 1967): 22–28.

Walters, Ronald. "African-American Nationalism." *Black World* 22 (October 1973): 9–27, 84.

_____."The New Black Political Culture." *Black World* 21 (October 1972): 4–17.

Washington, Joseph R., Jr. "Black Nationalism: Potentially Anti-Folk and Anti-Intellectual." *Black World* 22 (July 1973): 32–39.

Wildavsky, Aaron. "The Empty-Head Blues: Black Rebellion and White Reaction." *The Public Interest,* no. 11 (Spring 1968), pp. 3016.

Williams, John A. "Race, War and Politics." *Negro Digest* 16 (August 1967): 4–9.

Williams, Ronald. "Black Studies: The Work to Come." *Negro Digest* 19 (January 1970): 30–35.

Wilson, Charles E. "Lessons of the 201 Complex in Harlem." *Freedomways* 8 (Fall 1968): 399–406.

Wilson, James Q. "Liberalism v. Liberal Education." *Commentary* (June 1972), pp. 50–54.

_____."Liberalism and Purpose." *Commentary* (May 1972), pp. 74–76.

_____."Sick Sixties." *Atlantic* (October 1973), pp. 91–92.

Wilson, William J. "A Rejoiner to Vincent Harding." *Negro Digest* 19 (March 1970): 6–11.

Zangrando, Robert L. "Dr. Kenneth B. Clark vs. Black Power." *Negro Digest* 17 (July 1968): 36–41.

Newspapers

Atlanta Constitution, 14 October and 25 November 1975.

Boston Globe, 18 May 1975.

Chicago Sun-Times, 7 June 1975.

Los Angeles Times, 29 May 1975.

National Observer, 7 June 1975.

New York Times, 31 August 1969; 11 February, 18 August, 16 November 1975.

Wall Street Journal, 1 July 1975.

Washington Post, 13, 14 July, 21 July 1975.

Washington Star, 29 April 1973, 8 June 1975.

U.S. Government Documents and Publications

Congressional Record. 29 June 1973, 28 June 1973 (daily Ed.).

U.S. Bureau of the Census. *Current Population Reports: Special Studies,* Series P-23, No. 52. Washington: Government Printing Office, 1975.

————.*The Social and Economic Status of the Black Population, 1973.* Washington: Government Printing Office, 1974.

————.*The Social and Economic Status of the Black Population in the United States, 1974.* Washington: Government Printing Office, 1975.

U.S. Bureau of Labor Statistics. *Social and Economic Conditions of Negroes in the United States, 1963.* Washington: Government Printing Office, 1967.

A Report of the U.S. Commission on Civil Rights: The Federal Civil Rights Enforcement Effort—1974. By Arthur S. Fleming, chairman. Washington: Government Printing Office, 1975.

A Report of the U.S. Commission on Civil Rights: Twenty Years after Brown. By Arthur S. Fleming, chairman. Washington: Government Printing Office, 1975.

U.S. Congress. House of Representatives. Committee on Appropriations. *Public Works for Water and Power Development and Atomic Energy Appropriations.* Hearings before the House Committee on Appropriations. 92d Congress, 1st sess., 1971.

U.S. *Constitution.* Art. I, sec. 8.

U.S. Congress. House of Representatives. *Report No. 93-6.* 93d Congress 1st sess., 1973.

————.*Report No. 93-15.* 93d Congress, 1st sess., 1973.

————.*Report No. 93-20.* 93d Congress, 1st. sess., 1973.

————.*Report No. 93-21.* 93d Congress, 1st sess., 1973.

————.*Report No. 93-11.* 93d Congress, 1st sess., 1973.

U.S. Congress. Senate. Committee on Banking, Housing, and Urban Affairs. *Hearings on Withholding Funds for Housing and Urban Development Programs, Fiscal Year 1971, before the Senate Committee on Banking, Housing and Urban Affairs.* 92d Congress, 1st sess., 1972.

————.Judiciary Committee. *Hearings before a Subcommittee of the Senate Judiciary Committee on Separation of Powers.* 92d Congress, 1st sess., 1971.

————.*Report No. 93-1.* 93d Congress., 1st sess., 1971.

Court Cases

Albemarle Paper Company v. *Moody,* 422 U.S. (1975).

Betts v. *Brady,* 316 U.S. 455 (1942).

Brown v. *Board of Education of Topeka, Kansas,* 347 U.S. 483 (1954).

Brown v. *Board of Education of Topeka, Kansas,* 349 U.S. 294 (1955).

Cooper v. *Aaron,* 358 U.S. 122 (1958).

Green v. *County School Board of New Kent County, Virginia,* 391 U.S. 430 (1968).

Griffin v. *County School Board of Prince Edward County, Virginia,* 377 U.S. 218 (1964).

Griggs v. *Duke Power Company,* 401 U.S. 424 (1971).

Harris v. *New York,* 401 U.S. 222 (1971).

In re Gault, 387 U.S. 1 (1967).

Keyes v. *School District No. 1, Denver, Colorado,* 413 U.S. 186 (1973).

McKeiver v. *Pennsylvania,* 403 U.S. 528 (1971).

Milliken v. *Bradley,* 4 Pl. U.S. 815 (1974).

Miranda v. *Arizona,* 384 U.S. 436 (1966).

San Antonio Independent School District v. *Rodrigues,* 411 U.S. 1 (1973).

Swann v. *Charlotte-Mecklenburg Board of Education,* 402 U.S. 1 (1971).

Unpublished Papers

Coleman, James. "Recent Trends in School Integration." Paper presented at meeting of American Educational Research Association, Washington, D.C., April 1975.

Hook, Sidney. Statement before fact-finding hearings of Office of Federal Contract Compliance of the Department of Labor, 3 October 1975.

McKay, Robert B. "The Court, Congress and School Desegregation." Paper presented to U.S. Commission on Civil Rights, Consultation on School Desegregation: The Courts and Suburban Migration, 8 December 1975.

INDEX